MW01595835

LAWYERS' PROFESSIONAL LIABILITY

SECOND EDITION

LAWYERS'
PROFESSIONAL LIABILITY

SECOND EDITION

Stephen M. Grant

Linda R. Rothstein

of the Ontario Bar

 Butterworths

Toronto and Vancouver

The *Butterworth Group of Companies*

Canada:
75 Clegg Road, MARKHAM, Ontario L6G 1A1
and
1721-808 Nelson St., Box 12148, VANCOUVER, B.C. V6Z 2H2
Australia:
Butterworths Pty Ltd., SYDNEY
Ireland:
Butterworth (Ireland) Ltd., DUBLIN
Malaysia:
Malayan Law Journal Sdn Bhd, KUALA LUMPUR
New Zealand:
Butterworths of New Zealand Ltd., WELLINGTON
Singapore:
Butterworths Asia, SINGAPORE
South Africa:
Butterworth Publishers (Pty.) Ltd., DURBAN
United Kingdom:
Butterworth & Co. (Publishers) Ltd., LONDON
United States:
Michie, CHARLOTTESVILLE, Virginia

Canadian Cataloguing in Publication Data

Grant, Stephen M.
    Lawyers' professional liability

2nd ed.
Includes bibliographical references and index.
ISBN 0-433-39994-5

1. Lawyers – Malpractice – Canada. I. Rothstein, Linda R. (Linda Rose), 1955-   . II. Title.

KE347.M3G73 1998   346.7103'3   C98-932288-2
KF313.G73 1998

Printed and bound in Canada.

For Jessica, Matthew and Sara

FOREWORD

The law is protean and malleable. It moves and grows and is ever in the making. Within the contours of its landscape, lawyers are constantly challenged to keep faith with both the old and the new, for the old and the new are constantly colliding and intermingling. Anyone in the profession who fails the challenge risks a very great deal: personal esteem, professional reputation, financial security.

Given these circumstances, lawyers' errors giving rise to liability are inevitable. Fortunately, we have in Canada an accessible and invaluable reference guide to understanding the myriad issues surrounding lawyers' professional liability. *Lawyers' Professional Liability*, by Stephen M. Grant and Linda R. Rothstein, was first published nearly ten years ago and was immediately heralded as a complete, comprehensive reference source for general practitioners and specialists alike, indeed for anyone interested in understanding and applying the legal principles relevant to professional malpractice claims, notably claims alleging negligence and breach of fiduciary duty.

Now, for our even greater benefit, authors Grant and Rothstein have produced *Lawyers' Professional Liability* in a second, updated edition, and in this latest initiative they have made an already valuable source of reference even better than it was in its original manifestation. Lawyers all across Canada cannot help but be enriched by learning more of what lies at the root of their professional and fiduciary obligations and by discovering what precisely is their standard of care.

Lawyer's Professional Liability, second edition, is a gem of a work, clearly and intelligently organized, painstakingly indexed, and, no less importantly, smoothly and gracefully expressed. For the skill and care that went into the making of this most exemplary work, the profession is most grateful.

Harvey T. Strosberg, Q.C.
Treasurer, Law Society of Upper Canada
November 1998

PREFACE

The first edition of this book was published ten years ago. Since then there have been significant changes in the way lawyers practise law, driven mostly by technological advances and the explosion of legal information sources and commentaries. Lawyers no longer keep abreast of developments in the law by flipping through provincial law reports once a week. Instead, they scan long lists of reporting services and periodical indices, sift through legal newspapers and magazines, search the Internet for the latest updates or simply a little legal humour and the odd bit of gossip. In this mass of information about the law and lawyers flows a steady stream of legal malpractice cases. It seems not a week goes by without mention of a case or two.

Our review of the recent jurisprudence reflects this new reality. In fact, two of our predictions have materialized: first, there has been a considerable expansion in the scope of lawyers' liability, especially in the area of fiduciary duty; and, second, the merging of tort and contract has become yesterday's news. Most claims against lawyers today plead tort, contract and, if applicable, breach of fiduciary duty, with little distinction among the three.

One of the other notable differences today is the emphasis on legal malpractice prevention by the various law societies. Preferential insurance rates for sound practice management and discounts for continuing legal education attendance are two examples of economic incentives tied to loss prevention. A number of law societies have published checklists to enable lawyers, at least superficially, to avoid malpractice. These are available in hard copy as well as on some of the law societies' web sites. Even disciplinary prosecutions for negligent practice seem, at least anecdotally, to be more prevalent.

As usual, we owe thanks to a number of people, especially to Monica McCauley and Julie De Marco, two of our Gowlings' colleagues. Without them we would not have written this second edition.

We have tried to be complete in our review of the jurisprudence to October 1998.

Finally, as with the first edition, we donate all of our royalties to the Hospital for Sick Children in Toronto.

Stephen M. Grant
Linda R. Rothstein

Toronto
November, 1998

TABLE OF CONTENTS

TABLE OF CASES

M

N

Chapter 1

SOURCES OF LIABILITY AND LIMITATIONS

I. INTRODUCTION

The study of lawyers' professional liability offers a fascinating view of the law in transition. For years, the path to the successful prosecution of a legal malpractice action was impeded by rules of liability that were derived primarily from the law of contract. Thus, a client was without remedy if he could not establish a solicitor-client relationship, if he failed to sue his lawyer within six years of the "breach", whether or not he had yet suffered damages, or if he claimed damages that were not specifically recoverable in contract. Judicial reliance on customary professional practice in defining the requisite standard of care and the barrister immunity rule also contributed to the difficulty of establishing legal malpractice.

Recent years have seen a steady integration in Anglo-Canadian jurisprudence of the principles of contract and tort. This has culminated in the judicial recognition of the concept of concurrent liability in cases of lawyers' professional negligence. In addition, the courts have tended to elevate the standard of care by which a lawyer's professional services are measured. And in Canada at least, the proposition that a barrister can be sued for the negligent conduct of litigation including her conduct in the courtroom has received significant judicial support. The result has been a broad expansion in the scope of lawyers' professional liability.

There are several possible explanations for this development. The existence of compulsory professional liability insurance has been an important factor in influencing the courts to view an action against a lawyer more as a loss allocation device than as a forum for the ascription of fault.[1] It is also arguable that the courts are responding to growing dissatisfaction with the quality of professional services in general and legal services in particular. Moreover, the increasing

---

[1] Hamilton, "A Lawyer's Liability for Negligence — Care is not Enough" (1986), 44 *Advocate* 53. As authority for this proposition Mr. Hamilton cites, *inter alia*, Lord Denning, *The Discipline of Law* (London: Butterworths, 1979), at 282, and *Allied Finance & Investments Ltd. v. Haddow & Co.*, [1983] N.Z.L.R. 22 at 31. See also R.M. Mahoney, "Lawyers — Negligence — Standard of Care" (1985), 63 *Can. Bar Rev.* 221 at 241.

complexity of legislation and the common law makes providing legal advice and services at times a hazardous undertaking and thus may indirectly contribute to this trend.

Whatever the rationale, the expanding scope of lawyers' professional liability shows no sign of abating and represents a major shift in the law.

II. DEFINITIONS

In examining this area of the law, we use the term "legal malpractice", which has been imported from the American jurisprudence, interchangeably with "lawyers' professional liability". These terms mean a wrongful act or omission arising out of the performance of legal services which results in civil liability.[2] Thus, our analysis includes negligence, breach of an implied (and, to a lesser extent, express) contractual obligation, and breach of fiduciary duty. We do not examine a lawyer's liability for fraud, breach of trust or torts such as malicious prosecution, intentional interference with economic relations or defamation. These acts or courses of conduct do not distinguish the lawyer as a professional from anyone else in the same circumstances.

III. SOURCES OF LIABILITY

A. CONTRACTUAL DUTIES

1. The Retainer

The first and most obvious source of a lawyer's duties is the retainer. A retainer is "a contract whereby in return for the client's offer to employ the solicitor, the solicitor expressly or by implication undertakes to fulfil certain obligations."[3]

The retainer may be oral or, preferably, written; or it may be inferred from the conduct of the parties.[4] Prudence dictates that a lawyer make careful note of

---

[2] This is a paraphrase of the definition of "legal malpractice" in Mallen and Levit, *Legal Malpractice* (St. Paul, Minnesota: West Publishing Co., 1977), at 3. In the fourth edition (1996), at 1-9, Mallen and Levit offer a more detailed analysis of the term "legal malpractice".

[3] F.T. Horne, ed., *Cordery's Law Relating to Solicitors*, 8th ed. (London: Butterworths, 1988), at 49. This same term, as used in common legal parlance, has come to mean the fee or deposit of funds for the performance of the service or services. This usage is technically incorrect although the payment of the fee or deposit may be evidence that the relationship of solicitor and client has been established.

[4] See *Groom v. Crocker*, [1939] 1 K.B. 194 at 222, [1938] 2 All E.R. 394, *per* Scott L.J.: "The relationship is normally started by a retainer, but the retainer will be presumed if the conduct of the two parties shows that the relationship of solicitor and client has in fact been established between them." See also *Bank of Nova Scotia v. Omni Construction Ltd.* (1983), 22 Sask. R. 161 (C.A.); *Korz v. St. Pierre* (1987), 61 O.R. (2d) 609, 43 D.L.R. (4th) 528 (C.A.); leave to appeal to S.C.C. refused February 5, 1988; *Laiman v. Orzech*, unreported, December 13, 1993,

the duties she has been retained to perform in order to avoid or limit later disagreement.[5] It is especially advisable where the retainer is a limited one that does not require the lawyer to perform all of the legal services that might otherwise be necessary to accomplish the client's goals. In *ABN Amro Bank Canada v. Gowling, Strathy & Henderson,*[6] Mr. Justice Trafford held: "[a]ny attempt by a solicitor to limit his/her retainer to a scope less than required of a reasonably competent and diligent solicitor should be done in simple, concise and precise language reduced to writing. Any ambiguity in any such communication, whether it be written or oral, should be resolved against the solicitor."[7] A more recent decision, *669283 Ontario Ltd. v. Reilly,*[8] described these comments as *obiter* and found that the absence of any written documentation to confirm the limitation of the scope of the retainer is a relevant but not dispositive consideration. However, it is clear that if a dispute arises as to the scope of the retainer and it has not been reduced to writing, the onus of proof lies upon the lawyer.[9]

As a general rule, a solicitor is not required to provide services outside the scope of the retainer.[10] As well, the standard of care to be implied will be defined within the confines of the retainer. A solicitor will only be required to take the steps that a reasonably competent practitioner would take to carry out the retainer, even though a particularly conscientious practitioner might, in his client's general interests, pursue a line of inquiry beyond its strict limits.[11] However, caution should be exercised in allowing the client unilaterally to define the retainer where there are risks inherent in the client's proposed course of action of which the solicitor is or should be aware.[12] The failure to warn of these risks may attract liability.

Where a solicitor is possessed of information that need not be disclosed to fulfil the retainer but nonetheless affects the client's interests in the matter, his

---

Mandel J., Docs. 92-CQ-29257, 92-CQ-29257A, 92-CQ-31250CM, [1993] O.J. No. 2996 (Gen. Div.).

[5] *Edwards v. Curran,* unreported, September 25, 1989, Sirois J., Doc. No. Toronto 5156/86, [1989] O.J. No. 2576 (H.C.).

[6] (1994), 20 O.R. (3d) 779 (Gen. Div.).

[7] *Ibid.,* p. 794.

[8] January 22, 1996, Herold J., Doc. No. 3670/92, [1996] O.J. No. 273 (Gen. Div.).

[9] *Bergman v. Williams* (1980), 22 B.C.L.R. 317 (S.C.).

[10] *Bower v. Colwell* (1995), 170 N.B.R. (2d) 46 (Q.B.); *369145 British Columbia Ltd. v. Connell,* unreported, October 25, 1995, Williamson J., Doc. New Westminister 5015668, [1995] B.C.J. No. 2229 (S.C.); *Coughlin v. Comery,* unreported, Ont. Gen. Div., March 8, 1996, Hoilett J., Doc. No. 401522/90, [1996] O.J. No. 822, supp. reasons June 20, 1996; *Fasken Campbell Godfrey v. Seven-Up Canada Inc.* (1997), 142 D.L.R. (4th) 456 (Ont. Gen. Div.); *Woodglen & Co. v. Owens, Wright* (1996), 6 R.P.R. (3d) 259 (Ont. Gen. Div.), supp. reasons February 24, 1997, May 28, 1997 (Ont. Gen. Div.).

[11] *Bower, supra,* note 10.

[12] *Marbel Developments Ltd. v. Pirani* (1994), 18 C.C.L.T. (2d) 229 (B.C.S.C.); *Fellowes, McNeil v. Kansa General Insurance Co.,* unreported, October 14, 1998, MacDonald J., Doc. 94-CU-78160CM, [1998] O.J. No. 4050 (Gen. Div.).

duty to disclose the information is unclear. In *Baranick v. Counsel Trust Co.*,[13] the court held: "a law firm does not incur liability for not communicating something within its knowledge and which would be quite advantageous to the client, if that element is outside the agreed retainer". More recently, in *Canada Trustco Mortgage Co. v. Bartlet & Richardes*,[14] the Ontario Court of Appeal considered whether a solicitor retained by a lender in a mortgage transaction for certain limited purposes was obliged to advise of a zoning restriction he learned of in the course of carrying out the retainer. The client's written instructions indicated that it would be relying on an architect's or engineer's certificate on the zoning issue. For discussion purposes, the court accepted that the lawyer had a duty to advise the client of the zoning restriction irrespective of whether he was acting under a limited contract of retainer but went on to find that the solicitor was not liable because the omission had not caused the client's loss. The Court of Appeal's implicit acceptance of the duty to disclose information relevant to the client's interests but outside of the retainer raises considerable doubt about the reliability of *Baranick.*

Generally, a retainer exists only until the end of the matter at hand.[15] Unless otherwise stated, a solicitor contracts to conclude the service for which she was

---

[13] Unreported, September 24, 1993, Farley J., Doc. B 343/92, [1993] O.J. No. 2186 (Gen. Div.), affd unreported, March 1, 1994, Doc. C16581, [1994] O.J. No. 3814 (C.A.).

[14] (1996), 28 O.R. (3d) 768 (C.A.).

[15] In *Noel & Lewis Holdings Ltd. v. Owen* (1990), 44 B.C.L.R. (2d) 37 (C.A.), application for leave to appeal to S.C.C. dismissed (1990), 50 B.C.L.R. (2d) *xxviii*, Seaton J.A. (Craig J.A. concurring) considered whether there is an obligation on a solicitor to pursue an application for an extension of time to appeal, given the fact that the solicitor and plaintiff clients had an agreement that the fees and disbursements would be paid as they were rendered, and all communications from the solicitors regarding the appeal indicated that the solicitor would not proceed until all outstanding accounts had been settled. Seaton J.A. found, at pp. 44-45:

> [The solicitor] did proceed after trial to complete the matters before the federal court, including several further applications, and he dealt with the government and ultimately obtained the licence for the plaintiff. He had given notice that he would be unwilling to proceed with the appeal in the absence of payment. The solicitor had not agreed to go to appeal and he had made it clear that he was not agreeing to go ahead unless his accounts were paid. In my view, thereafter there was a modified retainer. The solicitor was probably obliged to keep the file alive for a time, not forever, and to render the services that were urgent. But he was not obliged to act as though there was a full retainer and he was taking the appeal.
>
> . . . . .
>
> In my view, there was no duty on [the solicitor] to press ahead vigorously with the application for an extension of time at that time.

Lambert J.A. agreed with the result, but for the reason that the solicitor had ascertained that the chances of success on appeal were next to nothing. At p. 46:

> Every step taken by a lawyer in vigorous prosecution of such an appeal would be a disservice to his client, at best, or a breach of duty to his client, at worst.
>
> . . . . .

initially hired.[16] A retainer may be terminated in numerous ways but most commonly upon completion of the transaction or proceeding, the failure of the client to pay fees as accounts are rendered,[17] the solicitor's retirement (or the dissolution of the law firm),[18] the death or bankruptcy of the client, the discharge of the solicitor or change of solicitors by the client, or the discharge of the client by the solicitor for good reason and with sufficient notice.[19]

2. Implied Duties

In circumstances in which a solicitor-client relationship has been established, and absent a written retainer, the contractual obligations of a lawyer to his client will be implied by the court. It is axiomatic that a lawyer implicitly contracts to exercise reasonable competence and diligence in the provision of legal services.[20] That implied promise is, of course, also the standard of care which determines negligence.[21] In addition, the retainer or contract between solicitor and client "gives rise to a complex of rights and duties of which the duty to exercise reasonable care and skill is but one".[22] This *dictum* was applied, for example, in

---

> It is possible to consider that [the solicitor] may have had a tactical obligation to file a notice of application for an extension of time in which to appeal, but he cannot have had any tactical obligation at all to press that application forward.

In *Skimming v. Goldberg*, [1993] 8 W.W.R. 59 at p. 69 (Man Q.B.), the court held that when a solicitor is retained to act on behalf of the client in the purchase of a unit in a building and prepare the necessary documentation for execution:

> A solicitor's retainer in a case such as this commences on the receiving of instructions and ceases when the matter has been completed. Completed in this case is when the matter is reported out.

[16] A solicitor must approve a draft order to which there is no genuine objection, even if such approval is contrary to the client's specific instructions, and even if the solicitor who appeared on the motion has ceased to act for the client. See *Chrysler Credit Canada Ltd. v. 734925 Ontario Ltd.* (1991), 5 O.R. (3d) 65 (Gen. Div.).

[17] *Noel & Lewis Holdings Ltd. (Trustee of) v. Owen, Bird, supra*, note 15.

[18] *Philps v. Mooney* (1997), 41 B.C.L.R. (3d) 304 (S.C.).

[19] See *Cordery, supra*, note 3, at chapter 3. See also Chapter 6, II. "Conduct of a Civil Action", B. "Withdrawing Services", regarding the withdrawal of services during the conduct of an action.

[20] See, for example, *Schmalzbauer v. Gares* (1990), 89 Sask. R. 254 (Q.B.), wherein a plaintiff instructed his solicitor to sell specific shares. He did not act on these instructions for 16 months. The solicitor was found in breach of his duty to his clients in not acting in a timely fashion; see also *Faber-Castell Canada Ltd. v. Woods*, unreported, March 9, 1994, Matlow J., Doc. 3681/83, [1994] O.J. No. 475 (Gen. Div.); *835039 Ontario Inc. v. Fram Development Corp.*, unreported, Trafford J., Doc. No. 53207/90, Toronto, August 9, 1994, [1994] O.J. No. 1725 (Gen. Div.), in which a solicitor was found negligent for failing to deliver an important notice, and for failing to have a system designed to detect such clerical errors.

[21] See Chapter 2, Section I. "General Principles" A. "Reasonable Comptence" and D. "Reasonable Diligence".

[22] *Midland Bank Trust Co. Ltd. v. Hett, Stubbs & Kemp*, [1979] Ch. 384 at 434, [1978] 3 All E.R. 571, *per* Oliver J. See also *Granville Savings & Mortgage Corp. v. Slevin*, [1993] 4 S.C.R. 279,

a case where the court held that the acceptance of an undertaking to discharge a mortgage, contrary to the terms of the agreement of purchase and sale, constituted a breach of the lawyer's implied duty to fulfil the terms of the agreement.[23] However, in the majority of cases, a lawyer's failure to complete a task or to perform it properly will be treated as a breach of the lawyer's general duty to exercise reasonable competence and diligence.

B. DUTIES IN TORT

1. Concurrent Liability

In *Central Trust Co. v. Rafuse*,[24] the Supreme Court of Canada ended years of judicial and academic debate[25] by holding that there is concurrent liability both in contract and in tort for acts or omissions arising in the course of a solicitor-client relationship.

Like the Supreme Court of Canada in *Central Trust*, late nineteenth-century and early twentieth-century authorities commonly held that it did not matter how an action against a solicitor was framed — in contract or in tort.[26] Still, there was authority to the contrary and the question was not directly addressed

---

where the solicitor obtained what the plaintiff had specifically requested (a "first mortgage"), but failed to advise the plaintiff of potential problems due to outstanding judgments on the property. The nature of the relationship was such that the plaintiff was clearly relying on the solicitor's skills. Given such a relationship, it is not open to a solicitor to act for a party and yet fail to advise them of potential problems regarding their "first charge" on the property.

23 *Polischuk v. Hagarty* (1983), 42 O.R. (2d) 417, 149 D.L.R. (3d) 65 (H.C.), revd on other grounds 49 O.R. (2d) 71, 14 D.L.R. (4th) 446 (C.A.). The case is discussed in greater detail in Chapter 2, Section II. "Ancillary Principles", A. "General and Approved Practice" and B. "Implied Terms of the Retainer".

24 [1986] 2 S.C.R. 147, 75 N.S.R. (2d) 109.

25 The cases and articles on this subject are voluminous. A sampling includes: *Groom v. Crocker*, [1939] 1 K.B. 194 (liability in contract only); *Schwebel v. Telekes*, [1967] 1 O.R. 541 at 543, 61 D.L.R. (2d) 470 (C.A.) (duty is only contractual); *Midland Bank Trust Co. Ltd. v. Hett, Stubbs & Kemp, supra*, note 22 (liability in tort); *Messineo v. Beale* (1978), 20 O.R. (2d) 49, 86 D.L.R. (3d) 713 (C.A.) (majority holding that basis of liability is contractual only, minority finding concurrent liability in tort and contract); J. Irvine, "Contract and Tort: Troubles Along the Border" (1979-80), 2 *Advocates' Q.* 160; Dwyer, "Solicitor's Negligence — Tort of Contract?" (1982), 56 *A.L.J.* 524; French, "The Contract/Tort Dilemma" (1983), 5 *Otago L.R.* 236; N.I. Rafferty, "The Tortious Liability of Professionals to Their Contractual Clients" in Steel and Rodgers-Magnet, eds., *Issues in Tort Law* (Toronto: Carswell, 1983).

26 Among the early authorities holding that a solicitor may be liable both in contract and in tort is *Nocton v. Lord Ashburton*, [1914] A.C. 932 at 956, [1914-15] All E.R. Rep. 45 (H.L.), *per* Viscount Haldane L.C. [Emphasis added]:

> My Lords, the solicitor contracts with his client to be skilful and careful. For failure to perform his obligation he may be made liable at law *in contract or even in tort*, for negligence in breach of a duty imposed on him. In the early history of the action of assumpsit this liability was indeed treated as one for tort.

until the English Court of Appeal concluded in *Groom v. Crocker*[27] that a solicitor's duties to his client were contractual only and derived from the retainer.

This remained the law in England, and for that matter the Commonwealth, until *Esso Petroleum Co. Ltd. v. Mardon*[28] and *Hedley Byrne & Co. Ltd. v. Heller & Partners Ltd.*,[29] both of which heralded major shifts in the law on a variety of fronts. In the former case, Lord Denning on behalf of the Court of Appeal rejected the *Groom v. Crocker* formulation of the law, propounding instead a theory of concurrent liability. *Hedley Byrne* greatly expanded the scope of professional responsibility by taking it outside the contractual relationship and creating liability for negligent misrepresentation. Still, neither *Esso* nor *Hedley Byrne* was a case involving solicitors.

In *Midland Bank Trust Co. Ltd. v. Hett, Stubbs & Kemp*,[30] Oliver J. of the High Court, after an exhaustive review of the authorities, concluded that a solicitor owes a duty to his client independent of his duties in contract. The decision was cited with explicit approval by the House of Lords in *Henderson v. Merrett Syndicates*.[31] Lord Justice Goff, with whom all of the other Lord Justices agreed, held: "the claimant may be entitled to take advantage of the remedy which is most advantageous to him, subject only to ascertaining whether the tortious duty is so inconsistent with the applicable contract that, in accordance with ordinary principle, the parties must be taken to have agreed that the tortious remedy is to be limited or excluded".[32] The English Court of Appeal subsequently imposed liability against a law firm on this basis.[33] The Court of Appeal also clarified in that case that the duty of care in tort may be wider than the duties imposed on the parties under a contract. The High Court of Australia has also endorsed concurrency of liability in contract and tort and the New Zealand courts appear to be moving steadily in the same direction.[34]

Returning then to *Central Trust*, the defendant solicitors were retained to provide an opinion to the plaintiff trust company on the validity of a mortgage that was the security for a large advance of funds. The mortgage was held to be void for its failure to comply with certain provisions of the Nova Scotia *Companies Act*[35] resulting in the worthlessness of the plaintiff's security. If the cause

---

[27] *Supra*, note 25.
[28] [1976] Q.B. 801, [1976] 2 All E.R. 5 (C.A.).
[29] [1964] A.C. 465, [1963] 2 All E.R. 575 (H.L.).
[30] *Supra*, note 22.
[31] [1994] 3 All E.R. 506 (H.L.); for a detailed analysis of the significance of the decision, see A.G. Guest, ed., *Chitty on Contracts*, 27th ed. (London: Sweet & Maxwell, 1994), Second Cumulative Supplement.
[32] *Ibid.*, at 532-33.
[33] *Holt v. Payne Skillington (a firm)* (1995), 49 Con. L.R. 99 (C.A.).
[34] *Bryan v. Maloney* (1995), 128 A.L.R. 163 (H.C.). The principle was approved again by the High Court of Australia by way of *obiter* in *RF Hill and Associates v. Van Erp* (1997), 71 A.L.J.R. 487, 142 A.L.R. 687; see also *Rowlands v. Collow*, [1992] 1 N.Z.L.R. 178 (H.C.).
[35] R.S.N.S. 1967, c. 42, s. 96(5) [am. 1982, c. 17, s. 14; 1983, c. 19, s. 4].

of action was based on contract, it was statute-barred; if it could be asserted in tort, it was timely.

In a well-reasoned judgment, Mr. Justice Le Dain, speaking for a unanimous court, held that: (1) the common law duty of care is created by a "sufficient relationship of proximity" and is not confined to relationships that arise apart from contract;[36] and (2) the duty of care thus created is independent of contract in that it is not founded on the specific obligations or duties established by the express terms of the contract.[37] However, he cautioned that concurrent liability in tort will not apply if its effect would be to permit the plaintiff to circumvent a contractual exclusion or limitation of liability for the act or omission that would constitute the tort.[38] The extent to which lawyers can rely on exclusionary clauses to limit their obligations is discussed in Section V. "Special Liability Problems", B. "Disclaimers of Liability" of this chapter.

2. Clients and Third Parties

When a lawyer's liability does not depend on contract but on a duty in tort to exercise care towards all persons in a relationship of sufficient proximity who reasonably rely upon the lawyer's expertise, it is easy to see that lawyers' professional liability will now encompass claims by various third parties as well as clients.[39]

C. FIDUCIARY DUTIES

Increasingly, the law of fiduciaries is the basis of a lawyer's obligations to clients and non-clients. A lawyer's fiduciary duties exist independently of his duties both in contract and in tort. We examine the nature and scope of a lawyer's fiduciary obligations in Chapter 3.

D. ETHICAL CODES

The Law Society of each of the provinces has enacted a Code of Professional Conduct which defines the ethical obligations of practising lawyers. In addition, in 1974, the National Council of The Canadian Bar Association adopted a *Code of Professional Conduct.*

These codes set out the ethical rules to which lawyers must conform in providing professional services; failure to comply can result in the imposition of

---

[36] *Central Trust Co. v. Rafuse, supra,* note 24, at 204 S.C.R. That is, the court adopted the test and language of the House of Lords in *Anns v. Merton London Borough Council,* [1978] A.C. 728.

[37] *Central Trust Co. v. Rafuse, supra,* note 24, at 205 S.C.R.

[38] *Central Trust Co. v. Rafuse, supra,* note 24, at 206 S.C.R.

[39] For a discussion of the scope of a lawyer's professional liability to third parties, see Chapter 4.

discipline by the Law Society of the province. Although the ethical rules contained in these codes are broadly drafted and encompass all aspects of a lawyer's professional responsibility, disciplinary action is usually restricted to cases of fraud, misappropriation and failure to maintain proper trust accounts; negligence is not a common basis for discipline unless it is gross and habitual.

It is important to distinguish between the breach of an ethical rule, which can result in disciplinary sanctions, and breach of a contract, tort or fiduciary duty, which can result in civil liability. Breach of an ethical rule does not necessarily found a civil cause of action[40] and, as noted, the fact that a lawyer is found liable for negligence does not usually render him subject to discipline. This does not mean, however, that the ethical rules that govern the profession and the rules of civil liability are mutually exclusive. In an appropriate case of legal malpractice, the court may use the relevant ethical standards in the course of identifying a specific legal obligation.[41]

Mr. Justice Sopinka explained the role of ethical codes of conduct in civil actions in *MacDonald Estate v. Martin*,[42] a case concerning the circumstances under which a law firm should be disqualified from continuing to act in litigation because of a conflict of interest. Writing for a majority of the court, he referred to Manitoba's *Code of Professional Conduct* as an expression of the standards to which the profession should adhere:

> A code of professional conduct is designed to serve as a guide to lawyers and typically it is enforced in disciplinary proceedings. . . . The courts, which have in-

---

[40]   *Meadwell Enterprises Ltd. v. Clay & Co.* (1983), 44 B.C.L.R. 188, [1983] 3 W.W.R. 742 (S.C.).

[41]   For example, *Foster v. Barry* (1983), 46 B.C.L.R. 59, [1983] 5 W.W.R. 315 (S.C.) (duty to be "candid and honest" in advising clients); *Vienneau v. Arsenault* (1982), 41 N.B.R. (2d) 82 (C.A.) (duty to inform client promptly when lawyer discovers a mistake). Cases defining fiduciary obligations in language which mirrors that of the appropriate ethical rules include: *Confederation Life Insurance Co. v. Shepherd, McKenzie, Plaxton, Little & Jenkins* (1992), 29 R.P.R. (2d) 271 (Ont. Gen. Div.), varied (1996), 88 O.A.C. 398 (C.A.); *McKinnon v. Conexco International Corp.*, unreported, February 17, 1992, Steele J., Doc. 16582/86, [1992] O.J. No. 292 (Gen. Div.); *MacDonald Estate v. Martin*, [1990] 3 S.C.R. 1235; *Skimming v. Goldberg*, [1993] 8 W.W.R. 59; scc *Morton v. Asper*, [1988] 1 W.W.R. 47 (Man. Q.B.), aff'd [1988] 2 W.W.R. 317 (Man. C.A.), for a case in which the rules regarding confidentiality were used to inform the court of the expected standard; see *Chrysler Credit Canada Ltd. v. 734925 Ontario Ltd.* (1991), 5 O.R. (3d) 65 (Gen. Div.) where the court looked to the rules of professional conduct to guide it in ascertaining obligations regarding lawyers' duties to the court and other members of the profession; and in *Lefebvre v. Gardiner* (1988), 27 B.C.L.R. (2d) 294 (S.C.), the court affirmed that the Law Society's Professional Conduct Handbook is pertinent to the issue of the scope of a solicitor's fiduciary obligation. In the United States, the judiciary is making greater use of professional conduct in malpractice cases to assist in defining the common law duty of care owed. In fact, it has been held that a professional ethical violation establishes a rebuttable presumption of malpractice. For a review of the American jurisprudence, see D.L. Draisen, "The Model Rules of Professional Conduct and their relationship to Legal Malpractice Actions: A Practical Approach to the Use of the Rules" (1997), 21 *J. Legal Prof.* 67.

[42]   *Ibid.*

herent jurisdiction to remove from the record solicitors who have a conflict of interest, are not bound to apply a code of ethics. Their jurisdiction stems from the fact that lawyers are officers of the court and their conduct in legal proceedings which may affect the administration of justice is subject to this supervisory jurisdiction. Nonetheless, an expression of a professional standard in a code of ethics relating to a matter before the court should be considered an important statement of public policy.[43]

These *dicta* have been followed by numerous courts in similar applications to have solicitors removed from the record for conflict of interest. Furthermore, the fact that a lawyer has been disciplined for professional misconduct is *prima facie* evidence of misconduct in an ensuing civil action, subject to rebuttal on the merits.[44]

IV. THE LIMITATION PERIOD

Every province in Canada has a complex scheme of statutes prescribing the time within which legal actions must be launched. Notwithstanding considerable jurisdictional variations in the number and content of these statutes of limitations, all of them distinguish causes of action arising in contract from those arising in tort. When the cause of action is characterized as contractual, the temporal scope of the lawyer's liability is fairly well defined: usually six years from the date of the "breach", that is, the date error was made, whether or not the client knew or could have known that there had been an actionable wrong committed. In contrast, when the claim is characterized as tortious, the limitation period does not begin to run until the error is discovered or ought to have been discovered by the client through the exercise of reasonable diligence.[45] Until recently, a multitude of legal malpractice claims were defended, often successfully, on the basis that a client's action against her lawyer lay in contract only and, accordingly, that the limitation period had expired.[46]

This defence was eliminated by the Supreme Court of Canada in *Central Trust*, which held that an action against a barrister or solicitor for the negligent performance of professional services lies concurrently in contract and in tort and, thus, the limitation period does not start to run until the negligence of the lawyer, or the material facts on which it is based, has been discovered or could have been discovered by the exercise of reasonable diligence. Interestingly, it is arguable that, in a case where the lawyer's error is not self-evident to a lay per-

---

[43] *Ibid.*, at 1245-46.

[44] *Terrace Developments Ltd. v. Terry*, unreported, May 25, 1992, Mandel J. (Ont. Gen. Div.), affd unreported, April 5, 1994, Doc. C12383, [1994] O.J. No. 683 (C.A.).

[45] *Kamloops (City) v. Nielsen*, [1984] 2 S.C.R. 2, [1984] 5 W.W.R. 1; *Central Trust Co. v. Rafuse*, [1986] 2 S.C.R. 147, 75 N.S.R. (2d) 109.

[46] See, for example, *Schwebel v. Telekes*, [1967] 1 O.R. 541.

son, the limitation period may not commence until the client or injured party has obtained expert opinion as to the negligence of the lawyer.[47]

V. SPECIAL LIABILITY PROBLEMS

A. BARRISTER'S LIABILITY

1. The Position in England, Australia and New Zealand

Until the House of Lords' decision in *Rondel v. Worsley*[48] in 1967, the conduct of barristers in the preparation and presentation of cases was immune from civil action; this was the so-called "barrister immunity rule". The generally accepted basis for the rule was that the absence of a contractual relationship between the barrister and the client precluded liability for negligent acts or omissions.[49] For the same reason, it had long been established that a barrister could not sue for his fees.[50]

When as a result of *M'Alister (or Donoghue) v. Stevenson*[51] and *Hedley Byrne & Co. Ltd. v. Heller & Partners Ltd.,*[52] it was held that a duty of care could exist independently of contract and that the duty applied to professional services, the old rationale was discarded in favour of a reformulated, less all-encompassing rule based on public policy. The majority judgments in *Rondel v. Worsley*[53] outlined the public policy justifications for a limited barrister immunity rule as follows:

(1)   the necessity of avoiding the conflict that would otherwise arise between a barrister's duty to the court and his concern to appease a possibly vengeful client;

(2)   the difficulty that would otherwise ensue from attempts to retry the original case in order to determine the merits of the client's claim;

(3)   the multiplicity of actions that would be encouraged by elimination of the rule;

---

[47]   This appears to be the rule in medical malpractice cases: see C.L. Campbell, "Current Trends & New Directions in the Law of Professional Liability", *Insight* (Toronto: Canadian Institute, 1987), citing *Gaudet v. Levy* (1984), 47 O.R. (2d) 577, 11 D.L.R. (4th) 721 (H.C.); *Law v. Kingston General Hospital* (1983), 42 O.R. (2d) 476 (H.C.); *Mandarino v. Blue Mountain Resorts Ltd.*, unreported, February 19, 1987 (Ont. Master).

[48]   [1969] 1 A.C. 191, [1967] 3 All E.R. 993 (H.L.).

[49]   *Swinfen v. Lord Chelmsford* (1860), 5 H. & N. 890, 157 E.R. 1436 (Ex.); *Kennedy v. Brown* (1863), 13 C.B. (N.S.) 677, 143 E.R. 268 (C.P.).

[50]   *Mostyn v. Mostyn* (1870), 5 Ch. App. 457; *Le Brasseur v. Oakley*, [1896] 2 Ch. 487 (C.A.).

[51]   [1932] A.C. 562, [1932] All E.R. Rep. 1 (H.L.).

[52]   [1964] A.C. 465, [1963] 2 All E.R. 575 (H.L.).

[53]   *Supra*, note 48.

(4)   the obligation of a barrister, unlike other professionals, to accept any
        client, however unsavoury;
(5)   the anomaly that would result from the absence of the rule in light of
        the absolute privilege all participants in a legal proceeding enjoy
        regarding what is said by them in court.

In *Rondel v. Worsley*, the extent of a barrister's immunity was not directly in
issue, although the law lords proposed various dividing lines between work that
would be covered by the immunity and work that would not.[54] However, the
court did appear to agree that the immunity no longer applied to all work undertaken by a barrister but only to that portion performed in the conduct and management of a case in court.

The situation was partially clarified in *Saif Ali v. Sydney Mitchell & Co.*,[55] in
which it was alleged that a barrister had been negligent in failing to name certain
persons as defendants in a civil action. The House of Lords, by a majority of
three to two, held that these facts did not permit a defence of barristers' immunity since the immunity only extends to pre-trial work that is "so intimately
connected with the conduct of the cause in court that it can fairly be said to be a
preliminary decision affecting the way that cause is to be conducted when it
comes to a hearing."[56] This judgment adopted the test that had been formulated
by the New Zealand Court of Appeal in *Rees v. Sinclair*.[57]

Since *Saif Ali*, the immunity rule has not been reconsidered by the House of
Lords. However, in *Kelley v. Corston*,[58] the English Court of Appeal recently
addressed the scope of its application. This was an appeal from the decision of a
district court judge striking out the plaintiff's claim in negligence against her
lawyer respecting a settlement for ancillary relief in family law proceedings
reached at the court on the morning of the hearing. Pursuant to the *Matrimonial
Causes Act, 1973*, this type of settlement must be approved by court order.

After a detailed review of *Rondel*, *Saif Ali* and recent trial level authorities
upholding the rule, all three Lord Justices held that the barristers' immunity rule
applied in the circumstances and dismissed the appeal. Lord Justices Pill and
Butler-Sloss found that it extends both to settlements concluded on the door-
steps of the courthouse because they were intimately connected with the conduct
of the case, and to settlements required to be approved by the court. Lord Justice
Judge found that the immunity does not apply to settlements reached except in

---

[54]   *Supra*, note 48; [1969] 1 A.C. at 231-32 *per* Lord Reid, at 247-54 *per* Lord Morris, 285-86 *per*
       Lord Upjohn, at 293-94 *per* Lord Pearson.
[55]   [1980] A.C. 198, [1978] 3 All E.R. 1033 (H.L.).
[56]   *Ibid.*, at 224 A.C., *per* Lord Diplock, quoting McCarthy P. in *Rees v. Sinclair*, [1974] 1
       N.Z.L.R. 180 at 187 (C.A.).
[57]   [1974] 1 N.Z.L.R. 180 (C.A.). See also *Thompson v. Howley*, [1977] 1 N.Z.L.R. 16 (S.C.);
       Biggar v. McLeod, [1978] 2 N.Z.L.R. 9 (C.A.).
[58]   [1997] 4 All E.R. 466 (C.A.), leave to appeal to the House of Lords refused. For a brief synop-
       sis of the decision, see *Barrister's Immunity from Suit in Settlement*, Times (20 August, 1997).

two specific instances: settlements reached after trial begins and those requiring court approval.

While the law lords emphasized that the barrister immunity rule is a narrow exception to liability for professional negligence, each of them agreed with the decision in *Saif Ali* that it covers pre-trial work that is intimately connected to the conduct of action. Leave to appeal the decision in *Kelley* to the House of Lords was refused. The immunity was extended by statute to solicitors when they were given advocacy rights in higher courts.[59] Thus, it appears that English law is settled in favour of immunity in these narrow circumstances.

Rees v. Sinclair is still the highest New Zealand authority on point. In 1988, the Australian High Court, following *Rondel* and *Saif Ali,* confirmed barristers' immunity for in-court negligence and work done out of court which leads to a decision affecting the conduct of the case in court.[60] There is no blanket immunity for advocates in the United States, but liability is rarely imposed for their conduct in court.[61]

2. The Canadian Position

In 1979, Mr. Justice Krever, giving judgment in the Ontario High Court decision of *Demarco v. Ungaro,*[62] held that the barrister immunity rule had no place in Ontario and that a lawyer is liable to a client for the negligent conduct of an action, including the lawyer's conduct in the courtroom. The case involved an application by the defendant lawyer to strike out certain paragraphs of the plaintiff's statement of claim on the ground that they disclosed no cause of action. One of the paragraphs in question contained an allegation that the defendant had "failed to lead evidence which he knew was available and which would have supported the Plaintiff's position".[63] Accordingly, the case forced a decision on the fundamental point, whether the English House of Lords decision in *Rondel v. Worsley* had any application in Ontario. In dismissing the defendant's application, Mr. Justice Krever concluded that whatever force the policy considerations outlined in *Rondel v. Worsley* might have in England, "the public interest . . . in Ontario does not require that our Courts recognize an immunity of a lawyer from action for negligence at the suit of his or her former client by reason of the conduct of a civil case in Court".[64]

---

[59] *Courts and Legal Services Act, 1990,* s. 62.

[60] *Giannarelli v. Wraith* (1988), 165 C.L.R. 543 (H.C.).

[61] For a comprehensive review of the American case law on this issue, see M. Newman, "The Case Against Advocates' Immunity: A Comparative Study" (1995), *Georgetown Journal of Legal Ethics* 267.

[62] (1979), 21 O.R. (2d) 673, 95 D.L.R. (3d) 385 (H.C.). Interestingly, the plaintiff was later non-suited at trial.

[63] *Ibid.,* at 388 D.L.R.

[64] *Ibid.,* at 404-05 D.L.R.

Until the Ontario Court of Appeal's recent decision in *Wong v. Thomson, Rogers*,[65] no Canadian appellate court had considered the point, although the *Demarco* decision had been cited with approval in several reported trial court decisions.[66] In *Wong*, the Court of Appeal upheld the dismissal of an action in negligence by a plaintiff against the law firm that represented her in a personal injury suit. Although liability had been admitted in the personal injury case, the jury awarded her only nominal special damages and no general damages. The plaintiff alleged that the law firm's negligence in failing to summons to trial a certain police witness and to tender a medical report from her family physician caused the adverse result. The trial judge, relying on the decision in *Demarco*, held that, while there is no immunity in Canada for negligence in the conduct of a trial, the court may only impose liability for egregious errors. The Court of Appeal upheld the trial judge's conclusion that there was no demonstrative causal connection between the conduct, the trial and the result, thereby implicitly approving the ratio in *Demarco*.

Since this decision, Ontario courts have held that lawyers will not be liable in negligence for decisions made in the course of a trial, such as declining to call certain witnesses[67] or failing to question a complainant in a sexual assault case as aggressively as the accused wished,[68] unless these decisions are egregiously wrong. It appears, therefore, that the rejection of the barristers' immunity rule in favour of liability only for very egregious errors is settled at least in Ontario.

---

[65] Unreported, June 15, 1994, Doc. C12538, [1994] O.J. No. 1318 (C.A.).

[66] Including *Karpenko v. Paroian, Courey, Cohen & Houston* (1980), 30 O.R. (2d) 776, 117 D.L.R. (3d) 383 (H.C.); *M. Hodge & Sons Ltd. v. Monaghan* (1985), 51 Nfld. & P.E.I.R. 173 (Nfld. S.C.), affd (1988), 71 Nfld. & P.E.I.R. 60 (Nfld. C.A.); *Stevenson v. Stanek* (1980), 2 Sask. R. 259, [1980] 4 W.W.R 239 (Q.B.); *Pelky v. Hudson Bay Insurance Co.* (1981), 35 O.R. (2d) 97 (H.C.); *Wechsel v. Stutz* (1980), 15 C.C.L.T. 132 (Ont. Co. Ct.); *Hunter v. Roe*, [1990] 6 W.W.R. 85 (Sask. Q.B.). Even before *Demarco v. Ungaro, Rondel v. Worsley, supra*, note 48, was given a restrictive interpretation in Canada: see *Gouzenko v. Harris* (1976), 13 O.R. (2d) 730 (H.C.) (*Rondel v. Worsley* not applicable to the failure to conduct examination for discovery); *Banks v. Reid* (1977), 18 O.R. (2d) 148, 81 D.L.R. (3d) 730 at 735 (C.A.) (in which the Court of Appeal concluded that the application of *Rondel v. Worsley* in that particular jurisdiction, "where practitioners are both barristers and solicitors", is questionable).

[67] *Bartolovic v. Bennett*, unreported, March 26, 1996, Borins J., Doc. 95-CU-86639, [1996] O.J. No. 961 (Gen. Div.), supp. reasons April 12, 1996; *Anastasakos v. Allen* (1996), 16 O.T.C. 413 (Gen. Div.); *Boudreau v. Benaiah* (1998), 37 O.R. (3d) 686 (Gen. Div.), but the court still found the defendant liable for falling below the standard of ordinary competence with respect to conduct unrelated to the conduct of the trial. See also *Fellowes, McNeil v. Kansa General Insurance Co.*, unreported, October 14, 1998, Macdonald J., Doc. 94-CU-78160CM, [1998] O.J. No. 4050 (Gen. Div.), where it was held that a solicitor did not breach the standard of care in retaining an expert witness whose qualifications were rejected by the trial judge, and in failing to request an adjournment to retain an appropriately qualified expert witness.

[68] *Anastasakos, supra*, note 67. Although Benotto J. did not grant the defendant lawyer's application for an order dismissing the claim because it was brought as a motion for determination of an issue before trial under R. 21 of the Ontario Rules of Civil Procedure, R.R.O. 1990, Reg. 194, as opposed to a motion for summary judgment under R. 20, she indicated that the claim would not have survived the "good hard look" test under R. 20.

B. DISCLAIMERS OF LIABILITY

In *Central Trust Co. v. Rafuse*,[69] the Supreme Court of Canada held:

> A concurrent or alternative liability in tort will not be admitted if its effect would be to permit the plaintiff to circumvent or escape a contractual exclusion or limitation of liability for the act or omission that would constitute the tort.[70]

And:

> While the solicitor's duty of care has generally been stated, for obvious reasons, in the context of contractual liability as arising as an implied term of the contract or retainer, the same duty arises as a matter of common law from the relationship of proximity created by the retainer. In the absence of special terms in the contract determining the nature and scope of the duty of care in a particular case, the duties of care in contract and in tort are the same.[71]

These passages raise the question of the extent to which a lawyer can "contract out" of her obligations to a client. An agreement or retainer that defines the nature and extent of legal services a lawyer has undertaken to provide is likely to be held to be valid and enforceable. However, an exculpatory clause or disclaimer, that is, a term in a contract that purports to lessen the scope or exclude altogether a lawyer's liability for negligence in the performance of legal services, may prove to be unenforceable.

In fact, in *Klingspon v. Ramsay*,[72] a disclaimer of liability was held to be ineffective against a third party. A solicitor required that a certain woman who was investing in his client sign an acknowledgment which stated:

> I hereby confirm and agree that with regard to the purchase of these shares [the solicitors] are acting as solicitors for the company only and *have not offered me any advice other than as to the good standing of the Company* and its capacity to issue the within shares, nor have I requested such advice. I am aware that any such advice should be sought from independent counsel. [Emphasis in original.]

The court held that, given the circumstances, it was foreseeable that the investor would rely on the solicitor. Thus, the solicitor had a duty to impress in plain language that he could give no assurances with respect to the financial stability of the client company.

In two provinces, Ontario and British Columbia, legislation exists that renders void any disclaimer contained in a contract for remuneration between a lawyer and

---

[69]   [1996] 2 S.C.R. 147, 75 N.S.R. (2d) 109.

[70]   *Ibid.*, at 206 S.C.R.

[71]   *Ibid.*, at 210 S.C.R.

[72]   [1985] 5 W.W.R. 411 (B.C.S.C.).

a client.[73] However, the provisions do not cover disclaimers that are not included in contracts respecting the lawyer's fees. Similar provisions exist in the procedural rules in other provinces.[74] There are no reported cases on this issue.[75]

Even in the absence of judicial precedent, one may confidently assume that, like any exculpatory clause, a disclaimer of liability in a contract between a lawyer and client will be construed *contra proferentem* and will not generally exclude liability for negligence if a narrower meaning can be attached to it.[76] It is at least arguable that the doctrine of fundamental breach will preclude reliance on a disclaimer where there has been a significant failure by the lawyer to perform his contractual obligations.[77]

Moreover, given a lawyer's fiduciary obligations, it seems unlikely that a disclaimer of negligence will be enforced. As discussed at greater length in Chapter 3, a contract of this kind, namely, one in which the lawyer attempts to gain an advantage for himself at the expense of his client, is presumptively invalid;[78] and in the absence of independent legal advice regarding the nature and consequences of the agreement, it is probably unenforceable.[79]

---

[73] In Ontario, the *Solicitors Act*, R.S.O. 1990, c. S.15, provides, *inter alia*:

> 16(1) . . . a solicitor may make an agreement in writing with his or her client respecting the amount and manner of payment for . . . any past or future services in respect of business done or to be done by the solicitor . . .
>
> . . . . .
>
> 22. A provision in any such agreement that the solicitor is not to be liable for negligence or that he or she is to be relieved from any responsibility to which he . . . would otherwise be subject as such solicitor is wholly void.

In British Columbia, the *Legal Profession Act*, R.S.B.C. 1996, c. 255, provides, *inter alia*:

> 87(1) Despite any law or usage to the contrary, a member of the society may contract, in writing, with a person as to the remuneration to be paid to the member for services rendered or to be rendered to the person.
>
> . . . . .
>
> (17) A provision in an agreement referred to in subsection (1) or (2) that the member is not liable for negligence, or that the member is relieved from responsibility to which the member would otherwise be subject as a member, is void.

[74] See, for example, Alberta Rules of Court, Alta. Reg. 390/68, r. 620(1); Nova Scotia Civil Procedure Rules, r. 63.21; Prince Edward Island Civil Procedure Rules, OIC EC 492/90, r. 57.12(1).

[75] Reference was made to Alberta r. 620(1) by the Alberta Court of Queen's Bench in *obiter* in *MacLeod Dixon v. Schroder Finanz Holding*, unreported, October 25, 1996, Doc. 9601-05005, [1996] A.J. No. 902 (Q.B.).

[76] See, generally, S.M. Waddams, *The Law of Contracts*, 3rd ed. (Aurora, Ont.: Canada Law Book Ltd., 1993), at 315.

[77] *Ibid.*, at 317-481.

[78] See Chapter 3, Section III. "Fiduciary Obligations Defined", A. "Duty of Loyalty", 1.

[79] *Quaere* whether the lawyer providing the independent legal advice is obliged to recommend that the client not sign the disclaimer, failing which, the lawyer providing the independent legal advice may himself be negligent.

Chapter 2

THE STANDARD OF CARE

I. GENERAL PRINCIPLES

A. REASONABLE COMPETENCE

The standard of care and skill expected of a lawyer is reasonable competence and diligence.[1] Thus, it is not sufficient to establish liability to show that a lawyer has made an error in judgment or shown ignorance of some particular part of the law; the error or ignorance must be that which a reasonably competent lawyer would not have made or demonstrated.[2] Although various nineteenth-century authorities held that a lawyer was not liable unless he had acted with *crassa negligentia* or "gross negligence",[3] this terminology is no longer in use and should be avoided.[4]

Expressed in these terms, the standard of care is the same whether the action is framed in contract or in tort. Indeed, except in recent cases, the "negligence" alleged against a lawyer refers to a contractual claim, based on the implied duty

---

[1]   *Fletcher & Son v. Jubb, Booth & Helliwell*, [1920] 1 K.B. 275 (C.A.); *Groom v. Crocker*, [1939] 1 K.B. 194, [1938] 2 All E.R. 394 (C.A.); *Aaroe v. Seymour*, [1965] O.R. 736, 6 D.L.R. (2d) 100 (H.C.), affd 7 D.L.R. 676 (C.A.); *Grima v. MacMillan*, [1972] 3 O.R. 214, 27 D.L.R. (3d) 666 (H.C.). Various authorities also describe the standard as the "ordinarily competent" or "ordinarily prudent" lawyer: *e.g.*, *Doiron v. La Caisse Populaire D'Inkerman Ltee* (1985), 61 N.B.R. (2d) 123, 17 D.L.R. (4th) 660 (C.A.); *B. & R. Farms Ltd. v. Ulmer* (1987), 55 Sask. R. 309 (Q.B.); *Gouzenko v. Harris* (1976), 13 O.R. (2d) 730 (H.C.); and *Samayoa v. Marks* (1974), 6 O.R. (2d) 419, 53 D.L.R. (3d) 42 (H.C.). Although these terms are used interchangeably with "reasonably competent", the standard is a *legal* concept that does not necessarily equate with the practices of "ordinary" lawyers. Accordingly, we prefer the phrase "reasonable competence".

[2]   This is a paraphrase of the formulation of the standard of care stated in R.A. Percy, ed., *Charlesworth on Negligence*, 5th ed. (London: Sweet & Maxwell, 1971), at para. 312.

[3]   *Beal v. South Devon Ry. Co. Ltd.* (1864), 3 H. & C. 337, 159 E.R. 560; *Faithful v. Kesteven*, [1908-10] All E.R. Rep. 292, 103 L.T. 56 (C.A.); *Purves v. Landell* (1845), 12 Cl. & Fin. 91, 8 E.R. 1332 (H.L.).

[4]   R.M. Jackson and J.L. Powell, *Professional Negligence*, 2nd ed. (London: Sweet & Maxwell, 1987), at para. 4.23, point out that certain cases, *e.g.*, *Purves v. Landell, supra*, note 3, which speak in terms of "negligence of crass description", suggest a greater indulgence of error than is now the case.

to take reasonable care that is part of the retainer.[5] As the Supreme Court of Canada explained in *Central Trust Co. v. Rafuse*:[6]

> While the solicitor's duty of care has generally been stated, for obvious reasons, in the context of contractual liability as arising as an implied term of the contract or retainer, the same duty arises as a matter of common law from the relationship of proximity created by the retainer. In the absence of special terms in the contract determining the nature and scope of the duty of care in a particular case, the duties in contract and in tort are the same.[7]

B. ERROR OF JUDGMENT

While it is often said that "an error of judgment is not negligence",[8] this statement creates conceptual confusion. Simply to contrast an error of judgment with negligence presumes a "false antithesis".[9] The question is not whether the conduct constitutes an error of judgment, but whether it is the kind of judgmental error that would have been made by a reasonably competent and diligent practitioner.[10]

This misstatement may simply reflect the reluctance of the courts to elevate the lawyer to the status of guarantor of her client's claims and interests,[11] or it

---

[5]   As explained in Section II. "Ancillary Prinicples", B. "Implied Terms of the Retainer", the existence of a contract of retainer, permitting the implication of contractual terms, can be seen as creating a more onerous standard of care or, more precisely, an additional duty of care, whereby the lawyer is obliged not only to apply reasonable competence and diligence but also to fulfil all the implied terms of the retainer. See, *e.g.*, *Polischuk v. Hagerty* (1983), 42 O.R. (2d) 417, 149 D.L.R. (3d) 65 (H.C.), revd on other grounds 49 O.R. (2d) 71, 14 D.L.R. (4th) 446 (C.A.); R.M. Mahoney, "Lawyers — Negligence — Standard of Care" (1985), 63 *Can. Bar Rev.* 221 at 224 and 234-36.

[6]   [1986] 2 S.C.R. 147, 75 N.S.R. (2d) 109.

[7]   *Ibid.*, at 210 S.C.R.

[8]   See, *e.g.*, *Karpenko v. Paroian, Courey, Cohen & Houston* (1980), 30 O.R. (2d) 776, 117 D.L.R. (3d) 383 (H.C.), in which the court mistakenly cited *Brenner v. Gregory*, [1973] 1 O.R. 252, 30 D.L.R. (3d) 672 (H.C.), as authority for this proposition.

[9]   *Whitehouse v. Jordan*, [1980] 1 All E.R. 650 at 662 (C.A.), *per* Lord Donaldson, dissenting, affd on this point [1981] 1 All E.R. 267 at 276-77, 281 and 284, [1981] 1 W.L.R. 246 (H.L.).

[10] *Ibid.* This was, however, a case of medical malpractice. Some commentators have suggested that in most legal malpractice cases this false dichotomy has been overlooked: Smith, "Liability for the Negligent Conduct of Litigation: the Legacy of *Rondel v. Worsley*" (1982-83), 47 *Sask. L. Rev.* 211 at 263-64, citing Martyn, "Informed Consent in the Practice of Law" (1979), 48 *Geo. Wash. L.R.* 307, and "Comment: Attorney Malpractice" (1963), 63 *Columbia L.R.* 1292 at 1299.

[11] See *Alexander v. Small* (1846), 2 U.C.Q.B. 298 at 300, *per* Robinson C.J.: "The Profession of law would be the most hazardous of all professions, if those who practice in any of its branches were to be held strictly accountable for the accuracy of their opinions." In *Roberge v. Bolduc*, [1991] 1 S.C.R. 374, the Supreme Court of Canada stated at p. 432 that a lawyer does not assume an obligation not to err. The obligation is one of means, not of result, and a simple error of law will not necessarily entail liability.

may be an acknowledgment of the frailty of judges and lawyers alike in the realm of legal opinion.[12] Recently, in articulating the standard of care to be applied in cases of lawyers' malpractice, some courts have emphasized that the issue is whether a reasonably prudent solicitor in the same circumstances would have made the error.[13] This way of phrasing the test is preferable because it recognizes that an error of judgment may constitute negligence, thus avoiding the false antithesis. However, if an error is made in the conduct of a trial, a lawyer may not be liable even if a reasonably competent practitioner would not have made the same mistake. The inquiry in these circumstances is whether the error was egregious.[14]

For the most part, the reasonableness of a lawyer's error is assessed on the basis of expert or other objective evidence that tends to demonstrate whether or not a reasonably informed and competent practitioner would have made the same mistake as was made by the defendant lawyer.[15] In *Pelky v. Hudson Bay Insurance Co.*,[16] a lawyer's pursuit of an unsuccessful *volenti* defence on behalf of his client was characterized as a non-negligent error in judgment because: (1) the evidence adduced at trial in support of the defence differed from the lawyer's pre-trial understanding of the facts of the case; (2) the defence was dismissed by the trial judge only after consideration of the onus of proof; (3) the Court of Appeal did not think the *volenti* argument so unmeritorious as to render argument on it unnecessary; and (4) expert evidence supported the lawyer's decision to proceed with the defence.[17]

Further, the reasonableness of the error is judged in relation to the time it was made, permitting determinations that reflect the "state of the art". Thus, in 1971, the failure of a lawyer to recognize that a lease option did not comply with the provisions of the *Planning Act* was held to be excusable and not negligent although by 1980, the time of trial, it may well have constituted negligence.[18]

---

[12] A most forthright acknowledgment of this kind is found in *Montriou v. Jefferys* (1925), 2 C. & P. 113 at 116, 172 E.R. 51 at 53 (N.P.).

[13] See *Schmalzbauer v. Gares* (1990), 89 Sask. R. 254 (Q.B.); *285614 Alberta Ltd. v. Burnet, Duckworth & Palmer* (1993), 8 Alta. L.R. (3d) 212 (Q.B.); *Yang v. Overseas Investments (1986) Ltd.*, [1995] 4 W.W.R. 231 (Alta. Q.B.); *Ainscough v. Rankin, Bond & McMurray*, unreported, November 11, 1997, Beames J., Doc. Vancouver C923042, [1997] B.C.J. No. 2500 (S.C.).

[14] See Chapter 1, Section V. "Special Liability Problems", A. "Barrister's Liability", 2. "The Canadian Position", regarding barristers' liability in Canada.

[15] Other objective evidence might consist of information or checklists published by the Law Society or bar association. In *G. & K. Ladenbau (U.K.) Ltd. v. Crawley & de Reya*, [1978] 1 All E.R. 682, [1978] 1 W.L.R. 266, the court considered evidence that the specific conduct complained of had been drawn to the attention of the profession in two warning letters.

[16] (1981), 35 O.R. (2d) 97 (H.C.).

[17] *Ibid.*, at 114.

[18] *Page v. Dick* (1980), 12 C.C.L.T. 43 (Ont. H.C.). Evidence established that in 1971 there were no reported cases dealing with the problem, and a leading book of precedents, which the defendant had utilized in drafting the lease, omitted reference to the issue. See also *Ainscough v. Rankin, Bond & McMurray*, *supra*, note 13, in which the defendant lawyer acted for the plain-

C. KNOWLEDGE OF THE LAW

While a lawyer is not bound to know all the law,[19] he must have a good knowledge of the statutes and common law relevant to his work. At a minimum, he must know the "standard and fundamental" aspects of the law in his area. A real estate lawyer, for example, must possess the basic knowledge that, in the purchase of real property, funds are not advanced until the current state of encumbrances against title is ascertained.[20] Of course, the line between good and perfect knowledge is difficult to draw; suffice it to say, it is not necessary that the lawyer's knowledge of the law be at his fingertips:

> A solicitor is not required to know all the law applicable to the performance of a particular legal service, in the sense that he must carry it around with him as part of his "working knowledge", without the need of further research, but he must have a sufficient knowledge of the fundamental issues or principles of law applicable to the particular work he has undertaken to enable him to perceive the need to ascertain the law on relevant points.[21]

However, a lawyer has a responsibility to ensure that her client is making fully informed decisions on all matters relevant to the retainer. To this end, the client must be provided with complete advice. A client is not fully informed if his solicitor is only able to give incomplete advice due to inadequate research. Thus, the required standard of care includes a combination of a good working knowledge of the relevant law and further research, as necessary.[22] The court in *Confederation Life Insurance Co. v. Shepherd, McKenzie, Plaxton, Little & Jenkins*[23] emphasized that a lawyer has a duty to inform his client about the legal effects of particular courses of action:

> Where, as in this case, a solicitor undertakes to provide advice and legal services in respect of a transaction which is governed or affected, in whole or in part, by a public statute such as the *Condominium Act*, the solicitor bears the burden of exercising reasonable care and skill to ascertain by an examination of the relevant

---

tiff client in a personal injury action that was tried in 1983. The plaintiff claimed, *inter alia*, that the defendant ought to have put into evidence certain medical reports. In dismissing the claim, the trial judge held in 1997 that the defendant solicitor followed the standard practice of barristers conducting personal injury actions between 1981 and 1983 in that respect. In *Shute v. Premier Trust Co.* (1993), 35 R.P.R. 141 (Ont. Gen. Div.), the court held that there was a duty on solicitors in 1988 to exercise caution to guard against signatures being forged on mortgage documents.

[19] *Montriou v. Jefferys, supra*, note 12.

[20] *Yang v. Overseas Investments (1986) Ltd., supra*, note 13.

[21] *Central Trust Co. v. Rafuse, supra*, note 6, at 208 S.C.R., *per* Le Dain J.; *Fellowes, McNeil v. Kansa General Insurance Co.*, unreported, October 14, 1998, Macdonald J., Doc. 94-CU-78160CM, [1998] O.J. No. 4050 (Gen. Div.).

[22] *285614 Alberta Ltd v. Burnet, Duckworth & Palmer, supra*, note 13.

[23] (1992), 29 R.P.R. (2d) 271 (Ont. Gen. Div.), varied on other grounds 88 O.A.C. 398 (C.A.).

legislation the manner in which that legislation may impact upon the transaction. The solicitor is obliged to advise his client of any risks or concerns which such legislation may give rise to. [Case citations omitted.] [24]

The scope of the obligation to ascertain the law on all relevant points by carrying out legal research has not yet been judicially defined. One author has argued that this may be a reflection of courts' tendency to focus on the *result* of inadequate research methods, such as missed limitation periods or the failure to fully advise a client of his legal position. In these cases, negligent research is only implicitly at issue.[25] Guidance from the bench on a standard of legal research sufficient to avoid liability would be a welcome development in this area of the law, especially as fluency in technologically sophisticated research techniques becomes part of the skills set of the ordinarily competent solicitor.

Dugdale and Stanton have usefully observed that greater leniency is generally accorded lack of familiarity with substantive law principles than ignorance of matters of procedure; the latter is viewed as less likely to raise problems of professional judgment.[26] Thus, failure to be aware of or comply with a limitation period is always negligence, whether or not the provision is generally known or recently amended,[27] whereas failure to recognize that an esoteric doctrine of mortgage law invalidates a client's transaction is not.[28] Likewise, failure to follow the correct assessment appeal procedure is negligence even if there is doubt as to the appropriate procedure and evidence of the prevailing local practice supports the defendant solicitor's choice of procedure.[29] Generally, where there are two courses of action open to a lawyer, one of which is doubtful and the

---

[24] *Ibid*, at 297.

[25] K. Whitely, *Research Malpractice* (1990), 15 *Canadian Law Libraries* 51.

[26] Dugdale and Stanton, *Professional Negligence*, 2nd ed. (London: Butterworths, 1989), at 283. They are, however, careful to point out that this distinction "should not be elevated to a rule of law".

[27] As most recently stated in *Glivar v. Noble* (1985), 8 O.A.C. 60 at 67, *per* Blair J.A.:

> In all matters where the exercise of a client's rights is restricted by time limitations it seems to me that it is the duty of a solicitor to be certain what those time limits are before presuming to advise the client or to take any proceedings on his behalf. This is particularly true of statutes like the *Assessment Act* which are regularly amended and frequently used.

See also *Fletcher & Son v. Jubb, Booth & Helliwell*, [1920] 1 K.B. 275 (C.A.).

[28] See *Bannerman, Brydone Folster & Co. v. Murray and Another*, [1972] N.Z.L.R. 411 (failure by the defendant to determine that an option in a mortgage offended a corollary to the rule prohibiting clogs on the equity of redemption). See also the oft-cited American decision in *Lucas v. Hamm*, 364 P. 2d 685 (Cal. S.C., 1961), in which the defendant's unfamiliarity with the rule against perpetuities was held not to be negligence.

[29] *Glivar v. Noble, supra*, note 27. Although the court did not expressly acknowledge the doubt, the evidence referred to in the judgment suggests the procedure adopted by the defendant had, in the past, proven successful on occasion.

other assured of success, the pursuit of the doubtful course will constitute negligence.[30]

Omission of a legal principle or statutory provision from the standard textbooks[31] tends to establish its obscurity and may relieve against liability in a case where a lawyer's ignorance of the principle or provision is alleged to be negligence.[32] Conversely, the fact that a statutory provision has been in existence, unchanged, for many years and is not obscure is significant even if expert evidence is tendered to establish that the provision is not generally known.[33]

While the erroneous interpretation of an ambiguous or confusing statutory or contractual provision is not negligence,[34] failure to advert to the difficulty and bring it to the attention of the client may create liability.[35]

---

[30] *Levy v. Spyers* (1856), 1 F. & F. 3 at 5, 175 E.R. 599 (N.P.): "It is negligence where there are two ways of doing a thing, and one is clearly right and the other doubtful, to do it the doubtful way."

[31] Note that in *Ron Miller Realty v. Honeywell, Wotherspoon* (1991), 4 O.R. (3d) 492 (Gen. Div.), affd 16 O.R. (3d) 255*n* (C.A.), the court found the defendants negligent notwithstanding the introduction of evidence that revealed that the relevant section of the bar admission course had not dealt with the provision in question until the current year, and it currently did not cover the relevant provisions in any detail.

[32] *Page v. Dick, supra*, note 18; *Stephens v. Allen*, [1922] 1 W.W.R. 264 at 268 (P.C.): "but the question as to whether a solicitor is negligent or not in omitting to give effect to a statutory provision cannot be disentangled from the consideration of whether the statute that is involved is one which is of constant and common occurrence in practice or whether it is one unfamiliar and remote".

[33] *Elcano Acceptance Ltd. v. Richmond* (1985), 47 C.P.C. 256, 31 C.C.L.T. 201 (Ont. H.C.), revd on other grounds 55 O.R. (2d) 56, 9 C.P.C. (2d) 260 (C.A.).

[34] *Dunlop v. Woollahara Municipal Council*, [1982] A.C. 158, [1981] 2 W.L.R. 693 (P.C.) (construction of two clauses in a planning scheme); *Fletcher & Son v. Jubb, Booth & Helliwell, supra*, note 27, at 280.

[35] In *Central Trust Co. v. Rafuse*, [1986] 2 S.C.R. 147, 75 N.S.R. (2d) 109, the Supreme Court of Canada held that the fact the relevant statutory provision was hotly litigated resulting in conflicting judicial interpretations was no defence if the lawyer was not aware of the provision and, accordingly, failed to bring it to his client's attention as a potential obstacle to its course of action. See also *Richards v. Cox*, [1943] K.B. 139, [1942] 2 All E.R. 624 (C.A.). Conversely, in *Ormindale Holdings Ltd. v. Ray, Wolfe, Connell, Lightbody & Reynolds* (1980), 116 D.L.R. (3d) 346 (B.C.S.C.), affd 36 B.C.L.R. at 390, 135 D.L.R. (3d) 577 (C.A.), the defendants recommended a method of tax avoidance which was ultimately determined to be illegal. However, this advice was held not to be negligent, even though the plaintiffs were not told that the method could fail, because they were experienced businessmen who were aware of the daring nature of the scheme. In *285614 Alberta Ltd. v. Burnet, Duckworth & Palmer* (1993), 8 Alta. L.R. (3d) 212 (Q.B.), a solicitor structured a transaction, believing that it fit within the rules of the *Income Tax Act*, R.S.C. 1985, c. 1 (5th Supp.). However, the solicitor did no research on the subject, and failed to advise the clients that the law was unclear in the area. The solicitor was found negligent for giving the clients incomplete advice. The court held that it was not necessary that the solicitor's professional judgment in an unclear area of the law prove correct, but the client must be informed that the law regarding the particular transaction is unclear, and that the transaction is therefore more risky.

D. REASONABLE DILIGENCE

In addition to meeting a standard of reasonable competence, a lawyer must meet a standard of reasonable diligence.[36] A lawyer who does not adequately or diligently protect the interests of the plaintiff will be found negligent. For example, in *Skirzyk v. Crawford*[37] counsel for the plaintiff in a personal injury action owed a duty to "at least communicate with [the client] to ascertain his degree of recovery and what steps ought to be considered or taken either to settle the plaintiff's claim or set it down for trial". In *Islington Investments Ltd. v. Day, Ault & White*[38] a solicitor acting on behalf of a vendor of real estate delayed making application to the Committee of Adjustment for a necessary severance of lands with the result that a final certificate of severance could not be obtained prior to closing. The closing was consequently aborted and the solicitor was held liable to the vendor for lack of reasonable diligence even though a backlog of applications protracted the process beyond the solicitor's previous experience. Similarly, in *Rempel v. Parks*,[39] a case where a solicitor instructed a sheriff to serve process within the prescribed time, it was no defence that the sheriff failed to advise of his inability to do so before the expiry date. No action for indemnity against the sheriff was available. Thus a solicitor bears ultimate responsibility for timely service and any failure to meet that responsibility is negligence.

E. SURROUNDING CIRCUMSTANCES

Consistent with general principles of negligence, the reasonableness of a lawyer's impugned conduct is adjudged in light of the surrounding circumstances such as the time available to complete the work, the nature of the client's instructions, and the experience and sophistication of the client.[40] In the case of *Bannerman, Brydone*,[41] for example, the solicitor had one day to review the relevant document and the client was already committed to the transaction in its deficient form. These were determining factors in the dismissal of the client's

---

[36] *Fletcher & Son v. Jubb, Booth & Helliwell, supra*, note 27; *Groom v. Crocker*, [1939] 1 K.B. 194, [1938] 2 All E.R. 394 (C.A.); *Aaroe v. Seymour*, [1965] O.R. 736, 6 D.L.R. (2d) 100 (H.C.), affd 7 D.L.R. 676 (C.A.); *Grima v. MacMillan*, [1972] 3 O.R. 214, 27 D.L.R. (3d) 666 (H.C.); *835039 Ontario Inc. v. Fram Development Corp.*, unreported, August 9, 1994, Trafford J., Doc. 53207/90, [1994] O.J. No. 1725 (Gen. Div.).

[37] (1990), 64 Man. R. (2d) 220 at 230 (Q.B.).

[38] (1978), 7 C.C.L.T. 46 (Ont. H.C.).

[39] (1984), 53 B.C.L.R. 167, [1984] 4 W.W.R. 689 (C.A.). The failure of the action for indemnity against the sheriff has been criticized by J. Cassels, "Annotation" (1985), 35 R.P.R. 90. See also *Jakeman v. Jakeman and Turner*, [1963] 3 All E.R. 889 at 896.

[40] On negligence generally, see J.G. Fleming, *The Law of Torts*, 9th ed. (Sydney: The Law Book Co., 1998), at 117; A.M. Linden, *Canadian Tort Law*, 6th ed. (Toronto: Butterworths, 1997), at 115. On the relevance of surrounding circumstances to a claim of solicitors' negligence, see *Bell v. Strathern & Blair* (1954), 104 *L. J.* 618.

[41] *Supra*, note 28.

action against the solicitor.[42] On the other hand, when a purchaser, acting in haste without making pre-purchase inquiries, relied on a budget document voluntarily prepared by an accountant, the accountant was found liable for negligent misstatement. The court held that the defendant ought to have made clear to the plaintiff the limitations of the document as it was foreseeable that the plaintiff would rely on the budget document given the plaintiff's haste and known lack of independent inquiry.[43] The level of the client's sophistication can be relevant to the standard of care in some circumstances. A client's lack of sophistication will often be an appropriate factor in legal malpractice actions and at the very least will oblige the lawyer to take greater care.[44] In fact, this duty to take greater care may even extend to third parties in certain situations. In *Klingspon v. Ramsay*,[45] a solicitor owed a duty to an unsophisticated third

---

[42]   See also *Millican v. Tiffin Holdings*, [1967] S.C.R. 183, 60 D.L.R. (2d) 469. *Contra, Elcano Acceptance, supra*, note 33, at 272-73 47 C.P.C.: "the standard of care required of a solicitor should not be lowered when a solicitor is rushed by a client". However, on the facts of the case, the court found that the client's efforts to rush the lawyer did not contribute to the lawyer's negligent omissions. In *Mardling v. Malvern*, unreported, September 6, 1984 (Ont. C.A.), a lawyer was held not to be negligent in failing to make appropriate searches in the purchase of a business where the client insisted on closing without allowing time for those searches.

[43]   *MacDonald v. Schmidt*, unreported, November 14, 1991, Holmes J., Doc. C884881, [1991] B.C.J. No. 3377 (S.C.). The standard of care would have been met if the accountant had given the plaintiff a written statement explaining the assumptions underlying the document, and if the accountant had given an appropriate disclaimer.

[44]   *Lapierre v. Young* (1980), 30 O.R. (2d) 319, 117 D.L.R. (3d) 643 (H.C.); *Ferris v. Rusinak* (1983), 50 A.R. 297, 9 D.L.R. (4th) 183 (Q.B.); *Caligiuri v. De Lucia* (1983), 25 Man. R. (2d) 98 (Q.B.). The court in *285614 Alberta Ltd. v. Burnet, Duckworth & Palmer* (1993), 8 Alta. L.R. (3d) 212 (Q.B.), held that a solicitor's duty to advise her client in all matters relevant to the retainer is heightened by a client's lack of sophistication. Conversely, in certain circumstances the sophistication of the client may militate against a finding of negligence on the part of the solicitor: *Ormindale Holdings Ltd. v. Ray, Wolfe, Connell, Lightbody & Reynolds, supra*, note 35.

[45]   *Klingspon v. Ramsay*, [1985] 5 W.W.R. 411 (B.C.S.C.). The plaintiff attended the offices of the solicitor who obtained the signatures for the closing of a financing transaction. The solicitor required the investor to sign a receipt which acknowledged that:

> I HEREBY confirm and agree that with regard to the purchase of these shares [the solicitors] are acting as solicitors for the company only and have not offered me any advice other than as to the good standing of the Company and its capacity to issue the within shares, nor have I requested such advice. I am aware that any such advice should be sought from independent counsel.

The court held that the investor's reliance was foreseeable, that it should have been obvious that the plaintiff had no real understanding of the dangers involved and, notwithstanding the acknowledgment, that she was turning to the solicitor for reassurance. Given that there was no need for the solicitor to close a transaction of this sort with an inexperienced and unrepresented investor, the intent must have been to convey a misleading impression regarding the viability of the project. Thus, the solicitor had a duty to impress upon the investor in plain and unambiguous words that the solicitor could give no assurances with respect to the financial stability of the company.

party investor, even though the solicitor attempted to avoid liability by requiring the investor to sign an acknowledgment that he did not offer any advice respecting the project!

Conversely, the fact that a client is a sophisticated business person will have a direct effect on the lawyer's obligations. This is especially true where the nature of the client's instructions and the terms of the retainer, both express and implied, indicate that the client himself is taking responsibility for steps that might otherwise be taken by the lawyer.[46] Thus, in *Spence v. Bell*,[47] when an astute businessman retained a lawyer to prepare a lease for a mobile home park but reserved to himself the key function of structuring the mortgage financing for the project, the lawyer was not negligent when a financial institution refused to advance mortgage funds because the lease was unacceptable.

A similar result may be found in *Woodglen & Co. v. Owens*.[48] An experienced real estate developer devised and co-ordinated an elaborate redevelopment plan, compartmentalizing various tasks among many professionals. The defendant lawyer was retained in connection with the redevelopment but was advised that another firm was representing the client in his dealings with the municipality. The developer's high degree of sophistication, knowledge, intelligence and creativity created the reasonable perception in the mind of the lawyer that he understood that a part lot control exemption might be lifted. In finding the lawyer not liable in the circumstances for failing to warn the client of the possibility that part lot control might be reinstated, Madam Justice Macdonald of the Ontario Court (General Division), explained the relevance of the client's sophistication this way:

> This does not mean, however, that the standard of care required of [the solicitor] is less than it would have been if [the client] was not a sophisticated client. Its rele-

---

[46] See Section II. "Ancillary Principles", B. "Implied Terms of the Retainer".

[47] (1982), 22 Alta. L.R. (21d) 193, [1982] 6 W.W.R. 385 (C.A.), leave to appeal to S.C.C. refused 41 A.R. 305. In his dissenting judgment, Mr. Justice Kerans, at 405-11 W.W.R., would have allowed the appeal on the basis that the solicitor was negligent in failing to draw a lease which conveyed good title. In our opinion, this is the better view. In *Hallmark Financial Insurance Brokers Ltd. v. Fraser & Beatty* (1990), 1 O.R. (3d) 641 (Gen. Div.), in an acquisition involving more than $1 million, the solicitor was entitled to assume, as his clients were experienced businessmen, that they would carefully review crucial portions of important legal documents, particularly because the clause in issue was a business component of the transaction, not a legal one. The court emphasized that this is not to say that a solicitor does not owe a duty to bring the business provisions of a contract, as distinct from the legal provisions of the contract, to the attention of a client.

[48] (1996), 6 R.P.R. (3d) 259 (Ont. Gen. Div.). See also *Fasken Campbell Godfrey v. Seven-Up Canada Inc.* (1997), 142 D.L.R. (4th) 456 (Ont. Gen. Div.), wherein a client, who was himself a lawyer, claimed that his solicitors did not advise him that he may be liable to an estate for personal advantages he gained from his position as executor. The court held that the duty to warn only arises where an ordinarily competent and prudent solicitor would have issued a warning, taking into account all of the surrounding circumstances, including the form and nature of the client's instructions and the client's sophistication.

vance is that it impacts on the application of the standard of care, to the particular facts as they were at the relevant times during the course of the retainer. More particularly, it impacts the determination of such matters as the duty to warn of risk. The duty to warn of risk is not correctly analysed if it is premised on the notion that the failure to do so automatically creates liability on the part of the solicitor. Liability is established only if an ordinarily competent and prudent solicitor would have issued a warning, in all the circumstances, of this case.[49]

In *Islington Investments Ltd. v. Day, Ault & White*,[50] when a solicitor failed to take immediate steps to process his client's application to the Committee of Adjustment with the result that it could not be granted on a timely basis, it was no defence that circumstances beyond the control of the solicitor, in particular a large backlog of applications, contributed to the delay. It is irrelevant whether the lawyer is retained for a fee or whether she volunteers her services.[51] In *Duchesse of Argyll v. Beuselinck*[52] one case it was suggested that the standard of care may be higher if large fees are charged. Finally, solicitors who hold themselves out as experts in a given area of the law may be required to meet the higher standard of "reasonably competent experts":

> Where a solicitor holds himself out to his client as having particular expertise in a given area of law, such as in respect of sophisticated real estate transactions, a higher standard applies. The requisite standard is not that of a reasonably competent solicitor or ordinary prudent solicitor, but that of a reasonably competent expert in commercial real estate transactions. [Case citations omitted.][53]

II. ANCILLARY PRINCIPLES

A. GENERAL AND APPROVED PRACTICE

Many cases of professional negligence, including barristers' and solicitors' negligence, are defended on the basis that the conduct complained of is consistent with "general and approved", "prevailing" or "customary" practice.[54] Whether or not the defence affords the professional complete immunity from liability has

---

[49] *Woodglen & Co. v. Owens, supra*, note 48, at 295.

[50] *Supra*, note 38.

[51] *Kitchen v. Royal Air Forces Assn.*, [1958] 2 All E.R. 241, [1958] 1 W.L.R. 563 (C.A.).

[52] [1972] 2 Lloyd's Rep. 172. This case is discussed in greater detail in Section II. "Ancillary Principles", E. "Standard for Specialists".

[53] *Confederation Life Insurance Co. v. Shepherd, McKenzie, Plaxton, Little & Jenkins* (1992), 29 R.P.R. (2d) 271 (Ont. Gen. Div.), varied on other grounds (1996), 88 O.A.C. 398 (C.A.); *Fellowes, McNeil v. Kansa General Insurance Co.*, unreported, October 14, 1998, Macdonald J., Doc. 94-CU-78160CM, [1998] O.J. No. 4050 (Gen. Div.). See also Section II. "Ancillary Principles", E. "Standard for Specialists", regarding the standard of care applicable to specialists.

[54] These terms appear to be used interchangeably.

for some years been the subject of divergent judicial opinion[55] and academic debate.[56] In the case of lawyers specifically, the issue was for a time resolved by *Winrob v. Street & Wollen*[57] on the basis that evidence of a general and approved practice is "highly relevant" and "may establish a defence" unless it is "inconsistent with provident precautions against a known risk."[58] However, this defence seldom failed to absolve a lawyer of liability unless the practice was insufficiently established by the evidence.[59]

A series of recent decisions has substantially weakened the defence of general and approved practice in cases of legal malpractice. The foremost of these is *Edward Wong Finance Co. Ltd. v. Johnson, Stokes & Masker*,[60] a decision of the Privy Council on appeal from the Court of Appeal of Hong Kong. The plaintiff appellant was a financial institution that had retained the defendant firm of solicitors to act on its behalf in a land transfer, in which the plaintiff was advancing the purchase moneys and taking a mortgage as security. In accordance with the long-established practice of Hong Kong solicitors, the defendant firm advanced the mortgage funds to the vendor's solicitor on his undertaking to complete the transaction by perfecting the plaintiff's security, in particular, by discharging an existing encumbrance and registering the plaintiff's mortgage. When the vendor's solicitor absconded with the mortgage moneys without discharging the existing mortgage, the plaintiff sued the defendant for the funds it had advanced and effectively lost. The evidence at trial unequivocally established that the "Hong Kong style of closing" adopted by the defendant was used in 99 per cent of

---

[55] One line of cases characterizes proof of conformity to prevailing practice as a conclusive defence: see *McDaniel v. Vancouver General Hospital*, [1934] 3 W.W.R. 619, [1934] 4 D.L.R. 593 at 597 (P.C.): "A defendant charged with negligence can clear his feet if he shows that he has acted in accordance with general and approved practice"; cited with approval in *MacLeod v. Roe*, [1947] S.C.R. 420 at 424 and 430, [1947] 3 D.L.R. 241; *Vermont Construction Inc. v. Beatson*, [1977] 1 S.C.R. 758, 67 D.L.R. (3d) 95; *London & Lancashire Guarantee & Accident Co. v. Drolet*, [1944] S.C.R. 82; *Bolam v. Friern Hospital Management Committee*, [1957] 2 All E.R. 118, [1957] 1 W.L.R. 582 (Q.B.). Another line of authorities has held that proof of compliance with prevailing practice is not conclusive: see *Bank of Montreal v. Dominion Gresham Guaranty & Casualty Co.*, [1930] A.C. 659, [1930] 4 D.L.R. 689 at 693 (P.C.): "Neglect of duty does not cease by repetition to be neglect of duty"; *Lloyds Bank Ltd. v. E.B. Savory & Co.*, [1933] A.C. 201 at 235, [1932] All E.R. Rep. 106 (H.L.): "the practice on its very face, is inconsistent with provident precautions against a known risk and the mere fact that it is usual and long established is not a sufficient justification".

[56] *Cf.* Linden, *supra*, note 40 at 177-80; A.M. Dugdale and K.M. Stanton, *Professional Negligence*, 2nd ed. (London: Butterworths, 1989), at 240-43; and P.C. Weiler, "Groping Towards a Canadian Tort Law: The Role of the S.C.C." (1971), 21 *U.T.L.J.* 267, with R.M. Mahoney, "Lawyers — Negligence — Standard of Care" (1985), 63 *Can. Bar Rev.* 221.

[57] (1959), 28 W.W.R. 118, 19 D.L.R. (2d) 172 (B.C.S.C.), cited with approval in *Grima v. MacMillan*, [1972] 3 O.R. 214, 27 D.L.R. (3d) 666 (H.C.).

[58] *Ibid.*, at 175 D.L.R.

[59] For example, the defence was successful in *Grima v. MacMillan*, *supra*, note 57; *Brenner v. Gregory*, [1973] 1 O.R. 252, 30 D.L.R. (3d) 672 (H.C.); *Hauck v. Dixon* (1975), 10 O.R. (2d) 605, 64 D.L.R. (3d) 201 (H.C.); and *Smaldon v. Lawrence* (1983), 31 R.P.R. 126 (Ont. Co. Ct.).

[60] [1984] A.C. 296, [1984] 2 W.L.R. 1 (P.C.).

Hong Kong transactions, that it had proved to be of benefit to purchasers and vendors because it accelerated transactions, that this was the first occasion that the practice had backfired, and that there were no warning signs that ought to have put the defendant on guard against a possible defalcation by the vendor's solicitor. Nevertheless, the Privy Council held that the firm was negligent in following the practice since it involved a "foreseeable risk" which could have been avoided by alternate means and the firm had failed to do so.

In *Edward Wong*,[61] the Privy Council held that in assessing whether a lawyer falls short of the standard of care he owes to his clients, three questions must be asked:

(1)   did the practice engaged in by the lawyer involve a foreseeable risk;

(2)   if so, could that risk have been avoided;

(3)   if so, was the lawyer negligent in failing to take the avoiding action.[62]

This is a novel formulation of the standard of care; it departs from the traditional criterion defined as reasonable competence and diligence. Indeed, the omission of the word "reasonable" from the test is curious since general principles of negligence law hold that negligence is the creation of *unreasonable* risks.[63] While it was undisputed in *Edward Wong* that the practice adopted by the defendant firm of solicitors involved some, presumably foreseeable, risk, the defendant argued the risk was nevertheless reasonable to take in the circumstances.[64] Unfortunately, this argument was not addressed by the court in its reasons and, further, the judgment does not make clear whether the defendant firm's failure to avoid a foreseeable risk is the same as a failure to maintain reasonable competence and diligence or whether the defendant was liable notwithstanding that it had acted in a reasonably competent and diligent fashion.

Edward Wong was considered in *Polischuk v. Hagerty*,[65] where the Ontario Court of Appeal upheld the conclusion of Henry J. at trial that the defendant solicitor was liable notwithstanding that he had "acted in accordance with the general practice followed by solicitors in the circumstances at that time; he used reasonable skill and judgment, according to the standards of the profession."[66] The defendant lawyer in *Polischuk*, like the defendant in *Edward Wong*, accepted an undertaking from the vendor's lawyer in the course of a real

---

[61]   *Ibid.*

[62]   *Ibid.*, at 306 A.C.

[63]   See A.M. Linden, *Canadian Tort Law*, 6th ed. (Toronto: Butterworths, 1997), at 116; J.G. Fleming, *The Law of Torts*, 9th ed. (Sydney: The Law Book Co., 1998), at 117.

[64]   *Edward Wong, supra*, note 60, at 299-300. The facts of the case are summarized at p. 27, *supra*. The defendant pointed to the evidence that suggested any risk was outweighed by the economic benefits to the client in utilizing the practice.

[65]   (1983), 42 O.R. (2d) 417, 149 D.L.R. (3d) 65 (H.C.), revd on other grounds 49 O.R. (2d) 71, 14 D.L.R. (4th) 446 (C.A.).

[66]   *Ibid.*, at 425 42 O.R.

estate transaction, namely, to use a portion of the purchase moneys to discharge a prior mortgage. The undertaking was breached, the vendor's solicitor died without refunding the purchase price or discharging the existing mortgage, and the vendors left the country. Henry J. held that the defendant had failed in his obligation to complete the transaction in accordance with the terms of the agreement of purchase and sale, which contained the usual clause that the purchasers were to take title free of existing encumbrances. In rejecting the defence based on prevailing practice, Henry J. reasoned:

> While solicitors in London had adopted the practice followed by the defendant, as a practical way of closing transactions, where a discharge of mortgage was not readily available to carry out the vendor's obligation, I cannot accept that the profession was justified in imposing such practice upon the lay public, their clients, without their knowledge and consent.[67]

Edward Wong was expressly adopted in *Glivar v. Noble*[68] by the Ontario Court of Appeal, which rejected the trial judge's acceptance of prevailing practice as determinative of the proper standard of care. The defendant solicitor had been retained, *inter alia*, to appeal an assessment of his client's buildings. In accordance with the prevailing practice in his community, the solicitor challenged the assessment at the Assessment Review Court, which lacked jurisdiction in the matter. The trial judge found the defendant's choice of forum was incorrect and that the Supreme Court was the appropriate appellate forum, but he characterized the solicitor's error as non-negligent because it reflected prevailing practice.

On appeal, Blair J.A., speaking for a unanimous court, held that the trial judge had erred in accepting prevailing practice as the appropriate standard of care and, applying the *Edward Wong* test of "foreseeable risk", determined that an appeal to the Assessment Review Court was indeed a foreseeable risk since the defendant was aware that the tribunal did not always entertain jurisdiction in the kind of case in question. The Court of Appeal suggested that the rejection of prevailing practice was not a new development in that the *Edward Wong* test was consistent with the line of cases that had rejected practices "inconsistent with prudent precautions against a known risk."[69] However, the test of "known risk" is arguably less onerous than that of "foreseeable risk". Moreover, the former test had seldom been applied against a defendant. This standard was applied recently in *Yamada v. Mock*.[70] A mortgage on a matrimonial home was signed by a woman posing as the mortgagor wife. The solicitor, who acted for

---

[67] *Ibid.*, at 425-26 42 O.R.
[68] (1985), 8 O.A.C. 60.
[69] *Ibid.*, at 66, citing, *inter alia*, *Brenner v. Gregory, supra*, note 58, and *Major v. Buchanan* (1975), 9 O.R. (2d) 491, 61 D.L.R. (3d) 46 (H.C.).
[70] (1996), 29 O.R. (3d) 731 (Gen. Div.).

both sides of the transaction, was found liable to the mortgagee in negligence for failing to ask the impostor for identification. The court held: "I see the risk in these circumstances to be plainly foreseeable and, regardless of the practice, the law would impose liability on the solicitor to deal with the foreseeable risk."[71]

It appears to have been settled that, while evidence of prevailing or customary practice is a very relevant consideration, it will not be determinative of solicitors' negligence actions. In *Roberge v. Bolduc*,[72] the Supreme Court of Canada considered whether a notary was negligent when he erred in his assessment of whether a title defect had been cured. Madam Justice L'Heureux-Dubé, speaking for a unanimous court, made these statements about the weight to be given to expert evidence of general and accepted practice:

> This brief overview of both doctrine and jurisprudence indicates that courts have discretion to assess liability despite uncontradicted evidence of common professional practice at the relevant time. The standard, in regard to the particular facts of each case, must still be that of a reasonable professional in such circumstances.
>
> . . . . .
>
> The fact that a professional has followed the practice of his or her peers may be strong evidence of reasonable and diligent conduct, *but it is not determinative*. If the practice is not in accordance with the general standards of liability, i.e., that one must act in a reasonable manner, then the professional who adheres to such a practice can be found liable, depending on the facts of each case.[73] [Emphasis in original.]

Several courts have followed the reasoning in *Roberge*.[74]

In factually unique circumstances where it cannot be said that there is an accepted standard of practice, the standard of care is a question of law to be determined by the court in accordance with the unusual circumstances.[75] Where the court does not have the benefit of expert evidence as to the prevailing practice, it

---

[71] *Ibid.*, at 734.

[72] [1991] 1 S.C.R. 374.

[73] *Ibid.*, at 436-37.

[74] See, for example, *Ron Miller Realty v. Honeywell, Wotherspoon* (1991), 4 O.R. (3d) 492 (Gen. Div.), affd 16 O.R. (3d) 255*n* (C.A.); *Gauvreau v. Paci*, unreported, June 4, 1993, Gordon J., Doc. 8915/91, [1993] O.J. No. 1429 (Gen. Div.), revd on other grounds, unreported, June 28, 1996, Doc. C15906, [1997] O.J. No. 2396 (C.A.), application for leave to appeal refused, June 19, 1997, [1997] S.C.C.A. No. 549.

[75] *R.E.A.D. Enterprises v. Picadilly Investments Ltd.*, unreported, July 31, 1997, Errico J., Doc. C950415, [1997] B.C.J. No. 1806 (S.C.).

must decide the content of the standard from general principle and reason and then compare it to the services provided by the lawyer.[76]

B. IMPLIED TERMS OF THE RETAINER

It is apparent that the standard of care is directly related to the scope of the retainer. Oliver J. explained the relationship between the standard of care and the retainer in *Midland Bank Trust Co. Ltd. v. Hett, Stubbs & Kemp*:[77] "It may be that a particularly meticulous and conscientious practitioner would, in his client's general interests, take it upon himself to pursue a line of enquiry beyond the strict limits comprehended by his instructions. But that is not the test."[78] Thus, in *Buckland v. Mackesy*[79] a solicitor who was retained to advise a client on the terms of a lease, and did so satisfactorily, was not liable for subsequently failing to remind the client that the date for exercising an option to terminate the lease was approaching. Similarly, in *Hilloak Finance Services Ltd. v. Pichelli*,[80] solicitors acting for a mortgagee pursuant to a limited retainer were not negligent for not inquiring into zoning or work orders.

However, the converse proposition is also true: a solicitor who applies reasonable competence and diligence to her task may nevertheless be held liable if the task she undertakes does not satisfy all the terms of her retainer. As set out in *Midland Bank v. Hett, Stubbs & Kemp*: "A contract gives rise to a complex of rights and duties of which the duty to exercise reasonable care and skill is but one."[81] The problem is that in most cases the terms of the contract or retainer are not settled in writing and may be implied by the court. This obviously can lead to inconsistent and unpredictable results.

The leading case on the issue of the implied terms of the retainer is *Polischuk v. Hagerty*,[82] in which the plaintiff purchasers retained the defendant to carry out the terms of an agreement of purchase and sale of a residential property, but gave him no explicit instructions. He was simply, in the words of the trial judge, "to close the transaction and protect their interests."[83] The agreement provided that the vendors would deliver an executed discharge of an existing mortgage on closing, but shortly beforehand the defendant received a letter from the vendor's solicitor advising that his undertaking to do so would be provided instead. When

---

[76] *Hussey v. Parsons* (1997), 153 Nfld. & P.E.I.R. 354 (Nfld. T.D.).

[77] [1979] Ch. 384, [1978] 3 All E.R. 571.

[78] *Ibid.*, at 583 All E.R. This reasoning was applied by the English Court of Appeal more recently in *National Home Loans Corp. plc v. Giffen Couch & Archer (a firm)*, [1997] 3 All E.R. 808 (C.A.).

[79] (1968), 112 Sol. Jo. 841 (C.A.). See also *R. & L. Contracting Ltd. v. A.* (1981), 28 B.C.L.R. 342 (C.A.).

[80] Unreported, June 21, 1989, Fitzpatrick J., Doc. 913/85, [1989] O.J. No. 2560 (H.C.).

[81] *Supra*, note 77, at 611 All E.R.

[82] *Supra*, note 65.

[83] *Supra*, note 65, at 422 42 O.R.

the vendor's solicitor failed to discharge the existing mortgage, the plaintiffs obtained judgment against the vendors that remained unsatisfied. They then sued their solicitor for breach of contract in failing to provide them with a good and marketable title free from all prior mortgages.

In setting out the terms of the retainer between the plaintiff and the defendant, the trial judge held that two essential obligations were implied: (1) "to exercise reasonable care and skill according to the standards of the profession"; and (2) to "complete the contract of purchase and sale on behalf of the clients, according to its terms."[84] The court held that the defendant met his first obligation but failed to meet the second.[85] On appeal, the Ontario Court of Appeal upheld the trial judge's conclusions on liability, but allowed the plaintiff's appeal on damages and substantially increased the award.[86]

It is interesting to compare the *Polischuk* reasoning with the reasoning in *Edward Wong* in that both decisions were based on very similar facts. The test proposed in *Edward Wong*, avoidance of foreseeable risks, seems peculiarly a creature of tort law not unlike the doctrine of informed consent in medical negligence.[87] It could, therefore, be used in future to assess the liability of lawyers in relation to non-client third parties. In contrast, the implied retainer doctrine is exclusively a creature of contract law, the obligations of a lawyer being defined in accordance with the reasonable expectations of the parties to the contract. Hence this liability criterion would appear to be inapplicable to a lawyer's relationship with non-contractual plaintiffs.[88] By way of further contrast, the traditional liability criterion,

---

[84]   *Supra*, note 65, at 424 42 O.R.

[85]   R.M. Mahoney, "Lawyers — Negligence — Standard of Care" (1985), 63 *Can. Bar Rev.* 221 at 235, argues that "there was nothing forcing implication [of the second obligation]. The defendant's obligation . . . might just as easily have been altered by implication to include the ability to complete the transaction in the manner adopted by right thinking solicitors faced with similar circumstances." *Contra*, D. Dooley, "Liability of Solicitors for Accepting Undertakings — *Polischuk v. Hagerty*" (1985), 6 *Advocates' Q.* 123.

[86]   *Polischuk v. Hagerty* (1984), 49 O.R. (2d) 71, 14 D.L.R. (4th) 446 (C.A.).

[87]   Indeed, *Edward Wong* can, in certain respects, be seen as an example of the lawyer's duty to warn his client before undertaking a risky course of action; although, as discussed at pp. 27-29, *supra*, it goes further than the earlier cases dealing with the duty to warn, such as *Winrob v. Street & Wollen* (1959), 28 W.W.R. 118, 19 D.L.R. (2d) 172 (B.C.S.C.), and *Major v. Buchanan*, *supra*, note 69, in requiring disclosure of foreseeable as well as known risks. Moreover, to the extent the *Edward Wong* test is seen as a kind of informed consent doctrine (a lawyer has a duty to inform a client of the risks of a transaction and to obtain his or her consent before proceeding), it is clear that the Privy Council's approach to the issue of causation is very different from that of the Supreme Court of Canada in *Reibl v. Hughes*, [1980] 2 S.C.R. 880, 14 C.C.L.T. 1, the leading Canadian authority on informed consent in medical negligence. See Chapter 7, at Section I, A.

[88]   However, it is unlikely that the courts will entertain the notion of an apparent dichotomy between the standard of care required by the law of contract and the standard of care required under the rubric of tort law. The court held in *Graybriar Industries Ltd. v. Davis & Co.* (1990), 46 B.C.L.R. (2d) 164 at 180 (S.C.), affd, 72 B.C.L.R. (2d) 190 (C.A.), quoting from *Canadian Imperial Bank of Commerce v. Pomeroy*, unreported, December 16, 1986, Hogarth J. (B.C.S.C.):

expressed in terms of reasonable competence and diligence, while originally arising as part of a lawyer's implied contractual duty, is equally consistent with negligence principles.

This trend away from a single definition of the standard of care, reasonable competence and diligence, and toward a standard that also assesses the conduct of the defendant against the reasonable expectations of his client and the availability of alternative precautions against a foreseeable risk, will in all likelihood expose lawyers to increased liability. The reasonable expectations of the client will be ascertained in light of the client's sophistication and reliance upon the lawyer's expertise. If the client is properly informed as to his potential exposure, especially if the client is fairly sophisticated in the relevant type of transaction, then the solicitor has met the appropriate standard of care.[89]

Courts are willing to imply as a term of the retainer a duty to warn the client of potential risks of a particular transaction or course of action. For example, in *Confederation Life Insurance Co. v. Shepard, McKenzie, Plaxton, Little & Jenkins*[90] a lawyer retained to provide services in respect of a transaction affected by a public statute has been held liable for breach of the implied duty to warn by failing to advise his client of the risks to which the legislation may give rise. In another case, *Barrie v. 687844 Ontario Ltd.*, a solicitor breached the implied duty when he did not warn his mortgagee client that a bonus paid to the client by the mortgagor may constitute interest, causing the effective rate of interest to be a criminal rate and rendering a guarantee of the mortgage unenforceable.[91] It is also a breach of the implied duty to fail to warn an unsophisticated client of the risks of personally guaranteeing a business loan.[92]

The imposition of this duty ensures that clients are properly informed regarding the legal effect of a particular fact situation. The court in *Graybriar Industries Ltd. v. Davis & Co.*[93] canvassed the law[94] with respect to a duty to warn:

> The law is clear, as the plaintiff suggests, that if a solicitor fails to live up to the standard of care required of him, a client offended may sue him in contract or in tort. . .

> I do not believe, however, that in the absence of an express contractual term it can be said, nor has it been argued, that because the action is founded in tort as opposed to contract or vice versa, the duty of the solicitor is greater in the one case than in the other.

[89] *Legare v. Miller*, unreported, March 8, 1991, Chadwick J., Doc. 25616/88, [1991] O.J. No. 403 (Gen. Div.).

[90] (1992), 29 R.P.R. (2d) 271 (Ont. Gen. Div.), varied on other grounds (1996), 88 O.A.C. 398 (C.A.). See also *Haag v. Marshall* (1989), 1 C.C.L.T. (2d) 99 (B.C.C.A.), in which a solicitor was found to have breached his duty to his clients in failing to warn them of the possible results of certain situations.

[91] (1994), 43 R.P.R. (2d) 267 (Ont. Gen. Div.).

[92] *Couture v. Lamontagne*, [1997] 5 W.W.R. 23 (Sask. Q.B.), revd on other grounds [1998] 6 W.W.R. 481 (C.A.), application for leave to appeal to S.C.C. dismissed with costs June 11, 1998.

[93] *Supra*, note 88.

[94] Specifically, the following cases: *R. & L. Contracting Ltd. v. A* (1981), 28 B.C.L.R. 342 (C.A.); *Income Trust Co. v. Watson* (1984), 26 B.L.R. 228 (Ont. H.C.); *Canadian Imperial Bank of*

In digest with specific reference to those cases: ". . . a solicitor should warn his client of the risks . . ." (*R & L*); "If he fails to warn the client of the risk . . . the solicitor will be liable . . ." (*R & L*), "a lawyer is obliged to act as a 'prudent solicitor'" (*C.I.B.C.*); and the duty includes ". . . the duty to inquire to provide such warnings on the basis of a reasonable knowledge of the law, facts and practical implications of the results . . ." (*Olorenshaw*).[95]

Of course, the existence of the duty to warn will depend at least in part on the nature and extent of the retainer and the sophistication of the client. A court will consider whether a reasonably prudent solicitor would have relayed the warning in the circumstances.[96] As explained by Madam Justice Macdonald in *Woodglen & Co. v. Owens*:

> The duty to warn of risk is not correctly analysed if it is premised on the notion that the failure to do so automatically creates liability on the part of the solicitor. Liability is established only if an ordinarily competent and prudent solicitor would have issued a warning, in all of the circumstances, of this case.[97]

C. THE LOCALITY RULE

The English courts have not seen fit to apply the "locality rule" to cases of legal malpractice, that is, to apply different standards of care to lawyers practising in different communities or localities.[98] In contrast, Canadian courts often define the standard of care in terms of the geographical area, usually the city where the solicitor practises.[99] However, the rule, probably imported from the law of medical malpractice, has seldom been approved expressly. *Marbel Developments*

Commerce v. Pomeroy, *supra*, note 88; *Olorenshaw v. International Chem-Pro Industries Inc.*, [1989] B.C.W.L.D. 1888 (S.C.).

[95] *Supra*, note 88 at 181.

[96] *Woodglen & Co. v. Owens* (1996), 6 R.P.R. (3d) 259 (Ont. Gen. Div.); *Fasken Campbell Godfrey v. Seven-Up Canada Inc*, (1997), 142 D.L.R. (4th) 456 (Ont. Gen. Div.).

[97] *Woodglen & Co. v. Owens, supra*, note 96, at 295.

[98] A.M. Dugdale and K.M. Stanton, *Professional Negligence*, 2nd ed. (London: Butterworths 1989), at 240-43; Masel, *Professional Negligence of Lawyers, Accountants, Bankers and Brokers* (North Ryde, NSW: CCH Australia, 1981), at 86. However, the Privy Council, on hearing the appeal in *Stephens v. Allen*, [1922] 1 W.W.R. 264, appeared to consider local practices relevant to the question of liability (at 267): "The question of negligence with regard to the performance of a solicitor's duty must to some extent be affected by local conditions and the local circumstances."

[99] *Grima v. MacMillan*, [1972] 3 O.R. 214, 27 D.L.R. (3d) 666 (H.C.); *Hauck v. Dixon* (1975), 10 O.R. (2d) 605, 64 D.L.R. (3d) 201 (H.C.); *Elcano Acceptance Ltd. v. Richmond* (1985), 47 C.P.C. 256, 31 C.C.L.T. 201 (Ont. H.C.), revd on other grounds 55 O.R. (2d) 56, 9 C.P.C. (2d) 260 (C.A.); *Page v. Dick* (1980), 12 C.C.L.T. 13 (Ont. H.C.); *Gauvreau v. Paci*, unreported, June 4, 1993, Gordon J., Doc. 8915/91, [1993] O.J. No. 1429 (Gen. Div.), revd on other grounds, unreported, June 28, 1996, Doc. C15906, [1996] O.J. No. 2396 (C.A.), application for leave to appeal dismissed June 19, 1997, [1997] S.C.C.A. No. 549.

Ltd. v. Pirani,[100] a decision of the British Columbia Supreme Court, expressly rejected the argument that the standard of care may vary between large downtown and small suburban or rural law firms.

The justification for the rule in cases of medical malpractice — to reconcile the once vast disparity between the facilities, equipment, and assistants available to the urban practitioner as compared to the rural one[101] — does not readily lend itself to the provision of legal services given that disparities of resources are as large between firms within a city or geographical area as those between firms in different cities. Nor is it clear from the Canadian authorities whether the rule is really a variation of the "prevailing practice defence" in the sense that a local practice is considered sufficient to constitute a "general practice"; or whether, quite apart from the question of prevailing practice, it calls on the court to fix the standard of care having regard to the resources and skills of the practitioners within a particular locality. Of course, the latter interpretation of the rule invites a patchwork of different standards for different communities with inconsistent and intolerable results. To the extent that the rule enjoys continued acceptance, it should be viewed as a kind of prevailing practice defence, affording some, if not conclusive, evidence of the reasonableness of the defendant solicitor's conduct.[102]

D. THE USE OF EXPERT EVIDENCE

Given the diminished impact of prevailing practice on the standard of care, it is not surprising that expert evidence tending to establish or support the practice or, for that matter, the requisite standard of care,[103] has been the subject of increasing critical comment by the courts. First, the courts have become more vigilant about the nature of the expert evidence adduced, rejecting as irrelevant evidence of a particular witness's approach to the conduct in question;[104] that is, an expert witness must be in a position to opine as to general and approved

---

[100] (1994), 18 C.C.L.T. (2d) 229 (B.C.S.C.).

[101] Ellen Picard, *Legal Liability of Doctors and Hospitals in Canada* (Toronto: Carswell, 1978), at 118.

[102] This was the balance struck by Osborne J. in *Campbell v. Delrue*, February 15, 1985, [1985] O.J. No. 1028 (H.C.).

[103] It is important to note that expert evidence regarding professional liability is not binding on the precise question of law which the judge is called upon to decide: *Roberge v. Bolduc*, [1991] 1 S.C.R. 374, at 431.

[104] *McLaren Maycroft & Co. v. Fletcher Dev. Co. Ltd.*, [1973] 2 N.Z.L.R. 100; *Clements v. Wyatt* (1979), 9 R.P.R. 1 (Ont. H.C.); *De Yong v. Weeks* (1984), 55 A.R. 305 (C.A.), leave to appeal to S.C.C. refused 58 A.R. 38n. *Cf. Grima v. MacMillan, supra*, note 99, in which all the expert witnesses appear to have testified with respect to their personal views and experiences without judicial rebuke.

practice and not simply with respect to his personal regimen.[105] Secondly, expert evidence that purports to define the standard of care may be disregarded when the parties' witnesses offer opposing views such that "it takes [the court] to a draw".[106] Moreover, the relevance and weight of expert opinion is decreased in a case where the uniqueness of the conduct complained of renders doubtful the existence of a standard or customary practice.[107]

This does not mean that counsel either prosecuting or defending legal malpractice claims should refrain from adducing expert evidence. Although the adjudication of legal malpractice cases sometimes covers familiar ground for judges, the increasing complexity and specialization of legal practice makes expert evidence about the standard of care a critical factor in most cases.[108]

E. STANDARD FOR SPECIALISTS

It is no defence to a negligence claim that the defendant lawyer is inexperienced; an inexperienced lawyer must subscribe to a standard of reasonable competence and diligence that takes no account of her years at the bar.[109] What of the converse proposition: is the experienced lawyer or the lawyer who has developed a specialist practice held to a higher standard of care? The comments of Megarry J. in *Duchess of Argyll v. Beuselinck*[110] support the imposition of a specialist standard:

> . . . if the client employs a solicitor of high standing and great experience, will an
> action for negligence fail if it appears that the solicitor did not exercise the care

---

[105] *Midland Bank Trust Co. Ltd. v. Hett, Stubbs & Kemp*, [1979] Ch. 384, [1978] 3 All E.R. 571; *Sutherland v. Public Trustee*, [1980] 2 N.Z.L.R. 536 (S.C.); *Marbel Developments Ltd. v. Pirani, supra*, note 100.

[106] *Elcano Acceptance Ltd. v. Richmond, supra*, note 99, at 267 C.P.C. See also *Papadopoulos v. Anklewicz* (1987), 60 O.R. (2d) 198, 35 M.P.L.R. 105 (H.C.), in which the court accepted the statement of J. Irvine in "Annotation to *Brain v. Mador*" (1985), 32 C.C.L.T. 158 at 159, that where there are "genuine rifts of respectable professional opinion . . . no Ontario judge should label as negligent conduct performed in adherence to one or other of the contending bodies of opinion . . ."; *285614 Alberta Ltd. v. Burnet, Duckworth & Palmer* (1983), 8 Alta. L.R. (3d) 212 (Q.B.), in which the court held that, where one expert condemns the approach of another, the court must decide the issue.

[107] *De Yong v. Weeks, supra*, note 104; *R. & L. Contracting Ltd. v. A.* (1981), 28 B.C.L.R. 342 (C.A.); *R.E.A.D. Enterprises Ltd. v. Picadilly Investments Ltd.*, unreported July 31, 1997, Errico J., Doc. C950415, [1997] B.C.J. No. 1806 (S.C.).

[108] As Cromarty J. expressed it in *Morris v. Jackson* (1984), 34 R.P.R. 269 at 298 (Ont. H.C.): "In my opinion a Judge of this Court who in practice has been both a barrister and solicitor, can and may assess a solicitor's professional behaviour without expert evidence to assist him." See also *Neagle v. Power*, [1967] S.A.S.R. 373 at 376. But see *Grover Holdings Ltd. v. Weir* (1987), 54 Sask. R. 68, 44 R.P.R. 64 at 68 (Q.B.).

[109] *Rowswell v. Pettit*, [1969] 1 O.R. 22, 1 D.L.R. (3d) 268 (C.A.), affd [1970] S.C.R. 865, 11 D.L.R. (3d) 737, *sub nom. Wilson v. Rowswell*.

[110] [1972] 2 Lloyd's Rep. 172.

and skill to be expected of him, though he did not fall below the standard of a reasonably competent solicitor? If the client engages an expert, and doubtless expects
to pay commensurate fees, is he not entitled to expect something more than the
standard of the reasonably competent? I am speaking not merely of those expert in
a particular branch of the law, as contrasted with a general practitioner, but also of
those of long experience and great skill as contrasted with those practising in the
same field of law but being of a more ordinary calibre and having less experience.
The essence of the contract of retainer, it may be said, is that the client is retaining
the particular solicitor or firm in question, and he is therefore entitled to expect
from that solicitor or firm a standard of care and skill commensurate with the skill
and experience which that solicitor or firm has. The uniform standard of care
postulated for the world at large in tort hardly seems appropriate when the duty is
not one imposed by the law of tort but arises from a contractual obligation existing
between the client and the particular solicitor or firm in question. If, as is usual,
the retainer contains no express term as to the solicitor's duty of care, and the
matter rests upon an implied term, what is that term in the case of a solicitor of
long experience or specialist skill? Is it that he will put at his client's disposal the
care and skill of an average solicitor, or the care and skill that he has?. . . I wish to
make it clear that I have not overlooked the point, which one day may require
further consideration.[111]

The opinion of Megarry J. has yet to be considered by an English or Commonwealth appellate court, although it was referred to with approval by the
English Court of Appeal (Civil Division) in *Martin Boston & Co. v. Roberts*.[112]
In that case, a firm of solicitors acted for a client in an action against him by a
numbered company. A motion for security for costs brought by the firm on the
client's behalf was dismissed and the firm filed a notice of appeal. On the firm's
recommendation, the client accepted a personal guarantee signed by a director
of the plaintiff numbered company in lieu of proceeding with the appeal. At
trial, the plaintiff's action was dismissed with costs awarded in favour of the
client and the plaintiff appealed. The client accepted a second personal guarantee from the director in respect of his costs of the appeal. The appeal was dismissed and costs were again awarded to the client.

The personal guarantees proved worthless and the firm's efforts to recover
the costs awards were to no avail. When the firm subsequently sued the client
for unpaid fees, he counterclaimed alleging negligence in respect of their assessment of the enforceability of the guarantees. In a concurring judgment, Lord
Justice Simon Brown held:

It may be, as a passage in Megarry J.'s judgment in the *Duchess of Argyll* case
suggests, that different standards apply, depending on the different level of experi-

---

[111] *Ibid.*, at 183-84.
[112] The Times (17 March 1995).

ence, expertise and, indeed, expensiveness of individual solicitors. For present purposes, however, it seems to me immaterial to explore the accuracy of that proposition or how far it may be taken.[113]

Megarry J.'s opinion was reviewed by Mr. Justice Smith of the Ontario High Court in the course of his reasons in *Elcano Acceptance Ltd. v. Richmond.*[114] On the facts of the case before him, Smith J. found the defendants liable as either generalists or specialists, but he expressed a preference for an "approach that recognizes a distinction between the specialist and the generalist practitioners when defining the standard of care".[115] Importantly, however, Smith J. was not prepared to go as far as Mr. Justice Megarry's proposed distinction between lawyers of "long experience and great skill" and those of "more ordinary calibre and having less experience". This latter distinction, as Dugdale and Stanton have pointed out, would be difficult to apply and, rather ironically, would compel the court to assess the defendant's skill before deciding whether he was negligent.[116]

Conversely, the rationale that supports the imposition of a specialist standard is not easily dismissed. Megarry J. has observed that imposing a higher standard of care appears to be fairer in instances where the solicitor has "held himself out" as having special expertise in a particular area of practice,[117] although cases of "implied" holding out — by the charging of higher fees than normal — are not as apparent. A specialist standard has long been accepted in the law of medical negligence[118] and while the legal profession does not yet utilize the kind of formal and objective criteria for establishing specialist status that prevails in medicine, the legal profession is becoming increasingly specialized. The courts are aware of this increased specialization and the response seems to be that solicitors who hold themselves out as experts in a given area of the law may be required to meet the higher standard of "reasonably competent experts":

> Where a solicitor holds himself out to his client as having particular expertise in a given area of law, such as in respect of sophisticated real estate transactions, a higher standard applies. The requisite standard is not that of a reasonably compe-

---

[113] *Ibid.*

[114] *Supra*, note 99.

[115] *Ibid.*, at 267 47 C.P.C. Unlike Megarry J., Smith J. concluded that a specialist standard is equally applicable to tort and contract claims.

[116] Dugdale and Stanton, *supra*, note 98, at 238.

[117] For Canadian cases which the court considered in determining the standard of care (whether the defendant solicitor held himself out as an expert), see *Confederation Life Insurance Co. v. Shepherd, McKenzie, Plaxton Little & Jenkins* (1992), 29 R.P.R. (2d) 271 (Ont. Gen. Div.), varied on other grounds (1996), 88 O.A.C. 398 (C.A.) and *R.E.A.D. Enterprises, supra*, note 107.

[118] See *Wilson v. Swanson*, [1956] S.C.R. 804, 5 D.L.R. (2d) 113; *Challand v. Bell* (1959), 27 W.W.R. 182, 18 D.L.R. (2d) 150 (Alta. S.C.).

tent solicitor or ordinary prudent solicitor, but that of a reasonably competent expert in commercial real estate transactions. [Case citations omitted.][119]

However, many involved in the legal profession believe that the personal qualifications and expertise of a defendant lawyer should not dictate whether or not a specialist standard is applied.[120] The public interest in promoting competent legal services is not greatly enhanced by the imposition of a higher standard of care in all cases where a specialist is sued, even if the specialist has performed a routine task. Rather, what is important is that all those who undertake legal matters requiring expertise, whether they are specialists or generalists, be judged by the same standard as that expected of the reasonably competent and diligent lawyer specializing in the area of law in question.

F. ETHICAL STANDARDS

The Rule contained in Chapter II, "Competence and Quality of Service", of the *Code of Professional Conduct* of the Canadian Bar Association provides:

(a) The lawyer owes a duty to his client to be competent to perform the legal services which the lawyer undertakes on his behalf.
(b) The lawyer should serve his client in a conscientious, diligent and efficient manner and he should provide a quality of service at least equal to that which lawyers generally would expect of a competent lawyer in a like situation.

The language of paragraph (b) clearly distinguishes this ethical standard — defined in terms of what "lawyers generally would expect" — from the standard of care that is used by the court for purposes of determining negligence. This distinction is emphasized by the Commentary that accompanies the Rule.[121]

However, the courts may make reference to other rules contained in codes of professional conduct in determining that a particular act or omission falls below the requisite standard of care. For example, in *Pelky v. Hudson Bay Insurance Co.*,[122] the court made reference to the Law Society of Upper Canada *Rules of Professional Conduct* in identifying the obligation of a solicitor to communicate offers of settlement to his client; the court concluded that a failure to communicate a settlement offer constituted negligence. Likewise in *Kern-Hill Co-op*

---

[119] *Confederation Life Insurance Co.*, *supra*, note 117.
[120] See, for example, L.N. Klar et al., *Professional Negligence*, ed. by L.D. Rinaldi (Toronto: Carswell, 1995), at 32.
[121] Canadian Bar Association, *Code of Professional Conduct*, adopted by Council, August 25, 1974, at 4-6 and particularly Commentary 8: "A mistake even though it might be actionable for damages in negligence would not necessarily constitute a failure to maintain the standard set by the Rule, but evidence of gross neglect in a particular matter or a pattern of neglect or mistake in different matters may be evidence of such a failure regardless of tort liability."
[122] (1981), 35 O.R. (2d) 97 (H.C.).

Furniture Ltd. v. Shuckett,[123] the *Code of Professional Conduct* of the Canadian Bar Association was referred to in defining one of the duties of a solicitor, that is, to refrain from withdrawing his services except for good cause and upon appropriate notice. Failure to comply with this ethical standard was equated with negligence. Finally, many of the cases dealing with conflict of interest[124] refer to ethical guidelines. Although the guidelines do not have the force of law, they help to inform the court of the standard expected of members of the profession.[125]

---

[123] (1975), 58 D.L.R. (3d) 157 (Man. C.A.).

[124] See, for example, *MacDonald Estate v. Martin*, [1990] 3 S.C.R. 1235; *R. v. Leask* (1996), 140 D.L.R. (4th) 176 (Man. Prov. Ct.); *Rosin v. MacPhail* (1997), 142 D.L.R. (4th) 309 (B.C. C.A.).

[125] *McKay v. Cowan* (1989), 39 B.C.L.R. (2d) 192 (S.C.); See also *Morton v. Asper*, [1988] 1 W.W.R. 47 (Man. Q.B.), affd [1988] 2 W.W.R. 317 (Man. C.A.); *Planned Insurance Portfolios Co. v. Crown Life Insurance Co.* (1989), 68 O.R. (2d) 271 (H.C.J.); *Enerchem Ship Management Inc. v. Coastal Canada (The)* (1988), 83 N.R. 256 (Fed. C.A.).

Chapter 3

FIDUCIARY OBLIGATIONS

I. FIDUCIARY RELATIONSHIPS DEFINED

A. FIDUCIARY RELATIONSHIPS GENERALLY

Until recently, the term "fiduciary" was one of the most ill-defined in the common law[1] and the precise fiduciary obligations of barristers and solicitors, indeed professionals in general, had seldom been carefully analyzed.[2] In the result, a number of cases involving lawyers invoked the language of fiduciary obligations without adequate explanation and thereby created unnecessary conceptual confusion.[3]

During the last 15 years, the Supreme Court of Canada has provided considerable guidance on the nature of fiduciary relationships and obligations. Traditionally, only relationships which fell into a few status-based categories were considered fiduciary. Among them were the relationships between solicitor and client, doctor and patient and trustee and beneficiary. In 1984, Chief Justice Dickson articulated a new basis for the identification of fiduciary relationships in *Guerin v. R.*, a case in which the Crown was found to owe fiduciary obligations to native peoples:

> It is sometimes said that the nature of fiduciary relationships is both established and exhausted by the standard categories of agent, trustee, partner, director, and the like. I do not agree. *It is the nature of the relationship, not the specific category of the actor involved that gives rise to the fiduciary duty.* The categories of fiduciary, like those of negligence, should not be considered closed.[4] [Emphasis added.]

---

[1] Finn, *Fiduciary Obligations* (Sydney: The Law Book Co. Ltd., 1977), at 1.

[2] A useful discussion is, however, contained in D.F. Partlett, *Professional Negligence* (Melbourne: The Law Book Co. Ltd., 1985), at 119-58.

[3] See, *e.g.*, *Tracy v. Atkins* (1977), 83 D.L.R. (3d) 46 (B.C.S.C.), affd 16 B.C.L.R. 223, 105 D.L.R. (3d) 632 (C.A.), discussed in Chapter 4, Section II. "Breach of Fiduciary Duty", B,"Fiduciary Obligation to Third Parties".

[4] [1984] 2 S.C.R. 335 at 384.

In the ensuing years, the Supreme Court of Canada and lower courts attempted to establish criteria for the identification of fiduciary relationships outside of the status-based categories, although a definite test does not yet seem to have evolved. The first of the Supreme Court of Canada decisions to explore the subject in detail was *Frame v. Smith*,[5] in which the majority found that a custodial parent does not owe a fiduciary obligation to a non-custodial parent to comply with an access order. Madam Justice Wilson, in dissent, identified the essential features of fiduciary relationships:

> Relationships in which fiduciary obligations have been imposed seem to possess three characteristics:
>
> (1) The fiduciary has scope for the exercise of some discretion or power.
> (2) The fiduciary can unilaterally exercise that power or discretion so as to affect the beneficiary's legal or practical interests.
> (3) The beneficiary is peculiarly vulnerable to or at the mercy of the fiduciary holding the discretion or power.[6]

The criteria developed by Wilson J. were soon adopted by a majority of the Supreme Court in *International Corona Resources Ltd. v. Lac Minerals Ltd.*[7] A senior mining company received confidential information about certain geological findings from a junior mining company during the course of negotiations for a joint venture. It subsequently acquired the property itself and the junior mining company sued for breach of fiduciary duty and breach of confidence. Mr. Justice Sopinka, writing for the majority on this point, applied the reasoning of Wilson J. in *Frame* and concluded that there is no inherent vulnerability between two sophisticated business actors negotiating at arm's length. Thus, no fiduciary duties were owed. Dissenting on this issue, Mr. Justice La Forest held that fiduciary obligations exist not only in relationships that are inherently vulnerable, but also where vulnerability arises out of the special circumstances of the relationship as a matter of fact.

Sopinka and La Forest JJ. revisited their debate about the centrality of the concept of vulnerability to the existence of a fiduciary relationship in 1994 in *Hodgkinson v. Simms*.[8] Simms, an accountant, recommended that his client, Hodgkinson, invest in Multi-Unit Residential Buildings ("MURBs") but did not disclose the fact that he received a commission from the MURB developers for every investment made by his clients.

La Forest J. held that a party becomes a fiduciary to another where he has an obligation to act for the benefit of another person pursuant to a statute, an

5   [1987] 2 S.C.R. 99.

6   *Ibid.*, at 136.

7   [1989] 2 S.C.R. 574.

8   [1994] 3 S.C.R. 377.

agreement or a unilateral undertaking that carries with it a discretionary power. Outside the established categories of fiduciary relationships, the question to ask is whether, given all the circumstances, one party could reasonably have expected that the other party would act in the former's best interests with respect to the subject-matter at issue.[9] The criteria identified by Wilson J. "constitute *indicia* that help recognize a fiduciary relationship rather than ingredients that define it".[10] Vulnerability "is nothing more than the corollary of the ability to cause harm, *viz.*, the susceptibility to harm" and thus should not be overemphasized in assessing the existence of fiduciary relationships.[11] Discretion, influence, vulnerability and trust are non-exhaustive examples of evidentiary factors to be considered in making this determination. There must be some measure of reliance by the beneficiary, but the wholesale surrender of decision-making power to the fiduciary is not necessary. There must also be evidence of a mutual understanding between the parties that one of them has undertaken to relinquish her own self-interest to act solely on behalf of the other party. Applying his view of the fiduciary concept to the facts, La Forest J. concluded that in providing the investment advice, Simms had exercised a power and discretion that had been placed in him by Hodgkinson and therefore owed him a fiduciary duty of loyalty.

In *Hodgkinson*, Sopinka J. again held, this time in dissent, that vulnerability is an essential feature of the fiduciary relationship. There must be total reliance and dependence on the fiduciary by the beneficiary in order for fiduciary obligations to arise. Where a client retains the power and ability to make her own decisions, an advisor may be under a duty of care not to make any misrepresentations. However, she does not have a fiduciary duty of loyalty unless she has unilateral power over the client's affairs. A fiduciary relationship did not arise on the facts of this case because there had not been a total surrender of decision-making power by the client to the accountant.

Mr. Justice La Forest's opinion appears to have prevailed in *Hodgkinson*, although there was no clear majority in the case.[12] The Sopinka-La Forest debate has been the subject of considerable judicial and academic comment[13] but the Supreme Court has not extensively considered fiduciary principles since

---

[9]   We have remarked on the trend away from a vulnerability requirement towards a "reasonable expectation of the parties" in S.M. Grant and J.L. De Marco, "Professional Liability's Widening Net" (1997), 19 *Advocates' Q. 456*.

[10] *Hodgkinson v. Simms, supra*, note 8, at 409.

[11] *Ibid.*, at 430.

[12] La Forest and Sopinka JJ. each had the support of two justices. The seventh justice, Mr. Justice Iacobucci, wrote a very brief judgment concurring with La Forest J.'s reasons but stating without explanation that *Lac Minerals* was distinguishable from the case at bar.

[13] See, for example, *Stewart v. Canadian Broadcasting Corp.* (1997), 150 D.L.R. (4th) 24 (Ont. Gen. Div.), supp. reasons (1997), 152 D.L.R. (4th) 102 (Ont. Gen. Div.); L.I. Rotman, "The Vulnerable Position of Fiduciary Doctrine in the Supreme Court of Canada" (1996), 24 Man. L.J. 60; J.D. McCamus, "Prometheus Unbound: Fiduciary Obligation in the Supreme Court of Canada" (1997), 28 *Can. Bus. L.J.* 107.

Hodgkinson. The future of the vulnerability concept in fiduciary doctrine was rendered more uncertain with the retirement of La Forest J. and the sudden passing of Sopinka J.

The effect of the Supreme Court of Canada's development of the law in this area has been a significant expansion in the types of relationships to which fiduciary obligations have attached. Fiduciary obligations have been imposed on professionals such as accountants, architects, engineers, financial advisors and insurance agents, as well as in some non-professional contexts such as the relationship between parent and child.[14] In general, the law of fiduciary duty is becoming increasingly prevalent in the area of professional liability and, as one commentator has suggested, threatens to "swallow whole much of the law of torts and a considerable portion of contractual obligation".[15]

B. LAWYERS' FIDUCIARY OBLIGATIONS

Fiduciary obligations are playing an ever-increasing role in the liability of lawyers. In both *Lac Minerals* and *Hodgkinson*, La Forest J. explained that where a relationship has as its essence discretion, influence over interests, and inherent vulnerability, a strong but rebuttable presumption arises out of the inherent purpose of the relationship that one party has a fiduciary duty to act in the best interests of the other.[16] Because the lawyer-client relationship clearly falls into that category, *prima facie*, lawyers owe fiduciary duties to their clients in addition to the duties owed in contract and tort.

As for the content of the fiduciary obligation, it is important to emphasize that fiduciary duty is a creature of equity and, accordingly, must be contrasted with common law duties arising in contract and in tort.[17] However, "a fiduciary's obligations are prescribed in the case of a solicitor by the retainer, that he will act in a skilful, competent manner and act openly, honestly and in the best interests of his or her client. His duty is no more."[18] Further, although it is clear that a single course of conduct may give rise to liability both as a fiduciary and in negligence, the test of liability in each category is different.[19]

---

14   *M.(K.) v. M.(H.),* [1992] 3 S.C.R. 6.
15   McCamus, *supra,* note 13, at 115.
16   *Lac Minerals, supra,* note 7, at 647; *Hodgkinson, supra,* note 8, at 409.
17   44(1) *Halsbury's Laws of England,* 4th ed. Reissue (London: Butterworths, 1995), para. 148, at 121-22, citing *Nocton v. Lord Ashburton,* [1914] A.C. 932, [1914-15] All E.R. Rep. 45 (H.L.).
18   Flinn J., summarizing the article by Gautreau J., "Demystifying the Fiduciary Mystique" (1989), 68 *Can. Bar Rev.* 1 in *Canada Trustco Mortgage Co. v. Bartlet & Richardes* (1991), 3 O.R. (3d) 642 at 657 (Gen. Div.), affd 28 O.R. (3d) 768 (C.A.).
19   For example, in our view, the court in *Tracy v. Atkins, supra,* note 3, erroneously merged the test of liability for breach of fiduciary duty with the test of liability for negligence. Partlett, *supra,* note 2, at 120-21, cites *Boyd v. Ewachniuk,* [1975] 4 W.W.R. 210 at 215 (B.C.S.C.), as another example. In that case, the court held that a solicitor-client relationship establishes a fiduciary duty to take care. Partlett links this error to the confusion created by the jurisdiction that equity developed to grant compensation for breaches of equitable obligations. In this regard, we have noted elsewhere

The numerous obligations that are characterized as "fiduciary" can be seen as flowing essentially from three principles. A lawyer must:

(1)   represent his or her client with undivided loyalty;

(2)   preserve his or her client's confidences; and

(3)   make full disclosure of all relevant and material information relating to his or her client's interests.

The clearest example of a breach of fiduciary duty is a breach of trust, which we do not examine in this work. Although there are numerous cases of this kind, for the most part they involve some dishonesty on the part of the lawyer and, therefore, are beyond the definitional scope of this book. It is important to emphasize, however, that breaches of fiduciary obligations are not usually deliberate. Moreover, the fact that a lawyer was acting in good faith affords no defence when a breach of fiduciary duty has been established.[20]

One further matter requires comment. The law respecting a lawyer's fiduciary obligations, perhaps more than any other area of legal malpractice law, is intertwined with the rules of ethics contained in the various Law Societies' Codes of Professional Conduct. In *Hodgkinson*, Mr. Justice La Forest explained: "the rules set by the relevant professional bodies are of guiding importance in determining the nature of the duties flowing from a particular professional relationship".[21]

Nevertheless, the relationship between the two is seldom clear-cut; in some cases the ethical canon mirrors the legal obligation and in other cases the legal obligation is derived from the ethical rule. Fortunately, with respect to the three overriding fiduciary obligations of a lawyer — the duty of loyalty, the duty of disclosure, and the duty of confidentiality — the nature of the obligation is described similarly in the cases and in the codes of conduct.[22] This consistency makes sense; fiduciary obligations play a similar role to that of codes of conduct

---

the mistaken tendency of Canadian courts to describe an award of compensation for a breach of fiduciary duty as an award of damages: see McGregor, ed., *McGregor on Damages*, 16th ed. (London: Sweet & Mawxell Ltd., 1997), at 3. For further discussion of the inappropriateness of equating the duty of care in tort with fiduciary duty, see Shepherd, *The Law of Fiduciaries* (Toronto: Carswell, 1981), at 48-49. *Cox v. Pemberton Holmes Ltd.* (1991), 53 B.C.L.R. (2d) 92 (S.C.), supp. reasons 55 B.C.L.R. (2d) 118 (S.C.), affd (1993), 80 B.C.L.R. (2d) 331 (C.A.), carefully distinguishes between fiduciary obligations and the tort of negligence.

20   *Ott v. Fleishman* (1983), 46 B.C.L.R. 221, [1983] 5 W.W.R. 721 (S.C.); *Morkin v. Boras*, [1979] 5 W.W.R. 479 (Alta. C.A.), affd [1978] 2 W.W.R 385 (S.C.).

21   *Supra*, note 8, at 425.

22   For example, the Rule in Chapter V of the Canadian Bar Association's *Code of Professional Conduct*, Revised ed. (1996), dealing with conflict of interest (the duty of loyalty), provides, *inter alia*: "The lawyer shall not advise or represent both sides of a dispute and, save after adequate disclosure to and with consent of the clients or prospective clients concerned, shall not act or continue to act in a matter when there is or is likely to be a conflicting interest." See also the Rule in Chapter IV regarding confidential information.

in ensuring that clients are protected from the inherent risk of abuse by their lawyers in professional dealings with them.[23]

The fact that a lawyer alleged to have breached a fiduciary duty is not, in fact, in breach of any rule of professional conduct may be of considerable assistance in defending the claim.[24] However, although conformity with an ethical rule can influence a court's determination of whether a breach has occurred, it cannot exempt a lawyer from any fiduciary obligation because it cannot abrogate a client's legal or equitable rights.[25] Thus, a lawyer may be found in breach of fiduciary duty even though she has not breached a rule of professional conduct.[26]

II. TO WHOM THE OBLIGATIONS ARE OWED

A. CLIENTS

In most cases, the source of a lawyer's fiduciary obligations will be the solicitor-client relationship. Once this relationship is proven, the lawyer stands in a fiduciary relationship with the client whether the lawyer provides exclusively legal services or undertakes to serve the client's business interests as well.[27] Indeed, when fiduciary obligations are breached, it is often in the context of a business venture with the client.[28]

In the same way that solicitor-client privilege attaches to communications prior to a retainer, fiduciary obligations may arise even before a solicitor-client relationship is formally established.[29] Fiduciary duties do not attach to all work performed by the lawyer for the client. As one judge has explained: "I do not

---

[23] For cases in which a rule of professional conduct was referred to in deciding a claim of breach of fiduciary obligation see: *Confederation Life Insurance Co. v. Shepherd, McKenzie, Plaxton, Little & Jenkins* (1992), 29 R.P.R. (2d) 271 (Ont. Gen. Div.), affd 88 O.A.C. 398 (C.A.); *McKay v. Cowan* (1989), 39 B.C.L.R. (2d) 192 (S.C.); *Morton v. Asper*, [1988] 1 W.W.R. 47 (Man. Q.B.), affd [1988] 2 W.W.R. 317 (C.A.). For a discussion of ethical codes as a source of liability see Chapter 2, Section II. "Ancillary Principles", F. "Ethical Standards".

[24] *Phillis v. Burns* (1997), 38 O.T.C. 241 (Gen. Div.).

[25] *Stewart v. Canadian Broadcasting Corp., supra*, note 13.

[26] *Ibid.*

[27] There are numerous examples. A sampling includes: *Morkin v. Boras, supra*, note 20; *Demerara Bauxite Co. Ltd. v. Hubbard*, [1923] A.C. 673, [1923] All E.R. Rep. Ext. 841 (P.C.); *Cavallin v. King* (1984), 51 B.C.L.R. 149 (S.C.); *Cassey v. Morrison* (1989), 67 O.R. (2d) 65 (H.C.), at 69, upheld on appeal, except for one variation in the damages order: 15 O.R. (3d) 223 (C.A.). On the other hand, in *Lefebvre v. Gardiner* (1988), 27 B.C.L.R. (2d) 294 (S.C.), the court found that although the plaintiff may have been in a position of vulnerability *vis-à-vis* the defendant, and although the defendant knew that the plaintiff was relying on certain information provided by the defendant, at no time did the plaintiff expect the defendant to act in the plaintiff's interest or on his behalf.

[28] For example, see *Korz v. St. Pierre* (1987), 61 O.R. (2d) 609, 43 D.L.R. (4th) 528 (C.A.), leave to appeal to S.C.C. refused February 25, 1988.

[29] See M.V. Ellis, *Professional Fiduciary Duties* (Toronto: Carswell, 1995) and the decision in *Descoteaux v. Mierzwinski*, [1982] 1 S.C.R. 860, discussed therein at 9-2 to 9-3.

suggest that a fiduciary duty attached to every aspect of [the lawyer's] work for [the client] when he was his counsel. In the midst of a fiduciary relationship, not all of the fiduciary's actions are subject to such a duty."[30]

B. FORMER CLIENTS

It is clear that fiduciary obligations may persist even after the termination of the solicitor-client relationship.[31] Whether a fiduciary relationship exists between a solicitor and the former client, as well as the nature of the obligations owed, will be determined by reference to the original retainer. In *R. v. Speid*,[32] the Ontario Court of Appeal held that a solicitor has a fiduciary duty not to act against a former client in respect of the same subject-matter she was retained on; the fiduciary duty endures when the retainer is completed.

The relationship between solicitor and former client is not one of the *prima facie* fiduciary relationships. Thus, courts will now apply the criteria discussed in *Frame, Lac Minerals* and *Hodgkinson* to determine whether a fiduciary relationship currently exists between the lawyer and former client.[33] In *Stewart v. Canadian Broadcasting Corp.*,[34] a noted criminal defence lawyer discussed a former client's case on a television program over the protestations of the former client some ten years after the solicitor-client relationship ended. One of the services found to comprise part of the retainer was the improvement of negative public perceptions about the client that resulted from substantial publicity about the case. The new relationship was fiduciary because the relationship was not independent of the original retainer. The court found that the solicitor breached his fiduciary duty of loyalty to the former client by attracting attention to the case and preferring his self-interest, both financial and self-promotional, over the interests of the former client.

Where a lawyer does business with a former client, she will owe a fiduciary duty to make full disclosure if she has an advantage over the former client because of the confidential information she learned about the client during the retainer, or if she gained the client's trust and respect because of her expert knowledge and special position as advisor. In *Korz v. St. Pierre*,[35] a decision of the Ontario Court of Appeal, it was held that, because of the advantage the solicitor had as a result of the previous solicitor-client relationship, a solicitor engaged in a business venture with former clients owed to them a fiduciary obligation to make "a full disclosure of his position".[36] In a more recent decision, *Kalla v. Wolkovicz*, a solicitor who

---

[30] *Supra*, note 13 at 129-30 D.L.R. See also *Canada Trustco Mortgage Co. v. Bartlet & Richardes, supra*, note 18, 28 O.R. at 774.

[31] *Korz v. St. Pierre, supra*, note 28; *McMaster v. Byrne*, [1952] 1 All E.R. 1362 (P.C.).

[32] (1983), 43 O.R. (2d) 596 (C.A.).

[33] *Stewart, supra*, note 13, at 161.

[34] *Ibid.*

[35] *Supra*, note 28.

[36] *Supra*, note 28, at 618 O.R.

entered into a real estate transaction with former clients without disclosing a secret profit he made on the sale was held not to be in breach of his fiduciary duty because the previous solicitor-client relationship did not create any advantage for the defendant solicitor and the price charged had been fair.[37] Conversely, in *McKinnon v. Conexco Internatinal Corp.*,[38] a solicitor who invested with a long-time client of his firm in a newly formed company was found to have breached his fiduciary duty to the client when he failed to inform him that the firm was not acting for him in the venture and to advise him to obtain independent legal advice.

C. THIRD PARTIES

A fiduciary relationship can arise between a lawyer and a stranger to the solicitor-client relationship. The circumstances under which such a relationship will arise, and the scope of the duties that may be owed to third parties, are examined in detail in Chapter Four.

III. FIDUCIARY OBLIGATIONS DEFINED

A. DUTY OF LOYALTY

1. Self-Interest

The Supreme Court of Canada has defined the fiduciary duty of loyalty as including two central obligations: the fiduciary's personal interests must not conflict with the interests of the beneficiary, and the fiduciary must not profit at the beneficiary's expense.[39]

The House of Lords' decision in *Boardman v. Phipps*[40] is one of the earliest and best known illustrations of a lawyer's duty of undivided loyalty conflicting with his personal interests. In that case, Boardman, a solicitor, acquired a personal interest in a company in which his client, the Phipps family trust, had a substantial holding. The beneficiaries of the trust were fully informed of the stake Boardman was acquiring and it was not disputed that he did so in order to enhance the value of the trust's interest in the company. Indeed, the scheme proved highly profitable for all concerned. Nevertheless it was contended by the plaintiff, one of the beneficiaries, and ultimately accepted by a majority of the

---

[37]   Unreported, February 9, 1994, Haley J., [1994] O.J. No. 257 (Gen. Div.). However, the defendant was found in breach of fiduciary duty because of the conflict of interest that arose when he had his partner act on the transaction with the former clients.

[38]   *McKinnon v. Conexco International Corp.*, unreported, February 17, 1992, Steele J., Doc. 16582/86, [1992] O.J. No. 292 (Gen. Div.).

[39]   *International Corona Resources Ltd. v. Lac Minerals Ltd.*, [1989] 2 S.C.R. 574, and *Hodgkinson v. Simms*, [1994] 3 S.C.R. 377.

[40]   [1967] 2 A.C. 46, [1966] 3 All E.R. 721 (H.L.).

House of Lords, that Boardman held the shares as constructive trustee for and on behalf of the family trust and was liable to account to the plaintiff beneficiary for his share of the profits. While the decision in *Boardman v. Phipps* is still considered good law, the rule that brands a fiduciary as a constructive trustee for his client,[41] even in a case where there has been full disclosure of the fiduciary's interest and the transaction benefits the client, is seldom applied.

Where a solicitor's personal interests conflict with those of his client, the duty of disclosure requires that the solicitor meticulously disclose all relevant facts. In *Cassey v. Morrison*,[42] the Ontario Court of Appeal held that a solicitor who entered into a business partnership with his clients to own and operate a restaurant was liable for breach of fiduciary duty for failing to disclose the existence of a chattel mortgage and the precise details of a mortgage on the building.[43] The disclosure must be made as soon as the solicitor becomes aware of the fact that his personal interests conflict with those of her client.[44]

Breaches of the fiduciary duty of loyalty often flow from transactions between solicitor and client. However, a court may uphold such a transaction if the lawyer is able to discharge the onus of proving the overall fairness of it. For example, in *Milligan v. Gemini Mercury Sales Ltd.*,[45] Mr. Justice Goodman, then of the Ontario High Court, outlined the requirements that must be met in order to discharge this reverse onus:

(i)   the solicitor must have "made full disclosure of all material facts within his knowledge";

(ii) "the transaction [must be] just and fair . . . insofar as the client is concerned";

(iii) "the client [must have] received the advantage of the best professional assistance which if he had been involved in a transaction with a third party he could possibly have afforded"; and

(iv) [where independent legal advice has not been provided], "having regard to the facts of [the] case, [it] was not indispensable".[46]

---

[41] Although in *Boardman* the plaintiff was not Boardman's client but was a beneficiary of Boardman's client, the trust.

[42] *Supra*, note 27.

[43] *Ibid.*, at 244 15 O.R.

[44] See *MacDonell v. M&M Developments Ltd.* (1998), 157 D.L.R. (4th) 240 (N.S.C.A.), where the Nova Scotia Court of Appeal found a solicitor to be in breach of his fiduciary duty to his client, the defendant corporation, for the sole reason that he did not advise the owner that he had discovered he had a personal claim to lands owned by the company until the owner of the company, who lived overseas, came to Nova Scotia one-and-a-half to two months after the lawyer made the discovery.

[45] (1977), 1 B.L.R. 63 (Ont. H.C.).

[46] *Ibid.*, at 80. A similar statement of these principles is found in the English cases: see, *e.g.*, *Demerara Bauxite Co. Ltd. v. Hubbard, supra*, note 27.

The court concluded that the solicitor had in fact demonstrated the fairness of the transaction and, accordingly, allowed the solicitor's action for specific performance to exercise an option to purchase certain shares. Usually, however, it is difficult for a lawyer to discharge this heavy onus;[47] and there is even greater difficulty in demonstrating the fairness of the transaction when the client lacks business experience or sophistication.[48] Objective evidence that the transaction was just and fair is critical; for example, the fact that the purchase price is approximately equal to fair market value is some evidence of the fairness of the transaction.[49]

There is some authority for the proposition that a solicitor is in breach of her fiduciary obligation of loyalty when her personal, as opposed to pecuniary, interests conflict with those of the client. In *Stewart v. C.B.C.*,[50] a prominent criminal defence lawyer was found in breach of his fiduciary duty of loyalty to a former client by preferring his personal interests in self-promotion over the best interests of the client by discussing the client's case on a television programme over the client's objections. In *Szarfer v. Chodos*,[51] another lawyer breached his fiduciary duty to his client by engaging in an affair with the client's wife. In the course of his representation of the client in a wrongful dismissal action, the lawyer learned that the couple was experiencing marital difficulties and subsequently initiated an affair with the client's wife. Associate Chief Justice Callaghan of the Ontario High Court characterized the behaviour as a breach of the lawyer's fiduciary duty of confidentiality and his duty not to permit his own interests to come into conflict with those of his client, which is tantamount to a breach of the duty of loyalty.[52]

A fiduciary must not only act, but must also be seen to act, with undivided loyalty to her client. It is incumbent upon her to avoid both direct conflicts and the appearance of a possible conflict. Thus, in *Moffat v. Wetstein*,[53] a solicitor was removed from the record on a motion by the opposing party because the

---

[47] See *McGrath v. Goldman*, [1976] 1 W.W.R. 743, 64 D.L.R. (3d) 305 (B.C.S.C.) (solicitor found in breach of fiduciary duty when client lent money to a venture in which solicitor had an interest); *Taylor v. Murphy* (1980), 24 B.C.L.R. 198 (S.C.) (solicitor in breach of fiduciary duty in acting for purchasers on sale of solicitor's land); *Cavallin v. King, supra*, note 27 (solicitor found to have breached fiduciary duty when joint venture with clients went sour); *MacDonald v. Lockhart* (1980), 42 N.S.R. (2d) 29, 118 D.L.R. (3d) 397 (C.A.), varied 44 N.S.R. (2d) 261, leave to appeal to S.C.C. refused 118 D.L.R. (3d) 397*n* (solicitor lent money to client to assist in a corporate reorganization); *Stritzl v. Wassenaar*, unreported, July 23, 1996, Doc. 329/95, [1996] O.J. No. 2636 (Div. Ct.), leave to appeal refused, unreported, September 19, 1996, Doc. M18886, [1996] O.J. No 3166 (C.A.) (contract between a solicitor and a client company granting the solicitor an interest in the company in exchange for payment for professional services rendered to the company).

[48] See *Morris v. Jackson* (1984), 34 R.P.R. 269 (Ont. H.C.).

[49] *Kalla v. Wolkowicz, supra*, note 37.

[50] (1997), 150 D.L.R. (4th) 24 (Ont. Gen. Div.).

[51] (1986), 54 O.R. (2d) 663 (H.C.), leave to appeal to Ont. C.A. dismissed November 10, 1988.

[52] *Ibid.*, at 677.

[53] (1996), 29 O.R. (3d) 371 at 384 (Gen. Div.).

solicitor had a personal interest in the proceedings that was adverse to her client's interest. The court removed the solicitor in spite of the fact that the client had waived the conflict and the court was satisfied that her loyalty to her client would not be affected by her personal interests. It reasoned that, in the absence of independent legal advice, a reasonably informed person would not be satisfied that the impropriety of permitting the solicitor to continue to act was cured by the waiver.

Where a solicitor's interests conflict with those of her client because she has gained an advantage for herself at the expense of her client, a presumption of undue influence arises.[54] In order to rebut the presumption, it is necessary to show that "the person liable to be influenced has formed an independent and informed judgment after full, free and informed thought".[55] In effect, this is equivalent to the reverse onus set out in *Milligan v. Gemini Mercury Sales Ltd.* Although there is some uncertainty in the jurisprudence as to whether the client must have been advised to obtain independent legal advice, it is safe to assume that a referral elsewhere will almost always be necessary to discharge the reverse onus.[56] A court will not be satisfied with less than a complete rebuttal of the presumption.[57]

The presumption commonly arises where a solicitor does business with a client. In cases where the presumption is not rebutted, the business transaction is often held to be void. For example, in *Coss (Trustee of) v. Shuckett*[58] the Manitoba Court of Appeal declared a mortgage of land given as security for a loan advanced by the defendant lawyer's wife to his client void *ab initio* because of the lawyer's breach of the fiduciary duty of loyalty to the client.

2. Acting for Both Sides

The principle of undivided loyalty also precludes a lawyer from acting for two clients adverse in interest unless, having been fully informed of the conflict and clearly understanding its implications, they have agreed in advance to her doing

---

[54] *Malicki v. Yankovich* (1981), 33 O.R. (2d) 537 (H.C.), supp. reasons (1983), 42 O.R. (2d) 522 (H.C.), affd (1983), 41 O.R. (2d) 160 (C.A.); *Rochdale Credit Union Ltd. v. Barney* (1984), 48 O.R. (2d) 676, 14 D.L.R. (4th) 116 (C.A.), leave to appeal to S.C.C. refused 8 O.A.C. 320; *Hawrish v. Scott Industries Ltd.*, unreported, July 11, 1994, Doc. 849, [1994] S.J. No. 362 (C.A.); *Walker v. Rec Software Inc.*, unreported, November 30, 1995, Allan J., Doc. Vancouver C953361, [1995] B.C.J. No. 2519 (S.C.).

[55] *National Westminster Bank v. Morgan*, [1983] 3 All E.R. 85 at 93 (C.A.).

[56] See *Malicki, supra*, note 54, at 556, in which the Ontario High Court of Justice found that there is not an absolute requirement of independent legal advice in every fiduciary relationship; and *Walker, supra*, note 54, at para. 21, in which the British Columbia Supreme Court held that independent legal advice is necessary to rebut the presumption of undue influence where a solicitor has entered into a business agreement with his client respecting legal services which form the basis of the fiduciary relationship.

[57] *Malicki, supra*, note 54, at 556-67.

[58] (1990), 65 Man. R. (2d) 161.

so. There is ample authority on the point: the leading Canadian case is still *Davey v. Woolley, Hames, Dale & Dingwall.*[59] The defendant law firm was retained by both sides of a commercial transaction, namely, a purchaser, Howe, and a vendor, Davey. The two sides had apparently worked out a deal for Howe to purchase Davey's business and then asked the law firm to put the agreement into legal language. Their agreement included an option to purchase which could be assigned (and, in fact, was) to a company controlled by Howe. That company was also a client of the law firm and one in which Woolley, a senior partner in the firm, had a financial interest. Disputes arose under the agreement, and the plaintiff, Davey, claimed damages for negligence and breach of fiduciary duty against the law firm for its failure to protect his financial interests by not obtaining more adequate security from Howe. The action was dismissed at trial.

On appeal, the Court of Appeal held that the firm had breached its fiduciary duty to the plaintiff notwithstanding that, before the closing of the transaction, the defendant firm had arranged for the plaintiff to sign an acknowledgment that the firm was acting for both sides of the transaction and Woolley had a personal financial interest in one of the companies. The court reasoned that the plaintiff's consent was a case of "too little, too late", since Stevens, the lawyer primarily responsible for the transaction, "failed to take proper stock of the situation when he was first approached by the plaintiff".[60]

The court also cast doubt on the practice of solicitors, whether in rural communities or elsewhere, of acting for both vendor and purchaser even in a straightforward real estate transaction:

> . . . the solicitor unquestionably assumes a dual role at his own risk, the onus being on him in any lawsuit that ensues to establish that the client has had "the best professional assistance which, if he had been engaged in a transaction with a third party, he could possibly have afforded" . . . Even on the simple real estate deal the consequences of conflict can manifest themselves in a failure to make the requisition that allegedly should have been made and would have been made if the solicitor had been motivated solely by a concern for the plaintiff.[61]

These comments go somewhat further than those of Chief Justice Laskin in the 1979 case of *McCauley v. McVey*,[62] which recognized that in small communities there will be cases where other solicitors will not be available to act on the other side of a transaction. While judicial tolerance for the dual retainer is

---

[59] (1982), 35 O.R. (2d) 599, 133 D.L.R. (3d) 647 (C.A.), leave to appeal to S.C.C. refused 37 O.R. (2d) 499*n*.

[60] *Ibid.*, at 604 O.R.

[61] *Ibid.*, at 602 O.R., *per* Wilson J.A. (as she then was), quoting Lord O'Hagan in *McPherson v. Watt* (1877), 3 App. Cas. 254 at 266 (H.L.); also quoted in *London Loan & Savings Co. v. Brickenden,* [1933] S.C.R. 257 at 262, *per* Crocket J.

[62] [1980] 1 S.C.R. 165, 98 D.L.R. (3d) 577.

apparently decreasing, the practice continues to be widespread, particularly in those communities that seemingly cannot absorb the increased fees resulting from the separate representation of vendors and purchasers.

In cases where a solicitor undertakes a dual retainer she must at a minimum take three essential steps: (1) disclose the fact of the joint retainer; (2) advise that if a potential or actual conflict of interest arises, she will have to cease acting for at least one of the parties and refer that party to independent legal advice; and (3) explain that solicitor-client privilege will not apply as between the parties and she is obliged to disclose all relevant information to both of them.[63] The failure to advise of the joint representation and the possibility of a future conflict of interest may in itself amount to a breach of fiduciary duty, even if no such conflict subsequently arises.[64]

Lawyers who are contemplating acting for both sides of a transaction would do well to keep in mind the words of McKinlay J.A. in *Commerce Capital Trust Co. v. Berk*:[65]

> Courts have traditionally imposed a high duty of disclosure upon solicitors who have placed themselves in a position of conflict by acting for both parties in a mortgage transaction . . . . Scrupulous behaviour is of particular importance where one of the clients is a person with whom the lawyer has had a long-standing relationship — personal or professional.[66]

Indeed, in many of the cases involving lawyers acting for both sides, breach of fiduciary duty results when a lawyer prefers the interests of one client over the other by failing to disclose material facts.[67] Courts have found lawyers who acted for both the vendor and the purchaser in a real estate transaction[68] or the mortgagor and mortgagee on a loan[69] to have breached their fiduciary duty for withholding relevant information from one of the parties.

---

[63] *Ridge View Development & Holding Co. v. Simper*, [1989] 5 W.W.R. 133 (Alta. Q.B.); *Hussey v. Parsons*, (1997), 152 Nfld. & P.E.I.R. 1 (Nfld. T.D.).

[64] *Hussey, supra,* note 63, at 194 The defendant solicitor in *Harris v. First Western Ontario Properties Inc.*, [1995] O.J. No. 2190 (Gen. Div.), was also found liable for failing to disclose a conflict of interest and to obtain consent to continue to act; see also *Skimming v. Goldberg* (1993), 89 Man. R. (2d) 27 (Q.B), in which a solicitor was held liable for failing to disclose that he was acting for both sides.

[65] (1989), 68 O.R. (2d) 257 (C.A.).

[66] *Ibid.,* at 260.

[67] For a more detailed exploration of the fiduciary duty to disclose in the context of a dual retainer, see Section III. "Fiduciary Obligations Defined", B. "Duty of Disclosure", 1. "Duty to Disclose Conflict of Interest Situations", A. "Self-Interest".

[68] *Recha v. Yeamans* (1993), 135 N.B.R. (2d) 360 (C.A.), where the solicitor also had a personal interest in the transaction as he was the guarantor of a mortgage on the property and also held a small mortgage on it himself; *Barrett v. Reynolds* (1997), 163 N.S.R. (2d) 127 (S.C.).

[69] See, for example, *Dimitry Investments Ltd. v. Stern*, unreported, December 9, 1991, Van Camp J., Doc. 74849/91 Q, [1991] O.J. No. 2182 (Gen. Div.), affd, unreported, September 10, 1992, Doc. C9827, [1992] O.J. No. 1864 (C.A.).

In most cases, where a solicitor decides to act for both sides, he will be found in breach of fiduciary duty if one of the clients ultimately suffers a loss, but there are exceptions. In *Gkotsis v. Lasalle Hotel Co. (Kingston) Ltd.*,[70] the court found that the disputed clause in the lease between the parties "which is now said to be the foundation of the suggested conflict of interest was drawn to the attention of the plaintiffs, who, knowing of its tenor, elected to leave it in the lease"[71] and thus relieved the solicitor, who had acted for both sides of the transaction, of liability.

The fiduciary duty of loyalty may not be breached if a lawyer who acts for both parties to a transaction can show that her representation of them was not affected by her divided loyalty. In *Phillis v. Burns*,[72] a solicitor who acted for both a mortgagor and mortgagee pursuant to a limited retainer to register a valid second mortgage, and not to conduct an executions search, was not liable for breach of fiduciary duty when she did not advise the mortgagee of the number of executions registered against the guarantor.

B. DUTY OF DISCLOSURE

A lawyer's duty of disclosure has been described as follows:

> A lawyer fails in his duty if he fails to make disclosure of all relevant facts to his client. Once he has been retained by a client he cannot escape from his duty to make full disclosure for any reason whatsoever. The public interest requires that the courts enforce this rule without exception.[73]

1. Duty to Disclose Conflict of Interest Situations

The duty manifests itself in at least three contexts.

a. Self-Interest

First, the lawyer must disclose any personal interest he or a member of his firm has in the client's transaction as well as any information relating to the transaction which comes into his possession from another client or former client.[74] *Henfrey &*

---

[70] Unreported, September 4, 1986 (Ont. H.C.). See also *Nufort Resources Inc. v. Eustace* (1985), 29 B.L.R. 282 (Ont. H.C.).

[71] *Gkotsis v. Lasalle Hotel Co. (Kingston) Ltd., supra*, note 70, at 15.

[72] (1997), 38 O.T.C. 241 (Gen. Div.).

[73] *Jacks v. Davis*, [1980] 6 W.W.R. 11 at 16, 12 C.C.L.T. 298 (B.C.S.C.), *per* Anderson J.; affd 39 B.C.L.R. 353, [1983] 1 W.W.R. 327 (C.A.).

[74] See, *e.g.*, *Tri-crest Investment Corp. v. Davidson & Co.* (1988), 24 B.C.L.R. (2d) 248 (S.C.). Obviously, this is one of the major risks of acting on both sides of a transaction: receiving confidential information from one client that affects the other client's interests. Moreover, in some cases, a lawyer may have a duty to make full disclosure to a former client with whom he continues business dealings. In *Terrace Developments Ltd. v. Terry*, May 25, 1992, Mandel J.,

Co. Ltd. v. A Law Firm[75] is an example of a lawyer failing to disclose a personal interest in a client's transaction. A company on the verge of bankruptcy owed the defendant firm substantial fees that remained outstanding after various requests for payment. Nevertheless, the firm acted for the company on the bankruptcy and on the sale of certain of its assets. Without advising the client, the firm applied the closing funds to its outstanding accounts. On application by the trustee in bankruptcy, the payment was set aside on the basis that the firm had failed to make disclosure in advance of its intention to impound the money. In *MacDonnell v. M&M Developments*,[76] the Nova Scotia Court of Appeal emphasized the necessity of disclosing the personal interest as soon as it becomes known. A solicitor was found in breach of fiduciary duty for waiting to disclose a personal interest in lands owned by a corporate client until the company's president, who lived overseas, came to Nova Scotia one-and-a-half to two months after the personal interest was discovered.

In *Korz v. St. Pierre*,[77] the solicitor, Korz, failed to disclose to his former clients, with whom he had entered into a business venture, the fact that he was judgment proof. The Court of Appeal, in reversing the trial judge, held that he was obliged to make this disclosure:

> As a result of the possession by the lawyer of special and confidential information pertaining to clients, he should not take advantage of that position of superiority if he enters into a transaction with them. If he is entering into such a transaction, the lawyer is bound to make a full disclosure of his position so that the client is not placed at a disadvantage. The ethics of the profession and fairness require that such a disclosure be made. To hold otherwise would place lawyers in an unfairly advantageous position. They would be able to benefit from the special and confidential information obtained from their clients in the course of advising them on legal problems, while permitting lawyers to surreptitiously avoid the very risks they know are being assumed by their clients. This principle must apply in many instances to former clients as well as current clients.[78]

In *Cassey v. Morrison*,[79] a solicitor who engaged in a business partnership with clients for the ownership and operation of a restaurant was held to have breached his fiduciary duty for not revealing material facts, including the existence of a chattel mortgage and the precise details of a mortgage on the building. The Ontario Court of Appeal summarized this obligation of disclosure:

Doc. No. 23783/77 (Ont. Gen. Div.), affd [1994] O.J. No. 683 (C.A.), a solicitor who acted for X in X's attempt to purchase a parcel of property put in a bid for the same property on behalf of Y (the solicitor had an interest as an investor in Y). The solicitor breached her fiduciary duty to X in not revealing to X the existence of Y, and further for not revealing her interest in Y.

[75] (1983), 46 B.C.L.R. 227, 149 D.L.R. (3d) 736 (S.C.).

[76] (1998), 157 D.L.R. (4th) 240 (C.A.).

[77] (1987), 61 O.R. (2d) 609, 43 D.L.R. (4th) 528 (C.A.).

[78] *Ibid.*, at 618 O.R.

[79] *Cassey v. Morrison* (1993), 15 O.R. (3d) 223 (C.A.).

The law holds solicitors to a high standard of disclosure even when they do not have a personal interest in the enterprise involved. When they do have a personal interest, they must be meticulous in matters of disclosure.[80]

b. Acting for Both Sides

Examples of a breach of duty arising from acting for both sides of a transaction are legion. In *Bailey v. Ornheim*,[81] an early decision on the issue, a solicitor was held to have breached his duty of disclosure when, in acting for both the mortgagor and prospective mortgagee, he failed to advise the latter of "certain information which he knew could be vital to her decision to carry on or to stop the transaction".[82] The court held that the solicitor was obliged to reveal to the mortgagee everything he knew of the security, the purpose of the loan and the financial stability of the mortgagor.

A similar conclusion was reached in 1980 by the Ontario High Court in *Lapierre v. Young*,[83] where the defendant's solicitor failed to advise his client, an unsophisticated lender that he was also acting for the borrower, the recent sale price of the property was less than the total of two mortgages on the property, the first mortgage was in arrears, the borrower was prepared to pay a higher rate of interest than had been negotiated, and the owner of the property was a numbered company with no other assets. Further early illustrations of the principle by lower courts can be found in *Ferris v. Rusnak*,[84] *Morris v. Jackson*[85] and *Carlofsky v. McGuire*.[86]

More recently, courts of appeal have imposed liability for breach of fiduciary duty on solicitors acting for both sides of a transaction. Most of the cases involve lawyers acting for multiple parties in real estate deals. For example, the solicitor in *Commerce Capital Trust Co. v. Berk*, [87] who acted for both a mortgagee and a mortgagor, was found by the Ontario Court of Appeal to be in breach for failing to disclose several material facts to the mortgagee. In *Recha v. Yeamans*, the New Brunswick Court of Appeal explained the obligations and risks of representing both parties in a real estate transaction:

> A lawyer who acts for both parties runs a major risk. The lawyer cannot be heard to say in his or her own defence: Vendors you have engaged my right ear while you, purchasers, have engaged my left ear; everything that passes into these ears shall be assessed by me and I shall be the censor of what information each of you

---

[80] *Ibid.*, at 224.

[81] (1962), 40 W.W.R. 129, 35 D.L.R. (2d) 402 (B.C.S.C.).

[82] *Ibid.*, at 409 D.L.R.

[83] (1980), 30 O.R. (2d) 319, 117 D.L.R. (3d) 643 (H.C.).

[84] (1983), 50 A.R. 297, 9 D.L.R. (4th) 183 (Q.B.).

[85] (1984), 34 R.P.R. 269 (Ont. H.C.).

[86] (1979), 28 Chitty's L.J. 225 (Ont. H.C.).

[87] (1989), 68 O.R. (2d) 257 (C.A.).

shall receive. A solicitor is not a mere repository of relevant information which the solicitor decides shall or shall not be passed on to the client. The solicitor, on the contrary, is a receiver of and then a conduit or channel of relevant information for the benefit of the client and for final analysis and decision by the client. It is the informed client, not the solicitor, who bears the responsibility for the ultimate decision.[88]

The court found the solicitor who acted for both parties to a purchase and sale in breach of this unqualified duty for failing to disclose to purchasers that the contract price was higher than both the original purchase price and an appraisal, and that he had earlier guaranteed a loan to the vendors, who were long-standing clients of the defendant, which loan was to be discharged on the sale of the property.

c. Acting for Parties with Common Interests

A lawyer is equally obliged to make full disclosure where she acts for more than one party on the same side of a transaction. The clients cannot raise solicitor-client privilege as between themselves and the solicitor must disclose relevant information to all of them. In these situations, the clients' interests may appear to be coincident but a conflict of interest may arise between them at any time; hence, full disclosure is necessary to guard against a finding of breach of fiduciary duty.

Two recent appeal level cases illustrate this principle. In *Ramrakha v. Zinner*,[89] the Alberta Court of Appeal found a solicitor who acted for all of the purchasers of a shopping mall to be in breach of fiduciary duty for failing to disclose that one of them was making a secret profit on the transaction. Similarly, in *McKitterick v. Duco, Geist & Chodos*,[90] the Ontario Court of Appeal held that a lawyer representing five purchasers of a restaurant breached his fiduciary duty to four of them when he failed to disclose that the fifth purchaser, who had originally retained the lawyer and orchestrated the purchase, did not provide his required advance to the business on closing. In another recent decision, *Martin v. Goldfarb*,[91] a solicitor who acted for co-venturers in various business transactions was held liable for breach of fiduciary duty for failing to inform one of them that the other was a disbarred lawyer with a criminal past.

---

[88] *Recha v. Yeamans, supra*, note 68, at 376.

[89] (1994), 24 Alta. L.R. (3d) 240 (C.A.), supp. reasons (1994), 25 Alta. L.R. (3d) 145 (C.A.). For an early Court of Appeal decision in which a solicitor who acted for both the vendor and purchaser in a real estate transaction was held liable for failing to disclose a secret profit, see *Jacks v. Davis, supra*, note 73.

[90] (1994), 76 O.A.C. 310 (C.A.).

[91] (1997), 30 O.T.C. 321 (Gen. Div.) appeal of damages assessment allowed, and a new trial ordered to assess damages, unreported, August 26, 1998, Doc. CZ 7477, [1998] O.J. No. 3403 (C.A.).

2. Duty to Provide Complete Advice

Secondly, and quite apart from those circumstances in which the duty of disclosure arises in a conflict of interest situation, a lawyer owes a duty to disclose to her client all information relevant to the matter for which she has been retained.[92]

The disclosure is not restricted to material facts but includes an explanation of their legal significance. In many cases this fiduciary duty will parallel the duty at common law to advise and warn, that is, to provide advice so that the client fully appreciates the risks of a transaction.[93] If the requisite intent can be proved, the failure to advise and inform may also constitute fraud.[94] However, the Ontario Court (General Division) in *Fasken Campbell Codfrey v. Seven-Up Canada Inc.*[95] recently chose to treat the failure to advise of the risks associated with a transaction as a question of negligence as opposed to fiduciary duty:

> In my view, a claim for breach of fiduciary duty involves situations in which the solicitor takes advantage of the solicitor-client relationship by failing to make proper disclosure, acting for both sides without informing the client, breaching confidence, or other like behaviour. The claim here is not based upon allegations of this quality but rather upon failure to render appropriate advice.
>
> ... The claim in the case at bar is that the solicitor failed to warn about the risks of a transaction. In my view, the claim of the defendants in essence lies in negligence.

a. Referral to Independent Legal Advice

Breach of the duty to advise and inform is commonly exemplified by a failure to advise a client to seek and obtain independent legal advice. This failure was at the core of *Cavallin v. King*,[96] where King, the defendant solicitor, and the plaintiffs (husband and wife) were involved in a joint business venture. King knew that the husband, who was the spouse primarily involved in the transaction, had a very informal approach to business. This fact, together with the fact

---

[92] The obligation to disclose all relevant information to a client encompasses a duty to give good, informed advice that is based on thorough research: see *Alberta (Workers' Compensation Board) v. Riggins* (1990), 107 A.R. 314 (Q.B.), affd (1992), 131 A.R. 205 (C.A.); *285614 Alberta Ltd. v. Burnet, Duckworth & Palmer* (1993), 139 A.R. 31 (Q.B.). See also *Dimitry Investments Ltd. v. Stern*, unreported, December 9, 1991, Van Camp J., Doc. 74849/91 Q, [1991] O.J. No. 2182 (Gen. Div.), affd, unreported, September 10, 1992, Doc. C9827, [1992] O.J. No. 1864 (C.A.).

[93] The nature of this duty is discussed in Chapter 2.

[94] See *Greenglass v. Rusonik; Rusonik v. Conder* (1981), 21 R.P.R. 264 (Ont. H.C.), affd unreported, March 18, 1983 (C.A.). See also *McKinnon v. Conexco International Corp.*, unreported, February 17, 1992, Steele J., Doc. 16582/86, [1992] O.J. No. 292 (Gen. Div.).

[95] (1997), 142 D.L.R. (4th) 456 at 483 (Gen. Div.).

[96] (1984), 51 B.C.L.R. 149 (S.C.).

that King had a personal interest in the transaction, necessitated that he advise the plaintiffs to obtain independent legal advice. Mr. Justice Wallace of the British Columbia Supreme Court found that King had failed to do so. He held King liable for the plaintiffs' loss and, on the nature and scope of the solicitor's duty in this situation, commented:

> The duty to advise the plaintiffs to seek independent legal advice on the appropriateness of accepting his solicitor's invitation to invest in a joint venture is but one method of demonstrating the solicitor has met the fiduciary obligation of satisfying the court that the transaction was a just and fair one from the client's point of view, having regard to all the circumstances — that the terms of the transaction were as advantageous to the client as it would have been had the solicitor been advising him on the merits of a venture in which the solicitor had no interest.[97]

Where a presumption of undue influence arises in respect of a transaction between a lawyer and a client which is disadvantageous to the client, as explained earlier in this chapter,[98] in order to rebut the presumption, the lawyer will almost certainly be required to establish that she recommended independent legal advice.[99] A lawyer who does not engage in a transaction with her client, but has a personal interest in the client's matter, may also be in breach of fiduciary duty if she does not disclose her personal interest and recommend independent legal advice. This type of breach occurred in *Fisher v. Guardian Insurance Co. of Canada*,[100] where a solicitor learned from another lawyer at his firm that a client of the firm wanted to invest money in mortgages and suggested that the client lend money to a company in which he had a 21.5 per cent interest. The client granted the mortgage in favour of the company but was not advised of the solicitor's interests or advised to consult independent counsel.

If a solicitor represents both sides in a transaction, and a conflict of interest arises, she has a fiduciary duty to advise one of the clients to obtain independent legal advice. For example, in *St. Mars v. Bell*,[101] a solicitor who acted for parties with opposing interests in the knowledge that one of them was in the process of swindling the other was found to have breached his fiduciary duty by failing to inform the client of the necessity of obtaining independent legal advice. *Shoppers Trust Co. v. Dynamic Homes Ltd.*[102] makes it clear that a solicitor may be obliged to advise someone who is not her client to seek independent legal advice if a fiduciary relationship has arisen between the solicitor and the non-client. In that case, a solicitor who acted for both parties to a mortgage transaction was

---

[97] *Ibid.*, at 156.
[98] See Section III. "Fiduciary Obligations Defined", A. "Duty of Loyalty", 1. "Self Interest".
[99] *Walker v. Rec Software Inc.*, unreported, November 30, 1995, Allan J., Doc. Vancouver C953361, [1995] B.C.J. No. 2519 (S.C.).
[100] (1993), 87 B.C.L.R. (2d) 34 (S.C.), varied (1995), 3 B.C.L.R. (3d) 161 (C.A.).
[101] (1990), 70 D.L.R. (4th) 224 (S.C.).
[102] (1992), 10 O.R. (3d) 361 (Gen. Div.).

held to owe a fiduciary duty to the mortgagee's functionally illiterate wife to ensure that she obtained independent legal advice before signing a substantial mortgage on the then unencumbered matrimonial home.

There are other decisions that emphasize the importance of advising a client to seek independent legal advice in instances where, because of a conflict, a lawyer cannot fulfil her obligation to explain the legal significance of the transaction to her client,[103] or one to whom she owes a fiduciary obligation.[104] The obligation arises whether the conflict is between the lawyer's self-interest and the interest of the client, or between the interests of clients on a joint retainer. The failure to refer clients for independent legal advice in conflict situations is likely to be an increasing source of claims against lawyers.

3. Materiality, Causation and the Duty to Disclose

A lawyer will only be liable for material non-disclosures that occasion the clients' loss. In *Commerce Capital Trust Co. v. Berk*,[105] Madam Justice McKinlay of the Ontario Court of Appeal held that a client need not show that it would not have proceeded with the transaction if all of the facts were known in order to satisfy the test of materiality. A fact is material if, measured objectively, it would have been important to the client in making the decision to proceed. If the undisclosed facts are material, a court will not speculate about the course the client would have taken had full disclosure been made. The onus is on the solicitor to prove on the balance of probabilities that, in spite of the non-disclosure of material facts, the client would have continued with the transaction.[106]

---

[103] See, *e.g.*, *Copperview Haven Ltd. v. Waverley Park Estates Ltd.* (1984), 55 B.C.L.R. 230, [1984] 4 W.W.R. 673 (C.A.); *Exploits Sales & Services Ltd. v. Fox Farm Village Ltd.* (1984), 48 Nfld. & P.E.I.R. 266 (Nfld. C.A.); and *Klein v. Hine & Hine*, unreported, September 13, 1985 (B.C.S.C.). See also *Bertolo v. Bank of Montreal* (1986), 57 O.R. (2d) 577, 33 D.L.R. (4th) 610 (C.A.); *St. Mars v. Bell*, *supra*, note 101. Where failure to advise the client to seek independent advice is not the cause of the client's loss, no liability will attach to the solicitor: *Blown v. Johnstone* (1988), 20 B.C.L.R. (2d) 177, [1988] 2 W.W.R. 178 (C.A.). However, the court should not be too quick to find that a breach of duty was not the cause of the plaintiff's loss: see *Lee v. Nursery Furnishings Ltd.*, [1945] 1 All E.R. 387 (C.A.); *Bonnington Castings Ltd. v. Wardlaw*, [1956] 1 All E.R. 615 (H.L.), as cited in *St. Mars v. Bell*, *supra*, note 101. Further, in the absence of evidence of undue influence, fraud, misrepresentation or *non est factum*, the failure of a spouse to obtain independent legal advice prior to executing a guarantee will not in every case entitle the lawyer to escape liability: *Bank of Montreal v. Featherstone* (1989), 68 O.R. (2d) 541 (C.A.); *Shoppers Trust Co. v. Dynamic Homes Ltd.*, *supra*, note 102.

[104] In *Shoppers Trust Co. v. Dynamic Homes Ltd.*, *supra*, note 102, the solicitor owed a fiduciary obligation to the wife who encumbered the matrimonial home. The wife was not a client. The solicitor breached his fiduciary duty in not advising the wife to obtain independent legal advice.

[105] (1989), 68 O.R. (2d) 257 (C.A.).

[106] *Ibid.*, at 261; English courts appear to take the opposite approach to causation in breach of fiduciary duty cases. Lord Justice Evans of the English Court of Appeal suggested in *Swindle v. Harrison*, [1997] 4 All E.R. 705 at 716-17 that, unless the plaintiff can show that the breach

In *Hodgkinson*,[107] Mr. Justice La Forest affirmed the reverse onus for establishing causation for material non-disclosures citing the decision in *Commerce Capital*. In this case, an accountant failed to disclose his personal interest in an investment opportunity he recommended to his client. In response to an argument by the accountant that the client would have made the investment even if the disclosure had been made, La Forest J. held:

> . . . the submission runs up against the long-standing equitable principle that where the plaintiff has made out a case of non-disclosure and the loss occasioned thereby is established, the onus is on the defendant to prove that the innocent victim would have suffered the same loss regardless of the breach . . . [108]

The reverse onus appears to have been widely accepted in cases of breach of solicitors' fiduciary duty.[109] The Ontario Court of Appeal in *Canada Trustco Mortgage Co. v. Bartlet & Richardes*[110] recently held that a trial judge erred in not placing the onus on the defendant solicitors to show that the mortgagee client would have proceeded with a loan for the construction of an apartment building even if the solicitors had disclosed a restriction on the use of the property.

C. DUTY OF CONFIDENTIALITY

In the course of providing professional services, lawyers learn many of their clients' confidences and secrets. Preservation of the solicitor-client relationship demands the vigorous protection of this knowledge. However, it is not only information furnished to a lawyer by a client that is confidential: all information received on behalf of a client in a professional capacity is confidential.[111] The requirement of confidentiality continues indefinitely even though the solicitor-client relationship may have terminated.[112] However, in *Stewart v. Canada Broadcasting Corp.*[113] a lawyer who discussed the facts of a former client's case in a television broadcast some ten years after the solicitor-client relationship

---

was the equivalent of fraud, the onus will be on the plaintiff to show that she would not have proceeded with the transaction had full disclosure been made.

[107] [1994] 3 S.C.R. 377.

[108] *Ibid.,* at 441.

[109] *Ridge View Development & Holding Co. v. Simper,* [1989] 5 W.W.R. 133 (Alta. Q.B.); *Dimitry Investments Ltd. v. Stern,* unreported, December 9, 1991, Van Camp J., Doc. 74849/91 Q, [1991] O.J. No. 2182 (Gen. Div.), affd unreported, September 10, 1992, Doc. C9827 (Ont. C.A.); *Ramrakha v. Zinner, supra,* note 89; *Martin v. Goldfarb, supra,* note 91.

[110] *Canada Trustco Mortgage Co. v. Bartlet & Richardes* (1991), 28 O.R. (3d) 768 at 775 (C.A.). However, the Court of Appeal held that, on the facts of the case, the solicitors would have succeeded in meeting the reverse onus and dismissed the client's appeal.

[111] *Ott v. Fleishman* (1983), 46 B.C.L.R. 321, [1983] 5 W.W.R. 721 (S.C.).

[112] *Ibid.*

[113] (1997), 150 D.L.R. (4th) 24 at 128 (Ont. Gen. Div.).

ended was found not to have breached the fiduciary duty of confidentiality because the information discussed was in the public domain.

Perhaps the most questionable application of the duty occurred in *Szarfer v. Chodos.*[114] The defendant solicitor learned that marital difficulties were being experienced by his client, the plaintiff, who had retained the solicitor to conduct an action for damages for wrongful dismissal. The client's wife and the solicitor, for whom she occasionally worked as a legal secretary, engaged in a clandestine affair. The client, when he learned of this, suffered a severe depression and sued the solicitor. Associate Chief Justice Callaghan of the Ontario High Court, in finding liability against the solicitor, held: "The fiduciary relationship between a lawyer and his client forbids a lawyer from using any confidential information obtained by him for the benefit of himself or a third person *or to the disadvantage of his client*".[115] The judge concluded that the affair, which led to a conflict of interest between the solicitor and client and which caused harm to the client, was probably actionable in itself but, in addition, the solicitor's use of confidential information to advance the affair was a sufficient basis upon which to hold the solicitor liable.

Even if the disclosure of confidential information is well motivated, liability will be incurred. In *Ott v. Fleishman,*[116] the plaintiff wife retained the defendant lawyer to institute divorce proceedings and hired a private investigator to obtain evidence of her husband's adultery. When the plaintiff subsequently advised the defendant that she was having an affair with the investigator, he withdrew from the case and notified the relevant authorities; he believed the investigator's conduct to be improper and was concerned to prevent a possible fraud on the court in the divorce proceedings. In an action against the lawyer for damages, the British Columbia Supreme Court held that, having received the plaintiff's admission in his confidential capacity, there were no circumstances that permitted him to disclose the information.[117]

The extent of a lawyer's confidentiality obligation is of increasing concern with the increased mobility of lawyers between firms. In *MacDonald Estate v. Martin,*[118] the Supreme Court of Canada considered the circumstances in which the duty of confidentiality will prevent a law firm from continuing to act when it acquires a lawyer from a firm representing an opposing party. A lawyer who has

---

[114] (1986), 54 O.R. (2d) 663, 27 D.L.R. (4th) 388 (H.C.), affd November 10, 1988 (C.A.).

[115] *Ibid.*, at 676 O.R. [Emphasis in original].

[116] *Supra*, note 111.

[117] It should be noted that the court characterized the cause of action as a breach of contract and not as a breach of fiduciary duty. In *Rademaker, MacDougall & Co. v. Number Ten Holdings Ltd.* (1983), 47 B.C.L.R. 376 (S.C.), varied 60 B.C.L.R. 301 (C.A.), a lawyer was also held liable for a breach of confidentiality which the trial court said constituted a negligent breach of contract. In *Guay v. La Société Franco-Manitobaine* (1985), 37 Man. R. (2d) 16 (Q.B.), the duty of confidentiality was considered to be part of a lawyer's duty of care. For whatever reasons, none of these cases characterized the duty of confidentiality as part of a lawyer's fiduciary obligations.

[118] *MacDonald Estate v. Martin*, [1990] 3 S.C.R. 1235.

relevant confidential information cannot act against his client or former client. Once it is shown by the client that there existed a previous relationship which is sufficiently related to the retainer from which it is sought to remove the solicitor, the court should infer that confidential information was imparted unless the solicitor establishes that no information was imparted which could be relevant.[119] The British Columbia Supreme Court has held that *MacDonald Estate* should only be applied in cases where an actual solicitor and client relationship existed.[120] Otherwise, the countervailing principle that a litigant not be deprived of his or her choice of lawyer without good cause will be compromised too greatly.

---

[119] *Creamer v. Hergt* (1991), 55 B.C.L.R. (2d) 141 (S.C.).
[120] *Ibid.*

Chapter 4

LIABILITY TO THIRD PARTIES

I. INTRODUCTION

Until the latter part of the 1970s, a lawyer's liability to non-clients for negligently performed legal services was extremely limited; it arose primarily in cases where a solicitor had expressly undertaken a task for the benefit of the third party and then, through inadvertence or otherwise, failed to perform it. In these cases, the third party brought an action against the solicitor for breach of the undertaking.[1]

Since then, the scope of a lawyer's obligations to third parties has expanded considerably. It is now well established that, in addition to liability for breach of an express undertaking, a lawyer may incur liability to non-clients[2]

(1) for breach of fiduciary duty where a fiduciary relationship has been created between the lawyer and third party;
(2) under the tort of negligence causing economic loss,
    (a) on the basis of the principles enunciated in *Hedley Byrne & Co. Ltd. v. Heller & Partners Ltd.*,[3] that is, in cases where the third party reasonably relies on the lawyer's special skill and knowledge; and

---

[1] *E.g., Witten, Vogel, Binder & Lyons v. Leung* (1983), 148 D.L.R. (3d) 418 (Alta. Q.B.); *Hoffman & Dorchik v. Agnew, Nykyforuk, Purdy & Davis* (1985), 36 Sask. R. 257, [1985] 1 W.W.R. 656 (Q.B.). For a more recent example, see *Saunder v. Gnanapandithen* (1995), 25 O.R. (3d) 379 (Gen. Div.). For a discussion of solicitors' liability for breach of an undertaking, see F.T. Horne, ed., *Cordery's Law Relating to Solicitors*, 8th ed. Reissue (London: Butterworths, 1988), at 110-12, and 44(1) *Halsbury's Laws of England*, 4th ed. (London: Butterworths, 1995), at para. 255. In addition to liability for breach of an undertaking, two nineteenth-century authorities have held that a solicitor's breach of duty to the court may create liability to a third party: *Batten v. Wedgewood Coal & Iron Co.* (1886), 31 Ch. D. 346; *Re Dangar's Trusts* (1889), 41 Ch. D. 178, [1886-90] All E.R. Rep. Ext. 1445.
[2] This is, of course, apart from liability for such things as fraud, malicious prosecution, defamation, situations in which the court deems an implied retainer, *etc.*
[3] [1964] A.C. 465, [1963] 2 All E.R. 575 (H.L.).

(b) for breach of a duty of care arising out of a sufficient relationship of proximity that in the reasonable contemplation of the solicitor will be likely to cause damage to the third party;[4]

(c) under a "Third Party Beneficiary" claim; and

(d) for the tort of negligent misrepresentation.

II. BREACH OF FIDUCIARY DUTY

A. ESTABLISHING THE EXISTENCE OF A FIDUCIARY OBLIGATION

As discussed in Chapter 3,[5] the solicitor-client relationship is one of the categories that have *prima facie* been traditionally viewed as fiduciary. However, depending on the nature of the relationship, lawyers may owe fiduciary obligations to persons who are not their clients. The challenge is to identify the types of relationships in which a solicitor owes fiduciary duties to third parties. Courts will now be guided by the criteria outlined by the Supreme Court of Canada in the *Frame, Lac Minerals* and *Hodgkinson*[6] decisions that enable us to identify fiduciary relationships outside the traditional categories.

Basically, where a solicitor undertakes to act for the benefit of a third party, a court will consider whether elements of discretion, influence, vulnerability and trust are present on the facts of the case. Mr. Justice Sopinka has held that inherent vulnerability is an essential element of a fiduciary relationship while Mr. Justice La Forest maintained that vulnerability is not essential and may arise on the facts of the case.[7] Given that La Forest J.'s view appears to have prevailed in *Hodgkinson,* however, the third party's vulnerability and total reliance on the skill and knowledge of the solicitor will not likely be crucial to the classification of the relationship as fiduciary. Some measure of reliance by the third party on the solicitor, but not the wholesale surrender of decision-making power, will be necessary for the imposition of fiduciary obligations.[8]

B. FIDUCIARY OBLIGATIONS TO THIRD PARTIES

Even before the recent expansion of liability for breach of fiduciary duty in the non-traditional categories of relationships, lawyers had been held to owe fiduciary obligations to third parties. One of the first cases to do this was

---

[4] *Anns v. Merton London Borough Council,* [1978] A.C. 728, [1977] 2 All E.R. 492 (H.L.).

[5] See Chapter 3, Section I. "Fiduciary Relaionships Defined", A. "Fiduciary Relationships Generally".

[6] *Frame v. Smith,* [1987] 2 S.C.R. 99; *International Corona Resources Ltd. v. Lac Minerals Ltd.,* [1989] 2 S.C.R. 574; *Hodgkinson v. Simms,* [1994] 3 S.C.R. 377.

[7] See Chapter 3, Section I. "Fiduciary Relationships Defined", A. "Fiduciary Relationships Generally".

[8] *Ibid.*

Tracy v. Atkins.[9] The defendant solicitor was retained by the purchaser in a real estate transaction. The vendors were not represented. The transaction originally called for a substantial down payment and a vendor take-back first mortgage to secure the balance of the purchase price. Before closing, the defendant was advised by his client that the deal had collapsed because of lack of financing. However, a few days later the client presented the defendant with a letter, purportedly signed by the vendors, that "instructed" the defendant to register the vendor take-back mortgage subsequent to the registration of another mortgage procured by the purchaser to finance the transaction. The vendors had signed the letter, which had been prepared by the purchaser, without realizing that a new mortgage was to have priority over their own. The defendant undertook all the requisite conveyancing work including the registration of both mortgages. He did not refer to the prior mortgage in the Statement of Adjustments nor in the vendors' mortgage; he forwarded both documents to the vendors. Nor did he attempt to communicate with the vendors directly to clarify or confirm their "instructions".

Although not concluding that the defendant owed the vendors a contractual duty of care created by an implied if not an express retainer, Ruttan J. held that the "circumstances" nevertheless established a fiduciary relationship. This fiduciary relationship arose, he reasoned, by application of the principles enunciated in *Hedley Byrne*, namely, the existence of a special relationship in which the vendors were relying on the defendant to provide information and advice, and the defendant knew or ought to have known of this reliance. In short, the trial judge held that a solicitor standing in a "*Hedley Byrne* relationship" with a third party will attract double-barrelled liability: in equity, for breach of a fiduciary duty, and in tort, for breach of a duty of care.

It is far from clear that the authorities cited by Ruttan J. actually support this conclusion,[10] and in any event, the imposition of a fiduciary obligation in addition to a duty of care is probably superfluous and may explain why the Court of Appeal chose not to comment on this aspect of this judgment. Indeed, the trial judge appears to have ignored altogether a more solid conceptual footing for the imposition of a fiduciary obligation: the sudden reinstatement of the deal on terms unfavourable to the vendors and without consideration created the likelihood of conflict[11] between the defendant's obligations to the purchaser, his client, and to the vendors, who not only were unrepresented but also purported to

---

[9]   (1977), 83 D.L.R. (3d) 46 (B.C.S.C.), affd 16 B.C.L.R. 223, 105 D.L.R. (3d) 632 (C.A.).

[10]   In addition to *Hedley Byrne*, Ruttan J. relied on *Nocton v. Lord Ashburton*, [1914] A.C. 932, [1914-15] All E.R. Rep. 45 (H.L.), and *Robinson v. National Bank of Scotland*, [1916] S.C. (H.L.) 154, which held essentially that a duty of care may arise out of a fiduciary relationship, and not, as Ruttan J. concluded, that circumstances giving rise to a duty of care necessarily create a fiduciary relationship. See *Tracy v. Atkins, supra*, note 9, at 54 (S.C.).

[11]   See Section III. "Negligence", A. "Reasonable Reliance on Special Skill and Knowledge or Sufficient Relationship of Proximity" 2. "The Unrepresented Third Party", for a discussion of cases which have found a fiduciary obligation to exist in situations where a conflict arises.

instruct him. In short, we are of the view that the trial judge inappropriately merged the principles applicable to the finding of a fiduciary duty, a matter of equity, with those applicable to the duty of care in tort.

Although the judgment of the British Columbia Court of Appeal did not comment on this aspect of the trial judgment, preferring to uphold the appeal on the basis of a duty of care in tort,[12] the reasons for judgment of Ruttan J. have been cited with approval. In *Palmeri v. Littleton; Renke v. Littleton*,[13] the court relied on *Tracy v. Atkins* to conclude that a solicitor who was acting for the purchaser in a real estate transaction was liable to the vendors as a fiduciary even though they had obtained independent legal advice. Unfortunately, the judgment does not identify "the circumstance" that formed the basis of this determination.

In *Burman's Beauty Supplies v. Kempster*,[14] the solicitor drafted a mortgage in favour of the third party plaintiff. The mortgage contained a standard clause certifying that there were no outstanding liens or encumbrances. In fact, the solicitor himself held the first mortgage on the property. The court held that this clause was a representation by the solicitor upon which the plaintiff reasonably relied. A fiduciary relationship arose by application of the principles found in *Hedley Byrne*. The solicitor breached his fiduciary duty to the plaintiff and was consequently precluded from enforcing his first mortgage.

In *Cavallin v. King*,[15] a lawyer who participated in a joint venture was held liable to his co-venturers for breach of fiduciary duty. The defendant solicitor invited the plaintiffs to participate in a joint venture to acquire and develop certain properties in which the solicitor acted both as director of the joint venture and a participant who provided legal and other services as his contribution to the venture. The court decided that while the defendant owed no duty of care to the plaintiffs personally, but only to the joint venture, a conflict of interest arose as a result of the plaintiffs' financing a project in which the defendant was to participate as a co-venturer and hence the plaintiffs and defendant stood in a fiduciary relationship. In another instance, in *Bonneville v. Temelini & Zito*[16] a lawyer who acted as a mortgage broker owed a fiduciary obligation to his principal. However, in these cases, the defendant's status as a lawyer was virtually irrelevant to the characterization of the relationship as fiduciary: it was his status as a mortgage broker or joint venturer that attracted his fiduciary obligations.

---

[12] See discussion of this aspect of the decision in Section III, "Negligence", A. "Reasonable Reliance on Special Skill and Knowledge or Sufficient Relationship of Proximity", 2. "The Unrepresented Third Party".

[13] [1979] 4 W.W.R. 577, 7 B.L.R. 113 (B.C.S.C.).

[14] (1974), 48 D.L.R. (3d) 682, 4 O.R. (2d) 626 (Co. Ct.).

[15] (1984), 51 B.C.L.R. 149 (S.C.).

[16] (1981), 21 R.P.R. 206 (Ont. H.C.). See also *Courtright v. C.P. Ltd.* (1983), 45 O.R. (2d) 52, 5 D.L.R. (4th) 488 (H.C.), affd 50 O.R. (2d) 560, 18 D.L.R. (4th) 639 (C.A.) (solicitor entering into employment contract with corporation owes fiduciary duty of full disclosure to employer corporation).

More recently, in *Shoppers Trust Co. v. Dynamic Homes Ltd.,*[17] the *Frame* criteria were applied to find that the solicitor who acted on behalf of both a mortgagor and a mortgagee owed a fiduciary duty of care to the mortgagor's wife to ensure that she obtained independent legal advice as to the consequences of signing a mortgage that encumbered the matrimonial home. The court held that the existence of a fiduciary relationship between a solicitor and a third party will depend on the facts of the case. In this case, the fiduciary duty was owed because the wife was unrepresented and functionally illiterate, the matrimonial home was previously unencumbered and it was held in her name alone.

A fiduciary obligation was owed to a third party investor in *McKinnon v. Conexco International Corp.*[18] McKinnon was a long-time client of the defendant law firm. He and a partner of the firm invested in a development project. A room was set aside in the offices of the firm for the use of the investors and McKinnon attended the office almost daily to consult with them. Although he did not formally retain the firm in this matter, McKinnon believed it was acting for all the investors in the deal. The firm breached its fiduciary obligation by not advising McKinnon to obtain independent legal advice. The partner who was an investor in this project breached his fiduciary duty by not making sure that his view of the project viability was made known to McKinnon.

In *Filipovic v. Upshall,*[19] a group of syndicators led the plaintiff investors to believe that they would receive a beneficial interest in land in return for their investment. In fact, they only obtained shares in a company which held the property. Further, two substantial mortgages were placed on the property without the investors' knowledge. When the plaintiffs lost their investment, they brought an action against the solicitors who acted for the corporation on the purchase of the property, alleging negligence and breach of fiduciary duty. They claimed that the solicitors owed a fiduciary obligation to disclose that they were acquiring shares in the holding company as opposed to a beneficial interest in the land, and that the company had granted the mortgages. In dismissing the plaintiffs' case, the court held that it was reasonable for the solicitor to have acted on the instructions of the company's principals because he had been assured that the plaintiffs were aware of the nature of the transaction and had no reason to suspect otherwise. Fiduciary obligations did not arise on the facts of this case because there was no scope for the exercise of discretion by the solicitor and no relationship of reliance, trust or confidence that existed between the investors and him. The solicitor owed a common law duty which flowed through the company to the investors but it was discharged when he met his obligations to the company.

---

[17] (1992), 10 O.R. (3d) 361 (Gen. Div.); see also *Hants County Business Development Centre Ltd. v. Poole,* unreported, December 2, 1997, Kelly J., Doc. S.W. 1618, [1997] N.S.J. No. 546 (S.C.).

[18] [1992] O.J. No. 292, unreported, February 17, 1992, Steele J., Doc. 16582/86, (Gen. Div.).

[19] [1998] O.J. No. 2256 (Gen. Div.)

III. NEGLIGENCE

There are several categories of economic loss under the tort of negligence. Broadly speaking, relational economic loss is the term used to refer to pure economic loss flowing to one person as a consequence of damage having been done to the property of another. Non-relational economic loss is the term used to refer to pure economic loss flowing from conduct which is not capable of causing personal injury or physical damage to property.[20] The damages claimed by third parties against lawyers almost exclusively fall into this second category of pure economic loss.

The challenge faced by third parties claiming against solicitors in negligence for pure economic loss is in establishing that they were owed a duty of care by the solicitor. This may be accomplished by demonstrating that the solicitor undertook to apply his special skill or knowledge for the assistance of the third party, and that the third party relied on that undertaking, or establishing that there was a sufficient relationship of proximity between the parties.

A. REASONABLE RELIANCE ON SPECIAL SKILL AND KNOWLEDGE OR SUFFICIENT RELATIONSHIP OF PROXIMITY

1. General Principles

The watershed decision of the House of Lords in *M'Alister (or Donoghue) v. Stevenson* [21] permitted recovery on the basis of the neighbour principle for damage caused in the absence of a contractual or fiduciary relationship, but only for property damage and physical injury. Recovery for pure economic loss was still largely precluded until the House of Lords carved out a specific exception to the exclusionary rule in *Hedley Byrne* for negligent misrepresentations. Significantly, Lord Morris of Borth-y-Gest ruled that a more general duty of care will be owed where a solicitor undertakes to apply his skill for the benefit of a non-client who relies on him:

> . . . if someone possessed of a special skill undertakes, quite irrespective of contract, to apply that skill for the assistance of another person who relies on such skill, a duty of care will arise.[22]

Reliance was an essential feature of the "special relationships" giving rise to the duty of care on the basis of *Hedley Byrne*.

---

[20] *Canadian National Railway Co. v. Norsk Pacific Steamship Co.* (1992), 91 D.L.R. (4th) 289, [1992] 1 S.C.R. 1021.

[21] [1932] A.C. 562 (H.L.).

[22] *Supra*, note 3, at 594 All E.R.

Canadian courts adopted *Hedley Byrne* and interpreted it broadly. The decision of the House of Lords in *Anns v. Merton London Borough Council* [23] articulated an even broader test for recovery of economic loss. It did not require an undertaking to apply special skill for the benefit of another person and reliance by that person upon it. To establish a duty of care under *Anns*, Lord Wilberforce held that a plaintiff need only show: (1) foreseeability and sufficient proximity between the loss and the negligent act; and (2) no policy considerations that barred recovery.

The *Anns* test was later rejected by the House of Lords in *Murphy v. Brentwood District Council.* [24] but has been repeatedly endorsed by the Supreme Court of Canada and remains good law in this country. [25] In *Kamloops (City) v. Nielsen,* [26] Madam Justice Wilson confirmed the *Anns* test for determining whether a duty of care exists and restated it this way:

(1)   is there a sufficiently close relationship between the parties . . . so that, in the reasonable contemplation of the [professional], carelessness on its part might cause damage to that person? If so,

(2)   are there any considerations which ought to negative or limit (a) the scope of the duty and (b) the class of persons to whom it is owed or (c) the damages to which a breach of it may give rise?

When the test for duty of care described by Lord Wilberforce in *Anns* and adopted in *Kamloops* is used to establish liability between a lawyer and a third party, in theory, the absence of actual reliance by the third party within the meaning of *Hedley Byrne* is not determinative. [27] Rather, the special relationship that arises when a third party relies on the skill of a solicitor who has undertaken to apply that skill for the third party's benefit is simply an example of a relationship of proximity on which a duty of care may be based. [28] Nevertheless, the factual circumstances that gave rise to a relationship of sufficient proximity almost always involve a degree of reliance, such that it is difficult to know whether this type of relationship may arise in the absence of reliance. [29]

---

[23]   *Supra*, note 4.

[24]   [1991] 1 A.C. 398.

[25]   *Kamloops (City) v. Nielsen*, [1984] 2 S.C.R. 2; *B.D.C. Ltd. v. Hofstrand Farms Ltd.,* [1986] 1 S.C.R. 228; *Canadian National Railway Co. v. Norsk Pacific Steamship Co., supra*, note 21; *London Drugs Ltd. v. Kuehne & Nagel International Ltd.*, [1992] 3 S.C.R. 299; *Winnipeg Condominium Corp. No. 36 v. Bird Construction Co.,* [1995] 1 S.C.R. 85.

[26]   *Supra*, note 25, at 10-11.

[27]   However, for a contrary view, see *Seale v. Perry*, [1982] V.R. 193, *per* Murphy J.

[28]   *Tracy v. Atkins, supra,* note 9, at 638 105 D.L.R.; *Allied Finance & Invts. Ltd. v. Haddow & Co.,* [1983] N.Z.L.R. 22 at 29. The *Anns* test for proximity has been applied to a case of legal malpractice in which a lawyer engaged in a business venture with former clients: *Korz v. St. Pierre* (1987), 61 O.R. (2d) 609, 43 D.L.R. (4th) 528 (C.A.), leave to appeal to S.C.C. refused February 25, 1988.

[29]   In *Junior Books Ltd. v. Veitchi Co. Ltd.*, [1982] 3 All E.R. 201 at 214 (H.L.), Lord Roskill stated: "The concept of proximity must always involve, at least in most cases some degree of

There is some authority which suggests that a third party must establish a degree of reliance in order to impose a duty of care on a solicitor on the basis of *Anns*. The British Columbia Court of Appeal held in *Kamahap Enterprises Ltd. v. Chu's Central Market Ltd.* [30] that foreseeability of economic loss is not in itself sufficient to establish a sufficient relationship of proximity giving rise to a *prima facie* duty of care under *Anns*; "something more" is required. The additional requirement will usually be reasonable reliance. *Kamahap* considered the duty owed to the other party in an arms-length commercial transaction where, for policy reasons, it will usually be undesirable to impose a duty of care. Whether reliance is necessary to establish a sufficient relationship of proximity in other circumstances is somewhat uncertain at this time.[31]

Some doubt was cast by the Supreme Court of Canada in *Canadian National Railway v. Norsk*[32] on the appropriateness of the proximity test in cases of relational economic loss. The court's concern stemmed from the high potential for indeterminate liability in the category of pure economic loss. Lawyers' malpractice cases will rarely fall into this category because they seldom involve economic loss that is connected to damage to a person or property.

At present, a solicitor may be found to owe a duty of care to a third party under the *Hedley Byrne* doctrine if he undertakes to apply his special skill or knowledge for the third party's benefit and that undertaking is relied upon, or on the basis of *Anns* principles, if the solicitor and the third party are in a sufficient relationship of proximity so as to give rise to a duty of care which need not be negated for any policy reasons. When a duty of care does arise, a solicitor may avoid liability by expressly clarifying that he does not intend to assume the duty.[33]

For example, in *Tracy v. Atkins* the British Columbia Court of Appeal upheld the trial judge's finding of a duty of care based on *Hedley Byrne* because the

---

reliance." Note that reliance is generally not required in the case of disappointed beneficiaries: Section III. "Negligence".

[30] (1989), 40 B.C.L.R. (2d) 288 (C.A.); see also *Kripps v. Touche Ross & Co.* (1992), 94 D.L.R. (4th) 284 (B.C.C.A.), in which the court refused to find a sufficient relationship of proximity between the auditors of negligently prepared financial statements and investors who did not rely on the financial statements.

[31] For a detailed analysis of this issue, see D. Rolph, "Solicitors' Liability to Non-Clients in Negligence" (1993), 15 *Advocates' Q.* 129.

[32] *Supra*, note 20. Madam Justice McLachlin, writing for the majority, held that proximity is the controlling concept in determining recoverability for all economic loss. Mr. Justice Stevenson, writing for himself, held that, while the court should not depart from the general formulation of the duty of care articulated in *Anns*, *supra*, note 4, and adopted in *Kamloops*, *supra* note 26, he expressed reservations about the use of the concept of proximity and stated that it was incapable of providing a principled basis for drawing the line on the issue of liability. Mr. Justice La Forest, in dissent, echoed Stevenson J.'s concerns. The court declined an opportunity to choose between the approaches to the concept of proximity in *D'Amato v. Badger*, [1996] 2 S.C.R. 1071, another case involving relational economic loss.

[33] *Marko v. Perry* (1980), 18 B.C.L.R. 263 (Co. Ct.); *Pham v. Woo* (1996), 39 Alta. L.R. (3d) 7 (Q.B.); *Free v. Baumgartel Gould*, unreported, November 17, 1997, Prowse J., Doc. Vancouver C932662, [1997] B.C.J. No. 2566 (S.C.).

solicitor had undertaken to perform all of the conveyancing work that would ordinarily be done by the vendor's solicitor, such as the registration of the mortgage. The solicitor knew or ought to have known that the plaintiff vendors were relying on him to protect their interests. Chief Justice Nemetz affirmed the applicability of *Hedley Byrne* in cases involving the negligent performance of legal services in addition to the giving of negligent advice: "It is true that *Hedley Byrne, supra*, dealt with negligence arising from the giving of advice. *A fortiori* it is my opinion that in cases of negligence arising from the giving of legal services the same *rationale* should apply."[34] These circumstances also gave rise to a sufficient relationship of proximity and thus a duty of care arose on the basis of *Anns*. The solicitor's duty in the circumstances was to contact the plaintiffs to inquire into the instructions he had received. The loss suffered by the plaintiffs was a direct consequence of the solicitor's careless failure to meet this duty to inquire.

2. The Unrepresented Third Party

In most of the cases in which a solicitor is found to owe a duty of care to a third party, the third party is not independently represented. Liability is imposed on the basis of *Hedley Byrne* where the solicitor undertakes, either expressly or impliedly, to provide legal services to an unrepresented third party who relies on that undertaking.

A duty of care has also been imposed on solicitors in favour of unrepresented third parties based on a sufficient relationship of proximity as established by *Anns*. However, these cases overwhelmingly, if not exclusively, involve an undertaking by the solicitor and a measure of reliance by the unrepresented plaintiff. Interestingly, the vast majority of the cases in this area involve the purchase and sale of real estate or financing transactions where only one party to the agreement has counsel.

There are several early illustrations of the principle that a solicitor may owe a duty of care to an unrepresented third party. *Tracy v. Atkins*,[35] which we have previously discussed, is an example. The third party plaintiffs "instructed" the defendant solicitor to register a mortgage on their behalf. Both the trial court and the Court of Appeal properly concluded that, in doing so, the defendant ought to have been aware that the plaintiffs were relying on him to protect their interests. The court in *Dorndorf v. Hoeter*[36] came to a similar conclusion. The defendant, a notary public, acted for the vendors in the sale of ten acres of property in which he had a ten per cent interest. He received a cheque representing a down payment and a letter from the unrepresented purchasers which the court found should have alerted him to the probability that they were relying on him

---

[34] (1997), 83 D.L.R. (3d) 46 (B.C.S.C.), affd 16 B.C.L.R. 223, 105 D.L.R. (3d) 632 at 638 (C.A.).
[35] *Ibid.*
[36] (1981), 29 B.C.L.R. 71, 122 D.L.R. (3d) 758 (S.C.).

to protect their interests. The court also found that he had a duty to ensure they did not continue in that belief.[37] Analogous reasoning was applied in *Clarence Constr. Ltd. v. Lavallee*,[38] in which a solicitor retained by the purchaser in a real estate transaction was held liable to the vendor for breach of a duty of care because he had performed duties that would ordinarily have been performed by the vendor's solicitor — preparation of the Statement of Adjustments and a vendor take-back second mortgage, and remittance of the balance on closing to the vendor. However, the solicitor failed to ensure that the vendor understood the nature of the second mortgage which contained a clause permitting the purchaser to obtain a prior mortgage. The solicitor in *MacDonald v. Nugent*,[39] who was acting on behalf of an estate, was found liable when he gave a third party incorrect advice about the availability of the estate's assets for purchase. In *Klingspon v. Ramsay*,[40] the defendant lawyer attempted to avoid liability to an unrepresented third party, who had invested in a company that the lawyer represented, by having her sign an acknowledgment that he had *"'not offered . . . any advice other than as to the good standing of the Company'"*.[41] The attempt backfired: the court determined that this acknowledgment would have the effect of confirming the plaintiff's false impressions about the company's financial soundness and, given the circumstances, the defendant had a duty to impress upon her in plain and unambiguous language that he could give no assurance about the solvency of the company or the security of her investment.

In *Begusic v. Clark Wilson & Co.*[42] solicitors who acted for a developer were liable to the unrepresented purchaser of a co-op unit because they performed conveyancing work for her for a fee. They should have known that she might consider them to be her solicitors and rely on them to protect her interests. Thus, a duty of care arose to advise the plaintiff of a provision for rent revision in the head lease. In *Peake v. Vernon & Thompson*,[43] a mortgage company's lawyer undertook to file transfer documents. The court held that the lawyer owed a duty to the non-client purchaser to file the documents on time.

In *Paton v. Shaw*,[44] the defendant solicitor acted for the purchaser of the plaintiff's company. He undertook to do all of the work in the transaction, including the corporate work which would ordinarily be carried out by the vendor's solicitors. The defendant failed to change the company's directors and Revenue Canada subsequently found the plaintiff liable as a director for sub-

---

[37] The plaintiffs had no difficulty in establishing actual reliance since the vendors had told them the defendant solicitor would act for them.

[38] (1980), 111 D.L.R. (3d) 582 (B.C.S.C.), affd [1982] 2 W.W.R. 760, 132 D.L.R. (3d) 153 (C.A.).

[39] (1977), 14 A.R. 476 (C.A.).

[40] (1985), 65 B.C.L.R. 132, [1985] 5 W.W.R. 411 (S.C.).

[41] *Ibid.*, at 413 W.W.R.

[42] (1992), 92 D.L.R. (4th) 273 (B.C.S.C.).

[43] (1990), 49 B.C.L.R. (2d) 245 (S.C.).

[44] (1995), 134 Nfld. & P.E.I.R. 271 (P.E.I.T.D.).

stantial unpaid taxes. The Prince Edward Island Supreme Court (Trial Division) found both that a sufficient relationship of proximity arose when the defendant undertook to perform the services, and that the plaintiff relied on him to do so, such that in the reasonable contemplation of the solicitor, carelessness on his part might cause damage to the plaintiff. The court articulated this broad legal principle against which the factual situation in cases such as these ought to be assessed:

> Where a lawyer, acting in his capacity as a lawyer in a transaction in which one of the parties is unrepresented, undertakes to do, in addition to the legal work he ordinarily would do for the party who retained him, legal work which ordinarily would be done by the unrepresented party's lawyer (if he had one), and the unrepresented party actually and justifiably relies on the lawyer in that respect, then if the lawyer knows or ought to know the unrepresented party is relying on him, he has placed himself in a sufficient relationship of proximity vis-à-vis the unrepresented party to incur a duty of care towards him and the lawyer is liable for any reasonably foreseeable loss that results from a breach of that duty of care.[45]

Although reliance may not be necessary to establish a sufficient relationship of proximity under *Anns*, the absence of foreseeable reliance by unrepresented plaintiffs has effectively prevented the imposition of a duty of care in some cases. For example, in *Kwak v. Odishaw*,[46] the defendant solicitor prepared a promissory note to be signed by the plaintiff in favour of his client. Although the defendant recommended that he review the note with a lawyer before signing it, the plaintiff failed to do so. The court held that the case was distinguishable from *Tracy v. Atkins*[47] as it could not be said that the defendant knew or ought to have known that the plaintiff was relying on him to provide advice with respect to the plaintiff's obligations under the note and a companion contract. The court went on to say: "it is [not] necessary to decide whether the circumstances of this case were such that the lawyer was bound to advise [the plaintiff] to take the note to his own lawyer. It was a prudent and proper thing to do in these circumstances . . . [and] certainly all that he had to do."[48]

The lack of reliance by the plaintiffs in *C.T. Industries Ltd. v. M & T Rentals Ltd.*[49] also prevented the imposition of a duty of care. The defendant solicitor, who had been retained by the purchaser, failed to discover arrears of municipal

---

[45] *Ibid.*, at 287. For another example of a case in which the existence of a sufficient relationship of proximity was determined on the basis of whether the plaintiffs relied on the defendants, see *Dinelle Holdings Ltd. v. Hansen*, unreported, February 5, 1992, Scarth J., Doc. Prince George 8255, [1992] B.C.J. No. 236 (S.C.).

[46] (1984), 59 B.C.L.R. 54, [1985] 2 W.W.R. 222 (C.A.).

[47] *Supra*, note 34.

[48] *Supra*, note 46 at 229 W.W.R. See also *Gerlock v. Safety Mart Foods Ltd.*, [1983] 2 W.W.R. 569 (B.C.C.A.).

[49] (1982), 41 B.C.L.R. 22 (Co. Ct.).

taxes on the property to be purchased. The purchasers sued the vendors, and the vendors joined the solicitor as a third party claiming that he was in breach of his duty to them in failing to make a proper tax search. The court held, *inter alia*, that the vendors had not relied on the solicitor since they were aware of the arrears at all material times.

In *Dinelle Holdings Ltd.*,[50] a solicitor who acted for the purchasers of a bakery but also prepared the documents securing the unpaid portion of the purchase price on behalf of the unrepresented vendors did not owe a duty of care to the vendors to insist that they obtain independent legal advice and to make it clear that they were not acting for them. The court found it troubling that the defendant solicitors attended on the execution of the security documents which subsequently proved to be flawed. However, the solicitor ought not to have reasonably known that the vendors were relying on him because he suggested that they take the documents to their own solicitors for execution. Similarly, in *Hutchinson v. Ventresca*,[51] the solicitor's client, a real estate agent, persuaded the plaintiffs to invest in a commercial property and represented that the defendant solicitor would act for them on the transaction. The solicitor never met or spoke with the plaintiffs, although without his authorization his secretary sent them a bill for the preparation of a trust agreement. The plaintiffs lost all of their money but their action against the solicitor was dismissed because they had relied on the real estate agent, not the solicitor. In *Lobelio v. Pichini*,[52] the defendant solicitor was retained by a borrower of funds to prepare a promissory note. At a meeting between the solicitor, the borrower and the plaintiff, an unrepresented and unsophisticated lender, the promissory note was executed and the solicitor helped the lender make out a cheque for the loan proceeds. The plaintiff was led by her sister, or the borrower, or both, to believe that the solicitor would protect her interests but did not communicate this belief to the solicitor and he did nothing to confirm that he was acting for her. When the loan was not repaid, the plaintiff commenced an action against the solicitor in negligence. The court accepted that the plaintiff had relied on the solicitor but concluded that the reliance was neither reasonable nor reasonably foreseeable in the circumstances. A solicitor does not owe a duty of care to a non-client simply because others have led her to believe that the solicitor will act in her interest.

At least one case has held that the fact that a solicitor knows that his client is acting as agent for an unrepresented third party is sufficient to create a duty of care in favour of the unrepresented third party. In *Midland Mortgage Corp. v. Jawl & Bundon*,[53] the plaintiff entered into an agreement with a trust company to lend money to a borrower to redevelop certain property under a long-term lease. A commitment letter from the trust company to the plaintiff provided that all mortgage documentation was to be prepared by solicitors mutually acceptable to

---

[50] *Supra*, note 45.
[51] Unreported, July 9, 1996, Doc. 9670/91 (Ont. Gen. Div.).
[52] Unreported, June 5, 1998, Doc. C-32715/95, Dunn J. (Ont. Gen. Div.).
[53] (1997), 28 B.C.L.R. (3d) 288 (S.C.).

them. Because security was taken in the trust company's name and held for the plaintiff and other investors, an agency relationship arose between them. The defendant solicitors advised the trust company to execute a mortgage which eventually proved to be insufficient when a default occurred. The plaintiff lost the funds it had advanced to the borrower and brought an action in negligence against the solicitors.

The court held that there was sufficient proximity between the plaintiff and the solicitors to give rise to a duty of care in connection with the preparation of the security documents and related advice because the solicitors were aware of the agency relationship between their client and the plaintiff. A duty of care also arose on the basis that the solicitors, being persons of special skill, undertook to apply that skill for the assistance of the plaintiff who relied on them to do so. The court expressed doubt that the reasonableness of the reliance is determinative: "That requirement exists in respect of the tort of negligent misrepresentation. If it is necessary for me to do so, I find that [the plaintiff's] reliance on the Defendants was reasonable."[54] The solicitors breached the duty of care by failing to advise the trust company of the deficiency in the security.

A lawyer dealing with an agent acting within the scope of his authority may treat the agent as having authority to represent and bind the agent's principal.[55] He will owe the principal a duty of care, but is not required to look beyond the agent and communicate with the principal directly unless it is apparent that the agent is not properly representing the principal or is failing to convey the solicitor's advice to the principal. Of course, a lawyer who himself acts as agent for a third party will owe the obligations that are normally owed by an agent to his principal.[56]

3. The Third Party with Independent Legal Advice

The fact that a third party is individually represented or obtains some measure of independent legal advice does not immunize a lawyer from a claim by the third party. If a lawyer, by words or conduct, undertakes to perform legal services ordinarily performed by the third party's lawyer, or offers legal advice to the third party, a relationship of reliance may be created under the *Hedley Byrne* principle even if the third party has her own lawyer. The duty of care to third parties with legal representation may also be based on the *Anns* concept of a

---

[54] *Ibid.,* at 317.

[55] *Sinclair v. Smith* (1982), 41 B.C.L.R. 374 (S.C.); *Feschuk v. Hudema* (1994), 126 Sask. R. 26 (Q.B.).

[56] See *Hongkong Bank of Canada v. Phillips* (1997), 119 Man. R. (2d) 243 (Q.B.), in which the defendant lawyer was found to have been an agent of the third party plaintiff because he held a mortgage in his own name for the benefit of the plaintiff and other investors. The plaintiff invested in the mortgage at the suggestion of the lawyer's client. The fact that the plaintiff was unrepresented does not appear to have weighed very heavily in the court's decision to impose liability.

sufficient relationship of proximity. Issues concerning the duty of care owed to the opposing party in litigation or to a party adverse in interest to a solicitor's client are considered in greater detail under the heading of "Conflict of Interest Situations".

In *Marko v. P.*,[57] a case illustrative of the point that a solicitor may owe a duty of care to a third party who has independent legal advice, the solicitor for the mortgagor assumed the duty of registering a mortgage but failed to do so. He was held liable to the mortgagee notwithstanding that the mortgagee had his own solicitor. Similarly, in *Free v. Baumgartel Gould*,[58] solicitors for borrowers assumed full responsibility for securing the assignment of a term deposit as security for a loan but did not properly complete the task. Although they had been separately represented, the lenders brought an action against them. The determining factor was that the relationship of the solicitors to the lender was sufficiently proximate that they could foresee that their conduct could damage the lender. Proximity was evidenced by the fact that the solicitors knew or reasonably should have known that the lender was relying on them to secure the assignment.

In *Wynston v. MacDonald*,[59] where the mortgagor's solicitor did not undertake the "obligations of a solicitor" to either the mortgagee plaintiff or the plaintiff's solicitor, he did not incur liability for the inadequacy of the mortgage security and did not need to disclose facts contrary to the interests of his clients. The principles of *Hedley Byrne* were determined to be inapplicable since the mortgagor's solicitor could not reasonably foresee that the mortgagee would place reliance on him. This reasoning was applied more recently by the Ontario Court (General Division) in *Seaway Trust Co. v. Markle*[60] to conclude: "[t]he duty of a solicitor who is not a party to, but knows of a fraud upon the opposite party in a commercial transaction where all parties have, and rely upon, their own solicitors, is, according to *Wynston, supra*, not to himself misrepresent the transaction." The solicitor who acted for a mortgagee did not have a duty to ensure the propriety of the transaction for the independently represented mortgagor; rather, it was his duty not to disclose facts contrary to the interests of his client.

---

[57]　(1980), 18 B.C.L.R. 263, [1980] 3 W.W.R. 565 *sub nom. Marko v. Perry* (Co. Ct.). The mortgagee's solicitor was also sued and the court apportioned liability equally between the two solicitors.

[58]　Unreported, November 17, 1997, Prowse J., Doc. Vancouver C932662, [1997] B.C.J. No. 2566 (S.C.).

[59]　(1979), 27 O.R. (2d) 67, 105 D.L.R. (3d) 527 (H.C.), affd 32 O.R. (2d) 108, 119 D.L.R. (3d) 256 (C.A.).

[60]　(1991), 7 C.C.L.T. (2d) 83 at 91 (Ont. Gen. Div.).

4. Conflict of Interest Situations

A court will be reluctant to impose on a lawyer an obligation to a third party if it will conflict with the duties owed by the lawyer to his clients. Such conflicts commonly arise where the third party is the opposing party in litigation or is adverse in interest to the lawyer's client in a commercial transaction.

a. Duty to the Opposite Party in Litigation

It remains doubtful whether or not a duty to the opposite party will be imposed in the context of litigation. If, when conducting a lawsuit, a lawyer owes a duty of care to his client's opponent, his duty to his own client may be undermined. This was the concern of the Alberta Court of Appeal in *German v. Major*,[61] in which the defendant barrister had been retained by the Attorney General to prosecute the plaintiff for tax evasion. The plaintiff was ultimately acquitted and then sued the defendant for, *inter alia*, negligence, alleging that the defendant had failed to take care in the investigation and prosecution of the case. While the court was prepared to assume that the plaintiff and the defendant stood in a sufficient relationship of proximity to satisfy the first part of the *Anns* test, it held that there were substantial policy considerations that ought to limit the scope of the duty in the circumstances. First, the imposition of the duty would mean the retrial of many criminal cases in a civil court; second, the duty of counsel is to represent her client's interests and the law should not impose upon her a conflicting duty to refrain from acting in a manner detrimental to the other side.

The Supreme Court of Canada has affirmed that a Crown attorney is not immune from liability for malicious prosecution if the accused can establish both that there was an absence of reasonable and probable cause for commencing the proceedings and that the prosecution was motivated by an improper purpose or motive.[62] The Saskatchewan Court of Appeal has determined that a Crown attorney may also be liable for abuse of statutory power, conspiracy or even negligence if the prosecution was actuated or contributed to by malice or improper purpose.[63] In the absence of malice or improper purpose, however, it is clear that a Crown cannot be liable for negligent prosecution. The plaintiff in *Walker v. Ontario*[64] claimed damages for malicious and negligent prosecution against the Crown attorney who prosecuted a sexual assault charge against him. In granting the defendant's motion for summary judgment, the Court quoted extensively from *German v. Major* to conclude that, although a Crown attorney owes a duty

---

[61] (1985), 39 Alta. L.R. (2d) 270, 20 D.L.R. (4th) 703 (C.A.).

[62] *Nelles v. Ontario,* [1989] 2 S.C.R. 170; see also *Al's Steak House & Tavern v. Deloitte & Touche* (1997), 13 C.P.C. (4th) 90.

[63] See *Milgaard v. Kujawa* (1994), 123 Sask. R. 164 (C.A.), in which the court refused to strike out as disclosing no reasonable cause of action a statement of claim which alleged that prosecutors conspired to and did intentionally and with malice breach their duty to disclose information that tended to exculpate the plaintiff with the purpose of causing him harm.

[64] (1997), 32 O.T.C. 19 (Gen. Div.).

of care to an accused, he will not be liable for the conduct of the prosecution unless there is evidence of bad faith. The duty of prosecuting counsel during the trial is to ensure that the accused is tried fairly.[65] This is similar to the position taken by the New Zealand Court of Appeal in *New Zealand Social Credit v. O'Brien*.[66] The court acknowledged that a solicitor may make himself liable to the opposing party for malicious prosecution, in which case malice on the part of the solicitor himself must be proven, but determined that the opposing party had no cause of action for breach of a professional duty of care.

Family law practitioners have been the subject of a number of actions by opposing parties in matrimonial proceedings, perhaps because of the highly emotional nature of the issues in dispute. The allegations have included that the defendant solicitor poisoned the plaintiff's relationship with his children,[67] assisted the client in dissipating assets[68] and commissioned affidavits which the solicitor ought to have known were false.[69] In each case, the opposing party was found not to have a cause of action against the solicitor. This common result was explained as follows:

> . . . the plaintiff's position is tantamount to an assertion that all counsel who represent litigants owe a fiduciary duty or a duty to take care to the other party to the litigation. This is patently absurd, as in the course of counsel's representation of her own client, much may be done that is intentionally and necessarily directed toward injuring the other party's interests. . . . I do not intend to say that [the solicitor] could in no circumstances be held to owe a duty of care to the [opposing party]. But I do say that before such a duty can be found to exist, facts must be proved in evidence — and alleged in pleadings — which describe the relationship and the circumstances from which the duty arose.[70]

Another illustration of the courts' extreme reluctance to impose a duty on a solicitor to the opposite party in the context of litigation is the case of *Garrant v. Cawood*.[71] The plaintiff, who was unrepresented, was unfamiliar with the appli-

---

[65] See also *Canada v. Reynen* (1993), 70 F.T.R. 158, revd in part 96 F.T.C. 240*n*. For a decision relying on *German v. Major*, *supra*, note 62, to conclude that a lawyer owes no duty of care to the opposing party in a civil action, see *Gone Hollywood Video Ltd. v. Skrabek* (1997), 199 A.R. 318 (Q.B.).

[66] [1984] 1 N.Z.L.R. 84.

[67] *Jensen v. MacGregor* (1992), 65 B.C.L.R. (2d) 224 (S.C.); *Brignolio v. DesMarais, Keenan*, unreported, November 7, 1995, D. Lane J., Doc. C-1298/95, [1995] O.J. No. 3499 (Gen. Div.), motion to set aside an order dismissing the appeal dismissed, unreported, April 26, 1996, Docs. 18176, C23315/96, [1996] O.J. No. 4812 (C.A.).

[68] *Re Kern & Kern* (1986), 54 O.R. (2d) 11 (H.C.); *Crooks v. Manolescu*, unreported, January 9, 1995, Master Bolton, Doc. Vancouver C943158, [1995] B.C.J. No. 17 (S.C.).

[69] *Crooks, supra*, note 68.

[70] *Ibid.*, at paras. 10-13.

[71] (1984), 40 Sask. R. at 162 (Q.B.), affd 40 Sask. R. 155, [1985] 6 W.W.R. 31, *sub nom. Garrant v. Moskal; Garrant v. Cawood* (C.A.).

cable legal principles. Not surprisingly, the court determined that the plaintiff's claim disclosed no cause of action. However, the court went on to say that it is highly doubtful whether a cause of action could be found to exist between a lawyer and his client's opponent "even if it could be proved that counsel participated in dishonest and fraudulent conduct, and counselled perjury, which resulted in the opposite party being deprived of rights or property".[72]

b. Duty to Party Adverse in Interest

Outside of the litigation context, courts have exhibited considerable reluctance to find that a solicitor owes a duty of care to someone who is adverse in interest to her client. The third party adverse in interest need not be adverse in the sense of being on the "other side" of the transaction. For example, in normal circumstances, a solicitor acting for a corporation does not owe a duty to individual officers, directors and shareholders to protect their individual legal interests.[73] In *McGauley v. British Columbia*,[74] unsophisticated investors in TIHC (a co-operative) wanted the duty to warn to extend beyond the co-operative to each investor in their personal capacity. Although the individual investors relied on the defendant for information regarding the security of their investment, the solicitor's client was TIHC, not the individual investors.

A solicitor will not normally owe a duty to his client's debtor. In *Re Abacus Cities Ltd.*,[75] a solicitor negligently advised a bank about the appointment of a receiver for the plaintiff, the bank's debtor, knowing and intending that it would rely on the advice. The plaintiff was harmed as a foreseeable result of the bank's reliance. Irrespective of the fact that the plaintiff did not itself rely on the advice, the court held that, because of the conflict of interest created, as a matter of policy, no duty of a solicitor to his client's debtor should be recognized in law:

> A solicitor owes a duty to his client, when that client is a creditor, to give advice to the client, as best he can and with care and prudence, with the object of further-

---

[72] *Ibid.*, at 164 Sask. R. The American courts have expressed a similar reluctance: see R.E. Mallen and J.M. Smith, *Legal Malpractice*, 4th ed. (St. Paul, Minn.: West Publishing Co., 1996).

[73] *McMurchie v. Boyle & Co.*, unreported, September 30, 1996, Humprhies J., Doc. Vancouver C936664, [1996] B.C.J. No. 2054 (S.C.). Note that the Ontario Court (General Division) has potentially confused this issue by holding that a solicitor for a corporation owes a duty of care to the shareholders to carry out her duties to the corporation in a reasonably professional and competent manner and with the utmost good faith. The duty flows through the corporation to the shareholders but does not arise independently of the corporation itself and is fully discharged if the solicitor meets his obligations to the corporation. While this decision suggests that a solicitor may be liable to shareholders for breaches of duty owed to the corporation, it confirms that no other obligations are owed to them as individuals.

[74] (1990), 44 B.C.L.R. (2d) 217 at 236 (S.C.). However, the Court of Appeal allowed the TIHC investors one last chance to plead a cause of action from the perspective of the plaintiffs in their personal capacity, independent of the claims of TIHC; see *McGauley v. British Columbia* (1991), 56 B.C.L.R. (2d) 1 (C.A.).

[75] (1986), 39 C.C.L.T. 7 (Alta. Q.B.), affd (1987), 44 C.C.L.T. 199 (Alta. C.A.).

ing his client's interests against the client's debtor. If the solicitor were held to owe a duty to the debtor to use reasonable care in arriving at the solicitor's understanding of the law or the facts, and therefore in formulating the advice he gives his client as to what action should be taken to collect the debt or enforce the security, that duty would often impede the effective execution of his duty to his client. . . . As a matter of policy no such duty of care should be recognized by our law.[76]

As well, a solicitor will not generally owe a duty of care to protect the economic interests of a party that is contractually related to the solicitor's client. Two British Columbia Court of Appeal decisions support this general rule. In *Kamahap Enterprises Ltd. v. Chu's Central Market Ltd.*,[77] the court considered whether a duty was owed to the purchaser by the solicitor for the vendor in a commercial transaction for the sale of property. The court held that a party to a commercial transaction cannot owe a duty in tort to protect the economic interests of the other party to the transaction in carrying their bargain into effect. In the absence of reliance, a solicitor acting for that party cannot owe a duty that his principal did not have.[78] Analogous reasoning was applied in *McPhail's Equipment Co. v. "Roxanne III" (The)*[79] where the defendant lawyer, who acted for the vendor of a vessel, failed to sign and return documents delivered to him by the purchaser in time for closing and would not agree to extend the closing deadline. The court upheld the dismissal of the purchaser's motion to add the lawyer as a defendant in an action against the vendor.

Where there is absolutely no relationship between the solicitor's client and the third party plaintiff, a duty of care will be even harder to establish. For example, a solicitor acting for the purchaser in a transaction does not owe a duty of care to a judgment creditor having a writ of execution over the vendor's assets not to distribute the proceeds of the sale to the vendor.[80]

Because courts are critical of lawyers who act on both sides of a transaction,[81] it is not surprising that there are cases in which a court has found a positive obligation on a lawyer to look after the interests of non-clients, even when the imposition of this duty creates a conflict of interest. However, the duty usually arises in situations where the solicitor has contractual relations

---

[76] *Ibid.*, at 18.
[77] (1989), 40 B.C.L.R. (2d) 288 (C.A.). See also *Seaway Trust Co., supra*, note 60.
[78] *Kamahap Enterprises, supra*, note 78, at 296.
[79] (1995), 2 B.C.L.R. (3d) 393 (C.A.).
[80] *Pham v. Woo* (1996), 39 Alta. L.R. (3d) 7 (Q.B.).
[81] See, for example, *Davey v. Woolley, Hames, Dale & Dingwell* (1982), 35 O.R. (2d) 599, leave to appeal to S.C.C. refused 37 O.R. (2d) 499n; *Dinelle Holdings Ltd. v. Hansen*, unreported, February 5, 1992, Scarth J., Doc. Prince George 8255, [1992] B.C.J. No. 236 (S.C.).

with one side, yet is obligated to both sides because of some reasonable reliance on the lawyer by the non-contractual party.[82]

The decision of the New Zealand Court of Appeal in *Allied Finance & Investments. Ltd. v. Haddow & Co.*[83] suggests that lawyers involved in all manner of commercial transactions, when providing "certificates" or "opinions" about the status of their client's property interests, may attract liability to third parties who are separately represented but rely to their detriment on these certificates. The plaintiff, a financial institution, lent money to the defendant solicitors' client, H, on the security of a yacht that the plaintiff understood H was buying. The defendant firm "certified" that the security instrument executed by its client was "fully binding" upon him and that there were "no other charges whatsoever on the yacht".[84] In fact, to the knowledge of the defendant firm, the yacht was being purchased by a company of which H was a director and controlling shareholder. H did not intend to use the money to buy any interest in the yacht himself. The court held the defendant firm liable to the plaintiff because providing the certificate, which was an exercise of professional expertise, was misleading, and reliance on the certificate by the plaintiff was to be contemplated.[85] A Canadian court has distinguished this decision on the basis that the duty arose from the giving of the certificate, not from any general duty on the part of solicitors to persons who are not their clients.[86]

B. THE "THIRD PARTY BENEFICIARY" CLAIM

Although a few cases have suggested that a solicitor cannot be liable to a non-client in the absence of reliance on him by the non-client,[87] we find an exception in the case law respecting third party beneficiaries. Recovery by a "third party beneficiary" is well accepted for disappointed beneficiaries under a will. Moreover, there is a perceptible trend in favour of extending liability to other "third party beneficiaries" — to anyone upon whom a client instructs his lawyer to confer a benefit and whom it is reasonably foreseeable will be harmed by the solicitor's negligence in carrying out those instructions.

---

[82]   See *Clarence Construction Ltd. v. Lavallee* (1980), 111 D.L.R. (3d) 582 (B.C.S.C.), affd [1982] 2 W.W.R. 760, 132 D.L.R. (3d) 153 (B.C.C.A.), wherein a duty was found where the third party plaintiffs reasonably relied on the solicitor.

[83]   [1983] N.Z.L.R. 22. In *Allied Finance*, the court premised its finding of liability on both the wider *Anns* doctrine and the narrower concept of reliance within the meaning of *Hedley Byrne*.

[84]   *Ibid.*, at 23.

[85]   This was because the court found that the plaintiff's solicitors had no way of independently verifying the ownership of and encumbrances on the yacht (at 30-31). In our view the facts of this case border on fraud, although it appears that fraud was neither pleaded nor argued. *Cf. Greenglass v. Rusonik; Rusonik v. Conder* (1981), 21 R.P.R. 264 (Ont. H.C.), affd unreported, March 18, 1983 (C.A.).

[86]   *Seaway Trust Co. v. Markle* (1991), 7 C.C.L.T. (2d) 83 at 89 (Ont. Gen. Div.).

[87]   See Section II." Breach of Fiduciary Duty", A. "Establishing the Existence of a Fiduciary Obligation".

1. The Wills and Estates Cases

a. The English Jurisprudence

Until recently, the leading English case, albeit a decision of first instance, on the issue of a solicitors' liability to the intended beneficiaries of a failed bequest was *Ross v. Caunters*.[88] The defendant solicitors prepared on behalf of a testator a will in which the plaintiff was named as a residuary beneficiary. When the will was sent to the testator for execution, the solicitors failed to warn him that it should not be witnessed by the spouse of a beneficiary. The plaintiff's husband witnessed the will but this defect was not discovered until after the testator's death. The gift to the beneficiary was declared void under the applicable wills legislation. The solicitors admitted their negligence but claimed that their duty of care did not extend to the plaintiff.

Vice-Chancellor Megarry held: "A solicitor who is instructed by his client to carry out a transaction that will confer a benefit on an identified third party owes a duty of care towards that third party in carrying out that transaction."[89] Applying the principles enunciated in *Anns*, Megarry V.-C. reasoned that the beneficiary was someone to whom the solicitor owed a duty of care because she was within his "direct contemplation as someone . . . so closely and directly affected by his acts or omissions [in carrying out his client's instructions] that he [could] reasonably foresee that the third party [would be] likely to be injured by those acts or omissions."[90]

Vice-Chancellor Megarry emphasized that the plaintiff was a named beneficiary and was not a member of an indeterminate and unascertained class.[91] Whether or not this means that the beneficiaries of class gifts, for example, "the children of A", have a claim against a negligent solicitor is not clear from the judgment and has yet to be considered in a subsequent case.[92]

The rejection of the *Anns* test by the House of Lords in *Murphy v. Brentwood District Council*[93] caused some doubt in England as to the validity of the conclusion in *Ross v. Caunters*. The issue was recently revisited by the House of Lords in *White v. Jones*,[94] and the court confirmed by a narrow majority the li-

---

[88] [1980] Ch. 297, [1979] 3 All E.R. 580. It has, however, received widespread academic approval: M.M. Litman and G.B. Robertson, "Solicitor's Liability for Failure to Substantiate Testamentary Capacity" (1984), 62 *Can. Bar Rev.* 457; Banakas, "Professional Negligence: the New Principles Considered — I" (1985), 129 *Sol. Jo.* 372; Cane, "Negligent Solicitors and Disappointed Beneficiaries" (1980), 96 *L.Q.R.* 182 and "Negligent Solicitors and Doubly Disappointed Beneficiaries" (1983), 99 *L.Q.R.* 346.

[89] *Ross v. Caunters, supra*, note 88, at 322-23 Ch.

[90] *Ibid.*, at 323 Ch.

[91] *Ibid.*, at 320-21 Ch.

[92] For a discussion of this problem, see Bates, "Liability of Solicitors for Negligence to Beneficiaries Under a Will" (1985), 59 *Aust. L.J.* 327 at 330-31.

[93] [1991] 1 A.C. 398.

[94] [1995] All E.R. 691 (H.L.).

ability of lawyers to disappointed beneficiaries in negligence. In this case, the testator wrote to the defendant solicitors instructing them to prepare a new will providing for a gift to two daughters whom he had previously excluded from his estate. The firm had still not put the dispositions into effect when the testator died over two months later. The daughters sued the solicitors for damages in negligence.

Each of the five law lords delivered separate speeches. Three of them imposed a duty of care based on an extension of the *Hedley Byrne* doctrine because of the solicitors' assumption of the responsibility for the task and the injustice that would result if neither the testator nor the beneficiary had a remedy against the solicitor. Reliance by the third party was not required in these narrow circumstances. Lords Keith and Mustill, in dissent, found that *Ross v. Caunters* is no longer good law because it relied on *Anns,* which had since been disapproved by the House of Lords. In their view, a duty of care can only be owed under *Hedley Byrne* by a solicitor to a non-client where there was a direct relationship between them and the non-client relied in some way on the solicitor.

A few recent English decisions have emphasized that a fundamental consideration in *White v. Jones* was that no one would have a remedy against the negligent solicitor if a duty of care to the beneficiary were not recognized, the estate having suffered no loss. However, in cases where the estate does have remedy against the solicitor, no duty of care can be owed to a disappointed beneficiary.[95] In *Panford v. Gilberts Accountants (A Firm),*[96] a case involving a will prepared by an accountant, the English Court of Appeal recently held that the duty owed by the draftsperson of a will to a disappointed beneficiary cannot be greater than that owed to the testator.

b. The Canadian Jurisprudence

Interestingly, at least one case held a solicitor liable to a disappointed beneficiary even before the decision in *Anns,* and before it was applied to disappointed beneficiaries in *Ross v. Caunters.* In *Whittingham v. Crease & Co.,*[97] a disappointed beneficiary sued the testator's solicitor claiming that he had been negligent in permitting the beneficiary's spouse to execute the will, which, in turn, invalidated a bequest to the beneficiary. In holding that the *Hedley Byrne* doctrine applied to these facts, Mr. Justice Aikins of the British Columbia Supreme Court reasoned:

> The plaintiff was present and . . . had an interest in the proper completion of the will; he, in my view, relied on [the defendant] to see to it that the will was properly witnessed. This reliance did not stem from a contractual relationship. It stemmed

---

[95] *Punford v. Gilberts Accountants (A Firm)*, [1998] E.W.J. No. 445 (Eng. C.A.); see also *Carr-Glynn v. Fearsons (a firm)*, [1997] 2 All E.R. 614 (Ch. D.).

[96] *Supra*, note 95.

[97] (1978), 88 D.L.R. (3d) 353, 6 C.C.L.T. 1 (B.C.S.C.).

from what may best be described as the practical realities of the situation. Viewed practically, the conclusion in my view is inescapable that the plaintiff, keenly interested in the will being effective, relied on the solicitor to see to it that it was. He relied on the implied representation to which I have referred.[98]

Mr. Justice Aikins acknowledged that this was not the kind of reliance identified in the jurisprudence in that the plaintiff did not act on the strength of the defendant's implied representation to use reasonable care in attending to the execution of the will. Nevertheless, he concluded that there was no need for the plaintiff to act on the implied representation in order to suffer a loss and that the solicitor could reasonably foresee his negligence would, by itself, cause the very loss that in fact occurred.

It has been persuasively argued that this so-called "passive reliance"[99] is insufficient to create a duty of care and that the concept of reliance articulated in *Hedley Byrne* has been inappropriately diluted.[100] Subsequent cases side-stepped this conceptual difficulty by formulating a principle of liability to third parties that derives more from *M'Alister (or Donoghue) v. Stevenson*[101] and *Anns v. Merton London Borough Council*[102] (that is, on the principles of "proximity") than it does from *Hedley Byrne* (and the principles of "reliance"). Many cases followed *Ross v. Caunters* and relied on *Anns* to hold lawyers liable to disappointed beneficiaries.[103] In *Linsley v. Kirstiuk*,[104] it was held that the trustee's solicitors owed a duty of care to the beneficiaries, who necessarily relied on the solicitors to act properly. If the solicitors did not act properly, it would be the beneficiaries' interests which would suffer.

However, the adoption of the *White v. Jones* decision by the Saskatchewan Court of Queen's Bench in *Carl v. Wilhelm*[105] as the definitive statement of the law in this area signifies that *Hedley Byrne* is still relevant to the issue of lawyers' liability to disappointed beneficiaries. Here, the defendant solicitors incorporated the testator's successful farming operation. Some ten years later, the testator executed a will drafted by the defendant solicitors purporting to bequeath land to the plaintiff, an employee of the testator. The gift failed because the corporation owned the land. In an action against the solicitors by the employee *qua* disappointed beneficiary, the court reviewed the English and Canadian jurisprudence and relied on *White v. Jones* to support the conclusion that,

---

[98]   *Ibid.*, at 372 D.L.R.
[99]   In *Ross v. Caunters, supra,* note 88, Megarry V.-C., discussing *Whittingham v. Crease & Co.,* describes it as a case of "passive reliance" since the plaintiff knew of the will and the bequest to him, and distinguishes this situation from one where the beneficiary knows nothing of the intended gift until after the testator's death and there is, therefore, no reliance at all.
[100]   L.N. Klar, "A Comment on *Whittingham v. Crease*" (1979), 6 C.C.L.T. 311.
[101]   [1932] A.C. 562, [1932] All E.R. Rep. 1 (H.L.).
[102]   [1978] A.C. 728, [1977] 2 ALL E.R. 492 (H.L.).
[103]   See, for example, *McQuarrie v. Jacobs* (1987), 12 B.C.L.R. (2d) 216 (S.C.).
[104]   *Linsley v. Kirstiuk* (1986), 28 D.L.R. (4th) 495 (B.C.S.C.).
[105]   (1997), 160 Sask. R. 4 (Q.B.).

under the *Hedley Byrne* principle, the assumption of responsibility by a solicitor to his client is extended to intended beneficiaries.

At present, therefore, it appears that either *Anns* or *Hedley Byrne* may give rise to liability in disappointed beneficiaries cases.

However, a duty of care should not be imposed on a solicitor in favour of a third party if it will conflict with the duty he owes to his client. The testator in *Smolinski v. Mitchell*[106] instructed the defendant lawyer to prepare a will including bequests to the lawyer and the testator's cousin. The solicitor drafted the will and delivered it two days later to the testator, who was hospitalized at the time. He advised the testator to obtain independent legal advice and have the will executed elsewhere. Because the testator was alert and mobile at the time and was discharged from the hospital the next day, the solicitor had no reason to suspect that he had received a prognosis of imminent death.

The testator died a little over a week later without having executed the will. His cousin brought a claim in negligence against the lawyer alleging that he owed him a duty to ensure the execution of the new will in a timely fashion. The British Columbia Supreme Court held that, although a lawyer's responsibility to carry out a client's testamentary wishes may extend to an intended beneficiary who may be foreseeably deprived of a legacy by the lawyer's negligence, this duty will not be imposed if it conflicts with a duty owed his client. In the circumstances, because the solicitor owed a duty of care to the testator to refer him for independent legal advice, he did not also owe an obligation to the defendant to see to the expeditious execution of the will.

A few recent cases suggest that solicitors may be liable to disappointed beneficiaries not only for the untimely execution of wills and the ineffectiveness of bequests, but for advice negligently given. In *Heath v. Darcus,*[107] a testator bequeathed her home to her six children. One of the daughters, D, had been living in the home when the testator died, and all of the other children agreed to allow her to continue living there indefinitely. They executed a quitclaim to D so that she could mortgage the property on the understanding that it would eventually be transferred to the estate for division. When O, one of the other daughters, died, the defendant solicitors were retained to conduct the probate of her estate. The solicitors met with the O estate and O's siblings and a consensus was reached that the solicitors should approach D about a trust claim against the home. D denied the trust, and the solicitors advised the O estate and the other siblings that the claim could not be pursued at that time.

Eleven years later, the O estate and the siblings brought an action against D for a declaration of a trust. Justice Spencer of the British Columbia Supreme Court concluded that a trust existed but that they were out of time to bring the claim. The O estate subsequently successfully sued the defendant solicitors on

---

[106] (1995), 10 B.C.L.R. (3d) 366 (S.C.).
[107] (1990), 48 B.C.L.R. (2d) 259 (S.C.), revd (1991), 60 B.C.L.R. (2d) 145 (C.A.).

the missed limitation period.[108] Some months later, in a separate action, Maczko J. held that the solicitors owed a duty of care to the other siblings as well.[109] The court summarized the law as follows:

> In my view the authorities are quite clear that a solicitor can put himself in a position of proximity which creates a duty of care even though he has not been retained or instructed by that person. If a solicitor undertakes to a client to perform a task for a third party he may have a duty of care to that third party whether or not the third party relied on that undertaking.[110]

The siblings admitted that they had not retained the defendants or instructed them to approach D about the trust claim, but the court held that a sufficient relationship of proximity arose out of the meetings with them in which one of the defendants undertook to contact D. The solicitors breached that duty of care by failing to advise of the limitation period. Even if the meeting had not taken place, the solicitors would be liable because they contracted with the estate to confer a benefit on the siblings. The decision suggests that the duty of care owed by a solicitor for an estate may extend not only to a disappointed beneficiary but to a non-beneficiary whose interests may be harmed by negligent advice to the estate.

The British Columbia Court of Appeal reversed Spencer J.'s finding with respect to the trust claim limitation period and thus cast doubt on the precedential value of this case. The appeal of Maczko J.'s decision on the scope of the duty of care owed was rendered moot and reversed without reasons.

In the course of their representation of the testator in divorce proceedings, the defendant solicitors in *Makhan v. McCawley*[111] were instructed to prepare a will benefitting the testator's children and a grandchild. Only preliminary steps had been taken towards equalization of net family property and the will had still not been executed when the testator died unexpectedly two months later. Her assets at the time consisted of property owned jointly with her husband and RRSPs which designated him as beneficiary. As a result, the testator's estranged husband was the beneficiary of her entire estate.

In an action against the solicitors, the children and grandchild claimed damages not only as disappointed beneficiaries under the unexecuted will, but also for the solicitors' alleged failure to advise the testator to sever the joint tenancies and change the beneficiary designations of her investments and to commence equalization proceedings. The defendant solicitors conceded that the plaintiffs had a cause of action as disappointed beneficiaries but asserted that they had no

---

[108] *Heath v. Ivens, McGuire, Souch and Ottho,* unreported, January 15, 1991, Maczko J., Doc. Vancouver C904424, [1991] B.C.J. No. 72 (S.C.).

[109] *Heath, Wells, v. Ivens, McGuire, Souch and Ottho,* unreported, July 18, 1990 (B.C.S.C.).

[110] *Ibid.*

[111] *Makhan v. McCawley* (1998), 158 D.L.R. (4th) 164 (Gen. Div.).

cause of action for the alleged failure to advise the testator as to the means of giving effect to her testamentary intentions. In dismissing a motion for summary judgment, the court noted that it was highly unlikely that the estate could bring an action against the solicitor given that the estranged husband was the executor.

2. Other Situations

The reasoning in *Ross v. Caunters* was applied in rather unusual circumstances in *Al-Kandari v. J.R. Brown & Co.*[112] The plaintiff had obtained an order granting her custody of her children. Her husband, a foreign national, had been granted access to the children on his undertaking to deposit his passport with his solicitors, the defendants, and they, in turn, had undertaken not to release it to him. With the plaintiff's solicitor's knowledge, the defendants agreed to release it to the husband's Embassy but failed to take adequate precautions to ensure it would not fall into the husband's hands. When it did and the husband was successful in abducting the children and fleeing the country, the plaintiff claimed that the defendants were liable to her for negligence. Although the court ultimately dismissed her claim on the basis that the intervening conduct of the Embassy in releasing the passport to the husband was not foreseeable, it held that the defendants had breached a duty of care they owed the plaintiff: "A solicitor who has authority from his client to give an undertaking, one of whose objects is to protect an identified third party, owes a duty of care towards that third party, in that the third party is a person within his direct contemplation."[113]

The English Court of Appeal upheld the trial judge's finding that the solicitor owed the wife a duty of care in the circumstances, but reversed his conclusion on the causation issue. It was reasonably foreseeable that the Embassy might inadvertently release the passport to the husband. Interestingly, the court held that when the solicitors gave an implied undertaking to retain the husband's passport and not release it to him, they were acting not as solicitors or agents of the husband but as independent custodians of the passport subject to the direction of the court and the joint direction of the parties. They owed the appellant a duty of care under the *M'Alister (or Donoghue) v. Stevenson* neighbour principle.

In another case that did not involve either a will or an estate, *Yang v. Overseas Investments (1986) Ltd.*,[114] the court referred to *Ross v. Caunters* as "the seminal decision which gives rise to the liability of the solicitor to others than his or her client". The plaintiffs invested a considerable amount of money in an investment company owned by the defendant lawyer and accredited under the federal government's immigration investor program for the development of a shopping centre. As a result of the lawyer's negligence in dealing with the funds

---

[112] [1987] 2 All E.R. 302 (Q.B.), affd on other grounds [1988] 1 All E.R. 833 (C.A.).

[113] *Ibid.*, at 308, *per* French J. The court maintains that this language is a rephrasing of one of Megarry V.-C.'s conclusions in *Ross v. Caunters*.

[114] [1995] 4 W.W.R. 231 at 261 (Alta. Q.B.).

entrusted to him, the plaintiffs lost their entire investment. The court found that the lawyer was in a solicitor-client relationship with the plaintiffs because he did the legal work in connection with the purchase of the property. However, it held in the alternative that if the plaintiffs were not clients of the defendant, he still owed them a duty of care as third parties to the retainer between him and his investment company. After a review of *Ross v. Caunters* and several other authorities, the court held:

> I conclude that the law is that a solicitor who is instructed by his client to carry out a transaction that will confer a benefit on an identified third party owes a duty of care towards that third party in carrying out that transaction if the third party is a person within his direct contemplation as someone who is likely to be so closely and directly affected by the solicitor's acts or omissions that the solicitor can reasonably foresee that the third party is likely to be injured by those acts or omissions.[115]

The court did not address the fact that, in effect, the lawyer would have been instructing himself to confer a benefit on the plaintiffs because he was the controlling mind of the client's investment company.

The broadly stated conclusion in *Yang* as to the circumstances in which a solicitor will owe a duty of care to a third party was relied on in *Texas Industries Ltd. v. Siewert*,[116] a case in which a lawyer took instructions from his client to place certain conditions on the payment of a loan to the client by the plaintiff lender. The solicitor clearly owed the plaintiff a duty to carry out the conditions, but that duty had been discharged.

There are many situations outside of the wills cases in which a client may instruct a solicitor to do something that confers a benefit on a third party, such as in estate or tax planning.[117] *Yang* and *Texas Industries* may portend the extension of a duty of care to third party beneficiaries in a variety of circumstances.

C. NEGLIGENT MISREPRESENTATION

1. General Principles

In addition to creating liability for situations of reasonable reliance on an undertaking to apply special skill, *Hedley Byrne* carved out an exception to the rule against recovery for economic loss for negligent misstatements. This exception was embraced in Canadian jurisprudence.[118] Until recently, the leading case on

---

[115] *Ibid.,* at 264.
[116] (1996), 194 A.R. 303 (Q.B.).
[117] See L.N. Klar, *Tort Law*, 2nd ed. (Toronto. Carswell, 1996), at 204.
[118] See, for example, *Fletcher v. Manitoba Public Insurance Co.*, [1990] 3 S.C.R. 191.

negligent misrepresentation was *Queen v. Cognos Inc.*[119] Mr. Justice Iacobucci laid out the requirements for a successful *Hedley Byrne* action for negligent misrepresentation in this case:

> (1) there must be a duty of care based on a "special relationship" between the representor and the representee; (2) the representation in question must be untrue, inaccurate, or misleading; (3) the representor must have acted negligently in making said misrepresentation; (4) the representee must have relied, in a reasonable manner, on said negligent misrepresentation; and (5) the reliance must have been detrimental to the representee in the sense that damages resulted.[120]

Liability for negligent misstatement may also arise under the principles set out in *Anns* where there is a sufficient relationship of proximity to impose a duty of care on the solicitor in favour of a third party.[121] Under *Anns*, the notion of proximity, as opposed to reliance, is used to set reasonable and workable limits on potential liability for economic loss due to negligent misstatement.[122] But, as we have seen in the negligence cases, the reliance concept may overlap with the proximity concept. If a plaintiff is found to have reasonably relied upon a solicitor's negligent misstatement, a relationship of sufficient proximity is usually established:

> The decisions of the Supreme Court in *Just* [*Just v. British Columbia*, [1989] 2 S.C.R. 1228, 64 D.L.R. (4th) 689] and *Rothfield* [*Rothfield v. Manolakos*, [1989] 2 S.C.R. 1259, 63 D.L.R. (4th) 449] reinforce my view that the reasonableness of the reliance alleged must be considered in determining whether or not the relationship between the parties is sufficiently proximate to give rise to a duty of care in cases of negligent misstatement. Those decisions also suggest that the reasonableness of an expectation of protection must be considered in cases where the alleged negligence is failure to warn. In all the judgments in both cases, the reasonableness of the victim's expectations was considered in determining whether or not the victim came within the class to whom the negligent party owed a duty of care.[123]

The Supreme Court of Canada in *Hercules Management Ltd. v. Ernst & Young*[124] recently merged the law of negligent misrepresentation with the law in other negligence cases involving economic loss. The plaintiff shareholders brought an action against the company's auditors for damages for negligent mis-

---

[119] [1993] 1 S.C.R. 87.

[120] *Ibid.*, at 110.

[121] *Kamahap Enterprises Ltd. v. Chu's Central Market Ltd.*(1989), 40 B.C.L.R. (2d) 288 (C.A.).

[122] *Dixon v. Deacon, Morgan, McEwen, Easson* (1989), 41 B.C.L.R. (2d) 180 (S.C.); *MacPherson v. Schachter* (1989), 1 C.C.L.T. (2d) 65 (B.C.S.C.).

[123] *McGauley v. British Columbia* (1990), 44 B.C.L.R. (2d) 217 at 232 (S.C.), revd on other grounds 56 B.C.L.R. (2d) 1 (C.A.).

[124] (1997), 146 D.L.R. (4th) 577.

representation, alleging that the annual audit reports were negligently prepared. They claimed damages for investment losses and the loss in value of their share holdings. Mr. Justice La Forest, speaking for a unanimous court, criticized the current approach of treating negligent misrepresentation cases differently than other negligence cases involving economic loss: "to create a 'pocket' . . . in which the existence of a duty of care is determined differently from other negligence cases would, in my view, be incorrect".[125] He held that the existence of a duty of care is to be determined through the application of the two-part test in *Anns*. With respect to the first part of the test, which requires a sufficient relationship of proximity to establish a *prima facie* duty of care, La Forest J. held:

> A *prima facie* duty of care will arise on the part of a defendant in a negligent misrepresentation action when it can be said (a) that the defendant ought reasonably to have foreseen that the plaintiff would rely on his representation and (b) that reliance by the plaintiff, in the circumstances, would be reasonable.[126]

Professor Feldthusen's[127] five general *indicia* of reasonable reliance were adopted, not as a strict test, but to assist in identifying reliance that is reasonable: (1) the defendant had a direct or indirect financial interest in the transaction in respect of which the representation was made; (2) the defendant was a professional or someone who possessed special skill, judgment or knowledge; (3) the advice or information was provided in the course of the defendant's business; (4) the information or advice was given deliberately, and not on a social occasion; and (5) the information or advice was given in response to a specific enquiry or request.[128]

Once a *prima facie* duty of care is established, according to the second part of the *Anns/Kamloops* test, the court should consider whether there are any policy considerations that should limit or negative that duty. La Forest J. held that considerations of whether the defendant had knowledge of the plaintiff (or class of plaintiffs) and whether the plaintiff used the statements at issue for the particular transaction for which they were provided are more appropriately taken into account at this stage of the enquiry.[129]

Applying this approach to the facts of the case, La Forest J. found that the auditors owed a *prima facie* duty of care to the shareholders because it was reasonably foreseeable that they would rely on the audited financial statements in conducting their affairs and would likely suffer harm if the reports were negligently prepared. However, this duty was negated for policy reasons because, although the auditors knew the very identity of all of the shareholders, the re-

---

[125] *Ibid.*, at 587.

[126] *Ibid.*, at 597.

[127] B. Feldthusen, "The Recovery of Pure Economic Loss in Canada: Proximity, Justice, Rationality, and Chaos" (1996), 24 *Man. L.J.* 1.

[128] *Hercules Management, supra*, note 125, at 598.

[129] *Ibid.*, at 591.

ports were prepared under statutory duty to allow the shareholders as a group to supervise the management of the company, not to assist them in making individual investment decisions. The use of the report for a purpose other than that for which it was prepared could lead to indeterminate liability.

As a result of *Hercules Management*, a plaintiff in a negligent misrepresentation action will be able to establish a duty of care if he can demonstrate that the defendant foresaw or ought to have foreseen that the plaintiff would rely on his representation, and that, in the circumstances, the plaintiff's reliance was reasonable. Once a *prima facie* duty of care is established, it is open to negation or limitation by policy considerations. One commentator has described this blending of the law of negligent misrepresentation with *Anns* principles as a welcome change and "a purely Canadian view, true to our earlier jurisprudence, true to the general principles of negligence law".[130]

Other cases have established that silence, that is, not disabusing a party of a misperception, may be sufficient to establish that a representation was made, but silence without proof of the other part of the test, that is, reasonably foreseeable reliance that is reasonable in the circumstances, will be insufficient to found a negligent misrepresentation claim.[131]

The adviser's statements are not required to be perfectly accurate. The same standard of care that applies in all other cases, that of the "reasonable person", applies in negligent misstatement cases.[132] However, where the defendant is a professional, the standard of the reasonable professional person applies.[133]

Liability will only be found if reliance is proven, it cannot be deemed.[134] Although there must be reliance in fact, the negligent misstatement need not be the only reason the plaintiff acted to her detriment.[135] The extent of the reliance, in light of other factors, is a consideration that is appropriate when ascertaining any contributory negligence, but it should not be taken into account in determining whether the reliance was reasonable.[136]

The adviser need not be in the business or profession of giving advice of the type relied upon in order to establish the reasonableness of the plaintiff's reli-

---

[130] A.M. Linden, *Canadian Tort Law*, 6th ed. (Toronto: Butterworths, 1997), at 430.

[131] *Gordelli Management Ltd. v. Turk* (1991), 6 O.R. (3d) 521 (Gen. Div.); *Fletcher v. Manitoba Public Insurance Co., supra*, note 119; *Spinks v. Canada*, [1996] 2 F.C. 563 (C.A.).

[132] *Queen v. Cognos Inc., supra*, note 120, at 121.

[133] Linden, *supra*, note 130, at 444.

[134] *Kripps v. Touche Ross & Co.* (1992), 94 D.L.R. (4th) 284 (B.C.C.A.).

[135] *Surrey Credit Union v. Willson* (1990), 73 D.L.R. (4th) 207 (B.C.S.C.). See also *United Citrus Ltd. v. Ceresne*, unreported, September 4, 1991 (Ont. Gen Div.), where the other investigative steps taken were deemed not to negate the reasonable reliance, but were deemed to raise the question of contributory negligence on the part of the plaintiff.

[136] See Fleming, *The Law of Torts*, 5th ed. (1977), at 633, as cited in *Dorsch v. Weyburn* (1985), 23 D.L.R. (4th) 379 at 393 (Sask C.A.). See *United Citrus Ltd. v. Ceresne, supra*, note 136, wherein, albeit the plaintiff took steps to investigate (other than solely relying on the financial statements), these other steps did not negate the reasonable reliance, but instead just raised the question of contributory negligence.

ance, but courts will only impose liability for negligent misrepresentation where a reasonable person would have relied on the particular advice coming from the particular adviser.[137] Similarly, where the recipient is himself knowledgable or experienced in the area in which the advice is given, it may not be reasonable for him to rely on the person making the representation.

As suggested by Professor Feldthusen, and affirmed by the Supreme Court in *Hercules Management*, the nature of the occasion at which the advice was given is an important consideration in determining whether a special relationship exists. Advice given on an occasion that is social, not business-related, is significantly less likely to give rise to a duty of care than advice given as part of a professional or business relationship.[138] Also, as Professor Klar has indicated, "the more speculative a statement is, and the less it is based on an assessment of ascertainable facts, the less reasonable the reliance on this statement will be, to the point that any reliance at all might legitimately be considered as unreasonable."[139] Although the advice will usually be given in response to a specific request, it need not have been for a duty of care to be imposed where the adviser knows or ought to know that the advice will be relied upon.[140]

2. Legal Malpractice

Actions by third parties against solicitors for negligent misrepresentation are not as common as claims framed in negligence and breach of fiduciary duty, although a solicitor clearly may be liable for negligent misrepresentation. The *Hedley Byrne* principle was applied in a case in which a negligent misrepresentation was made by the city solicitor in a letter to a developer concerning the zoning of lands the developer considered buying, even though the letter was not written in response to any enquiry by the developer.[141] It was clear that the solicitor knew and intended the developer to act in reliance on it.

One case, *Brummer v. Frydenlund*,[142] illustrates that, although a solicitor must be careful not to make careless representations that may be reasonably relied upon by a third party with whom he is in a relationship of proximity, he does not commit the tort of negligent misrepresentation when he makes off-handed comments or offers only an opinion. The plaintiff vendor entered into an interim agreement for the sale of his property with the defendant solicitor's client. Before closing, the plaintiff, who was also legally represented, became concerned about the purchaser's financial situation and instructed his solicitor to seek ad-

---

[137] *Sirois v. Federation des Enseignants du Nouveau-Brunswick* (1984), 28 C.C.L.T. 280 (N.B.Q.B.); *Dorsch v. Weyburn, supra,* note 136.

[138] L.N. Klar, *Tort Law,* 2nd ed. (Toronto: Carswell, 1996), at 185.

[139] *Ibid.,* at 188.

[140] *392980 Ontario Ltd. v. Welland* (1984), 6 D.L.R. (4th) 151 (Ont. H.C.).

[141] *Ibid.*

[142] Unreported, January 19, 1994, Koenigsberg J., Doc Vancouver C908116, [1994] B.C.J. No. 99 (S.C.).

ditional security for the balance of the purchase price. In response to this request, the defendant solicitor stated that he would accept the purchaser's covenant if he were in the plaintiff's shoes and that the purchaser was well off. The plaintiff claimed that the losses he suffered when the purchaser failed to complete the transaction resulted from his reliance on the defendant's negligent misrepresentation. The court dismissed the claim because the statements were general in nature, vague, off-hand and more opinion than fact, and the evidence showed that the plaintiff had not relied on them. Thus, they did not create a sufficient relationship of proximity to give rise to a duty of care.

Interestingly, in *Gran Gelato v. Richcliff (Group) Ltd.*,[143] the English Court of Appeal held that, although the plaintiff reasonably relied on the negligent lawyer, as agent of his client, the lawyer did not owe a duty of care to the plaintiff. The plaintiff expected the defendant solicitor to use his legal expertise in answering the plaintiff's enquiry as to whether there was anything that would affect tenants' enjoyment of a property in accordance with terms of the underlease. The defendant solicitor replied, "not to the lessor's knowledge". The misstatement was intended to be relied upon, was in fact relied upon, and the resulting losses were foreseeable. However, the court held that the law should not impose an independent duty of care in favour of a third party on a solicitor who is acting as agent for his client.[144] The decision in *Gran Gelato* has not yet been considered in any reported lawyers' malpractice case in Canada.[145]

D. RECOMMENDING INDEPENDENT LEGAL ADVICE

Perhaps the most effective, proactive method of negating liability potentially owed to third parties is for the solicitor to recommend in writing that the unrepresented third party obtain independent legal advice. This recommendation ought to emphasize that, as the solicitor is representing her own client, she cannot adequately look after the third party's interests. If this precaution is taken, it will be difficult for a third party to claim either that the solicitor owed him a duty of care or that he reasonably relied on the solicitor to look after his interests.[146]

When a lawyer and the third party are in a fiduciary relationship, it may not be sufficient for the lawyer to advise the third party to obtain independent legal advice; it may be necessary for the lawyer to ensure that such advice is actually

---

[143] [1992] 1 All E.R. 865.

[144] Of course, the negligent solicitor was liable to indemnify his client.

[145] It was referred to in a case about the duty of care owed to an insurer by an insurance broker who is acting as agent for an insured: *Adams-Eden Furniture Ltd. v. Kansa General Insurance Inc.* (1996), 113 Man. R. (2d) 142 (C.A.).

[146] See discussion under Section III. "Negligence", B. "The 'Third Party Beneficiary' Claim", 2. "Other Situations" regarding the extent to which a solicitor is immunized when the third party has obtained independent legal advice.

obtained.[147] Presumably, this requirement will be met if the lawyer takes reasonable measures to ensure that the third party does so.

Any duty of care owed by a solicitor to a third party is generally satisfied if the solicitor advises the third party to obtain independent legal advice;[148] the duty probably does not extend to ensuring that the third party in fact obtains independent legal advice.[149] In *Ristad v. Perry*[150] although there was sufficient proximity between the solicitor and third party to give rise to a duty of care, this duty was not breached because the solicitor advised the third party purchaser to obtain independent legal advice. In situations in which a conflict of interest arises in the midst of a transaction, the solicitor must renew his advice that the third party obtain independent legal representation.[151]

A lawyer who does not advise a third party to obtain independent advice does so at her peril. In *McKinnon v. Conexco International Corp.*,[152] which we discussed earlier in this chapter, the court found that the firm ought to have advised the investors to obtain independent legal advice.

On the other hand, in *Dorsch*,[153] the court did not impose upon the solicitor an obligation to recommend that the third parties seek independent legal advice. In fact, the third parties reasonably ought to have known that the solicitor was acting for the municipality, which was likely to be adverse in interest to them. There was no previous relationship between the solicitor and the third parties. *McKinnon* and *Dorsch* show that the closer the relationship between the lawyer and the third party, the more likely the solicitor will owe the third party a duty of care, and the more likely the third party will be found to have reasonably relied upon the lawyer.

The precaution of recommending independent legal advice will not necessarily protect a solicitor in every case.[154] In *Dinelle Holdings*,[155] for example, a solicitor wrote a post-closing letter to the third party plaintiffs. It clearly stated that she was acting for X and not for the plaintiffs, and that it was advisable that the

---

[147] *Shoppers Trust Co. v. Dynamic Homes Ltd.* (1992), 10 O.R. (3d) 361 at 367 (Gen. Div.).

[148] See discussion *infra*, at p. 97, regarding situations in which simply advising a third party to obtain independent legal advice is not sufficient to answer the duty owed to the third party. These cases are limited to situations in which the third party does not fully understand the ramifications of the disclaimer.

[149] See *Gerlock v. Safety Mart Foods Ltd.*, [1983] 2 W.W.R. 569 (B.C.C.A.), cited with approval in *Ristad v. Perry* (1989), 38 B.C.L.R. (2d) 326 (S.C.). This appears to be a lower standard than that required of a fiduciary, *i.e.*, the obligation to ensure the third party *obtains* independent legal advice.

[150] *Supra*, note 149.

[151] *Ibid.*, at 342.

[152] Unreported, February 17, 1992, Steele J., Doc. 16582/86, [1992] O.J. No. 292 (Gen. Div.).

[153] *Dorsch v. Weyburn, supra*, note 136.

[154] See Section III. "Negligence", A. "Reasonable Reliance on Special Skill and Knowledge", 2. "The Third Party with Independent Legal Advice" for situations in which a solicitor was held liable to a third party, even when independent legal advice had been obtained.

[155] *Dinelle Holdings Ltd. v. Hansen*, unreported, February 5, 1992, Scarth J., Doc. Prince George 8255, [1992] B.C.J. No. 236 (S.C.).

plaintiff obtain independent legal advice. However, the letter went on to say: "the [change requested] does not contain any more rights than you had previously nor does it contain any less rights than you had previously with respect to the security". The court held that, despite the lawyer's attempt to limit her liability, it was reasonably foreseeable that the plaintiff would rely on the solicitor's skill as a result of the statement.

Whether it is reasonable for the solicitor to know that the plaintiffs are likely to rely on his skill is a fact-specific determination. The courts impose a higher duty on a solicitor to ensure that an unsophisticated third party fully understands the extent to which the solicitor is or is not protecting the third party's interests.[156] On the other hand, where the third party is sophisticated and independent legal advice is recommended, a duty will generally not be owed:

> Where the non-client is claiming breach of a duty of care, my view is that the court should be slow to impose liability if the claimant is experienced, educated, intelligent and neither elderly nor infirm and when the claimant has been advised to obtain independent legal advice and has declined to do so.[157]

---

[156] *Klingspon v. Ramsay*, [1985] 5 W.W.R. 411 (B.C.S.C.). The extenuating circumstances in this case include an unsophisticated investor, coupled with an unsound investment that the solicitor was closing in order to convey a misleading impression regarding the viability of the project.

[157] *Ristad v. Perry, supra*, note 149, at 340. This was a case in which there was sufficient proximity between the solicitor and third party to give rise to a duty of care, but this duty was not breached because the solicitor advised the third party purchaser to obtain independent legal advice.

Chapter 5

VICARIOUS LIABILITY

I. INTRODUCTION

In this chapter, we examine the vicarious liability of lawyers for the acts and omissions of their partners, agents and employees. That is, we will consider the circumstances in which a lawyer will be held liable, absent his fault, for the conduct of others.

II. LIABILITY FOR AGENTS AND EMPLOYEES

A. EMPLOYEES

A lawyer is liable for the negligent acts of her employees including lawyers, clerks, paralegals, secretaries and other support staff. Indeed, the courts impose a test that approaches absolute liability; it is rare that even due diligence will afford a defence. In *835039 Ontario Inc. v. Fram Development Corp.*,[1] a lawyer was found negligent when, due to an honest mistake, his secretary failed to deliver, by fax, a notice required to extend the deadline for a contract. The lawyer was negligent even though he had emphasized to the secretary that this task was to be given priority. The lawyer is liable even where there has been no negligence by her either in delegating the task to the employee or in supervising the employee in the completion of the task. Thus, the lawyer in *Aetna Roofing (1975) Ltd. v. Conradi*,[2] who was completely unaware of her secretary's failure to file a builders' lien, was held liable for this omission even though the client, without any previous consultation with the defendant lawyer, had instructed the secretary to file the lien. The evidence revealed that the lawyer had advised the client to deal directly with her and not her secretary on "unusual" matters, such as this, but this afforded the lawyer no defence to the negligence claim.

---

[1]   Unreported, August 9, 1994, Trafford J., Doc. 53207/90, [1994] O.J. No. 1725 (Gen. Div.).
[2]   (1984), 52 A.R. 369 (Q.B.).

The *Aetna Roofing* case also illustrates the principle that when paralegals, secretaries or clerks undertake tasks requiring legal skills or expertise, the same standard of care applicable to lawyers will be used to assess their liability.[3]

Partners of a firm will be held liable for failing to supervise adequately its associate lawyers.[4]

B. AGENTS

The law dealing with a lawyer's liability for the negligent acts of his agent is not easily stated and is much confused in the jurisprudence. The legal characterization of a wrongdoer as the agent of a lawyer is not determinative of the lawyer's vicarious liability for that wrongdoer's acts or omissions. The issue of vicarious liability, a concept of tort law, normally turns on whether the wrongdoer is a servant or an independent contractor of the person sought to be held vicariously liable.[5] It does not depend on the nature and extent of the authority of the person who committed the tort, which is the critical factor in determining the existence of a principal-agent relationship. As *Bowstead* elucidates, an agent may be either a servant or an independent contractor, or in the case of a gratuitous agent, neither, but only the acts of the servant create vicarious liability.[6]

Nevertheless, some of the cases dealing with lawyers' vicarious liability do not reflect the legal distinctions between "agents", "servants" and "independent contractors". Indeed, the terminology of "master and servant" and "principal and agent" are often used interchangeably as are the phrases "course of employment" and "scope of authority".[7] Consequently, it is not possible to separate entirely the concept and language of agency from that of vicarious liability.

---

[3] See also *Bonneville v. Temelini & Zito* (1981), 21 R.P.R. 206 (Ont. H.C.); R.E. Mallen and J.M. Smith, *Legal Malpractice*, 4th ed. (St. Paul, Minn.: West Publishing Co., 1996), at 383, observe that as the professionalism of paralegals develops and as their status receives legislative recognition, there may be some justification for moving toward a different standard of care for paralegals, that is, the skill and knowledge ordinarily exercised by paralegals performing similar services. The movement afoot in some of the provinces, including Ontario, to enact legislation governing the rights and obligations of paralegals may stimulate a parallel development.

[4] See *McKay v. Cowan* (1989), 39 B.C.L.R. (2d) 192 (S.C.).

[5] F.M.B. Reynolds, ed., *Bowstead and Reynolds on Agency*, 16th ed. (London: Sweet & Maxwell, 1996), at 498-99. J.G. Fleming, *The Law of Torts*, 9th ed. (Sydney: The Law Book Co., 1994), at 414, says that the traditional test for distinguishing a servant from an independent contractor is the "control test": the servant is "subject to the command of the master as to the manner in which he shall do his work" (relying on *Yewens v. Noakes* (1880), 6 Q.B.D. 530 at 532 (C.A.), *per* Bramwell L.J.) while an "independent contractor undertakes to produce a given result but is not, in the actual execution of the work, under the order or control of the person for whom he does it" (citing *Queensland Stations v. F.C.T.* (1945), 70 C.L.R. 539 at 545, *per* Latham C.J.). According to Fleming (at 416) the courts are in the process of devising alternative tests such as the "organization" test, that is, "was the would-be servant part of his employer's organization?"

[6] *Bowstead, supra*, note 5.

[7] *Ibid.*, at 499.

In considering the issues that arise when a solicitor engages "agents" (for example, process servers, title searchers, expert consultants, or indeed other solicitors, to undertake some task on behalf of a client), it is sufficient to say that a lawyer will be held vicariously liable in essentially three situations:

(1)   Where the lawyer instigates or authorizes the wrongful act of the agent.[8] Of course, this is the easy case: the lawyer has effectively committed the tort herself, and the liability is not, therefore, truly vicarious.

(2)   Where the so-called "agent" has committed the wrongful act while acting during the course of his employment. In other words, the "agent" is viewed as a servant of the lawyer and not as an independent contractor. Still, it must be noted that in many of these cases the language of agency is used: words and phrases, such as "agent", "acting within the scope of his authority", and "apparent or actual authority," are commonly found. In *Lloyd v. Grace, Smith & Co.*,[9] for example, a solicitor was held liable for the fraud of his managing clerk. Even though the clerk was acting for his own gain and therefore "outside the scope of his actual authority," he was nevertheless found to be "acting as a representative of the solicitor's firm within his apparent authority" in conducting the firm's conveyancing business.[10]

(3)   Where the lawyer is in breach of her duty of care because of a failure to supervise or direct the agent properly, although the act leading to the breach may have actually been performed by the lawyer's agent.[11] Again, the liability is not actually vicarious. Thus, in *B & M Enterprises Ltd. v. Crosbie Enterprises Ltd.*,[12] the solicitor was found liable in damages to the defendants for the negligence of a bailiff hired by the solicitor on behalf of the defendant. The bailiff improperly carried out a distress against the plaintiff, and the trial judge concluded that the solicitor had failed to instruct the bailiff properly in the appropriate procedures to be employed.

A related issue that arises concerns a lawyer's obligations in referring a client to other professionals, including another lawyer. The only Canadian case to address the issue is *Patchett v. Oliver*,[13] in which C, a solicitor, introduced the plaintiff to O, another solicitor, to invest the plaintiff's money. O promised to invest the money in second mortgages and then converted the money to his own

---

[8]   *Ibid.*, at 499 and 502.
[9]   *Lloyd v. Grace, Smith & Co.*, [1912] A.C. 716, [1911-13] All E.R. Rep. 51 (H.L.).
[10]   See also *Uxbridge Permanent Benefit Building Society v. Pickard*, [1939] 2 K.B. 248, [1939] 2 All E.R. 344 (C.A.).
[11]   *Bowstead, supra*, note 5, at 498-99.
[12]   (1982), 39 Nfld. & P.E.I.R. 153 (Nfld. T.D.).
[13]   *Patchett v. Oliver*, [1977] 5 W.W.R. 299 (B.C.S.C.).

use. The plaintiff's action against C was unsuccessful since C was found to have honestly believed in O's integrity and had not in any way induced the plaintiff to invest his money with O. This accords with the English position that a solicitor whose retainer includes the recommendation of another professional will not be liable if the appointee turns out to be incompetent or untrustworthy, unless the solicitor knew or ought to have known of this fact before the recommendation was made.[14]

According to Mallen and Smith,[15] in the United States the case of *Tormo v. Yormark*[16] has paved new ground in holding that a New York lawyer was negligent in referring his client to a New Jersey lawyer to bring an action in New Jersey on the client's behalf. The New York lawyer's only evaluation of the New Jersey lawyer's qualifications was to ascertain from a legal directory that the lawyer was licensed to practise law in New Jersey. He was thus not aware that the lawyer had been indicted for fraud. The New Jersey lawyer settled the client's case and misappropriated much of the settlement funds. The court reasoned that, while ordinarily an attorney may rely on a professional licence to establish another lawyer's legitimacy, certain suspicious circumstances, such as the fact that the New Jersey attorney had specifically solicited the work, which solicitation the court considered to be unethical, required a more detailed investigation by the New York lawyer. Whether Canadian courts will impose a positive duty on a lawyer to conduct an adequate investigation before referring a client to another lawyer or professional remains to be seen.

III. LIABILITY FOR PARTNERS

A. GENERAL PRINCIPLES

Each province has a statute regulating the affairs of partnerships. These statutes govern law firms as well as ordinary commercial and other professional partnerships. For the most part, a lawyer's vicarious liability for the negligence or fraud of a partner is determined on the basis of the statute. Typically, lawyers enter into written partnership agreements which define (a) the nature of the partnership's business, and (b) the rights and obligations of the partners *inter se*. There are, in addition, partnerships that are created without a written agreement.

In the absence of a written agreement, a question may arise as to whether or not a partnership exists in fact or in law. In *Corbett v. McKee, Calabrese & Whitehead*,[17] for example, three lawyers practised under a firm name that was comprised of each of their surnames. However, one practised in one city and the

---

[14] See, generally, F.T. Horne, ed., *Cordery's Law Relating to Solicitors*, 8th ed. (London: Butterworths, 1988), at 145, and particularly footnote 173.

[15] *Supra*, note 3, at 390.

[16] 398 F. Supp. 1159 (D.N.J., 1975).

[17] (1984), 54 N.B.R. (2d) 107, 16 E.T.R. 200 (Q.B.).

other two in another city. Each office was responsible for its own expenses; neither office was accountable to the other and the fees of each office went to the lawyers who practised in it. In these circumstances, the court found that while there "outwardly appeared to be a partnership, the evidence clearly estab-lishe[d] that two separate businesses were being carried on under a common name".[18] In other words, the two offices did not constitute a single partnership. The fact lawyers do not share profits may in itself be sufficient to demonstrate that no partnership exists between them.[19]

As the court in *Corbett* made clear, persons who are not in fact partners may nevertheless be subject to vicarious liability because of a "holding-out" when the person seeking to establish liability deals with the ostensible partnership in the belief it is a partnership.[20] In *Corbett*, the court found that the two lawyers had held themselves out as partners of the third but they were not liable to the latter's client because the client intended to deal with the third lawyer only and was not concerned whether or not he had any partners. The plaintiff must dem-onstrate that she relied on the holding out to advance credit to the firm in order for ostensible partners to be vicariously liable for one another's conduct.[21] Moreover, she must show that she would, not that she might, have changed her course of action were it not for the holding out of partnership.[22]

Lack of reliance on a holding out of partnership prevented the imposition of vicarious liability on an ostensible partner in *Nationwide Building Society v. Lewis*,[23] a recent decision of the English Court of Appeal. The names of both defendant solicitors, L and W, appeared side by side on their letterhead under the firm name "Brian Lewis and Company Solicitors", although W was in fact L's employee. The plaintiff mortgagee retained the firm to investigate and re-port on title to a property but dealt exclusively with L. W did not play any role in the transaction. L, using the firm's letterhead, reported to the plaintiff about the title. When the plaintiff lost some of its investment, it sued both the solici-tors in negligence and breach of contract but called no evidence of reliance on the holding out of W as a partner. Like the corresponding Canadian statutes, partnership legislation in England provides that vicarious liability may be im-posed on a solicitor who represents himself as a partner if the client gives credit to the firm on the strength of that representation. W admitted that he was held out as a partner on the firm's letterhead, but the court held that reliance on holding out is an essential ingredient for the imposition of vicarious liability on ostensible partners both at common law and under the statute. Reliance will

---

[18] *Ibid.*, at 119 N.B.R.
[19] *Bet-Mur Investments Ltd. v. Spring* (1994), 20 O.R. (3d) 417 (Gen. Div.); *Westfair Foods Ltd. v. Coopers & Lybrand* (1997), 45 B.C.L.R. (3d) 186 (S.C.).
[20] *Supra*, note 17, citing *Ontario Silver & Antimony Co. v. Andrew* (1905), 5 O.W.R. 206 (H.C.), affd 6 O.W.R. 63 (C.A.), and *Johnston v. Brandon* (1919), 45 O.L.R. 369 (H.C.).
[21] *Bet-Mur Investments, supra*, note 19.
[22] *Westfair Foods Ltd., supra*, note 19.
[23] [1998] E.W.J. No. 218 (Eng. C.A.).

rarely be inferred because the client is usually in a better position to know and prove whether the client relied on the plaintiff. Further, knowledge of the holding out is a precondition of reliance. W was not vicariously liable for L's negligence because the evidence did not establish that the plaintiff knew of and relied upon the holding out.

Courts will consider factors such as the names appearing on the firm letterhead and sign, the name in which the firm bank account is held, as well as the sharing of office space, to determine whether there was a holding out of partnership.[24] However, the mere fact that an associate is married to a partner of a firm does not in itself establish a holding out of the spouse as a partner.[25] In order to ascertain whether lawyers' conduct amounts to holding out, a court will only consider their business activities and not their social relationship.

The issue of whether persons who are not in fact partners should be subject to vicarious liability may also arise in the situation where a former partner has retired from the partnership but the firm chooses to retain her name on the letterhead. In *Terry Martel Real Estate Ltd. v. Szpakowsky*,[26] the partnership was dissolved prior to the negligent act, but the retired partner permitted the firm to continue to use his name on the letterhead with "Ret'd" indicating his inactive status. The court held that a lawyer who is clearly not a partner at the relevant time can only be estopped from denying partnership if there is knowledge and reliance on the fact that the particular lawyer is a partner of the firm. In this case, the client did not rely on the fact that the retired partner was indeed a partner of the firm.

As a general rule a legal partnership and its members are liable for a tort or breach of contract or breach of fiduciary duty[27] committed by a partner acting within the ordinary course of business of the firm or with the authority of his partners. Importantly, the dissolution of the partnership does not discharge any liability that has arisen during its existence.[28]

Although the issue has not been conclusively resolved, there is authority for the proposition that damages that flow from a breach of fiduciary duty need not take into account considerations of remoteness, causality and mitigation.[29] Thus, although the dissolution of a partnership (with appropriate notification) will preclude a finding of liability for breaches that occur thereafter, a partner may be liable for damages accruing after the dissolution as a result of breaches that occurred while the partnership existed. The plaintiff in *McKay v. Cowan*[30] transferred his lottery winnings into the trust account of the defendant F's law firm

---

[24] *Bet-Mur Investments Ltd.*, *supra*, note 19; *Westfair Foods Ltd.*, *supra*, note 19.

[25] *Palter v. Zeller* (1996), 30 O.R. (3d) 796 (Gen. Div.).

[26] (1990), 70 D.L.R. (4th) 758 (Ont. H.C.).

[27] *Korz v. St. Pierre* (1987), 61 O.R. (2d) 609, 43 D.L.R. (4th) 528 (C.A.), leave to appeal to S.C.C. refused February 25, 1988.

[28] *Panamaroff v. Reid* (1962), 32 D.L.R. (2d) 126 (B.C.S.C.).

[29] *Canson Enterprises Ltd. v. Boughton & Co.*, [1991] 3 S.C.R. 534.

[30] *McKay v. Cowan* (1989), 39 B.C.L.R. (2d) 192 (S.C.).

and gave the defendant C limited authority to handle the funds for certain transactions. C misappropriated the funds during four distinct periods. At the time the funds were advanced, C was an associate in F's firm (period 1). He subsequently practised in partnership with F and another lawyer, S (period 2). The partnership was dissolved less than a year later, although F maintained an association with C for a time following the dissolution (period 3). Thereafter, C practised on his own (period 4).

F was found vicariously liable for the misappropriations that occurred not only while C was his employee and then his partner, but also during periods 3 and 4 after the dissolution of the partnership. The court reasoned that all of the misappropriated funds came from the original deposit of the plaintiff's winnings into the firm's account while C was an associate. No fresh funds had been injected. F breached his fiduciary duty to the plaintiff by negligently supervising C when he was an employee, and there was no intervening act that set off a new chain of damages that were unconnected to that original breach. Although the plaintiff knew that C made some investments without his prior authorization and was disturbed by that fact, he had no duty to mitigate by firing or reporting him. A client cannot be found to have acquiesced in a lawyer's dishonest conduct unless he knew or ought to have known that the lawyer was acting dishonestly.

Finally, retired partners may be held liable for acts that arise after the dissolution of the partnership. They will be held liable to those who know and rely on the fact that they are partners of the firm.[31] So, those who were clients and creditors of the partnership prior to the dissolution must be notified with clear evidence of the retirement.[32]

Principles of principal and agent are not applicable with respect to indemnity among partners. Internally, each of the several partners is individually a principal. Negligent work performed within the ordinary course of business should be viewed as a loss like any other, one that the partners share proportionately per the partnership agreement.[33]

---

[31] *Terry Martel Real Estate Ltd. v. Szpakowsky, supra,* note 26.

[32] The court in *Terry Martel, supra,* note 26, indicated that those who were clients and creditors of the partnership prior to the dissolution may very well estop the retired lawyer from denying partnership because of ambiguity created by the use of his name, without clear evidence of his retirement. The court indicated that the word following the retired partner's name should be "Retired" and not "Ret'd" to give notice and avoid any ambiguity. However, it should not be inferred that the word "Retired" following the name of the retired partner would be sufficient to avoid liability. The court did not go so far as to find that "Retired" on the letterhead was "clear evidence of retirement", especially in the case of those who were clients and creditors of the partnership prior to the retirement.

[33] *MacDonald v. Schmidt,* unreported, February 7, 1992, Holmes J., Doc. Vancouver C884881, [1992] B.C.J. No. 230 (S.C.).

B. NEGLIGENCE AND FRAUD

Section 11 of the Ontario *Partnerships Act*,[34] which was largely derived from the English statute and is substantially similar to the Partnerships Acts in effect in the other provinces, provides:

> 11. Where by any wrongful act or omission of a partner acting in the ordinary course of the business of the firm, or with the authority of the co-partners, loss or injury is caused to a person not being a partner of the firm, or any penalty is incurred, the firm is liable therefor to the same extent as the partner so acting or omitting to act.

The phrase "wrongful act or omission" is not restrictive and includes not only negligence but also misrepresentation, defalcation and fraud. The only qualification is that the allegedly wrongful act must be committed within the "ordinary course of business of the firm" or with the authority of the wrong-doer's partners in order to create vicarious liability.

In the leading Canadian case, *Public Trustee v. Mortimer*,[35] the partner of a law firm, Mortimer, acted as executor and trustee for an estate. During the years he was a partner in the firm, Mortimer stole substantial sums of money from the estate. The Public Trustee sued Mortimer and his partners, the latter on the basis of their vicarious liability under the *Partnerships Act*. They defended on the basis that Mortimer was acting in the capacity of executor and, therefore, not within the scope of the ordinary business of the firm.

The court indicated that it is a question of fact in every case whether a particular transaction is part of the ordinary course of business of the firm but "[t]he fact that a transaction is dealt with in the books of the firm is strong evidence that it is part of the ordinary course of the business of the firm."[36] The court outlined some of the *indicia* that must be reviewed in order to determine whether a particular lawyer's activity comes within the ordinary course of the business of the firm:

> (1) the terms of the general partnership agreement. In *Mortimer*, the agreement provided that all "offices and appointments held by any partner during the partnership were to be held for the benefit of the partnership";[37]

---

[34] R.S.O. 1990, c. P.5.

[35] (1985), 49 O.R. (2d) 741, 16 D.L.R. (4th) 404 (H.C.).

[36] *Ibid.*, at 750 O.R., citing the dissenting judgment of Brownridge J.A. in *Reitmeier v. Exner* (1970), 75 W.W.R 97, 12 D.L.R. (3d) 627 *sub nom. Reitmeier v. Kraft* (Sask. C.A.), approved by the Supreme Court of Canada at [1971] 5 W.W.R. 384, 23 D.L.R. (3d) 744n; *Rhodes v. Moules*, [1895] 1 Ch. 236 (C.A.); and *Dundonald (Earl) v. Masterman* (1869), 7 L.R. Eq. 504.

[37] *Public Trustee v. Mortimer*, *supra*, note 35, at 751 O.R.

(2) whether any junior lawyers of the firm have assisted in the tasks undertaken by the wrongdoing lawyer;

(3) whether the typing or bookkeeping of the work performed by the wrongdoing lawyer was done by employees of the firm;

(4) whether correspondence on the matter was on the firm's letterhead;

(5) whether the record of receipts and disbursements was kept in the firm's ledgers and whether any funds were deposited in the firm's bank accounts.[38]

In short, the characterization of an activity as coming within the ordinary course of the business of the firm will be determined objectively. In the *Mortimer* case, the court found that Mortimer had used the firm's letterhead, accounts, bookkeeping, and so on; as a result, Mortimer's partners were liable to the plaintiff under s. 11 of the *Partnerships Act.*

To determine whether the partner was acting in the normal course of the partnership's business, a court will first consider the nature of the impugned conduct, and then the nature of the firm's business.[39] There need not be a finding that it was usual for the firm to perform the services in the same negligent or dishonest manner as the services were delivered by the partner, for such a requirement would severely limit the vicarious liability created by the various provincial Partnerships Acts. It is the nature of the activity, and not the manner in which it was carried out, that is relevant. If the law firm is in the business of providing similar services to other clients, and the solicitor used the law firm as the facility for carrying out the transactions, a court is likely to conclude that the conduct is a part of its ordinary course of business.[40]

Some courts have little difficulty in finding that an act falls within the ordinary course of the business of the firm. In *Linsley v. Kirstiuk*,[41] the negligent trustee was a senior partner in a firm retained to act as solicitors in the administration of the estate. He was not an estates lawyer but some of the work he did as trustee was of the type normally carried on by estate lawyers. His knowledge of what was going on was imputed to the firm and both were held jointly and severally liable.

In *Purdy v. Ryan*,[42] a partner was retained by his mentally and physically disabled neighbour to tend to the administration of his mother's estate. According to an agreed statement of facts, the partner met with the client in the parking lot of a bank. He had the client endorse a cheque that the client had received from his father's estate and then the lawyer deposited it into his personal bank account, not the firm's. Subsequently, a cheque was sent by the administrator of

---

[38] *Ibid.*

[39] *Mancini (Trustee of) v. Falconi* (1994), 17 O.R. (3d) 512 (Gen. Div.); *McDonic Estate v. Hetherington (Litigation Guardian of)* (1997), 31 O.R. (3d) 577 (C.A.).

[40] *McDonic Estate, supra,* note 39, at 586-87.

[41] 28 D.L.R. (4th) 495 (B.C.S.C.).

[42] (1993), 136 N.B.R. (2d) 1 (Q.B.).

the father's estate to the firm's address to the attention of the partner for distribution to the client along with a release. This cheque was also deposited into the partner's personal account. The partner witnessed the client's signature on the release and endorsed it with the firm's address. The law firm argued that he stole the money as the client's neighbour, friend or otherwise, but not as a member of the firm. Although the court noted that there was less evidence that the partner was acting in the ordinary course of the firm's business than was present in other cases, it held the firm vicariously liable for both misappropriations because it was within the ordinary course of business of a law firm to arrange for the execution and delivery of legal documents in exchange for the delivery of a cheque to the client. What is most significant about this case is that the only evidence that the partner was acting in the ordinary course of the firm's business in respect of the first cheque was that the client was trusting him as his lawyer when he endorsed the cheque and gave it to him. The firm itself was not used as a vehicle for the transaction and the transaction occurred away from both the client's and the firm's offices.

In addition to liability under section 11, partners may be vicariously liable for the acts of one of their partners when that partner, "acting within the scope of his apparent authority", receives the money or property of a third person and misapplies it.[43]

The term "apparent authority", no doubt borrowed from the law of agency, renders a partner liable for certain acts of another partner even if they fall outside the ordinary course of business of the firm and even if they have not been authorized. In instances where an "innocent" partner, by words or conduct, represents or permits it to be represented that the wrongdoing partner has authority to act on behalf of the partnership, the innocent partner will be bound by those acts and liable to anyone relying on that representation.[44] Thus, in *Mortimer*, the court held that while there may be "some question" as to whether Mortimer, as executor and trustee, was acting in the ordinary course of the business of the firm, "there can be no doubt . . . that the firm, by permitting Mortimer to use the stationery, accounts, staff and other facilities of the firm in connection with his activities as executor and trustee, had vested Mortimer with apparent authority to receive the money or property of the estate which he subsequently misapplied".[45] The fact that the other partners had no knowledge of their colleague's dealings with the plaintiff is irrelevant to the question of apparent authority.[46]

---

[43] *Supra*, note 34, at s.12(*a*).

[44] As to the law respecting apparent (or ostensible) authority, see *Bowstead and Reynolds on Agency*, 16th ed. (London: Sweet & Maxwell, 1996), at 366-73.

[45] *Public Trustee v. Mortimer, supra*, note 35, at 752 O.R. See also *McDonic Estate v. Hetherington (Litigation Guardian of), supra,* note 39, where similar *indicia* led to a finding of apparent authority.

[46] *McDonic Estate v. Hetherington (Litigation Guardian of), supra,* note 39, at 587.

In *McKinnon v. Conexco International Corp.*,[47] Smela, a partner in a law firm, was approached with an investment opportunity. Smela became a client of his firm with respect to this transaction. The court held:

> . . . the breaches of fiduciary duty by any member of the firm, including Smela, are breaches by [the firm]. . . . Smela's liability is as a partner of [the firm]. Although he was named separately, the statement of claim was clear that he was a partner. There was no allegation of fraud against [the firm] and therefore it was reasonable to make Smela a separate party, but his personal fraud must be imputed to his duty as a partner of his own law firm. For these reasons the action against Smela personally is dismissed [48]

Sections 11 and 12 of the *Partnerships Act* may render a partner vicariously liable not only to clients, but also to third parties who have had no or limited dealings with the partnership. In this respect, section 11 applies to losses or injuries caused to "a person not being a partner of the firm", and section 12 applies to the misappropriation of the money or property of a "third person". In *Victoria & Grey Trust Co. v. Crawford*,[49] F, a partner in the defendant law firm, had received various cheques payable to the firm in connection with an estate he had been handling. The cheques were designed to close the estate, the administration of which was being transferred to a new trustee in California. F took one of the cheques drawn to the order of the firm, destroyed it and prepared a forged cheque in the same amount payable to himself. He then presented it at the plaintiff trust company which honoured it. After having made good the loss to the estate, the trust company, which had no other relationship with the defendant firm, sued F and the firm. Although sections 11 and 12 fall under a heading in the *Partnerships Act* that reads: "Relation of Partners to Persons Dealing with Them", the trial judge held the firm liable by finding "no indication in [section 11] that the Legislature intended to limit liability of persons who suffer loss to persons dealing with the partnership."[50]

---

[47] Unreported, February 17, 1992, Steele J., Doc. 16582/86, [1992] O.J. No. 292 (Gen. Div.).

[48] *Ibid.*, at paras. 22-24.

[49] *Victoria & Grey Trust Co. v. Crawford* (1986), 57 O.R. (2d) 484 (H.C.), affd unreported, September 29, 1988 (C.A.).

[50] *Ibid.*, at 488.

Chapter 6

LIABILITY IN SPECIFIC PRACTICE AREAS

I. INTRODUCTION

In this chapter, we sort cases of lawyers' professional negligence into particular practice areas to try to identify some of the recurring problems encountered by lawyers practising in a given field. The result is a kind of taxonomy of lawyers' negligence cases; it should not be viewed as an exhaustive review of prudent practice in each area.

II. CONDUCT OF A CIVIL ACTION

A. TAKING INSTRUCTIONS AND GIVING ADVICE

The extent of a litigation lawyer's obligation to give unsolicited advice or to recommend preventative action is at issue in many suits by dissatisfied clients. In the often-cited case of *Griffiths v. Evans*,[1] an employee who had been injured at work and who had been receiving worker's compensation consulted a solicitor because he feared a reduction in his weekly payments. The solicitor gave him advice on the compensation claim, obtained a lump-sum payment under the legislation on his behalf, but neglected to advise him that by seeking and accepting the lump-sum award he had forfeited any right to claim common law damages against his employer. The plaintiff claimed damages against the solicitor for this omission. While the majority of the court held that the solicitor was not negligent since he had been asked specifically to advise on workers' compensation and not on a civil action, Lord Denning, dissenting, observed that to absolve the solicitor of liability "attributes to the workman a legal knowledge of the difference between [worker's compensation and common law damages]. Many workmen do not in fact know the difference, and it would be most unfair to attribute such knowledge to them."[2] Lord Denning's reasoning might well prevail in cases brought on similar facts today. Recent decisions clearly show

---

[1] [1953] 2 All E.R. 1364, [1953] 1 W.L.R. 1424 (C.A.).

[2] *Ibid.*, at 1370 All E.R.

that judicial expectations of the nature and quality of lawyers' services have risen since *Griffiths* was decided.

A lawyer has an obligation to discuss with the client the various options presented by the fact situation.

> Once he agreed to act for the plaintiff, the defendant owed a duty to the plaintiff to at least communicate with him to ascertain his degree of recovery and what steps ought to be considered or taken either to settle the plaintiff's claim or set it down for trial.[3]

It is clear that the courts are willing to impose upon the solicitor a duty to warn the client of potential risks of particular transactions. There is every reason to believe that the litigation lawyer is under a similar obligation as the imposition of this duty ensures that clients are properly informed about the legal effect of a particular fact situation.[4] The court in *Graybriar Industries Ltd. v. Davis & Co.* [5] canvassed the law[6] respecting the duty to warn, which may be summarized as requiring a solicitor to warn his client of risks on the basis of a reasonable knowledge of the law, facts and practical implications of the results.

There is a corresponding obligation on the client in civil actions to provide information and instructions: "[i]t is incumbent on the client to explain the problem fully, provide all facts pertaining to the matter, including anything which might be detrimental to the possibility of a successful claim, and to give the lawyer instructions on proceeding after being fully advised. It is only then that a solicitor can act properly on behalf of the client."[7] A court will assess a litigator's performance of his obligations with reference to the information and instructions provided by the client.[8]

Even in the absence of clear instructions or a specific request, a solicitor may have an obligation to issue originating process when a client has consulted him

---

[3]   *Skirzyk v. Crawford* (1990), 64 Man. R. (2d) 220 (Q.B.).

[4]   In *Confederation Life Insurance Co. v. Shepherd, McKenzie, Plaxton, Little & Jenkins* (1992), 29 R.P.R. (2d) 271 (Ont. Gen. Div.), the court held that a lawyer is obliged to advise a client of any risks or concerns respecting the manner in which relevant legislation may impact upon a particular transaction. Similarly, in *Haag v. Marshall* (1989), 1 C.C.L.T. (2d) 99 (B.C.C.A.), a solicitor breached his duty to his clients in failing to warn them of the possible results of certain likely situations.

[5]   (1990), 46 B.C.L.R. (2d) 164 (S.C.).

[6]   Specifically, these following cases: *R. & L. Contracting Ltd. v. A* (1981), 28 B.C.L.R. 342 (C.A.); *Income Trust Co. v. Watson* (1984), 26 B.L.R. 228 (Ont. H.C.), affd February 14, 1986 (unreported); *Canadian Imperial Bank of Commerce v. Pomeroy*, unreported, December 16, 1986, Hogarth L.J.S.C., Doc. C843488, [1986] B.C.J. No. 2672 (S.C.); *Olorenshaw v. International Chem-Pro Industries Inc.*, Doc. Chilliwack 860009, [1989] B.C.W.L.D. 1888 (S.C.).

[7]   *Dawe v. Brown* (1995), 130 Nfld. & P.E.I.R. 281 at 289 (Nfld. T.D.).

[8]   *Ibid.*

about the commencement of an action and a limitation period is about to expire.[9] And where it is "implicit" in a client's instructions to issue a claim, a solicitor will be liable for failure to do so even if the failure arises by reason of an inability to contact the client to clarify his instructions.[10]

When retained by a partnership, a lawyer is obliged to take instructions from the managing partner[11] and is not negligent if he fails to keep the other partners informed of the progress of the action.[12]

The obligations of a civil litigation lawyer to report to a client are more complicated in a case where the lawyer is retained by a legal aid committee or an insurer to represent the client. In *Davy-Chiesman v. Davy-Chiesman*,[13] the court held that a solicitor acting for a legally-aided client owed a duty to the legal aid committee to inform it of any change in the circumstances of the litigation, in this case that the client no longer had a reasonable chance of success.[14]

B. WITHDRAWING SERVICES

Whenever a lawyer undertakes the prosecution or defence of an action or counterclaim and thereby makes herself the solicitor of record for a client, she owes a duty to the client not to withdraw her services except on proper notice, and where she fails to do so, she will be found negligent.[15] Withdrawal without justification also amounts to a breach of contract, because a court is likely to interpret the retainer as requiring the solicitor to continue to represent the client at least until the end of trial.[16] Furthermore, a lawyer may not be entitled to his fees

---

9   *Gray v. Solicitors* (1980), 17 B.C.L.R. 392, [1980] 3 W.W.R. 689 at 697 *sub nom. Gray v. Forbes* (S.C.): "[a solicitor has] an obligation . . . to issue a writ, even though there may have been some doubt or ambiguity in his own mind concerning his client's instructions"; but see *contra, Schopp v. McCrank* (1983), 24 Sask. R. 88 at 93 (Q.B.). At the very least, a solicitor has an obligation to advise the client that the limitation period is about to expire: *Prior v. McNab* (1976), 16 O.R. (2d) 380, 78 D.L.R. (3d) 319 at 332 (H.C.).

10   *Gray v. Solicitors, supra,* note 9.

11   *Tomlinson v. Broadsmith,* [1896] 1 Q.B. 386 (C.A.).

12   *Ibid.*

13   [1984] 1 All E.R. 321 (C.A.).

14   While to some extent, the obligation in this case can be seen to arise from a statutory duty pursuant to the U.K. Legal Aid (General) Regulations 1980, similar provisions are found in comparable Canadian statutes. The reporting obligations of counsel for an insurer are discussed in Chapter 8, Section II. "The Policy", B. "Rights and Obligations of the Insurer", 1. "Obligation to Defend".

15   *Hoby v. Built* (1832), 3 B. & Ad. 350, 110 E.R. 131; *North American Forest Products Ltd. v. Pelletier* (1981), 33 N.B.R. (2d) 424 (Q.B.), affd 35 N.B.R. (2d) 36 (C.A.).

16   *Kent v. Waldock* (1996), 26 B.C.L.R. (3d) 11 (C.A.). The defendant solicitor's refusal to continue with the trial unless a guardian *ad litem* was appointed for his client amounted to an anticipatory breach of contract, if not an actual breach. The court granted a declaration that the solicitor had no claim for fees or a solicitor's lien in respect of any proceeds from the subsequent settlement of the action. An award for general damages for breach of contract was not

unless withdrawal was proper in the circumstances.[17] Where a solicitor acting on behalf of a collection agency makes a claim on behalf of one of the creditors represented by the agency and a counterclaim is then filed against the creditor, the lawyer is obliged to give notice of withdrawal to the creditor; it is not sufficient for the lawyer to notify the agency.[18]

C. COMMENCEMENT OF THE ACTION

A disproportionately high number of claims by clients against lawyers result from missed limitation periods.[19] Failure to issue process within the relevant limitation period constitutes negligence,[20] but a lawyer who fails to do so will not be liable unless the client establishes that this failure has resulted in a loss.[21] The determination of this issue requires a trial of the merits of the statute-barred action within the trial of the negligence action against the lawyer.[22] Courts appear to take a two-step approach in these cases, considering first whether the plaintiff has established that she would likely have succeeded in the original claim had the limitation period not expired, and secondly, whether and to what extent she would have recovered on the judgment.[23] A plaintiff will only be entitled to nominal damages for the lawyer's negligence if he cannot show that he probably would have succeeded.[24] If for some reason it is not possible to conduct a trial within a trial, a court must assess the value of the plaintiff's lost op-

---

made because there was no evidence that the plaintiff would have recovered more than the amount of the settlement had the breach not occurred.

[17] For a decision that allowed the fees because the withdrawal was justified, see *Jakab v. Sauer, Mogan, De Jager & Volkenant* (1997), 152 D.L.R. (4th) 748 (B.C.S.C.).

[18] *Kern-Hill Co-op Furniture Ltd. v. Shuckett* (1975), 58 D.L.R. (3d) 157 (Man. C.A.).

[19] The Lawyers Professional Indemnity Company reports that 256 of the approximately 2,000 claims against lawyers in Ontario in 1997, and 10 per cent of claims costs, were attributable to missed limitation periods: "Limitation Period Cases", *LPIC: News*, Vol. 4 (Spring 1998), at 4.

[20] See *Fyk v. Millar* (1973), 2 O.R. (2d) 39, 41 D.L.R. (3d) 684 (H.C.) (Ontario *Highway Traffic Act*, R.S.O. 1970, c. 202); *Fletcher & Son v. Jubb, Booth & Helliwell*, [1920] 1 K.B. 275 (C.A.) (*Public Authorities Protection Act, 1893*, 56 & 57 Vict., c. 61); *Yarn v. Locke* (1983), 42 Nfld. & P.E.I.R. 140 (Nfld. T.D.) (Newfoundland *Highway Traffic Act*, R.S.N. 1970, c. 152); *Smith v. Wells* (1984), 47 Nfld. & P.E.I.R. 326 (Nfld. Dist. Ct.) (Newfoundland *Highway Traffic Act* and *Fatal Accidents Act*, R.S.N. 1970, c. 126); *MacDonald Construction Co. v. Ross* (1980), 32 Nfld. & P.E.I.R. 450 (P.E.I.S.C.) (P.E.I. *Insurance Act*, R.S.P.E.I. 1974, c. I-5); *Melanson v. Cochrane* (1985), 63 N.B.R. (2d) 91 (Q.B.), affd 68 N.B.R. (2d) 370 (C.A.) (New Brunswick *Limitation of Actions Act*, R.S.N.S. 1973, c. L-8); *Skirzyk v. Crawford, supra*, note 3. Similarly, failure to file a mechanic's lien within the limitation period is negligence: see *Aetna Roofing (1975) Ltd. v. Conradi* (1984), 52 A.R. 369 (Q.B.).

[21] See Chapter 7, Section II. "Damages", A. "Compensatory Damages", 1. "Pecuniary Losses", d. "Loss of Opportunity".

[22] *Prior v. McNab, supra,* note 9; *Fisher v. Knibbe* (1992), 3 Alta. L.R. (3d) 97 (C.A.); *Okafar v. Bond,* unreported, December 4, 1995, Roberts J., Doc. 92-CG-19492, [1995] O.J. No. 3811 (Gen. Div.); *Bueckert v. Mattison* (1996), 149 Sask. R. 81 (Q.B.).

[23] See, for example, *Bueckert v. Mattison, supra,* note 22.

[24] *Fisher, supra,* note 22.

portunity to bring the action. The Alberta Court of Appeal has summarized the various possible outcomes in solicitors' negligence cases involving missed limitation periods this way:

> After conducting the "trial within a trial" to determine what damages, if any, a negligent solicitor is liable for missing a limitation, three results are possible. First, the trial judge could find that had the case gone to trial the plaintiff would have been successful and in such case 100 per cent of the lost damages would be awarded against the solicitor. Second, the trial judge could find that the plaintiff would not have been successful therefore only nominal damages may be awarded against the solicitor. Finally, where time has passed to such an extent that a "trial within a trial" would be impossible, then the court must to the best of its ability calculate the value of the opportunity lost to the plaintiff and award damages against the solicitor on that basis.[25]

While in certain circumstances a lawyer can refuse to conduct a civil action on behalf of a client, for example, if she believes it has little or no change of success,[26] she may still have an obligation to advise a client as to the relevant limitation period, particularly when its expiration is imminent.[27] However, a lawyer will be held liable even if her failure to issue process arises from an inability to contact the plaintiff to confirm instructions, as long as it can be established that the plaintiff had originally given instructions to sue.[28] It has been held that where a lawyer fails to ascertain whether the defendant is alive before issuing process and after the expiry of the limitation period the action is determined to be a nullity because of the defendant's death, the solicitor is not negligent.[29] In another case, a solicitor was not liable for the expiration of a limitation period because he had been retained on a related but separate matter. The limited retainer defence applied.[30] A lawyer retains exclusive responsibility for the com-

---

[25] *Ibid.,* at 101-02.

[26] The comments of Bayda C.J.S., giving judgment for the Saskatchewan Court of Appeal in *Pound v. Nakonechny* (1983), 28 Sask. R. 222, 5 D.L.R. (4th) 427 at 443-44, are of particular interest: "The failure to advance a claim [on behalf of the plaintiff] of such dubious merit while there was available to the plaintiff a claim of much greater merit . . . particularly when both claims would only result in the same award of damages, is, in my respectful view, not a breach of duty, and probably is not even a case of bad professional judgment." See also *Holmes v. National Benzole Co. Ltd.* (1965), 109 Sol. Jo. 971: "A solicitor who, without any investigation of his client's claim, allowed or encouraged a client to pursue a claim which proper investigation would at any early state have shown to be a hopeless one was in breach of duty to his client."

[27] *Prior v. McNab, supra,* note 9, at 332 D.L.R.

[28] *Gray v. Solicitors, supra,* note 9.

[29] *Grima v. MacMillan,* [1972] 3 O.R. 214, 27 D.L.R. (3d) 666 (H.C.).

[30] *Coughlin v. Comery,* unreported, March 8, 1996, Hoilett J., Doc. 401522/90, [1996] O.J. No. 822 (Gen. Div.). The client retained the solicitor to deal with a dispute with the client's insurer concerning the termination of benefits for a disability arising from a slip and fall. The solicitor did not have an obligation to advise the client about causes of action relating to the slip and fall.

mencement of process within the limitation period even after he retains expert counsel to advise him as to the preparation of the proof of loss claim in an insurance case.[31] Likewise, a lawyer bears the ultimate and exclusive responsibility for the service of process and has no claim for contribution or indemnity against a sheriff who fails to advise the lawyer that he has been unable to effect service prior to the writ's expiry.[32]

The doctrine of promissory estoppel is a defence to a missed limitation period, but the party relying on promissory estoppel must meet the test established by the Supreme Court of Canada in *Maracle v. Travellers Indemnity Co. of Canada*.[33] He must establish that: (1) the other party, by words or conduct, made a promise or assurance intended to affect their legal relationship; (2) the promise or assurance was made with the intention that it be acted on; and (3) the party in fact acted on it or changed his position in some way. The fact that the other party admitted liability, engaged in settlement discussions and perhaps even made an offer to settle are factors from which a court may infer that a promise was made not to rely on the limitation period. However, promissory estoppel will not be established unless there are words or conduct from which a court could infer that the admission was to apply whether the case was settled or not, and that the only issue between the parties, should litigation ensue, is the issue of quantum.

D. FAILURE TO PROSECUTE AND DELAY

A lawyer's obligations in the conduct of an action do not end with the issuance and service of process; failure to complete pleadings or discoveries, or to set the action down for trial, or to do so without unreasonable delay, is also negligence.[34] Further, when an action is dismissed for want of prosecution through a lawyer's negligence, he has a duty to inform his client and his failure to do so may constitute fraudulent concealment and give rise to damages.[35]

E. SETTLEMENT OF ACTIONS

Although a client is normally bound by a settlement entered into by her lawyer, even if she has not authorized it, the client has an action against the lawyer for

---

[31] *Webb Real Estate Ltd. v. McInnis, Meehan & Tramble*, [1978] 2 S.C.R. 1357, 91 D.L.R. (3d) 190 *sub nom. Smith v. McInnis*.

[32] *Rempel v. Parks* (1984), 53 B.C.L.R. 167, [1984] 4 W.W.R. 689 (C.A.), revd in part 34 B.C.L.R. 253, [1982] 3 W.W.R. 670 (S.C.). But see critique of this result: J. Cassels, "Annotation" (1985), 35 R.P.R. 90.

[33] [1991] 2 S.C.R. 50.

[34] *Gouzenko v. Harris* (1976), 13 O.R. (2d) 730 (H.C.); *Skirzyk v. Crawford* (1990), 64 Man. R. (2d) 220 (Q.B.).

[35] *Vienneau v. Arsenault* (1982), 41 N.B.R. (2d) 82 (C.A.).

exceeding her authority.[36] Similarly, a lawyer has a duty to report all offers of settlement to her client even if she believes the offer is not satisfactory and, when acting for an insurer, the offer should be presented to the insurer as well.[37]

The obligations of a lawyer in recommending or not recommending a particular settlement proposal to a client are more difficult to define. In *Fawell v. Atkins*,[38] it was determined that the defendant solicitors were at fault in reaching a conclusion as to the merits of the plaintiff's case and recommending a settlement without first interviewing an important witness. However, it is less certain whether this conduct would have triggered liability on the views set out by Anderson J. in *Karpenko v. Paroian, Courey, Cohen & Houston*,[39] in which he held that "it would only be in a clear and exceptional case that the decision of counsel to recommend settlement could be successfully assailed."[40] This conclusion, suggesting a less rigorous standard of care in the case of settlement recommendations than in other areas of a lawyer's practice, was justified by Anderson J. on the basis of public policy:

> It is in the interests of public policy to discourage suits and encourage settlements. The vast majority of suits are settled. It is the almost universal practice among responsible members of the legal profession to pursue settlement until some circumstance or combination of circumstances leads them to conclude that a particular dispute can only be resolved at trial. I say nothing of the suits which are settled by reason of sloth, or inexperience, or lack of stomach for the fight. They have nothing to do with this case. What is relevant and material to the public interest is that an industrious and competent practitioner should not be unduly inhibited in making a decision to settle a case by apprehension that some Judge, viewing the matter subsequently, with all the acuity of vision given by hindsight, and from the calm and security of the Bench, may tell him he should have done otherwise.[41]

Although Mr. Justice Anderson correctly maintained that a settlement recommendation involves a complex consideration of a number of factors, he probably overstated the problem. In our view, the approach propounded in *Maillet v. Haliburton*[42] is preferable. In that case, after a trial by jury, the plaintiff was awarded $75,000 general damages for personal injuries resulting from a motor vehicle accident. When the judgment was appealed, the plaintiff's lawyer,

---

[36] *Fray v. Voules* (1859), El. & El. 839, 120 E.R. 1125; *Butler v. Knight* (1867), L.R. 2 Ex. 109; *Thompson v. Howley*, [1977] 1 N.Z.L.R. 16 (S.C.).

[37] *Pelky v. Hudson Bay Insurance Co.* (1981), 35 O.R. (2d) 97 (H.C.); *Sill v. Thomas* (1839), 8 C. & P. 762, 173 E.R. 707.

[38] (1981), 28 B.C.L.R. 32 (S.C.).

[39] (1980), 30 O.R. (2d) 776, 117 D.L.R. (3d) 383 (H.C.).

[40] *Ibid.*, at 790 O.R.

[41] *Ibid.*, at 790 O.R.

[42] (1983), 55 N.S.R. (2d) 311, 32 C.P.C. 33 (T.D.).

fearing that the award would be drastically reduced, advised the plaintiff to accept $40,000 in settlement, which she did. The court, on hearing the plaintiff's legal malpractice claim against her lawyer, determined that, prior to recommending settlement, the lawyer had adequately researched the relevant case law, had acquainted his client in considerable detail with the results of his research, and had cautioned her about the delay and costs attendant upon an appeal. The court held that in these circumstances the plaintiff's lawyer had acted in the manner of a reasonably competent lawyer, one who would have been sufficiently uncertain about the appeal outcome to conclude that settlement was advisable.

Alberta (Workers' Compensation Board) v. Riggins[43] was decided along comparable lines, finding the solicitor negligent. In his preparation for settlement discussions, the solicitor did not consider all heads of damage, nor did he research liability or properly assess the value of the claim. The court held that, even if the client had given consent to the settlement offer,[44] it would not have been informed consent, as the client would have been relying on deficient advice. The standard of care to be applied in these cases was expressed as that of a similarly situated, reasonably competent member of his profession.

Regardless of the strength of the policy rationale articulated in *Karpenko*, courts have continued to emphasize that it is only in the rarest of cases that solicitors will be found negligent in advising settlement.[45] One court has stated: "In the absence of finding the most glaring wrong-doing, particularly when concerned with advice to settle, it is inappropriate for the court to substitute its discretion for that of experienced counsel."[46] The burden on the plaintiff will be especially heavy where he was well informed and actively participated in the negotiation process.[47] When a solicitor does negligently advise settlement, she may be liable for the costs incurred by the client in having the settlement set aside.[48]

---

[43]   (1990), 75 Alta L.R. (2d) 13 (Q.B.), affd 5 Alta L.R. (3d) 66 (C.A.).

[44]   The Workers' Compensation Board was subrogated to the injured worker's cause of action, and the solicitor was retained by the Board. The injured worker instructed the solicitor to settle the action. The solicitor did so erroneously believing that he had received instructions from the Board.

[45]   See, for example, *Greig v. Waldock (Trustee of)*, unreported, October 7, 1997, Williamson J., Doc. Vancouver C940881, [1997] B.C.J. No. 2217 (S.C.); *Parker v. Ledwell, Larter & Driscoll* (1997), 159 Nfld. & P.E.I.R. 58 (P.E.I.T.D.). However, in *Parker*, the defendant solicitor's motion for summary judgment was dismissed. The plaintiff alleged that she was given negligent information and advice surrounding the settlement. It was too difficult a question to be decided on a summary judgment motion because it was necessary to examine the circumstances surrounding the acceptance of the settlement.

[46]   *Greig v. Waldock, supra,* note 45, at para. 32.

[47]   *Dykun v. Rogers*, unreported, October 27, 1994, Lee J., Doc. 9103-01722, [1994] A.J. No. 1110 (Q.B.).

[48]   *Irwin v. Howard Smith & Co.* (1997), 88 B.C.A.C. 138.

Finally, the British Columbia Court of Appeal has held in *Clark v. Poje*[49] that a lawyer has a duty to negotiate. However, he will not be liable for failing to reach a settlement unless the client can show that a more favourable result would have been obtained if the solicitor tried harder to effect a compromise. The test is not whether there was "meaningful negotiation" but whether the plaintiff acted as a reasonably competent solicitor in the circumstances.

F. PREPARATION AND CONDUCT OF TRIAL

Notwithstanding the rejection of the barrister's immunity rule by Canadian courts,[50] many cases reflect a continuing reluctance to second-guess the decisions made by a trial lawyer in the "heat of battle". Indeed, the court in *Demarco v. Ungaro*,[51] after refusing to apply the barrister's immunity rule, nevertheless concluded: "[It is] difficult to believe that a decision made by a lawyer in the conduct of a case will be held to be negligence as opposed to a mere error of judgment."[52] It now appears that lawyers will only be liable for negligence for "egregious errors" made in the conduct of a trial.[53]

The fact that trial counsel does not present every item of potential evidence or take every possible objection at trial does not generally lead to the conclusion that there has been negligence.[54] Strategic decisions and advocacy style are also not likely to found a successful action for negligence. In *Hunter v. Roe*,[55] an action by a client against a lawyer for negligence in the preparation and conduct of a trial, the Saskatchewan Court of Queen's Bench held:

---

[49] (1989), 38 B.C.L.R. (2d) 110 (C.A.). Note that this case did not involve negotiations for the settlement of an action. Rather, the defendant solicitor represented the plaintiff client on the sale of his property. The solicitor negotiated unsuccessfully with a judgment creditor for the removal of a judgment registered against the client's property. The client was forced to pay the judgment in order to complete the transaction and sued the solicitor for failing to engage in meaningful negotiations. For a review of the American jurisprudence respecting failure to settle, see J.K. Baker-Selesky, "Negligence in Failing to Settle Lawsuits: Malpractice Actions and Their Defences" (1995/1996), 20 *J. Legal Prof.* 191.

[50] See Chapter 1, Section V. "Special Liability Problems", A. "Barrister's Liability", 2. "The Canadian Position".

[51] (1979), 21 O.R. (2d) 673, 95 D.L.R. (3d) 385 (H.C.).

[52] *Ibid.*, at 693 O.R.

[53] *Supra*, note 50.

[54] *Garrant v. Moskal; Garrant v. Cawood* (1985), 40 Sask. R. 155, [1985] 6 W.W.R. 31 (C.A.); *B. Matthew Developments Ltd. v. Hanman*, May 11, 1989, Doc. Vancouver CA009544 (B.C.C.A.). However, if a lawyer makes a decision not to prepare or call further evidence on an important issue, in this case with respect to damages, he has an obligation to inform the client of this decision and the reasons therefor: *M. Hodge & Sons Ltd. v. Monaghan* (1985), 51 Nfld. & P.E.I.R. 173 (Nfld. T.D.); *Bartolovic v. Bennett*, unreported, March 26, 1996, Borins J., Doc. 95-CU-86639, [1996] O.J. No. 961 (Gen. Div.); *Anastasakos v. Allen* (1996), 16 O.T.C. 413 (Gen. Div.); *Boudreau v. Benaiah* (1998), 37 O.R. (3d) 686 (Gen. Div.).

[55] [1990] 6 W.W.R. 85 at 87 (Sask. Q.B.).

There were certainly no errors to be distilled from the evidence that can be categorized as being "so egregious" as to amount to negligence. A "clear case of error" has not been made out. Perhaps different strategies could have been taken in confronting some of the issues. No doubt one could say that a cross-examination could have been conducted in a different way. That is often so on reflection in nearly all cases. But after reviewing the transcript of evidence from the trial in Family Court, as well as the evidence on this trial, it is quite apparent to me that the plaintiff's allegation of negligence is not well founded.

Likewise, where a lawyer conducts a trial according to his client's express wishes, he ought not be held liable for any loss attributable to those instructions.[56] For example, in an action for damage to property, the plaintiff's lawyer followed the plaintiff's instruction to seek damages based on the cost of repairing the property, and, accordingly, adduced no appraisal evidence at trial as to the property's actual value. On appeal, the Court of Appeal applied a different valuation principle and, in the absence of valuation evidence, reduced the client's damages. The solicitor was found not to be negligent.[57]

In contrast, a lawyer who fails to interview or make reasonable efforts to interview an independent witness whose evidence may well have altered the result at trial is negligent.[58] However, a lawyer is not obliged to chase down every possible witness: for instance, a witness who he reasonably concludes is unlikely to testify in his client's favour,[59] or a witness whose evidence is reasonably assumed to be unnecessary since the point of his testimony will be well covered by three independent witnesses who have been subpoenaed for trial.[60]

A trial lawyer will be liable if she allows a trial to proceed without ascertaining that a material and necessary witness is in attendance;[61] if she fails to seek an adjournment so an important witness can be found to give evidence;[62] or if she retains an expert witness whom she knows to be an alcoholic and the witness fails to attend at trial with adverse effects for the lawyer's client.[63]

Failure to adequately prepare a witness for trial may constitute negligence although this would ordinarily be hard to establish and there may be some additional difficulty in demonstrating that the outcome of the trial would have been different if the witness had been properly prepared.

---

[56]   This does not mean that a lawyer is entitled to leave important decisions to the judgment of his client, and in any event, owes a duty to advise and warn the client of any risks inherent in a particular course of action.

[57]   *Moore v. Gillespie* (1980), 22 B.C.L.R. 329 (C.A.). However, if the client can demonstrate that he gave instructions based on erroneous advice or a lack of advice as to his options respecting remedy, a finding of negligence would then be appropriate.

[58]   *Fawell v. Atkins, supra,* note 38.

[59]   *Roe v. Robert MacGregor & Sons Ltd.,* [1968] 2 All E.R. 636, [1968] 1 W.L.R. 925 (C.A.).

[60]   *Crook v. Derbyshire,* [1961] 3 All E.R. 786 (C.A.).

[61]   *Reece v. Righy* (1821), 4 B. & Ald. 202, 106 E.R. 912.

[62]   *Allen v. Allen* (1960), 112 Sol. Jo. 965.

[63]   *Mercer v. King* (1859), 1 F. & F. 490, 175 E.R. 822 (N.P.).

The case of *Canadian Kawasaki Motors Ltd. v. MacLean*[64] was not a case of legal malpractice but was an action by a creditor against the alleged signatory of a guarantee; nevertheless, it provides a useful illustration of this principle. On the day of trial, the plaintiff company moved to dismiss its own action having discovered that the guarantee was a fraud. The trial judge was understandably appalled to learn that counsel for the alleged guarantor had never shown his client the guarantee, the one document upon which the plaintiff based its case, and that he had never conducted an examination for discovery of the plaintiff to ascertain the document's authenticity. Had the defendant been held liable for costs, no doubt she would have had a successful claim against her solicitor for negligent pretrial and trial preparation.

Conversely, it has been held that the failure of a lawyer to show a civil witness the transcript of his evidence in a previous trial is not negligence.[65]

Perhaps the most difficult allegation to establish in proving negligence concerns a lawyer's decision not to cross-examine a witness. In *Wechsel v. Stutz*,[66] the plaintiff, who had retained the defendant lawyer to conduct an assessment appeal, complained that the defendant had failed to cross-examine the assessors, called by the assessment department, on the documents filed by the department. The court seemed anxious to give the defendant the benefit of the doubt and concluded:

> The extent of a cross-examination of a witness or indeed whether he should be cross-examined at all *must be left to the judgment of counsel*. If, in the judgment of counsel, a witness cannot be broken down or at least the impact of his testimony reduced, it is sometimes preferable to forgo cross-examination. Cross-examination in some instances can result in a strengthening of the evidence by mere repetition. As mentioned earlier the defendant was an experienced counsel and if in fact he refrained from cross-examining witnesses it is reasonable to conclude that he had a reason for so refraining.[67]

---

[64] (1981), 45 N.S.R. (2d) 569, revd on issue of costs 45 N.S.R. (2d) 284 (C.A.).

[65] *Barclays Bank Ltd. v. Cole* (1967), 111 Sol. Jo. 585.

[66] (1980), 15 C.C.L.T. 132 (Ont. Co. Ct.).

[67] *Ibid.*, at 136 (emphasis added). The plaintiffs' argument no doubt was hindered by the fact that they were unrepresented, called no expert evidence and had no transcript of the assessment appeal proceedings. However, the court seems to go further than necessary in suggesting that the scope and nature of cross-examination is part of an advocate's untrammelled right to control the conduct of litigation. This view has been criticized by a number of commentators: for example, Smith, "Liability for the Negligent Conduct of Litigation: The Legacy of *Rondel v. Worsley*" (1982-83), 47 *Sask. L. Rev.* 211 at 246-56.

G. EXECUTION OF JUDGMENT

A lawyer is liable to his client for failing to carry out instructions to register a judgment thereby hindering the client in recovering his judgment debt;[68] but it is not clear whether a lawyer has a duty to proceed to execute a judgment in the absence of specific instructions to do so.[69] Prudence dictates, however, that in appropriate circumstances he enquire of the client as to whether the client wishes to proceed.

In addition, failure to issue execution in a timely way is negligence when there is evidence that, had immediate steps been taken, the plaintiff might have recovered the judgment debt.[70] In *Saucer v. Dunnaway*[71] the British Columbia Court of Appeal recently found a family law practitioner liable for failing to properly serve on a bank an order restraining it from distributing RRSP proceeds to a defaulting husband. The court held: "[b]y not taking the steps necessary to ensure that the Bank was properly provided with notice and omitting to obtain an acknowledgment of receipt of the order from the Bank, the [solicitor] did not discharge her duty to the [wife] with reasonable care or, alternatively, did not perform her contract for services with the plaintiff with reasonable care."

III. COMMERCIAL TRANSACTIONS

A. BUSINESS AND INVESTMENT ADVICE

The obligation of a lawyer to consider and advise on a client's business interests, as well as her legal interests, depends largely on the nature of the relationship between the lawyer and the client. The scope of the retainer, the degree to which the client reasonably relies on her lawyer to provide business advice, and the sophistication of the client in business matters are all relevant factors in ascertaining the extent of the lawyer's obligation. However, a law-

---

[68] *Hett v. Pun Pong* (1890), 18 S.C.R. 290.

[69] In *Hett, ibid.*, Strong J. expressed the view in *obiter* that a retainer to prosecute an action does not terminate when judgment is obtained and that it is the duty of the solicitor, without further instructions, to endeavour to execute the judgment. We are of the view that this overstates the lawyer's obligations and indeed, may result in wasted expenditure in cases where, for example, there is reason to believe that the judgment debtor is judgment proof. The better view is that a lawyer has an obligation to advise her client of the steps that can be taken in aid of execution and to obtain specific instructions. This would seem to accord with the opinions expressed in *Harrington v. Binns* (1863), 3 F. & F. 942, 176 E.R. 429, in which it was held that in order to maintain an action against a solicitor for failure to issue execution there must be evidence that execution would have benefited the plaintiff. For a case in which a lawyer was found negligent for failure to be aware of a statutory provision which would have assisted the plaintiff in collecting a judgment, see *Murphy v. Nicholson* (1984), 28 A.C.W.S. (2d) 399 (Ont. Co. Ct.).

[70] *Sweetman v. Lemon and Peterson* (1863), 13 U.C.C.P. 534 (C.A.).

[71] Unreported, July 16, 1997, Pitfield J., Doc. Vancouver C944884, [1997] B.C.J. No. 1679 (S.C.), at para. 32.

yer certainly has a responsibility to inform a client when their undertaking is not realistic.[72]

A solicitor who holds himself out as competent to give investment advice (and subsequently does so) is under a duty to do so in accordance with the standards of a reasonably competent investment counsellor.[73] In *Morris v. Jackson*,[74] for example, a lawyer who undertook to arrange the mortgage investments for an unsophisticated client, assuring her that he was supplying her with "good mortgages", was held negligent because he failed to obtain appraisals of the mortgaged properties. As it happened, the value of encumbrances grossly exceeded the value of the properties. Likewise, in *Brumer v. Gunn*,[75] a lawyer was found negligent for advising an unsophisticated elderly woman to invest all her money in speculative loans, for approving inadequate security for the loans, and for failing to advise her to discount the loans when the borrower's financial position deteriorated. Further, in cases where a lawyer is advised that an unsophisticated client intends to lend money to a limited company without assets, he should take steps to ensure the adequacy of the proposed security and is negligent if he fails to do so.[76] The court in *Graybriar* went even further, requiring a solicitor not only to inform a client that he was investing in a shell company, but to also explain the risks of such ownership:

> Any person who goes to a lawyer with respect to a land transaction is entitled to expect those lawyers to investigate the state of any title that is germane to the matter *and to explain to the client exactly what it is that is portrayed by the state of the title.* I find the defendants negligent and in breach of duty in not carrying out the latter part of that duty. [Emphasis in original.][77]

The additional duty owed to the unsophisticated client has been extended to apply to an unsophisticated investor who clearly is not a client. In *Klingspon v. Ramsay*,[78] a solicitor owed a duty to an unsophisticated third party investor, even

---

[72] In *Stephenson v. Rollo*, unreported, February 14, 1990 (Ont. H.C.J.) at p. 15, the court held:

> A solicitor who supports his client in a futile pursuit of his/her unrealistic ventures does not act responsible [*sic*]. If the solicitor advises the client in writing that he does not agree nor will he condone the pursuit of the hairbrain [*sic*] scheme on which the client embarks, he must disassociate himself from such undertaking.

[73] *Brumer v. Gunn* (1983), 18 Man. R. (2d) 155, [1983] 1 W.W.R. 424 (Q.B.).
[74] (1984), 34 R.P.R. 269 (Ont. H.C.).
[75] *Supra*, note 73. However, *Brock v. Gronbach*, [1953] 1 S.C.R. 207, [1953] 1 D.L.R. 785, appears to run contrary to this judgment.
[76] *Ferris v. Rusnak* (1983), 50 A.R. 297, 9 D.L.R. (4th) 183 (Q.B.).
[77] *Graybriar Industries Ltd. v. Davis & Company* (1990), 46 B.C.L.R. (2d) 164 at 181 (S.C.).
[78] [1985] 5 W.W.R. 411 (B.C.S.C.). The plaintiff attended the offices of the solicitor who obtained the signatures for the closing of a financing transaction. The solicitor required the investor to sign a receipt which acknowledged that:

though the solicitor attempted to avoid liability by requiring the investor to sign an acknowledgment that the solicitor did not offer any advice respecting the project!

Conversely, as in *Enola Apartments Ltd. v. Young*,[79] where the client has considerable sophistication and experience with investments and undertakes his own investigation of the investment properties, making only limited inquiries of his solicitor, there is no obligation on the solicitor to investigate or advise the client as to the value of the property. In this case, Reid J. stated that the result would have been different in these circumstances:

> If [the lawyer] were aware that the client were relying on him to advise on the value of the investment, that is to advise whether the investment was a prudent or imprudent one or a good or bad one, then that would, in my opinion, set up a duty in him without any explicit request from the client to consider the client's financial interest.[80]

Similarly, in a case where a lawyer who is consulted by experienced building contractors provides legally sound advice to terminate a contract with a troublesome subcontractor, the lawyer need not outline the financial risks entailed in such a course of action since these risks would be apparent to any experienced businessman in similar circumstances.[81]

In *Hallmark Financial Insurance Brokers Ltd. v. Fraser & Beatty*,[82] the solicitor prepared an agreement of purchase and sale based on a letter of intent which was negotiated by the parties to the transaction without the solicitor. The method of calculating the purchase price as drafted by the solicitor and contained in the agreement did not reflect the understanding of the parties as set out in the letter of intent. The solicitor was not negligent as the solicitor's interpre-

---

I HEREBY confirm and agree that with regard to the purchase of these shares [the solicitors] are acting as solicitors for the company only and have not offered me any advice other than as to the good standing of the Company and its capacity to issue the within shares, nor have I requested such advice. I am aware that any such advice should be sought from independent counsel.

The court held that the investor's reliance was foreseeable, that it should have been obvious that the plaintiff had no real understanding of the dangers involved and, notwithstanding the acknowledgment, that she was turning to the solicitor for reassurance. Given that there was no need for the solicitor to close a transaction of this sort with an inexperienced and unrepresented investor, the intent must have been to convey a misleading impression regarding the viability of the project. Thus, the solicitor had a duty to impress upon the investor in plain and unambiguous words that the solicitor could give no assurances with respect to the financial stability of the company.

[79] (1979), 30 R.P.R. 94 (Ont. H.C.).

[80] *Ibid.*, at 96.

[81] *R. & L. Contracting Ltd. v. A.* (1981), 28 B.C.L.R. 342 (C.A.). See also *Savonol Enterprises Ltd. v. Pollock* (1984), 30 Man. R. (2d) 27 (Q.B.).

[82] (1990), 1 O.R. (3d) 641 (Gen. Div.).

tation was not unreasonable; further, the clause in issue was found to be a business component of the transaction, as distinct from a legal provision in the agreement. The court further held that, because the clients were experienced businessmen, it was reasonable for the solicitor to assume the clients would review the important clauses of the agreement to ensure their instructions were being discharged. This decision has been severely criticized.[83]

Although a lawyer will not be negligent for bad judgment alone, she may be negligent for proffering bad advice. The lawyer, through experience and research, must be able to identify potential problem areas and advise clients of them. In one case, *285614 Alberta Ltd. v. Burnet, Duckworth & Palmer*[84] a solicitor believed a specific transaction fit within the provisios of the *Income Tax Act*[85] rules, but did no research on the subject and so failed to advise the clients that the law was unclear in this area. The lawyer was held negligent for his failure to advise the clients that the structure of the transaction may be invalid under the *Income Tax Act*:

> A reasonably competent corporate commercial lawyer, utilizing the relevant provisions of the *Income Tax Act* on a relatively frequent basis, should have been alert to the necessity to consider whether a demand note met the requirements of that section.[86]

When engaged in drafting the documents required for specific commercial transactions, the lawyer must be familiar with those statutes which affect such transactions. The court in *Elcano Acceptance Ltd. v. Richmond, Richmond, Stambler & Mills*[87] held that a reasonably competent solicitor undertaking to

---

[83] See M. Teplitsky, "Solicitors' Duty of Care in Carrying out Clients' Instructions: *Hallmark Financel Insurance Brokers Ltd. v. Fraser & Beatty*" (1993), 14 *Advocates' Q.* 111. Teplitsky notes that whether the solicitor's interpretation of the clause is unreasonable is irrelevant; the solicitor is not an arbitrator whose decisions can only be overturned if they are unreasonable. Rather, the solicitor had a duty to draft the agreement in accordance with the client's instructions. The real issue ought to have been whether a reasonably prudent lawyer would have noticed the ambiguity in the language and sought clarification from the client. Teplitsky further remarks that the assertion that the clause in issue was a business component as compared to a legal component of the transaction is without foundation. The solicitor was retained to draft a contract, and drafting is solicitors' work; it is irrelevant that the drafting involved a business issue. With respect to the comments made in *obiter*, that is, that the lawyer had the right to assume that the client would review the document and draw any errors to the lawyer's attention, Teplitsky observes that the responsibility for work should remain with the solicitor, and his responsibility should only be shifted with the client's consent.

[84] (1993), 8 Alta. L.R. (3d) 212 (Q.B.).

[85] S.C. 1970-71-72, c. 63.

[86] *285614 Alberta, supra,* note 83, at 220.

[87] (1989), 68 O.R. (2d) 165 (H.C.), supp. reasons 68 O.R. (2d) 641, affd 3 O.R. (S.C.) 123 (C.A.), with the court holding that the trial judge erred in two respects not relevant to this issue. The solicitor was negligent in failing to insert an annual interest rate in the promissory note as required by statute.

draft a promissory note should have known of and taken account of the requirements of the *Interest Act*.[88]

B. LOAN TRANSACTIONS

A lawyer acting for a client in a loan transaction is negligent if he fails to determine the existence of encumbrances on the proposed security,[89] if he fails
to properly draft the security documents or to provide for the usual security
devices,[90] or if he fails to advise that the structure of the transaction may render the security invalid.[91] In addition, he must ensure that his client understands the nature and effect of the transaction.[92] In a transaction to finance the
acquisition of a business, the solicitor for the lender must ensure that the
terms of the commitment letter and loan agreement are implemented unless
they are specifically instructed otherwise by the lender.[93]

A solicitor does not owe a duty to those on the other side of the loan transaction.[94] Understandably, as long as he otherwise fulfils his obligations a solicitor

---

[88]   R.S.C. 1970, c. I-18.

[89]   *Caligiuri v. De Lucia* (1983), 25 Man. R. (2d) 98 (Q.B.); *Burman's Beauty Supplies Ltd. v.
       Kempster* (1974), 4 O.R. (2d) 626, 48 D.L.R. (3d) 682 (Co. Ct.).

[90]   *Bjorninen v. Mercredi* (1983), 21 Man. R. (2d) 229, [1983] 4 W.W.R. 633 (Q.B.), varied 27
       Man. R. (2d) 67, [1984] 2 W.W.R. 646 (C.A.).

[91]   *Central Trust Co. v. Rafuse*, [1986] 2 S.C.R. 147, 75 N.S.R. (2d) 109.

[92]   *Caligiuri v. De Lucia, supra*, note 89.

[93]   *ABN Amro Bank Canada v. Gowling Strathy & Henderson* (1994), 20 O.R. (3d) 779 (Gen.
       Div.). In this case, the loan commitment letter and loan agreement to finance the acquisition of
       a lumber mill required that existing insurance policies be assigned to the borrower and that
       there be business interruption insurance in place on closing. The borrower did not produce evi-
       dence of business interruption insurance on closing and the solicitors closed without obtaining
       further instructions from the lender. Subsequently, the lumber mill was destroyed by fire and
       the solicitors were liable for the loss sustained by the lenders on the realization of its security.

[94]   The court in *Re Abacus Cities Ltd.* (1986), 39 C.C.L.T. 7 at 18 (Alta. Q.B.), affd 44 C.C.L.T.
       199 (Alta. C.A.) held:

       A solicitor owes a duty to his client, when that client is a creditor, to give advice to the cli-
       ent, as best he can and with care and prudence, with the object of furthering his client's in-
       terests against the client's debtor. If the solicitor were held to owe a duty to the debtor to
       use reasonable care in arriving at the solicitor's understanding of the law or the facts, and
       therefore in formulating the advice he gives his client as to what action should be taken to
       collect the debt or enforce the security, that duty would often impede the effective execu-
       tion of his duty to his client. To recognize that a solicitor could ever owe such a duty of
       care to his client's debtor would fetter the candour and vigour with which the solicitor
       should be encouraged to proffer advice to his client. To recognize the existence of such a
       duty would adversely affect the relationship between solicitor and client that is essential to
       the orderly regulation of rights and obligations between creditors and debtors. As a matter
       of policy no such duty of care should be recognized by our law.

       Similarly, in a normal conveyance, the vendor's solicitor does not owe a duty to the pur-
       chasers. The purchasers have a remedy against the vendor if there is a misrepresentation and

is not liable to his lender client for his failure to anticipate that the borrower is a rogue who will engage in criminal acts to defraud the client of money.[95]

C. INCORPORATING A COMPANY

It has been held that a solicitor retained to incorporate a company is negligent if she fails to file a list of the officers of the company and the required statutory report with the provincial company registration branch; if she fails to issue qualifying shares to the incorporating partners; or if she fails to advise the partners that if they do not hold shares their directorships will automatically expire after incorporation.[96] She will be liable for any expenses incurred in remedying the defects whether or not such remedial steps are successful.[97]

D. PURCHASE, SALE AND REORGANIZATION OF A BUSINESS

In *Enns v. Panju*,[98] the British Columbia Supreme Court held that a solicitor who, acting for a client in the purchase of a motel business, failed to include in the purchase agreement any representations or warranties as to the motel's financial viability either in the past or at the date of closing, was negligent even though the client had already executed an interim agreement with similar omissions. The court held that if a client expresses concern as to the company's financial condition, a lawyer must at least attempt to obtain the proper warranties and advise the client of the dangers of proceeding without them.

When acting for the vendor of a business, a solicitor must procure for the client adequate security for any unpaid balance of the purchase price.[99] He must also properly perfect any chattel mortgage, and advise the vendor that the registration of the mortgage must be renewed when it expires.[100] On closing, if the solicitor for the purchaser of a business undertakes to do the corporate work on

---

the vendor's solicitor will be liable to indemnify the client if the misrepresentation was due to negligence on the part of the solicitor. Of course, the solicitor owes a duty of care to the extent that the solicitor has stepped outside the role of solicitor for her client and accepts direct responsibility to the third party; *Gran Gelato Ltd. v. Richcliff (Group) Ltd.*, [1992] 1 All E.R. 865 (Ch.).

95 *Tiffin Holdings Ltd. v. Millican* (1964), 50 W.W.R. 673, 49 D.L.R. 92d) 216 (Alta. S.C.), revd 53 W.W.R 505, 53 D.L.R. (2d) 674 (C.A.), restd [1967] S.C.R. 183, 59 W.W.R 31. See also *Adams v. Mancuso* (1985), 34 A.C.W.S. 406 (Ont. H.C.). See also *De Yong v. Weeks* (1984), 55 A.R. 305, 33 Alta. L.R. (2d) 338 *sub nom. Deyong v. Weeks* (C.A.), leave to appeal to S.C.C. refused 58 A.R. 38*n*.

96 *MacCulloch v. Corbett* (1982), 49 N.S.R. (2d) 663, 133 D.L.R. (3d) 43 (C.A.).

97 *Ibid.* See also *P.A. Wournell Contr. Ltd. v. Allen* (1979), 34 N.S.R. (2d) 250, 100 D.L.R. (3d) 62 (S.C.), revd in part on other grounds 37 N.S.R. (2d) 125, 108 D.L.R. (3d) 723 (C.A.).

98 [1978] 5 W.W.R 244, 5 R.P.R. 248 (B.C.S.C.).

99 *Bjorninen v. Mercredi, supra*, note 90; *Gilkes v. Loucks* (1991), 79 Alta. L.R. (2d) 86 (C.A.); *Bru-Hill Ltd. v. House*, unreported, January 29, 1996, Metrvier J., Doc. 69136/92, [1996] O.J. No. 408 (Gen. Div.).

100 *Bru-Hill Ltd., supra*, note 99.

behalf of an unrepresented vendor and does not ensure that the vendor's name is removed as a director of the company, he will be liable for any director's liability incurred by the vendor subsequent to the sale.[101] With respect to the tax consequences of the sale of a business, the Nova Scotia Court of Appeal has held:

> In the ordinary case, a solicitor retained by a client who acts in the sale of the client's business, should be alert to, and give competent advice, with respect to the tax implications arising on the sale. If not knowledgable, he should advise his client to seek advice from one who possesses the expertise.[102]

A solicitor will be found liable if he permits a sale to proceed which contemplates the vendor relinquishing his right, without substitute security, to re-enter the premises being leased to the purchasers.[103] Similarly, in *Holt Holdings Ltd. v. Shumiatcher,*[104] the solicitor for the vendor of a business drafted an agreement for the sale of a business which assigned the lease of the business premises to the purchaser and provided that, in the event of default, the vendor could void the agreement and re-enter the premises. When the purchaser defaulted, the fact that the lease had been fully assigned prevented the vendor from re-entering the premises. Expert evidence indicated that the solicitor should have obtained a general security agreement on all the assets to be sold and should not have assigned the lease. It would have been more prudent to enter into a sub-lease with the purchaser, with a cross-default clause allowing the purchaser to re-enter in the event of a default. His handling of the transaction fell below the standard of a reasonably competent solicitor.

In *R.E.A.D. Enterprises Ltd. v. Picadilly Investments Ltd.,*[105] the vendor sold a hotel to the purchaser, who intended to demolish the building. The purchaser leased the hotel back to the vendor with the provision that it would give 30 days' notice of demolition so that the vendor could remove fixtures from the premises. Subsequently, the purchaser sold the property to a third party which gave the vendor notice to quit and prevented it from removing the fixtures. The court found the vendor's solicitor negligent for failing to advise the plaintiff that

---

[101] *Paton v. Shaw* (1995), 134 Nfld. & P.E.I.R. 271 (P.E.I.T.D.). The solicitor for the purchaser was liable to the third party vendor because the vendor justifiably relied on the solicitor's undertaking. For a more detailed discussion of solicitors' liability to unrepresented third parties, see Chapter 4, particularly Sections III. "Negligence", A. "Reasonable Reliance on Special Skill", 1. " General Principles" and 2. "The Unrepresented Third Party".

[102] *Silver v. Morris* (1995), 139 N.S.R. (2d) 18 at 22 (C.A.). However, in this case, the solicitor was not liable for failing to advise his client to transfer all or substantially all of her proprietorship assets to a corporation and then sell its shares in order to qualify for a capital gains exemption on the proceeds because the solicitor had warned the client that he had no tax law expertise. Moreover, the client herself was knowledgable about tax issues (the business she sold was an H & R Block franchise) and had access to specialized tax advice.

[103] *Loubardeaus v. W.* (1984), 33 Sask. R. 26 (Q.B.).

[104] (1993), 117 Sask. R. 120 (Q.B.), affd (1995), 134 Sask. R. 311 (C.A.).

[105] Unreported, July 31, 1997, Errico J., Doc. Vancouver C950415, [1997] B.C.J. No. 1806 (S.C.).

the purchase agreement did not provide that the lease could only be terminated on the demolition of the building, to ensure that the lease and the purchase agreement were consistent and to consider and advise the vendor of the effect of a sale of the property to a third party. In *Couture v. Lamontagne*,[106] a lawyer was also found negligent for failing to explain the risks of signing a personal guarantee of a loan for the purchase of a hotel and releasing some of the client's funds to the vendors before the guarantees were signed.

In *MacDonald v. Lockhart*,[107] a solicitor retained to structure the reorganization of his client's business, requiring both legal and financial advice, was successful in defending an action for negligence on the basis that, although his reorganization report lacked some accounting details, his basic recommendations were sound.

In *Hallmark Financial Insurance Brokers Ltd. v. Fraser & Beatty*,[108] a solicitor successfully defended an action for negligence on the basis that the clause which the clients claimed was negligently drafted was, in fact, a business component of the transaction, as distinct from a legal provision in the agreement. The solicitor's interpretation of the clients' wishes with respect to this clause was reasonable, and, given the sophistication of the clients, it was reasonable for the solicitor to assume that the clients would review the clause to ensure it reflected their intent.

E. ACTING FOR MORE THAN ONE PARTY

In addition to his fiduciary obligations,[109] a solicitor who acts for more than one party in a commercial transaction runs a greater risk of being held negligent. This problem is discussed in Section IV. "Real Estate Transactions", D. "Acting for More Than One Party" of this chapter.

IV. REAL ESTATE TRANSACTIONS

A. ACTING FOR A PURCHASER

A lawyer retained to act on a client's behalf in connection with the purchase of real estate is obliged to conduct a title search, even if not specifically instructed to do so, unless there is a clear understanding or there are instructions to the contrary.[110] A solicitor who discovers a title defect is negligent if she does not

---

[106] [1997] 5 W.W.R. 23 (Sask. Q.B.).

[107] (1980), 42 N.S.R. (2d) 29, 118 D.L.R. (3d) 397 (C.A.), varied 44 N.S.R. (2d) 261 (C.A.), leave to appeal to S.C.C. refused 118 D.L.R. (3d) 397*n*.

[108] (1990), 1 O.R. (3d) 641 (Gen. Div.).

[109] See Chapter 4.

[110] *Knox v. Veinote* (1982), 54 N.S.R. (2d) 666 (S.C.). See also *Jansons v. Iwanczuk* (1991), 17 R.P.R. (2d) 308 (Ont. Gen. Div). Ontario's *Registry Act*, R.S.O. 1990, c. R.20, s. 112, makes it

bring it to the purchaser's attention and provide a formal report or opinion on
title. [111] However, she is not negligent if she simply fails to research a title back
to a good root so as to avoid repeating, at unnecessary cost to the client, work
already done.[112] The proper drafting of a legal description of the property and
advising a client of the obligation to object to title defects within the time required by the agreement of purchase and sale are also routine matters and if they
are not done and damages are suffered as a result, liability will attach.[113]

Of course, a real estate lawyer has a duty to explain the meaning of legal
documents to the client[114] and will be liable, for instance, where she fails to advise and warn a purchaser about the conditions and material terms in the agreement of purchase and sale.[115]

In addition, a real estate solicitor will be liable if she fails to: obtain, in writing,
warranties orally agreed by the vendor;[116] point out to the purchaser the necessity
of obtaining fire insurance and the formalities required to transfer a fire insurance
policy;[117] ascertain whether a condition inserted in the agreement of purchase and
sale for the benefit of the purchaser has been fulfilled;[118] search relevant municipal
by-laws;[119] inform the purchaser of a registered right of way over the land;[120] properly requisition executions;[121] warn the purchaser of the risk of paying the purchase
proceeds to the vendor while undischarged mortgages remain registered on title;[122]

---

clear that there is no need to go beyond a 40-year search period unless there has been no conveyance within the 40-year period. See *Fire v. Longtin* (1994), 17 O.R. (3d) 418 (C.A.).

[111] *Spencer v. King* (1990), 111 N.B.R. (2d) 154 (Q.B.), affd (1991), 119 N.B.R. (2d) 358 (C.A.).

[112] *Smaldon v. Lawrence* (1983), 31 R.P.R. 126 (Ont. Co. Ct.).

[113] *Knox v. Veinote, supra*, note 110; *Mini-Mansion Const. Co. v. Agnew* (1983), 24 Sask. R. 1
(Q.B.), affd 38 Sask. R. 100 (C.A.).

[114] *Kragh-Hansen v. Kin-Com Const. & Devs. Ltd.* (1979), 13 R.P.R. 22 (B.C.S.C.).

[115] *Bowers v. Dives* (1980), 21 A.R. 318 (N.W.T.S.C.) (failure to warn of condition making completion dependent on client's ability to obtain financing).

[116] *Tooton v. Atkinson* (1985), 52 Nfld. & P.E.I.R. 167 (Nfld. Dist. Ct.).

[117] *Stronghold Invts. Ltd. v. Renkema* (1984), 51 B.C.L.R. 189, 7 D.L.R. (4th) 427 (S.C.).

[118] *Ingwerson v. Dykstra* (1983), 50 B.C.L.R. 88, 4 D.L.R. (4th) 355 (S.C.).

[119] *Ekkebus v. Lauinger* (1990), 73 O.R. (2d) 743 (H.C.). The solicitor should have searched municipal by-laws regarding hot tub requirements, however he would only have been liable for
remedying any defect, such as the cost of a new fence. The court did not address the question of
failing to advise the client to obtain a new survey. On the facts of this case, the solicitor was not
negligent as no duty was owed to the plaintiff (a child who fell into the hot tub and was injured), as the injuries to the child were not foreseeable when the contract for services in connection with the matter was entered into.

[120] *Moorcroft v. Doraty & Kebe* (1990), 71 O.R. (2d) 470 (H.C.), supp. reasons 72 O.R. (2d) 320
(H.C.). This decision was criticized in N.M. Fera, "Solicitor's Negligence: An Essay on the
Moorcroft Decision" (1991), 23 *Ottawa L. Rev.* 319. Fera argues that it is contrary to the decision in *Blinkhorn v. Ainsworth* (1985), 54 O.R. (2d) 182 (C.A.), in which it is implicitly held
that the solicitor for a purchaser will not be liable for failing to search for rights of way under
an agreement excluding them from good title.

[121] *Silva v. Atkins* (1978), 20 O.R. (2d) 570, 4 B.L.R. 209 (H.C.).

[122] *Neagle v. Power*, [1967] S.A.S.R. 373; *Grover Holdings Ltd. v. Weir* (1987), 54 Sask. R. 68, 44
R.P.R. 64 (Q.B.), is a more recent example of liability attaching to a failure to warn a purchaser
of the inadequacy of its security.

prepare mortgage documents in time, thereby endangering the transaction;[123] question the absence of a party's signature on an amendment to the terms of an agreement of purchase and sale;[124] advise the purchaser of an outstanding tile drain loan if it is an encumbrance against the property;[125] or ascertain the lawfully recoverable rent of an income-producing property.[126]

The solicitor for the purchaser of a rental property will also be negligent if she fails to review the leases, or ensure that there is sufficient security for a rental income warranty.[127]

The obligations of a solicitor concerning surveys and problems arising from the physical condition of the property appear to be evolving and, therefore, cannot be precisely catalogued. To some extent these obligations are determined on the basis of the solicitor's knowledge of the property in question and his ability to make an effective examination of its physical condition.[128] In one of the first cases to consider the issue, *Winrob v. Street & Wollen*,[129] the solicitor failed to review the plan filed in the Registry Office in order to establish the dimensions of the property to be purchased. After closing it was discovered that part of the lot the plaintiffs thought they were buying was actually owned by the municipality and formed part of a street. The court nevertheless dismissed the clients' claim against the solicitor on the basis that the solicitor was not obliged to ascertain and advise on the dimensions of the lot, there being no specific instructions respecting size. The court took the position that the defendant solicitors were not engineers or surveyors and did not consider whether they nonetheless had an obligation to advise the plaintiffs of the risks of proceeding without a survey. Likewise, the defendant solicitor in *Shaak v. McIntyre*[130] was found to have reviewed with the plaintiff purchasers a site survey that revealed that her house encroached on her neighbour's land. However, the court held that he would not have been liable to the plaintiff in negligence in any event because she had pre-

---

[123] *Lawrie v. Gentry Developments Inc.* (1989), 72 O.R. (2d) 512 (H.C.).

[124] *Kwok v. Griffiths*, unreported, January 19, 1996, Henderson J., Doc. Vancouver C936487, [1996] B.C.J. No. 84 (S.C.). A notary public who did not question the absence of the vendor's signature on an agreement to extend the closing date was liable for damages sustained by the purchaser when the notary public was not prepared to close on the original date and the vendors would not agree to an extension.

[125] *Smith v. Heimbecker*, unreported, November 5, 1990, McGarry J., Doc. 70/89, [1990] O.J. No. 2115 (Gen. Div.). Under Ontario's *Tile Drainage Act*, R.S.O. 1990, c. T.8, loans were encumbrances against the property and should be paid by the vendor on closing if the agreement of purchase and sale provides for unencumbered transfers of title.

[126] *Goody v. Baring*, [1956] 2 All E.R. 11, [1956] 1 W.L.R. 448 (Ch.); *669283 Ontario Ltd. v. Reilly*, unreported, January 22, 1996, Herold J., Doc. 3670/92, [1996] O.J. No. 273 (Gen. Div.); *Wong v. 407527 Ontario Ltd.* (1996), 1 R.P.R. (3d) 245 (Ont. Gen. Div.).

[127] *Wong, supra*, note 126.

[128] J. Swan and B.J. Reiter, "Solicitors' Responsibilities in Real Estate Transactions" (1979), 8 R.P.R. 155 at 174.

[129] (1959), 28 W.W.R. 118, 19 D.L.R. (2d) 172 (B.C.S.C.).

[130] Unreported, September 6, 1991, Ryan J., Doc. Vancouver A852424, [1991] B.C.J. No. 2607 (S.C.).

sented him with a concluded, unconditional agreement of purchase and sale. All that was required of the solicitor was that he take whatever steps were necessary to transfer title.

In *Brenner v. Gregory*,[131] the court accepted the proposition that the failure of a purchaser's solicitor to obtain a survey could constitute negligence in the appropriate circumstances. However, the court found that because the defendant solicitor knew the plaintiffs had seen the property numerous times before purchasing it and because they knew there was some question as to the location of the building on the property, the solicitor was not liable when it was determined that the building encroached on an adjoining property. In *Smith v. Wilf Vezeau Real Estate Ltd.*,[132] a solicitor was also not liable to a purchaser who thought he purchased a particular lot, but in fact bought one with identical dimensions two lots away. The purchaser had reviewed the survey extensively and repeatedly assured the solicitor that he understood the transaction.

It has been held in *Ravina v. Kanigsman, Cordon, Stern & Freeman*[133] that a lawyer certifying title for a purchaser must advise the purchaser to obtain a survey or a building location certificate and advise of the risks he runs if he fails to do so. The defendant firm had acted on the purchase of a building that turned out to be partly located on lands owned by the Canadian National Railway. Although the title search gave no indication of the railway's encroachment, Chief Justice Clark of the Nova Scotia Supreme Court Appellate Division said: "An objective assessment of the title information [available to the firm] should have raised some question . . . whether there was enough land to meet the description."[134] This, the court reasoned, indicated the need for a survey to clarify the situation.

Moreover, it is clear that a lawyer is negligent if he fails to inquire into problems raised by a survey.[135]

A solicitor has an obligation to check for outstanding work orders under the applicable municipal by-laws,[136] although her obligation to ensure compliance

---

[131] [1973] 1 O.R. 252, 30 D.L.R. (3d) 672 (H.C.).

[132] Unreported, December 27, 1991, Sheppard J., Doc. 1617, [1991] O.J. No. 2532 (Gen. Div.).

[133] (1987), 77 N.S.R. (2d) 406 (C.A.).

[134] *Ibid.*, at 411. See also *Aaroe v. Seymour*, [1956] O.R. 736, 6 D.L.R. (2d) 100 (H.C.), affd on other grounds 7 D.L.R. (2d) 676 (C.A.) (failure to obtain a survey to determine the location of an easement when Registry Office records raised a real doubt as to its location constitutes negligence); *Dreisorner v. Romney* (1986), 73 N.S.R. (2d) 123 (S.C.) (failure to insist on a survey or point out the risks of proceeding without one is negligence); *Marwood v. Charter Credit Corp.* (1971), 2 N.S.R. (2d) 743, 20 D.L.R. (3d) 563 (C.A.).

[135] *Nielsen v. Watson* (1981), 33 O.R. (2d) 515, 125 D.L.R. (3d) 326 (H.C.).

[136] *Kolan v. Solicitor*, [1970] 1 O.R. 41, 7 D.L.R. (3d) 481 (H.C.), affd [1970] 2 O.R. 686, 11 D.L.R. (3d) 672 (C.A.); *Campbell & Campbell v. Delrue & Delrue*, unreported, February 15, 1985 (Ont. H.C.); Swan and Reiter, *supra*, note 128, at 179. See also *Ahuntsic Investments Inc. v. Cheng* (1992), 28 R.P.R. (2d) 16 (Ont. Gen. Div), affd (1994), 39 R.P.R. (2d) 38 (Ont. C.A.), where an order of an inspector regarding compliance with a by-law was a work order and did not go to the root of title. Thus, any objections must be made within any agreed time limits.

with zoning by-laws is less clear. Certainly, where the solicitor specifically undertakes the responsibility to check that the purchaser's proposed use complies with zoning restrictions, she is negligent if she fails to do so.[137] In *Redmond v. Desmore*,[138] the Newfoundland Court of Appeal found a solicitor liable for failing to ensure that zoning was consistent with the use to which the purchaser wished to put the property. The subject property was zoned for a single-family dwelling but was listed as having two apartments in addition to the main living quarters. The real estate agent informed the purchaser that the apartments were not registered but negligently misrepresented that they could be registered with certain upgrades. Because the negligent misrepresentation entitled the purchaser to void the sale, the solicitor was liable for failing to discover the zoning restrictions.

However, in the absence of specific instructions, where the solicitor is consulted after the agreement of purchase and sale has been signed and the purchaser is not entitled to void the sale for any reason, the purchaser may have no recourse against his solicitor for failure to advise of zoning problems.[139] A lawyer who is retained by a purchaser after she has waived a zoning condition is entitled to assume that she satisfied herself on the issue and is not required to conduct any further enquiries.[140] The failure to make enquiries about unlevied local improvement changes (that is, where the local improvement is proposed but has not yet been constructed, or has been constructed but not yet levied) is not negligence.[141] Unless a solicitor is warned of a potential problem with a septic tank approval, he is under no obligation to review the certificate with the purchasers.[142]

Finally, the purchaser's lawyer must explain the risks of closing a transaction in escrow and take all possible steps to minimize those risks. She will be found negligent if she permits a real estate transaction to close in escrow without ob-

---

[137] *Fohrenkamm v. Plaxton*, [1973] 2 O.R. 518, 34 D.L.R. (3d) 470 (H.C.).

[138] (1997), 153 Nfld. & P.E.I.R. 181 (Nfld. C.A.).

[139] *Hauck v. Dixon* (1975), 10 O.R. (2d) 605, 64 D.L.R. (3d) 201 (H.C.). However, Swan and Reiter, *supra*, note 128, at 172-73, conclude that the result in this case may be based on an overly narrow view of the purchaser's rights in a real estate transaction. See also *Victoria & Grey Trust Co. v. Apple* (1984), 32 R.P.R. 230, 25 M.P.L.R. 220 (Ont. H.C.), in which the solicitor for the mortgagee was held liable for failing to ensure zoning by-law compliance because the mortgagee's commitment letter specifically required such compliance. The obligations of solicitors and municipalities regarding zoning by-laws and work orders are discussed in M.J. Winer and S.L. Ungar, "Investigating Zoning By-laws and Work Orders — Who is the Lawyer Anyhow? — *Victoria & Grey Trust Co. v. Apple et al; Corp. of City of Toronto (third party)*" in (1985), 5 *Advocates Q.* 506.

[140] *Kotowich v. Petursson* (1994), 91 Man. R. (2d) 160 (Q.B.).

[141] *Pirko v. Magder*, unreported, Doc. 1218/94, June 8, 1995 (Ont. Gen. Div.).

[142] *Green v. Dixon*, unreported, March 24, 1995, Tobias J., Docs. G8581, G8581A, [1995] O.J. No. 834 (Prov. Div.).

taining a deed and other closing documents. In addition, a solicitor should advise the purchaser of the risk of renovating a property prior to final closing.[143]

B. ACTING FOR A VENDOR

Solicitors acting for vendors in real estate transactions have been held negligent in the following circumstances: where the solicitor neglected to tell his client that the offer to purchase did not include assumption of the existing mortgage, one of the client's requirements of sale;[144] for failing to advise a client who held a vendor's lien on certain property of the risks involved in allowing a dwelling on the property to be demolished;[145] where the solicitor failed to set limits for a first mortgage when the second mortgage was to be held by his client in partial payment of the purchase price;[146] for failing to secure for the vendor a release of a second mortgage upon sale of the property;[147] where the solicitor inadvertently failed to deliver a notice pursuant to a condition in the agreement of purchase and sale extending the closing date as instructed;[148] for failing to obtain a release of the vendor's personal guarantee of a mortgage on the property;[149] and, where the agreement of purchase and sale was conditional on the vendor obtaining severance approval, for representing that final severance approval had been obtained when in fact it was conditional.[150]

In instances where the purchasers repudiate a real estate transaction, the vendor's solicitor is not negligent if, on his clients' instructions, he acts to reinstate the transaction but fails, particularly where failure is in part due to the intransigence of his client.[151] The solicitor for the vendor is not required to obtain an indemnification or assumption agreement from the purchaser named in the agreement of purchase and sale in respect of a mortgage where the purchaser directs that title be taken in the name of a third party on closing.[152] A solicitor must always obtain his client's approval to postpone closing.[153]

---

[143] *Palmeri v. Di Poce*, unreported, Doc. 43942/890, April 26, 1993 (Ont. Gen. Div.), affd unreported, March 19, 1998, Doc. C15445, [1998] O.J. No. 1164 (C.A.).

[144] *McMorran's Cordova Bay Ltd. v. Harman & Co.* (1980), 17 B.C.L.R. 173, [1980] 2 W.W.R. 499 (C.A.).

[145] *Major v. Buchanan* (1975), 9 O.R. (2d) 491, 61 D.L.R. (3d) 46 (H.C.).

[146] *Meadwell Enterprises Ltd. v. Clay & Co.* (1983), 44 B.C.L.R. 188, [1983] 3 W.W.R. 742 (S.C.).

[147] *Bossee v. Clavette* (1984), 56 N.B.R. (2d) 375 (C.A.).

[148] *835039 Ontario Inc. v. Fram Development Corp.*, unreported, August 9, 1994, Trafford J., Doc. 53207/90, [1994] O.J. No. 1725 (Gen. Div.).

[149] *Healey v. Kennedy* (1991), 93 Nfld. & P.E.I.R. 115 (Nfld. C.A.).

[150] *Jaouen-Malgorn v. Irani*, unreported, February 12, 1996, Sedgwick J., Doc. 7378/87A, [1996] O.J. No. 520 (Gen. Div.).

[151] *Hutzkal v. B.*, [1974] 6 W.W.R. 607 (Alta. S.C.).

[152] *DaCosta v. Maksymiw*, unreported, November 5, 1991, Montgomery J., Doc. 370751/89, [1991] O.J. No. 1943 (Gen. Div.), affd [1998] O.J. No. 4 (C.A.).

[153] *Jaouen-Malgorn v. Irani, supra*, note 150.

C. ACTING FOR A MORTGAGEE

The obligations of a lawyer acting for a mortgagee in a real estate transaction are analogous to those of a lawyer acting for a purchaser. A mortgagee's lawyer is negligent if she drafts a mortgage containing an incorrect legal description of the mortgaged property;[154] if she fails to ensure that the mortgage is duly registered;[155] if she fails to register mortgage discharges as soon as she gets them;[156] if she fails to ensure that both owners of the property sign the mortgage as mortgagors;[157] if she fails to explain the mortgage transaction to an unsophisticated mortgagor;[158] if she fails to obtain a first mortgage for her clients, as instructed;[159] if she fails to obtain two individual mortgages on different portions of land that would be separately enforceable, as instructed;[160] if she fails to obtain a postponement of a prior mortgage as instructed;[161] if she relies on an oral agreement to postpone and disburses the replacement mortgage funds without obtaining a written postponement;[162] if she fails to vacate or postpone liens before advancing funds under the mortgage;[163] and for failing to advise that the effective rate of interest on the mortgage may amount to a criminal rate.[164]

The solicitor for a mortgagee is also negligent if she fails to advise her client to obtain a survey or location certificate where a building or proposed building

---

[154] *Bank of Montreal v. Chedore* (1985), 63 N.B.R. (2d) 361 (Q.B.), affd 76 N.B.R. (2d) 99, 34 D.L.R. (4th) 177 (C.A.).

[155] *Marko v. P.* (1980), 18 B.C.L.R. 263, [1980] 3 W.W.R. 565 *sub nom. Marko v. Perry* (Co. Ct.); *Laiman v. Orzech*, unreported, December 13, 1993, Mandel J., Docs. 92-CQ-29257, 92-CQ-29257A, 92-CQ-31250CM, [1993] O.J. No. 2996 (Gen. Div.), affd unreported, December 5, 1996, Doc. C17514, [1996] O.J. No. 4290 (C.A.).

[156] *Penava v. MacIntyre*, unreported, June 14, 1989 (Ont H.C.J.)

[157] *Canada Permanent Trust Co. v. Letcher* (1980), 30 N.B.R. (2d) 55 (Q.B.), revd in part 35 N.B.R. (2d) 630 (C.A.), leave to appeal to S.C.C. refused 36 N.B.R. (2d) 180n. See also *Shute v. Premier Trust Co.* (1993), 35 R.P.R. (2d) 141 (Ont. Gen. Div.), where the solicitor ostensibly acted for Premier Trust Co., the husband and the wife, yet the solicitor did not meet nor did he speak with the husband. The solicitor delivered mortgage documents to the wife out of his control for transmittal to Morocco for execution by the husband. The solicitor made no effort to contact the husband, made no enquiries as to when the husband would return, nor did he at any time make enquiries as to whether he could confirm the husband's signatures and understanding of the documents.

[158] *Premier Trust Co. v. Beaton* (1990), 1 O.R. (3d) 38 (Gen. Div.).

[159] The solicitor was aware at all material times of judgments outstanding on the property. It is not open to the solicitor to act for a client yet fail to advise them of potential problems with respect to outstanding judgments. *Granville Savings & Mortgage Corp. v. Slevin*, [1993] 4 S.C.R. 279.

[160] *Woodglen & Co. v. Owens, Wright* (1996), 6 R.P.R. (3d) 259 (Gen. Div.), supp reasons February 24, 1997 and May 28, 1997 (Ont. Gen. Div.).

[161] *Federal Business Development Bank v. Royal Bank of Canada* (1985), 67 N.S.R. (2d) 18, 28 B.L.R. 279 (S.C.).

[162] *Federal Savings Credit Union Ltd. v. Hessian* (1979), 36 N.S.R. (2d) 166, 8 R.P.R. 32 (S.C.).

[163] *Ron Miller Realty Ltd. v. Honeywell* (1991), 4 O.R. (3d) 492 (Gen. Div.) revd as to quantum of damages (1993), 16 O.R. (3d) 255n (C.A.).

[164] *Barrie v. 687844 Ontario Ltd.* (1994), 43 R.P.R. (2d) 267 (Gen. Div.).

forms part of the mortgagee's security.[165] Courts have determined that a solicitor is not negligent for failing to enquire into zoning or work orders[166] or to inform the mortgagee of restrictive covenants and easements[167] provided that she is acting pursuant to a limited retainer. However, more recently, in *Canada Trustco Mortgage Co. v. Bartlet & Richardes*,[168] the Ontario Court of Appeal held that a solicitor may be required to disclose zoning restrictions of which she is aware, regardless of whether she is acting pursuant to a limited retainer.

A solicitor's obligation to advise a mortgagee on the adequacy of the proposed security, a matter involving both business and legal considerations, depends on the sophistication of the mortgagee, the nature of the retainer, the solicitor's knowledge of the property to be mortgaged, and the mortgagor's financial position. Thus, when acting for an unsophisticated mortgagee, a lawyer is negligent if she fails to advise her client that a recent sale price of the property is less than the mortgage moneys being advanced, that a first mortgage is in arrears, and that the borrower is prepared to pay a higher rate of interest.[169] Conversely, it has been held that a solicitor who acts for an experienced mortgagee in placing a second mortgage has no obligation to report on the standing of the first mortgage unless express instructions are given to do so, although she is negligent if she fails to enquire as to the status of corporation taxes.[170]

Whatever the mortgagee's sophistication, the mortgagee's lawyer will be adjudged negligent and in breach of his fiduciary duty if he fails to pass on information within his possession regarding the security, which may influence the mortgagee's decision to proceed with the transaction,[171] such as his awareness that an annexation order affecting the property is under appeal or that the property had been purchased by the current vendor three years previously for less

---

[165] *Financeamerica Realty Ltd. v. Gillies* (1983), 40 Nfld. & P.E.I.R. 169 (Nfld. C.A.).

[166] *Hilloak Finance Services Ltd. v. Pichelli*, unreported, June 21, 1989, Fitzpatrick J., Doc. 913/85, [1989] O.J. No. 2560 (Ont. S.C.).

[167] *Cox v. Pemberton Holmes Ltd.* (1991), 53 B.C.L.R. (2d) 92 (S.C.), supp. reasons 55 B.C.L.R. (2d) 118 (S.C.), revd on other grounds 80 B.C.L.R. (2d) 331 (C.A.); the disclosure of restrictive covenants and easements was not "naturally incidental" to the retainer.

[168] (1996), 28 O.R. (3d) 768 (C.A.).

[169] *Lapierre v. Young* (1980), 30 O.R. (2d) 319, 117 D.L.R. (3d) 643 (H.C.).

[170] *Abbey Discount Corp. v. Nicol*, [1972] 3 O.R. 360, 28 D.L.R. (3d) 268 (H.C.). The case of *Income Trust Co. v. Watson* (1984), 26 B.L.R. 228, 35 R.P.R. 71 (Ont. H.C.), upheld on an unrelated point February 14, 1986 (unreported), appears to be inconsistent with the principle that experienced mortgagees are ordinarily required to make their own enquiries as to the prudence of an investment. In this case, a solicitor acting for a sophisticated mortgagee was found negligent in advancing mortgage funds for a residential subdivision development prior to its registration because he failed to warn the client of the increased risk of advancing on an unregistered subdivision. As the annotation to the case points out, this result is difficult to justify since these risks would have been known to an experienced client.

[171] See *Carolfsky v. McGuire* (1979), 28 Chitty's L.J. 225 (Ont. H.C.). The fiduciary obligations of a solicitor in this situation are discussed in Chapter 3, Section III. "Fiduciary Obligations Defined", B. "Acting for More Than One Party".

than half of the proposed mortgage advance.[172] And where the solicitor for a mortgagee is specifically instructed to confirm the sale price of the property that is to be subject to the mortgage as well as the *bona fides* of the sale, he is negligent if he relies on a copy of the statement of adjustments and nothing more.[173]

When a solicitor deals with a mortgage broker representing various investors, he is not obliged to advise the investors personally on the proposed transaction but is entitled to rely on the broker to pass on his advice.[174]

In foreclosure proceedings, an ordinarily prudent solicitor would consider whether commission is payable to a listing agent before approving a draft consent order providing for payment of such a commission. It constitutes further negligence if the solicitor fails to take effective steps to set aside such a payment provision once it is discovered that commission is not payable.[175]

D. ACTING FOR MORE THAN ONE PARTY

In many cases, a real estate lawyer will be held liable for malpractice in circumstances in which she agrees to act for more than one party in the transaction — for example, purchaser and vendor, mortgagor and mortgagee. The lawyer will be in breach of her fiduciary duties if she fails to disclose that she is working for more than one party.[176] A lawyer may be negligent if she represents both sides of a transaction without advising one party to obtain independent legal advice.[177] If the solicitor also has a personal interest in the transaction, her obligation is more clearly defined: she must require one party to obtain independent legal advice.[178]

In acting for more than one party to a transaction, she is more likely to come into possession of information that may affect the decision of one of the parties to proceed with the transaction and will be found negligent and in breach of fiduciary duty if she fails to disclose it.[179] For example, in *Panko v.*

---

[172] *Greenglass v. Rusonik; Rusonik v. Conder* (1981), 21 R.P.R. 264 (Ont. H.C.), affd unreported, March 18, 1983 (Ont. C.A.).

[173] *Wynston v. MacDonald* (1979), 27 O.R. (2d) 67, 105 D.L.R. (3d) 527 (H.C.), affd 32 O.R. (2d) 108, 119 D.L.R. (3d) 256 (C.A.).

[174] *Sinclair v. Smith* (1982), 41 B.C.L.R. 374 (S.C.).

[175] *Mayo Holdings Ltd. v. Cunliffe* (1989), 41 B.C.L.R. (2d) 94 (C.A.).

[176] *Canson Enterprises Ltd. v. Boughton & Co.*, [1991] 3 S.C.R. 534; *Confederation Life Insurance Co. v. Shepherd, McKenzie, Plaxton, Little & Jenkins* (1992), 29 R.P.R. (2d) 271 (Ont. Gen. Div.); *Skimming v. Goldberg* (1993), 89 Man. R. (2d) 27 (Q.B.).

[177] For an example of a case where a solicitor acting for multiple parties to a loan avoided liability by referring them to independent legal advice when a conflict arose, see *470301 Alberta Ltd. v. Johnston* (1995), 31 Alta. L.R. (3d) 59 (Q.B.).

[178] *Harris v. First Western Properties Inc.*, unreported, June 20, 1995, Caswell J., Docs. C716/90, 21170/91U, [1995] O.J. No. 2190 (Gen. Div.).

[179] *Greenglass v. Rusonik; Rusonik v. Conder, supra*, note 171; *Carlofsky v. McGuire, supra*, note 171. In *Commerce Capital Trust Co. v. Berk* (1989), 68 O.R. (2d) 257 (C.A.), the solicitors (acting for both mortgagor and mortgagee) breached their fiduciary duty in failing to disclose to the mortgagee material facts regarding the transaction. The facts were material, not because the

Simmonds,[180] a solicitor acted for an elderly woman and her son-in-law in the transfer of the woman's property to the son-in-law and his wife. The woman believed she was merely helping them to arrange a small loan. The solicitor was held liable when his client, the mother, was defrauded by her daughter and son-in-law. The solicitor had failed to alert her to the possibility that she was either doing something against her best interests or at risk of being defrauded by her son-in-law and daughter. Similarly, in *Recha v. Yeamans*, [181] a lawyer who acted for both parties to an agreement of purchase and sale breached his fiduciary duty to the purchaser for failing to disclose that the purchase price was higher than both the price paid by the vendors and an appraisal of the property. The defendant lawyer in *Reisig v. Ross*,[182] who had acted for both parties in the preparation of a sub-lease, was found negligent for failing to define clearly the position of each party.[183] In *Szelazek v. Orzech*,[184] the lawyer acting for both parties to mortgages was found negligent for failing to advise the mortgagee of power of sale proceedings affecting one of the properties.

Typically, real estate lawyers are retained by spouses to effect a transfer, purchase or sale of property. In these cases, they must consider whether a conflict of interest arises and, if so, advise one of the spouses to obtain independent legal advice. In *Dwyer v. Spry*,[185] the plaintiff and her common law spouse accepted the defendant's advice to purchase a property in the man's name only. The defendant's partner subsequently registered a mortgage against the property without the plaintiff's knowledge or consent. When the plaintiff's spouse disappeared and foreclosure proceedings were threatened, the plaintiff sold the property at a loss. The court held that the defendant firm had breached its duty to the plaintiff in, *inter alia*, failing to advise her of the risks involved in putting the property in the name of her spouse and in failing to advise her to seek independent legal advice.[186]

---

transaction would not have proceeded had the facts been known, but because those facts would have been important in deciding whether to approve the loan. To avoid liability the solicitors would have had to demonstrate that the mortgagee would have proceeded with the loan if disclosure had been made. See also Chapter 3, Section III. "Fiduciary Obligation Defined", A. "Duty of Loyalty", 1. "Self Interest".

[180] (1983), 42 B.C.L.R. 50, [1983] 3 W.W.R 158 (S.C.).

[181] *Recha v. Yeamans* (1993), 135 N.B.R. (2d) 360 (C.A.). The solicitor also breached his fiduciary obligation to the purchaser by failing to disclose his personal interest in the transaction. He had previously guaranteed a loan to the vendors in relation to the refinancing of the property. The guarantee was to be discharged on the sale.

[182] (1984), 52 B.C.L.R. 183 (S.C.).

[183] See also *Bonneville v. Temelini & Zito* (1981), 21 R.P.R. 206 (Ont. H.C.) (solicitor, acting for both parties to a mortgage, was liable for negligently misrepresenting terms upon which the mortgage could be discharged).

[184] (1997), 23 O.T.C. 53 (Gen. Div.).

[185] (1981), 27 B.C.L.R. 253 (S.C.).

[186] See also *Ruxton v. Kelly, Peters & Associates Ltd.* (1985), 58 B.C.L.R. 317, [1985] 1 W.W.R. 66 (S.C.).

A solicitor acting for both parties to a mortgage transaction may have an obligation to verify the mortgagee's signature on the mortgage documents. In *Shute v. Premier Trust Co.*,[187] the defendant solicitor represented both the mortgagee and the mortgagor in respect of a mortgage on a matrimonial home. The court held that the mortgage was void because the wife had forged the husband's signature on the document and refused to find that an equitable mortgage arose on the facts. Because the solicitor never met or spoke with the husband at any time, he was liable in negligence to the mortgagor for the unsecured amount:

> I find there was a duty on a careful and prudent solicitor, in 1988, to ensure that the mortgage documents were properly executed by the mortgagors. [The solicitor] delivered the documents to [the wife] out of his control for transmittal to Morocco for execution by [the husband]. He took no steps to contact [the husband] in Morocco, nor did he make any inquiries to ascertain if he could speak to [the husband]. . . . He made no inquiries as to when [the husband] would return from Morocco, or whether he could confirm his signatures and understanding of the documents at any time. . . .
>
> Under these circumstances, I find that his professional dealings on this mortgage transaction fell below the standard required.[188]

A solicitor acting for both parties to a mortgage is negligent if the mortgage is signed by someone impersonating the mortgagee and the solicitor did not ask the imposter for identification before she signed.[189]

E. LEASEHOLDS

When retained by a lessee or sub-lessee, lawyers have been held negligent for failing to register the lease or sub-lease where registration is necessary to secure the tenancy;[190] for failing to examine the lease or, in the case of a sub-lessee, the head lease, to ensure that it permits the intended use;[191] for failing to make the sub-lessee aware of a rent revision provision in the head lease;[192] for failing to draw an enforceable lease option to purchase;[193] for failing to exercise a renewal option on time and advise the client of impediments to the exercise of the op-

---

187 (1993), 35 R.P.R. (2d) 141 (Ont. Gen. Div.).

188 *Ibid.*, at 160.

189 *Yamada v. Mock* (1996), 29 O.R. (3d) 731 (Gen. Div.).

190 *Reisig v. Ross, supra*, note 182.

191 *Hill v. Harris*, [1965] 2 Q.B. 601, [1965] 2 W.L.R. 1331 (C.A.); *C.W. Dixey & Sons Ltd. v. Parsons* (1964), 192 Estates Gazette 197; *Gargatzidis v. South Towne Developments Ltd.* (1980), 6 Sask. R. 151 (Q.B.).

192 *Begusic v. Clark, Wilson & Co.* (1992), 69 B.C.L.R. (2d) 273 (S.C.).

193 *Jacobson Ford-Mercury Sales Ltd. v. Sivertz*, [1980] 1 W.W.R. 141, 103 D.L.R. (3d) 480 (B.C.S.C.).

tion;[194] for failing to register an assignment of lease to the clients and to obtain the required consent of the landlord;[195] and for failing to review the terms of the lease with the client, especially unusual clauses that might affect the client's interests.[196]

When a lawyer is instructed to distrain and engages a bailiff for that purpose, he must provide specific instructions as to the proper execution of a distress warrant and is negligent if he fails to do so.[197]

V. WILLS AND ESTATES

A solicitor's obligations in the preparation of wills and the planning of estates are complicated by issues of third-party liability since suit is usually brought by a non-client third party, namely, a disappointed beneficiary or an executor. Although the scope of a solicitor's responsibility to these third parties is expanding rapidly, there is still considerable uncertainty as to its limits. We discuss this issue in Chapter 4.

Various judicial statements, usually by way of *obiter* in the context of actions contesting the testator's testamentary capacity, have identified the duties of a solicitor taking instructions in the preparation of a will. A solicitor retained for this purpose should receive his instructions directly from the testator and, in cases where that is not reasonably possible, should ensure that the will prepared expresses the true testamentary intentions of the testator prior to execution.[198] The lawyer must ascertain and document testamentary capacity[199] and must fully

---

[194] *120 Adelaide Leaseholds Inc. v. Thomson, Rogers* (1995), 43 R.P.R. (2d) 79 (Gen. Div.), supp. reasons (1995), 38 C.P.C. (3d) 69 (Ont. Gen. Div.).

[195] *Panamaroff v. Reid* (1962), 32 D.L.R. (2d) 126 (B.C.S.C.).

[196] *Sykes v. Midland Bank Executor & Trustee Co. Ltd.*, [1971] 1 Q.B. 113 (C.A.).

[197] *B & M Enterprises Ltd. v. Crosbie Enterprises Ltd.* (1982), 39 Nfld. & P.E.I.R. 153 (Nfld. T.D.).

[198] *Murphy v. Lamphier* (1914), 31 O.L.R. 287 (H.C.), affd 32 O.L.R. 19, 20 D.L.R. 906 (C.A.); *Re Worrell*, [1970] 1 O.R. 184, 8 D.L.R. (3d) 36 (Surr. Ct.).

[199] *Collicutt Estate (Re)* (1994), 128 N.S.R. (2d) 81 (Prob. Ct.), affd (1994), 134 N.S.R. (2d) 137 (C.A.). In M.M. Litman and G.B. Robertson, "Solicitor's Liability for Failure to Substantiate Testamentary Capacity" (1984), 62 *Can. Bar Rev.* 457, the authors provide a detailed review of the steps that should be taken to substantiate capacity in various circumstances, based on their analysis of the cases in which testamentary capacity has been litigated. An issue arises as to whether a solicitor should refuse to prepare a will when he is not satisfied that a testator possesses the requisite testamentary capacity. Litman and Robertson do not discuss the issue directly but appear to assume that a lawyer ought not to prepare a will in these circumstances. In the one reported case in which a solicitor's failure to substantiate testamentary capacity was directly challenged, *Philp v. Woods* (1985), 66 B.C.L.R. 42, 34 C.C.L.T. 66, Mr. Justice Hutchinson of the provincial Supreme Court suggested that the will should be prepared but it should include a statement highlighting the doubt as to competency (at 83 C.C.L.T.). See also P. Cory, "A Whirl with *Re Worrell*" (1971), 5 *Law Soc. Gazette* 274. In *Gonsalves v. Alameda County Super. Ct.*, 24 Cal. Rptr. 2d 52 (Ct. App. 1993), a California appellate court

inquire as to the nature and extent of the testator's property, personal position, and that of the family and designated beneficiaries.[200] A solicitor taking instructions for the preparation of a will from a client with impaired faculties should enquire about previous wills and determine the reasons for any changes.[201] Where the circumstances strongly suggest that testamentary capacity may be lacking, a solicitor should insist on a thorough mental examination before the testator executes the will. Certainly, where the testator is a patient in a psychiatric facility and has a history of mental illness, a solicitor should require a capacity assessment before he carries out the instructions of a testator to cut the testator's spouse of many years out of his will.[202]

When engaged in actually drafting the will, the lawyer must be familiar with those statutes that affect wills and estates administration. He must ensure that the will is validly executed and failure to do so will constitute negligence.[203] If a lawyer fails to attend to the execution of the will in a timely manner in the circumstances, he will generally be liable in negligence to the intended beneficiaries of an unexecuted will.[204]

A lawyer retained to prepare a will has a duty to advise a testator competently. Where, for example, a lawyer neglects to advise an unmarried client, who she knows is contemplating marriage, that the will will be revoked by marriage unless expressly made in contemplation of it, she will be liable.[205] But a solicitor has no obligation to persuade a testator client to accept her advice. Thus as in *Sutherland v. Public Trustee*,[206] where a testator refuses to provide for the contingency that his wife will predecease him, despite his solicitor's advice, the solicitor incurs no liability.

---

held that an attorney who fails to enquire into the testator's testamentary capacity is not liable to a former beneficiary who was disinherited by the will.

[200] *Murphy v. Lamphier, supra,* note 198; *Re Worrell, supra,* note 198; *Philp v. Woods, supra,* note 199.

[201] *Doyle v. Valente,* unreported, June 8, 1993, Spencer J., Doc. Vancouver C894120, [1993] B.C.J. No. 1270 (S.C.).

[202] *Fischer v. Fischer Estate,* unreported, April 7, 1993, Flinn J., Doc. 360/90, [1993] O.J. No. 910 (Gen. Div.).

[203] *Whittingham v. Crease & Co.,* [1978] 5 W.W.R. 45, 88 D.L.R. (3d) 353 (B.C.S.C.); *Ross v. Caunters,* [1980] Ch. 297, [1979] 3 All E.R. 580.

[204] *White v. Jones,* [1995] All E.R. 691 (H.L.); *Smolinski v. Mitchell* (1995), 10 B.C.L.R. (3d) 366 (S.C.). However, the court in *Smolinski* held that a solicitor will not owe a duty to the intended beneficiaries to see to the expeditious execution of the will if that duty conflicts with a duty owed to the testator. Delay in the execution of the will was also the basis of the claim in *Gartside v. Sheffield, Young & Ellis,* [1983] N.Z.L.R. 37 (C.A.), but the court declined to rule on the issue, determining only that the allegations constituted a valid cause of action and dismissing the defendant's application to strike the statement of claim. For a discussion of the relevant considerations in a case of delay, see Bates, "Liability of Solicitors for Negligence to Beneficiaries Under a Will" (1985), 59 *Aust. Law J.* 327 at 336.

[205] *Hall v. Meyrick,* [1957] 2 Q.B. at 458, [1957] 1 All E.R. 208, revd on other grounds [1957] 2 Q.B. 455, [1957] 2 All E.R. 722 (C.A.).

[206] [1980] 2 N.Z.L.R. 536.

Chapter 7

DAMAGES AND OTHER CONSEQUENCES OF MALPRACTICE

I. GENERAL PRINCIPLES

Damages are commonly defined as pecuniary compensation awarded to a successful plaintiff in an action for either tort or breach of contract. Actions in equity in which money is claimed, (for example, actions based on breach of fiduciary duty) are not technically actions for damages, but most of the cases concerning a lawyer's breach of fiduciary duty do not make this distinction, and a finding that a lawyer is in breach of fiduciary duty usually leads to an award of "damages". Accordingly, when we discuss the remedial principles applicable to cases of breach of fiduciary duty, we refer to pecuniary compensation or equitable relief as "damages".[1]

Damages are awarded in the form of an unconditional lump sum. The purpose of an award of damages, whether the action is framed in contract, tort or in equity, is to give the plaintiff compensation for the loss or injury he has suffered.[2] Generally, there are two categories of damages: pecuniary damages comprising all financial and material losses, and non-pecuniary damages comprising non-material losses such as physical injury and mental suffering.[3]

A. CONTRACT AND TORT

For both contract and tort actions, the starting point in calculating the measure of damages is "that sum of money which will put the party who has been injured, or who has suffered in the same position as he would have been in if he

---

[1] McGregor, ed., *McGregor on Damages*, 16th ed. (London: Sweet & Maxwell Ltd., 1997), at p. 3. See discussion of the remedial principles applicable to cases of breach of fiduciary duty in Section I, "General Principles", B. "Equitable Remedies".

[2] *Ibid.*, at p. 8.

[3] *Ibid.*

had not sustained the wrong."[4] Generally, the plaintiff bears the onus of establishing that her losses were caused by the defendant's negligence[5] although exceptions to this rule are evolving and are discussed under the heading "Limiting Principles". The plaintiff must also quantify and prove her damages.

The calculated damages may be reduced or eliminated by a variety of factors: the plaintiff's contributory negligence; a finding that the defendant's conduct was not the cause of the plaintiff's loss; a determination that the loss was not reasonably foreseeable, was not within the reasonable contemplation of the parties or was uncertain.

Apart from these general principles, the determination of damages in cases of lawyers' professional liability is complicated by two problems. First, many of the reported cases were decided before concurrent liability in contract and tort of a negligent lawyer had been clearly recognized by the courts, resulting in many of the reported damage assessments being premised exclusively on contractual liability.[6] Thus, it is not yet apparent to what extent the differences between tort and contract damages rules will continue to be a factor in cases of lawyers' professional liability. Secondly, to some extent, the reasoning in these cases is inconsistent with the courts' approach to damages in other cases;[7] for example, those involving other professionals.[8]

According to traditional theory, the measure of damages in contract can be distinguished from the measure of damages in tort in at least three respects:[9] (1) "expectation damages" are the normal measure in contract cases — the plaintiff recovers what she would have had if the contract had been performed, that is, her loss of bargain;[10] in tort, no question of loss of bargain arises — the plaintiff is restricted to a "reliance measure", that which will restore her to the status

---

[4] *Ibid.*, at p. 9, quoting Lord Blackburn in *Livingstone v. Rawyards Coal Co.* (1880), 5 App. Cas. 25 at 39 (H.L.). See also *Cassey v. Morrison* (1989), 67 O.R. (2d) 65 (H.C.), upheld on appeal, except for a variation in damages order: 15 O.R. (3d) 223 (C.A.).

[5] *Haag v. Marshall* (1989), 1 C.C.L.T. (2d) 99 (B.C.C.A.).

[6] See Chapter 1, Section I "Introduction".

[7] See, *e.g.*, J. Swan and B.J. Reiter, "Opinion Submitted to the Real Property Section, the Canadian Bar Association: Solicitors' Responsibilities in Real Estate Transactions" (1979), 8 R.P.R. 155 at 182-83 on the Ontario Court of Appeal decision in *Messineo v. Beale* (1978), 20 O.R. (2d) 49, 86 D.L.R. (3d) 713 (C.A.). This case and Messrs. Swan's and Reiter's critique are discussed in Section II "Damages", A. "Compensatory Damages", 1. "Peculiary Losses", (a) "Purchase and Sale of Land".

[8] For example, the causation issue in cases of failure to warn of risks has been treated rather differently in cases of medical malpractice than it has in legal malpractice cases: see *Reibl v. Hughes*, [1980] 2 S.C.R. 880, 14 C.C.L.T. 1. For a discussion of causation in legal malpractice cases, see Section II, "Damages", C. "Limiting Principles", 1. "Remoteness", a. "Causation".

[9] The distinction between the measure of damages in contract and tort is not troublesome in two instances: liquidated damages are, by definition, the result of agreement and apply only to contract cases; nominal damages, commonly awarded in contract actions, are not awarded in negligence cases. Nominal damages are discussed at Section II "Damages", B. "Non-Compensatory Damages", 2. "Nominal Damages".

[10] *Wertheim v. Chicoutimi Pulp Co.*, [1911] A.C. 301 at 307, [1908-10] All E.R. Rep. 707 (P.C.).

quo;[11] (2) the test of remoteness in contract is whether at the time of making the contract the damages claimed were within the "reasonable contemplation of the parties";[12] the test of remoteness in tort is whether the damages were "reasonably foreseeable";[13] (3) certain heads of damage recoverable in tort: for instance, damages for pain and suffering and punitive damages are not recoverable in contract,[14] and certain heads of damage recoverable in contract, principally damages for purely economic loss, are unrecoverable in most tort actions.[15]

Gradually, these distinctions are disappearing. After comparing the differently worded remoteness tests in contract and in tort, Scarman L.J. of the English Court of Appeal concluded in *H. Parsons (Livestock) Ltd. v. Uttley Ingham & Co. Ltd.*[16] that "[i]t may be that the necessary reconciliation is to be found, notwithstanding the strictures of Lord Reid [in an earlier case], in holding that the difference between 'reasonably foreseeable' (the test in tort) and 'reasonably contemplated' (the test in contract) is semantic, not substantial."[17] Mr. Justice Cory, speaking for the Ontario Court of Appeal in *Robert Simpson Co. v. Foundation Co. of Canada Ltd.*,[18] went even further:

> It seems anachronistic to be speaking in terms of "how the action is framed". The differences in result of an action based upon a breach of contract or a tortious act appear to be fast disappearing. For example, it is difficult for me to appreciate what, if any, difference that there might be either in the test to be applied in determining the remoteness of the damages or in the measure of damages flowing from the act that might be termed a breach of contract or a breach of duty owed to the plaintiff (apart from some agreement of the parties as to damages that is set out

---

[11] J.G. Fleming, *The Law of Torts*, 9th ed. (Agincourt: Carswell, 1997), at pp. 1-2. Also *British Trans. Commn. v. Gourley*, [1956] A.C. 185 at 206, [1953] 3 All E.R. 796 (H.L.), *per* Lord Goddard.

[12] *Hadley v. Baxendale* (1854), 9 Ex. 341, 156 E.R. 145; *Victoria Laundry (Windsor) Ltd. v. Newman Indust. Ltd.*, [1949] 2 K.B. 528, [1949] 1 All E.R. 997 (C.A.).

[13] *Overseas Tankship (U.K.) Ltd. v. Morts Dock & Engineering Co., The Wagon Mound (No. 1)*, [1961] A.C. 388, [1961] 1 All E.R. 404 (P.C.).

[14] Damages for mental distress not recoverable in contract: *Addis v. Gramophone Co.*, [1900] A.C. 488 (H.L.); *Groom v. Crocker*, [1930] 1 K.B. 194, [1938] 2 All E.R. 394 (C.A.). Punitive damages not recoverable in contract: *Cardinal Construction Ltd. v. Ontario* (1981), 32 O.R. (2d) 575, 122 D.L.R. (3d) 703 (H.C.), affd 38 O.R. (2d) 161, 128 D.L.R. (3d) 662 (C.A.); *Vorvis v. Insurance Corp. of B.C.* (1984), 53 B.C.L.R. 63, 9 D.L.R. (4th) 40 (C.A.).

[15] *Rivtow Marine Ltd. v. Washington Iron Works*, [1974] S.C.R. 1189, 40 D.L.R. (3d) 530. The case did not restrict recovery of economic losses in cases of concurrent liability or innocent misrepresentation. In any event, it is clear that since a lawyer's tortious duty of care is founded, *inter alia*, on the *Hedley Byrne* principle of a special relationship of proximity, the client has a right to recover for purely financial loss: *Central Trust Co. v. Rafuse*, [1986] 2 S.C.R. 147 at 206, 75 N.S.R. (2d) 109.

[16] [1978] Q.B. 791, [1978] 1 All E.R. 525 (C.A.).

[17] *Ibid.*, at 807 Q.B.; see also *Sykes v. Midland Bank Executor & Trustee Co. Ltd.*, [1970] 2 All E.R. 471 (C.A.).

[18] (1982), 36 O.R. (2d) 97, 134 D.L.R. (3d) 459.

in the contract). Perhaps the difference is now solely of significance upon a consideration of the commencement of the limitation period.[19]

More recently, the Ontario Court (General Division), in *Canada Trustco Mortgage Co. v. Bartlet & Richardes*,[20] held that the test in both contract and tort could be framed in terms of "reasonable foreseeability".

Likewise, recovery for economic loss has been allowed in tort in circumstances where they were once considered inapplicable,[21] and a number of cases have held that there is power to award punitive damages and damages for mental distress in breach of contract actions.[22] Moreover, the expectation measure of damages is no longer applied universally in breach of contract actions[23] and it has been criticized as inappropriate in certain cases of breach of contract where it has been applied.[24]

It is not yet clear to what extent the judicial recognition of concurrent liability in contract and in tort will result in a further blurring of these distinctions. In our view, however, the continued integration of tort and contract principles is the only logical course of action. Unfortunately, there will still be legal malpractice cases where a finding of concurrent liability is impossible because, for example, a limitation period has expired or because there is no contract between the parties.

---

[19] *Ibid.*, at 109-10 O.R. Additional statements to the effect that the tests of remoteness in contract and tort are essentially the same can be found in *Kienzle v. Stringer* (1981), 35 O.R. (2d) 85 at 89, 130 D.L.R. (3d) 27 (C.A.), leave to appeal to S.C.C. refused; 38 O.R. (2d) 159n, and *Canlin Ltd. v. Thiokol Fibres Canada Ltd.* (1983), 40 O.R. (2d) 687, 142 D.L.R. (3d) 450 at 459 (C.A.).

[20] (1991) 3 O.R. (3d) 642 (Gen. Div.), affd (1996), 28 O.R. (3d) 768 (C.A.), citing *Kienzle v. Stringer*, *supra*, note 19, as authority.

[21] See Chapter 4, Section III, "Negligence".

[22] Punitive damages recoverable in breach of contract action: *Brown v. Waterloo Regional Commissioners of Police* (1982), 37 O.R. (2d) 277, 136 D.L.R. (3d) 49 (H.C.) (issue not considered by Court of Appeal), revd on other grounds 43 O.R. (2d) 113, 150 D.L.R. (3d) 729; *Elkind v. Elks Stores Ltd.* (1983), 36 C.P.C. 242 (Ont. H.C.) (claim for punitive damages in wrongful dismissal action allowed); *Centennial Centre of Science & Technology v. VS Services Ltd.* (1982), 40 O.R. (2d) 253, 31 C.P.C. 97 (H.C.) (motion to amend statement of claim to include punitive damages allowed because the law has evolved to the point where these damages may be awarded in an exceptional case of wilful, wanton, malicious or other deliberate or unconscionable conduct leading to a breach of contract); *Edwards v. Harris-Intertype (Canada) Ltd.* (1983), 40 O.R. (2d) 558 (H.C.), affd 46 O.R. (2d) 286, 9 D.L.R. (4th) 319 (C.A.) (punitive damages can be awarded whether or not they have been specifically claimed). Damages recoverable for mental distress in breach of contract action: *Heywood v. Wellers*, [1976] Q.B. 446, [1976] 1 All E.R. 300 (C.A.), and see cases cited at notes 119 to 128, *infra*.

[23] See, *eg.*, the discussion of *Messineo v. Beale* (1978), 20 O.R. (2d) 49, 86 D.L.R. (3d) (C.A.), in Section II.

[24] Most of the criticism has surrounded the awarding of damages for loss of bargain in a case of innocent misrepresentation; see S.M. Waddams, *The Law of Contracts*, 3rd ed. (Aurora. Ont.: Canada Law Book Inc., 1993), at pp. 278 and 287.

B. EQUITABLE REMEDIES

Since fiduciary obligations are equitable in nature, when a fiduciary is found in breach of duty, the available remedies are not necessarily limited to damages but are in the court's discretion.[25] Other remedies may include an accounting of profits or the imposition of a constructive trust.[26] However, damages are the appropriate remedy in situations in which it is impossible to put the parties in the position they were in before the breach of fiduciary duty occurred.[27]

In the leading case of *Nocton v. Lord Ashburton*,[28] in which a solicitor had advised a client to release part of his mortgage security on a property in which the solicitor had an interest, the House of Lords held that although the pleadings precluded a claim for damages in negligence, this did not bar a remedy:

> When, as in the case before us, a solicitor has had financial transactions with his client . . . a Court of Equity has always assumed jurisdiction to scrutinize his action. It did not matter that the client would have a remedy in damages for breach of contract. Courts of Equity had jurisdiction to direct accounts to be taken, and in proper cases to order the solicitor to replace property improperly acquired from the client, or to make compensation if he had lost it by acting in breach of a duty which arose out of his confidential relationship to the man who had trusted him.[29]

The fiduciary will usually be required to make restitution by disgorging profits he has made where he has unjustly benefited from a conflict between his personal interest and his duty to his client.[30] Where a lawyer obtains an interest in property as a result of a breach of the fiduciary duty of loyalty, the appropriate remedy may be the imposition of a constructive trust. In *Soulos v. Korkontzilas*,[31] the Supreme Court of Canada imposed a constructive trust on a real estate broker who breached his fiduciary duty to his purchaser client. He failed to communicate information he received about the vendor's "bottom line" in the course of negotiations over the purchase price of a commercial building and arranged for his wife to purchase the property instead. The court held that the breach was sufficient to engage the conscience of the court to support a finding of constructive trust and require the transfer of the property to the client even

---

25   See *Walker v. Janzen Builders Ltd.*, [1985] 1 W.W.R. 529 (B.C.S.C.), affd [1986] 6 W.W.R. 722 (C.A.).
26   See M.V. Ellis, *Fiduciary Duties in Canada* (Toronto: Carswell, 1993).
27   *Cassey v. Morrison* (1989), 67 O.R. (2d) 65 (H.C.), affd on appeal (1993), 15 O.R. (3d) 223 (C.A.).
28   [1914] A.C. 932, [1914-15] All E.R. Rep. 45 (H.L.).
29   *Ibid.* at 956-57 A.C., *per* Viscount Haldane L.C.
30   *MacDonald v. Lockhart* (1980), 42 N.S.R. (2d) 29, 118 D.L.R. (3d) 397 (C.A.), varied 44 N.S.R. (2d) 261, leave to appeal to S.C.C. refused 118 D.L.R. (3d) 397n. Although not so expressed, this appears to be the basis upon which damages were awarded in *Cavallin v. King* (1984), 51 B.C.L.R. 149 (S.C.).
31   [1997] 2 S.C.R. 217.

though the value of the property had decreased since the breach and the client could show no loss.[32] However, where the imposition of a constructive trust is not appropriate, the measure of damages will be proportionate to the interest the plaintiff would have had in the property.[33]

A solicitor will not be liable for a secret profit of which she has no knowledge and in which she does not share.[34] The degree required to support liability for a secret profit in which the solicitor does not partake is actual knowledge, recklessness or wilful blindness.[35]

Historically, when damages were awarded for breach of fiduciary duty, they were not always limited by the principles of causation and remoteness as they were when the breach of duty arose in contract or tort.[36] Thus, in *Walker v. Janzen Builders Ltd.*,[37] the British Columbia Supreme Court held that because a client's losses were caused both by a solicitor's breach of fiduciary duty and market conditions, and it was impossible to balance these two causes with precision, the court should impose an "equitable solution", namely, cancel the client's obligation under a mortgage that had gone into default and award him any sale proceeds in excess of a prior mortgage.

The Supreme Court of Canada's decision in *Canson Enterprises Ltd. v. Boughton & Co.*[38] is now the leading case on the issue of the principles appropriate to the assessment of damages for breach of fiduciary duty. On the recommendation of T, the appellant co-venturers agreed to purchase real property for development purposes. Unbeknownst to the appellants, another corporation, Sun-Mark, purchased the property from the vendors on an interim basis and immediately re-sold it to the appellants for a profit. Sun-Mark and T shared the secret profit equally. The respondent solicitor acted for Sun-Mark on the interim purchase, and for both Sun-Mark and the appellants on the resale, but did not disclose to the appellants that the property was not purchased directly from the vendors. Instead, he took steps to conceal that the purchase had taken place through an intermediary.

The appellants proceeded with their development plans. A warehouse constructed on the property was damaged when its supporting piles began to sink because of the negligence of soil engineers and a pile-driving company, and judgment was obtained against them. However, the judgment could not be fully

---

[32] One of the conditions for the imposition of the trust is that acquisition of the asset results from deemed or actual agency activities of the defendant in breach of his equitable obligation to the plaintiff.

[33] *Terrace Development Ltd. v. Terry*, unreported, April 5, 1994, Doc. C12383, [1994] O.J. No. 683 (C.A.).

[34] *Canson Enterprises Ltd. v. Boughton & Co.* (1995), 11 B.C.L.R. (3d) 262 (C.A.).

[35] *Ibid.*, relying on *Air Canada v. M&L Travel Ltd.*, [1993] 3 S.C.R. 787.

[36] For a recent statement of this principle, see *Maghun v. Richardson Securities of Canada Ltd.* (1986), 58 O.R. (2d) 1 at 18, 34 D.L.R. (4th) 524 (C.A.).

[37] *Supra*, note 25.

[38] [1991] 3 S.C.R. 534.

recovered and the appellants sued the solicitor and his firm for the shortfall, alleging that the failure to disclose the secret profit constituted a breach of fiduciary duty. The action proceeded as a special case based on an agreed statement of facts. The sole issue was whether losses arising from the negligence of the engineers and pile drivers were recoverable from the solicitors. It was agreed that the appellants would not have proceeded with the transaction had they known about the secret profit.

The Supreme Court unanimously upheld the lower courts' decisions that the solicitors were liable for breach of fiduciary duty, but the court was divided as to the applicable remedial principles, particularly the appropriateness of applying common law principles of causation, remoteness and mitigation to limit recovery for an equitable breach. Mr. Justice La Forest found that the nature of the relief depended upon the nature of the fiduciary relationship. Where the fiduciary is also in the position of trustee (that is, where one has control of property which in the opinion of the court belongs to another), compensation will be assessed according to strict equitable remedial principles. On the other hand, in the case of a "mere breach of fiduciary duty", common law principles may be applied to limit the recovery. Thus, while the losses need not be foreseeable, the concepts of causation, mitigation and contributory negligence may be applied in the assessment of damages for breach of fiduciary duty. He also suggested that, as a result of the fusion of law and equity, the measure of damages should generally be the same: ". . . [t]he truth is that barring different policy considerations underlying one action or the other, I see no reason why the same basic claim, whether framed in terms of a common law action or an equitable remedy, should give rise to different levels of redress."[39]

Madam Justice McLachlin rejected La Forest J.'s distinction between trust situations and those involving a mere breach of fiduciary duty and found that it would be inappropriate to apply common law tort principles directly to equitable breaches. Recovery in equity did not depend on the foreseeability of the loss. Instead, McLachlin J. held that the losses must be related to the breach on a "common sense view of causation".[40] There is no obligation on a plaintiff to mitigate but she cannot be compensated for losses flowing from her unreasonable acts.

Mr. Justice La Forest's view appears to have prevailed but there was no clear majority on the court.[41] All of the justices agreed that the losses were not recoverable because they were not caused by the breach.

---

[39] *Ibid., per* La Forest J. at 581.

[40] *Ibid., per* McLachlin J. at 556.

[41] Eight justices participated in the decision. Three concurred with the reasons of La Forest J. and two with McLachlin J. The eighth justice, Mr. Justice Stevenson, held that the case had nothing to do with the fusion of law and equity. It if did, the rules of equity would prevail. He disagreed with La Forest J. (at 591) that the principles of contributory negligence were introduced by fusion.

In *McKitterick v. Duco, Geist & Chodos,*[42] the Ontario Court of Appeal relied on *Canson* to restrict the plaintiffs' compensation for breach of fiduciary duty to losses which were caused by the breach. The Court held that a two-part test for determining the amount of compensation to be awarded arose out of the decision in *Canson*. A court must first consider whether the losses flow from the breach and then determine whether there have been any intervening acts. A fiduciary will not be liable for losses flowing from any intervening acts of third parties or from the unreasonable intervening acts of the beneficiary.[43]

The defendant solicitor in *McKitterick* represented P and several other investors in the purchase of a restaurant but did not disclose to them that P did not make a required $200,000 advance to the business prior to closing. P oversaw the daily operations of the restaurant after closing and removed $252,000 from a company incorporated to operate the business. When the other investors learned of P's conduct, they excluded him from the business, quit their jobs and began running the restaurant themselves. They settled an action brought against them by P without claiming against the defendant solicitor or including him in the settlement negotiations. The Ontario Court of Appeal concluded that the losses from the first intervening act, P's removal of the $252,000, flowed from the solicitor's breach of fiduciary duty in failing to disclose that he had not made the requisite $200,000 advance to the business. The second intervening act was the investors' decision to settle with P without dealing with the defendant solicitor's potential liability. If they had intended to call the solicitor to account for their losses, they should have done so at that time. Thus, the court assessed the value of their losses as at the settlement date and refused to compensate them for any losses incurred afterwards. In particular, it overturned the trial judge's award of damages for actual and potential lost wages as they did not flow from the solicitor's breach.

Mr. Justice La Forest's analysis of the principles applicable to the assessed damages for a breach of fiduciary duty was applied by Mr. Justice Lederman of the Ontario Court (General Division) in *Martin v. Goldfarb.*[44] In this case, the plaintiff invested millions of dollars in various ventures with A. The defendant law firm acted on the transactions but did not disclose to the plaintiff that A was a disbarred lawyer with a recent criminal conviction for mortgage fraud. Lederman J. found the solicitors in breach of the fiduciary duty to disclose for failing to reveal A's true identity and criminal background to the plaintiff. He held that because it was a case of "mere breach of duty rather than abuse of a trust" the

[42] (1994), 76 O.A.C. 310. *Kalla v. Wolkowicz*, unreported, February 9, 1994, Haley J., Doc. 30172/91U, [1994] O.J. No. 257 (Gen. Div.), is another example of the application of the principles enunciated in *Canson* to the assessment of damages for breach of fiduciary duty by a solicitor.

[43] *Ibid.,* at 317-18.

[44] (1997), 31 B.L.R. (2d) 265 (Gen. Div.), revd in part August 26, 1998, Doc. C27477, [1998] O.J. No. 3403 (C.A.).

common law doctrines of remoteness, causation and mitigation applied to the assessment of damages.

Mr. Justice Lederman applied La Forest J.'s decision in *Canson*. He agreed that the plaintiffs should not recover higher damage awards merely because their claim is characterized as a breach of fiduciary duty as opposed to a breach of contract or tort. However, he relied on McLachlin J.'s comment in *Canson* that, in breach of fiduciary duty cases where the defendant has superior information, the degree of precision with which the plaintiff must identify the loss may be relaxed. Where it is clear that losses flow from a breach, a court ought to award damages regardless of the difficulty in calculating the precise figures. The evidence produced by the plaintiff about the losses attributable to the breach was not completely satisfactory, but Lederman J. assessed an admittedly arbitrary amount of compensation for the losses on each transaction that were attributable to the breach. Interestingly, it was one of the highest damages awards ever assessed against a solicitor for malpractice.[45]

There is authority for the proposition that if breach of fiduciary duty has been proved, the onus of proof on the causation issue is reversed and rests with the defendant.[46]

II. DAMAGES

A. COMPENSATORY DAMAGES

1. Pecuniary Losses

a. Purchase and Sale of Land

In *Messineo v. Beale*,[47] the Ontario Court of Appeal held that in a situation where a solicitor fails to detect a defect in title and the plaintiff buys the property, the measure of damages is the difference between the contract price and the actual value of the land with the defective title. The solicitor had failed to discover that the vendor did not own part of the land she purported to sell to the plaintiff; but since the value of the land the plaintiff bought was at least equal to a price the plaintiff had paid, the court held that the client had suffered no loss. The court reasoned that the failure of the defendant solicitor to discover that the vendor did not have good title to all the land was not the cause of the plaintiff's

---

[45] See N. Seeman, "Lawyer, Law Firm Must Pay $9 million: Liability Arises From Failure to Reveal Client's Background", *The Lawyers Weekly* (6 June 1997) 1.

[46] *Ferris v. Rusnak* (1983), 50 A.R. 297, 9 D.L.R. (4th) 183 (Q.B.); *Ruxton v. Kelly, Peters & Associates Ltd.* (1984), 58 B.C.L.R. 317, [1985] 1 W.W.R. 66 (S.C.); *Commerce Capital Trust Co. v. Berk* (1989), 68 O.R. (2d) 257 (C.A.); *Dimitry Investments Ltd. v. Stern*, unreported, December 9, 1991, Van Camp J., Doc. 74849/91 Q, [1991] O.J. No. 2182 (Gen. Div.), affd, unreported, September 10, 1992, Doc. C9827, [1992] O.J. No. 1864 (C.A.).

[47] (1978), 20 O.R. (2d) 49, 86 D.L.R. (3d) 713 (C.A.).

loss: it could not be shown that even if the solicitor had performed his duty, the plaintiff would have obtained all the land. Rather, the plaintiff would simply have been warned of the defect in time not to buy the land.[48]

Other cases have held that damages should be measured by the difference between the value of the property with the defects and its value without them or by the cost of remedying the defects.[49] It has been argued that the result of *Messineo* is that damages are awarded on the basis usually adopted in tort cases and not on the basis traditionally found in contract cases where liability is said to be strict.[50] In cases where the solicitor "certifies" title to his client, this is akin to a warranty and he should make good his client's expectations if the certificate proves false.

In our view, the measure of damages propounded in *Messineo v. Beale* is consistent with substantive principles of a solicitor's liability and the standard of care.[51] Moreover, the measure finds support in the leading English decision, *Ford v. White & Co.*,[52] which is favoured by the majority of academic commentators;[53] it is the measure ordinarily applied in analogous cases of professional negligence, for example, where a surveyor prepares an inaccurate survey of a property.[54] The British Columbia Supreme Court has held that the *Messineo*

---

[48]   The court found that this case was not one for specific performance with an abatement: *supra*, note 47, at 52 O.R. In cases where the plaintiff has been deprived of obtaining an abatement of the purchase price, by virtue of his solicitor's failure to warn of a defect, the damages ought to reflect that lost opportunity: see J. Swan and B.J. Reiter, "Opinion Submitted to the Real Property Section, the Canadian Bar Association Solicitors' Responsibilities in Real Estate Transactions" (1979), 8 R.P.R. 155, at 185-86 for examples of other cases which justify an award of damages greater than that in *Messineo*.

[49]   *Pilkington v. Wood*, [1953] Ch. 770, [1953] 2 All E.R. 810; *Clements v. Wyatt* (1979), 9 R.P.R. 1 (Ont. H.C.); *Tabata v. McWilliams* (1981), 33 O.R. (2d) 32, 123 D.L.R. (3d) 141 (H.C.), affd 40 O.R. (2d) 158, 140 D.L.R. (3d) 322 (C.A.); *Charette v. Provenzano* (1978), 21 O.R. (2d) 587, 7 C.C.L.T. 23 (H.C.), and accompanying "Annotation" by Lewis N. Klar in C.C.L.T. As Klar points out, although in *Charette* the court's award of damages to compensate for expenses incurred to comply with the easement that the defendants had failed to detect is not at odds with *Messineo*, the court also awarded the plaintiffs "the damage resulting in reduction in overall value of the improved property". This award was made even though the defendants were able to establish that the lot with the easement was worth at least as much as the plaintiffs had paid for it.

[50]   Swan and Reiter, *supra*, note 48, at 177-78.

[51]   See Chapter 2.

[52]   [1964] 2 All E.R. 755, [1964] 1 W.L.R. 885 (Ch.). See also *Lake v. Bushby*, [1949] 1 All E.R. 964 (K.B.) (measure of damages is the difference between the value of the property as it stood with a "secure" building and its value as diminished by the possibility that the local council might require the building to be pulled down).

[53]   For example, S.M. Waddams, *The Law of Damages* (Aurora, Ont.: Canada Law Book Inc., 1997), at p. 2.320; R.M. Jackson and J.L. Powell, *Professional Negligence*, 2nd ed. (London: Sweet & Maxwell, 1987), at p. 258; A.M. Dugdale and K.M. Stanton, *Professional Negligence*, 2nd ed. (London: Butterworths, 1989), at p. 361.

[54]   *Perry v. Sidney Phillips & Son*, [1982] 3 All E.R. 705, [1982] 1 W.L.R. 1297 (C.A.); a surveyor's negligent report failed to disclose defects. The measure of damages was held to be the difference in price between what the plaintiff paid for the property and its market value at the

principle is inapplicable where a solicitor is negligent in advising a vendor of real estate as to the correct terms of an offer to purchase, even where the amount offered was greater than the property was worth. The court reasoned that the vendor had nevertheless lost the opportunity to sell at an even higher price than that stipulated in the offer by reason of rising property values.[55]

Further, the *Messineo* measure of damages does not apply to circumstances in which the plaintiff would have obtained clear title to the property if the solicitor had properly completed the conveyance. In *Kienzle v. Stringer*,[56] the defendant solicitor prepared a deed to a property (the Oxford farm) from an estate without obtaining the consent of two of the beneficiaries in their personal capacity. Subsequently, the plaintiff entered into an agreement to purchase another property (the Kincardine farm) conditional on the sale of the Oxford farm. When the plaintiff tried to sell the Oxford farm, he was unable to convey good title because one of the beneficiaries refused to consent to the sale. Both transactions were aborted. The Ontario Court of Appeal held that this case could be distinguished from *Messineo v. Beale*:

> It would have been far different if the vendor [in *Messineo v. Beale*] had owned [the land] and the solicitor had omitted the property from the deed or in some other way had caused the plaintiff to lose the property. In that case, the plaintiff's damage would have been the value of the missing property despite the fact that value of what he received was greater than the purchase price.[57]

The plaintiff in *Kienzle* was awarded, *inter alia*, the amount necessary to buy out the beneficiary's interest as well as his loss of income as a result of having to remain on an unprofitable farm for the period necessary to remedy the title problems.

A further exception to the principle that damages should be measured by the difference between the purchase price and market value at the time of purchase is illustrated by the case of *Ferreira v. Amado*.[58] The plaintiffs purchased property from a vendor who insisted that the lot was 33 feet wide. Although the defendant, a notary public, was specifically requested to verify this measurement and was aware that the plaintiffs intended to remove the existing residence and build a new house on the property, the defendant negligently confirmed that the

---

time of the purchase if the defects had been noted. See also *MacLaren-Elgin Corp. Ltd. v. Gooch*, [1972] 1 O.R. 474, 23 D.L.R. (3d) 394 (H.C.).

[55] *McMorran's Cordova Bay Ltd. v. Harman & Co.* (1979), 17 B.C.L.R. 173, [1980] 2 W.W.R. 499 at 502 (C.A.). Unfortunately, the case does not make clear whether the opportunity to obtain a higher price was anything more than hypothetical, specifically, whether any evidence was adduced to establish that the plaintiffs may indeed have been able to obtain a more suitable offer.

[56] (1981), 35 O.R. (2d) 85, 130 D.L.R. (3d) 272 (C.A.), leave to appeal to S.C.C. refused 38 O.R. (2d) 159n.

[57] *Ibid.*, at 88 O.R.

[58] [1985] 1 W.W.R. 78, 33 R.P.R. 213 (B.C.S.C.).

lot was 33 feet wide when, in fact, it was less than 25 feet wide. As a result, the plaintiffs could not build on the property and, due to an unstable real estate market, eventually sold the property at a loss. The evidence established that, if damages were calculated as the difference between the purchase price and market value of the property at the time of the plaintiffs' purchase, they would not have suffered a loss. The court held, however, that had the defendant performed his duty, the plaintiffs would have refused to close and since they had lost that opportunity, they should not be the victims of the downturn in the market. Rather, they should be awarded the cost of repairing the unwanted property as well as their loss on the resale.[59]

The court in *Scott v. Sills*[60] reached the opposite conclusion on similar facts. The plaintiffs purchased property without knowledge of an easement which precluded them from building a pool in their backyard. The plaintiffs averred that they would not have purchased the property had they known of the easement. It was agreed that the existence of the easement caused no loss in value of the land. The loss of ability to install a pool was characterized by the court as "anticipatory damages",[61] and, as the plaintiffs were unable to prove actual pecuniary loss resulting from either breach of contract or negligence, nominal damages were awarded.

The Ontario Court of Appeal recently reconciled the *Messineo* and *Kienzle* principles with respect to the appropriate measure of damages in solicitors' negligence cases involving the purchase and sale of land. In *Toronto Industrial Leaseholds Ltd. v. Posesorski*,[62] the defendant solicitor acted on the purchase of an industrial property in 1979 but neglected to advise his clients that Toronto Industrial Leaseholds Limited ("TILCO") had an option to lease the property for ten years at a rent substantially below current market rates. The clients learned about it in 1981 when TILCO notified them that it intended to exercise the option and subsequently brought an action for a declaration that the option was valid. The clients joined the solicitor as a third party claiming contribution and indemnity based on the solicitor's negligence. The purchasers settled the main action with TILCO for $260,000. Negligence was admitted by the solicitor and the parties agreed that the clients would not have purchased the property had they known about the option.

In dissent, Mr. Justice Galligan quantified the damages as the amount paid to remove the option, specifically, the settlement amount of $260,000. Mr. Justice Doherty, writing for a majority of the court, criticized this approach as putting

---

[59] See also *Clements v. Wyatt, supra*, note 49, where the defendant failed to advise the plaintiffs of a title defect with the result that they were unable to market the property for resale as they had intended. The court did not consider the *Messineo* measure or indicate how the purchase price of the property compared with its market value; instead, it awarded the plaintiffs their loss of profits as well as legal fees and expenses incurred in rectifying their title problems.

[60] Unreported, October 11, 1990, Scott J., Doc. 12/89, [1990] O.J. No. 2085 (Gen. Div.).

[61] *Ibid.*, at 11-12.

[62] (1994), 21 O.R. (3d) 1 (C.A.), supp reasons 21 O.R. (3d) 383, 121 D.L.R. (4th) 766 (C.A.).

the clients in a better position than they would have been if the solicitor had informed them of the option. He held that *Messineo* was the widely accepted measure of damages in these cases and should be applied unless the party advocating a different approach demonstrates that it more effectively achieves the restitutionary goal. In addition to the difference between the purchase price and the market value at the time of purchase, a plaintiff is entitled to all consequential damages that are reasonably foreseeable.

Damages were considered by Doherty J. in three components: the clients paid more money than the property was actually worth, they lost the use of the funds represented by the overpayment, and they incurred certain additional costs and expenses that were the foreseeable consequence of the defendant's negligence. He summarized the law this way:

> . . . I do not regard the *Kienzle* case as a departure from *Messineo*. As indicated above, the two cases demonstrate that the initial measure of damages will depend on the nature of the solicitor's error. If the error caused the client to lose an interest in property he or she otherwise would have had, *Kienzle* is the appropriate starting point. If the error did not cause the client to lose an interest in property, but instead caused the client to enter into a transaction he or she would otherwise not have entered into, then *Messineo* is the appropriate starting point in the assessment of the client's damages. Further, as the Court of Appeal in *Kienzle* indicates, even where *Messineo* is the appropriate starting point, that measure of damages does not necessarily exhaust the client's claim. Consequential damages are recoverable if they were reasonably foreseeable. The Court of Appeal judgements in *Messineo* and *Kienzle* work together to describe the client's measure of damages. *Messineo* addresses the loss suffered the initial overpayment, and *Kienzle* speaks to the solicitor's liability for reasonably foreseeable consequential losses caused by the solicitor's negligence and occurring subsequently to the ill-advised purchase.[63]

In our view, this trilogy of cases — *Messineo, Kienzle* and *Toronto Industrial Leaseholds* — will govern the quantification of damages in solicitors' negligence cases involving title problems.[64] The *Toronto Industrial Leaseholds* decision has thus far been considered in only one subsequent case involving a title problem. In *789538 Ontario Ltd. v. Gambin Associates*,[65] the purchasers of industrial property were not advised of the presence of two easements and a right of way over the property. The court found that, in situations where the solicitor did not cause or fail to get rid of an encumbrance, but rather failed to discover

---

[63]   *Ibid.*, at 25.

[64]   For a helpful summary of the law in this area, see J.G. Hone and A.I. Schein, "Assessment of Damages for Solicitor's Negligence in Real Estate Transactions" (1996), 18 *Advocates' Q.* 478. The authors have also argued that the trilogy of cases will govern the quantification of damages in this area.

[65]   (1997), 45 O.T.C. 339 (Gen. Div.).

and report it to his client, thereby denying the client the opportunity to avoid the deal or negotiate a lower price, the damages should be calculated by referencel to the three heads set out in *Toronto Industrial Leaseholds* and may be awarded on that basis.

It seems clear that, at least in Ontario, in appropriate circumstances a defendant solicitor may be liable for damages relating to transactions which are secondary to the aborted transaction or delayed as a direct result of the solicitor's error. In *Kienzle*, Madam Justice Wilson, dissenting on this issue, would have awarded damages for the loss of the appreciation on the Kincardine farm, less the appreciation in the Oxford farm in addition to the other relief awarded by the court. In other words, she would have awarded damages arising out of the inability to complete a secondary transaction. In *Kasekas v. Tessler*,[66] an action for breach of contract by a vendor against a purchaser, the Ontario Court of Appeal adopted the reasoning of Wilson J. in *Kienzle* and awarded damages arising from the vendor's inability to complete the purchase of another property. The purchasers knew or certainly ought reasonably to have known that the vendors intended to buy a new home with their proceeds of sale. This decision was soon applied in solicitors' negligence cases in Ontario. In one case, *Froude v. Nash,*[67] the defendant solicitors overlooked the absence of the dedication and deeding of the property and certified good and marketable title to the plaintiff. The error was discovered several years later when the plaintiff attempted to sell the property. Liability was admitted, but the defendants disputed that damages for an aborted secondary purchase were recoverable. Applying *Kasekas*, the court held: "I do not find a fixed policy or rule that states all secondary transactions must be excluded from compensation. In my view, each case must be decided on its own facts, consistent with the control discipline of *stare decisis*."[68] In *Reid v. Barnes*,[69] Wilson J.'s reasoning was extended to a claim for damages caused because the plaintiffs were prevented from entering a rapidly rising real estate market in another city for six months because they could not deliver good title to their property. The defendants had certified good and marketable title when in fact the property was purchased in contravention of the *Planning Act*.[70]

In *Wong v. 407527 Ontario Ltd.*,[71] where a solicitor failed to obtain some form of security for a rental income warranty in an agreement to purchase a rental property, the measure of damages was held to be the lost rental income and legal fees. Damages for failing to advise the vendor of conditions attached

---

[66] (1989), 4 R.P.R. (2d) 110 (Ont. C.A.).
[67] Unreported, May 11, 1994, Crane J., Doc. 1883/94, [1994] O.J. No. 1100 (Gen. Div.).
[68] *Ibid.,* at para. 21.
[69] Unreported, May 11, 1994, Crane J., Doc. 1883/94, [1990] O.J. No. 2113 (Gen. Div.).
[70] R.S.O. 1990, c. P.13.
[71] (1996), 1 R.P.R. (3d) 245 (Gen. Div.). The court dismissed as "outrageous" the plaintiffs' claim for damages for overpayment and an alleged diminution in market value of the property. The purchase price was $975,000. The property was listed for sale the next year and the plaintiffs refused an offer of $1.5 million.

to a Committee of Adjustments severance approval were limited to the cost of defending and settling the claims brought by the purchasers.[72]

Finally, there is English authority that supports the proposition that a plaintiff saddled with a title defect will not be restricted to the difference between the contract price and the market value where the property has been acquired for a business use and the defect affects the business's profitability.[73] More recently, in *Kennedy v. Van Emden*[74] the English Court of Appeal has confirmed that, as a general rule, damages will be quantified as the diminution in value assessed as at the date of breach. In this case, damages were assessed for the defendant solicitors' failure to advise the plaintiffs of onerous rent review provisions in an underlease.

b. Loss of Profit

Loss of profit is a recognized head of damage in a case of lawyers' professional liability, but in the majority of cases these losses have been found to be too remote to sustain an award.[75] Thus, in *MacCulloch v. Corbett*,[76] a case where a solicitor was retained to incorporate a company and negligently failed to issue qualifying shares to the plaintiff directors with the result that their directorships expired and the company was no longer validly constituted, the plaintiffs' claim for loss of profits based on the alleged future profitability of the company was said to be "too vague and speculative to justify an award."

However, in *Reisig v. Ross*,[77] damages for loss of profit were awarded where a solicitor failed to register a sub-lease for the plaintiff, who ran a successful business on the sub-leased premises. The court held that the plaintiff, who was eventually forced out of business, had suffered the loss of a five-year lease and, in the absence of evidence that he would have given up his business during the term of the sub-lease, was entitled to his loss of earnings for the balance of the term. Similarly, in *Beiser v. A Law Firm*,[78] where a law firm failed to file a strata plan and prospectus within the statutory period thereby preventing the use of the plaintiffs' property as a strata title property, the plaintiffs were awarded their lost profit, that is, the difference between the value of the property as a single title property and as a strata title property. In another case, *Shaw Industries Ltd. v. Palmer*,[79] the British Columbia Supreme Court awarded damages for loss of

---

[72] *Jaouen-Malgorn v. Irani*, unreported, February 12, 1996, Sedgwick J., Doc. 7378/87A, [1996] O.J. No. 520 (Gen. Div.).

[73] *Simple Simon Catering Ltd. v. Binstock Miller & Co.* (1973), 228 Estates Gazette 527 (C.A.).

[74] [1996] N.L.O.R. 3325 (Eng. C.A.).

[75] See the discussion of remoteness of damages at Section II, "Damages", C "Limiting Principles", 1. "Remoteness".

[76] (1982), 49 N.S.R. (2d) 663, 133 D.L.R. (3d) 43 (S.C.).

[77] (1984), 52 B.C.L.R. 183 (S.C.).

[78] (1984), 53 B.C.L.R. 305, [1984] 4 W.W.R. 551 (S.C.).

[79] Unreported, November 10, 1992, Meredith J., Doc. Vancouver C914082, [1992] B.C.J. No. 2435 (S.C.).

profit when the defendant solicitor failed to take steps to complete the purchase of two out of four lots on behalf of the plaintiff purchasers who were in the business of building homes. The plaintiffs successfully sued the vendors for specific performance but construction was delayed on the second two lots for about a year as a result of the litigation. The court awarded the difference between the profit realized on the sale of the first two lots and that realized on the second two plus the cost of the specific performance proceedings.

Originally, where a secondary transaction (for example, the purchase of a second property dependent on the sale of the first) results in loss of profit, the loss was not recoverable from a negligent solicitor.[80] However, as discussed,[81] the court will now permit recovery for lost profit when the loss is reasonably foreseeable.

c. Inadequate Security

If, as a result of a lawyer's negligence in acting for a lender in a secured transaction, the client suffers a loss, the measure of damages is the difference between the value of the security which the client actually received, and that which she was entitled to receive in the event of default.[82] In a case in which this formula for assessing the loss poses practical difficulties, for example, because the asset secured has not yet been liquidated, the court may award the plaintiff judgment for the net amount owing on the loan, and upon payment of that amount, assign the loan to the defendant.[83]

d. Loss of Opportunity

(1) To Bring or Defend Proceedings

Negligence in the conduct of litigation may deprive a litigant of the right to bring or defend a proceeding or may yield an unsatisfactory result at trial or on appeal. In the often-cited English Court of Appeal decision in *Kitchen v. Royal Air Forces Assn.*,[84] the defendant law firm failed to commence an action under the *Fatal Accidents Act* within the limitation period. The plaintiff's husband had been electrocuted in his home while using domestic electrical equipment, but it

---

[80] *Kienzle v. Stringer* (1981), 35 O.R. (2d) 85, 130 D.L.R. (3d) 272 (C.A.), leave to appeal to S.C.C. refused 38 O.R. (2d) 157n, *per* Zuber J.A. at 90 O.R. Wilson J.A. dissented on this point, at 91 O.R.

[81] See Section II.A.1.9.

[82] *Rowswell v. Pettit*, [1969] 1 O.R. 22, 1 D.L.R. (3d) 268 (C.A.), affd [1970] S.C.R. 865, 11 D.L.R. (3d) 737, *sub nom. Wilson v. Rowswell*, applied in *Morris v. Jackson* (1984), 34 R.P.R. 269 (Ont. H.C.) and *Bailey v. Ornheim* (1962), 40 W.W.R. 129, 35 D.L.R. (2d) 402 (B.C.S.C.); *Carson v. Huebner* (1989), 80 Sask. R. 207 (Q.B.); *Presidential Management & Development Corp. v. Sugarman*, unreported, February 3, 1998, Kiteley J., Doc. 95-CU-88630CM, [1998] O.J. No. 382 (Gen. Div.).

[83] *Rowswell v. Pettit, supra,* note 82.

[84] [1958] 2 All E.R. 241, [1958] 1 W.L.R. 563 (C.A.).

was not clear that negligence could be established against the original defendant. On the question of whether the plaintiff had proved anything other than nominal damages against the defendant law firm, Lord Evershed stated that an "all or nothing" approach was inappropriate. Rather:

> If, in this kind of case, it is plain that an action could have been brought, and, that if it had been brought, it must have succeeded, the answer is easy. The damaged plaintiff then would recover the full amount of the damages lost by the failure to bring the action originally. On the other hand, if it can be made clear that the plaintiff never had a cause of action, that there was no case which the plaintiff could reasonably ever have formulated, then it is equally plain that she can get nothing save nominal damages for the solicitors' negligence. I would add, as was conceded by counsel for the plaintiff, that in such a case it is not enough for the plaintiff to say: "Though I had no claim in law, still, I had a nuisance value which I could have so utilised as to extract something from the other side, and they would have had to pay something to me in order to persuade me to go away".

> The present case, however, falls into neither one nor the other of the categories which I have mentioned. There may be cases where it would be quite impossible to try "the action within the action", as counsel for the second defendants asks. It may be that for one reason or another the action for negligence is not brought until, say, twenty years after the event, and in the process of time the material witnesses, or many of them, may have died or become quite out of reach for the purpose of being called to give evidence. In my judgment, assuming that the plaintiff has established negligence, what the court has to do . . . is determine what the plaintiff has lost by that negligence. The question is: Has the plaintiff lost some right of value, some chose in action of reality and substance? In such a case it may be that its value is not easy to determine, but it is the duty of the court to determine that value as best it can.[85]

Parker and Sellers LL.J. agreed that there was a scale of possibilities, from certainty of victory at one end to certainty of failure at the other, and that anything above a certainty of failure gave a right to something more than nominal damages.[86] In the result, the Court of Appeal upheld the trial judge's award of damages which was equal to two-thirds of the full amount recoverable under the statute. This approach was approved by the House of Lords in *Davies v. Taylor*[87] and has since been applied in a number of Canadian and Commonwealth decisions.[88] In *Fisher v. Kribbe*, the Alberta Court of Appeal has summarized the

---

[85] *Ibid.*, at 250-51 All E.R.

[86] *Ibid.*, *per* Lord Parker at 252, and *per* Lord Sellers at 254.

[87] [1974] A.C. 207, [1972] 3 All E.R. 836 (H.L.).

[88] In Canada, see *Prior v. McNab* (1976), 16 O.R. (2d) 380, 78 D.L.R. (3d) 319 (H.C.); *Gouzenko v. Harris* (1976), 13 O.R. (2d) 730 (H.C.); *Gorieu v. Simonot* (1982), 19 Sask. R. 74, [1982] 6 W.W.R. 221 (Q.B.); *Skirzyk v. Crawford* (1990), 64 Man. R. (2d) 220 (Q.B.), appeal dismissed

various possible outcomes in solicitors' negligence cases involving missed
limitation periods as follows:

> After conducting the "trial within a trial" to determine what damages, if any, a
> negligent solicitor is liable for missing a limitation, three results are possible. First,
> the trial judge could find that had the case gone to trial the plaintiff would have
> been successful and in such case 100 per cent of the lost damages would be
> awarded against the solicitor. Second, the trial judge could find that the plaintiff
> would not have been successful therefore only nominal damages may be awarded
> against the solicitor. Finally, where time has passed to such an extent that a "trial
> within a trial" would be impossible, then the court must to the best of its ability
> calculate the value of the opportunity lost to the plaintiff and award damages
> against the solicitor on that basis.[89]

An evaluation of the plaintiff's chances of success in the original action
formed the basis of the damage calculation in *Cook v. Swinfen*,[90] a case in which
the plaintiff, as a result of a lawyer's negligence, lost the opportunity not to
bring proceedings, but to defend them.

Even if the plaintiff can establish the probability of her success in the original
action, she will be awarded nominal damages only if it is demonstrated that she
had no chance of actually collecting a judgment against the original wrong-
doer.[91] Apart from this restriction, however, the plaintiff is often
"overcompensated" in cases where the plaintiff establishes less than a 100 per
cent chance of success, but nevertheless recovers 100 per cent of her loss.[92] In

---

June 11, 1991. *Fisher v. Knibbe* (1992), 3 Alta. L.R. (3d) 97 (C.A.); *Okafar v. Bond,* unreported, December 4, 1995, Roberts J., Doc. 92-CG-19492 [1995] O.J. No. 3811 (Gen. Div.);
Bueckert v. Mattison (1996), 149 Sask. R. 81 (Q.B.). However, at least two earlier Canadian
cases appear to have imposed a higher burden on the plaintiff, requiring that he establish not
simply that his original action was not certain to fail, but that it "probably" would have succeeded: *Fyk v. Millar* (1973), 2 O.R. (2d) 39, 41 D.L.R. (3d) 684 (H.C.) (which purports to rely
on *Kitchen, supra,* note 84) and *Burns & Dutton Concrete & Construction Co. Ltd. v. Yule*
(1968), 1 D.L.R. (3d) 699 (B.C.S.C.), affd 8 D.L.R. (3d) 683 (C.A.). In New Zealand and Australia, *Kitchen* has been applied in *Thompson v. Howley,* [1977] 1 N.Z.L.R. 16, and *Tutunkoff v.
Thiele* (1975), 11 S.A.S.R. 148. In Great Britain, see *Buckley v. National Union of General and
Municipal Workers,* [1967] 3 All E.R. 767 (Manchester Assizes).

[89] *Fisher, supra,* note 88, at 101-02.

[90] [1967] 1 All E.R. 299, [1967] 1 W.L.R. 457 (C.A.).

[91] *Melanson v. Cochrane* (1985), 63 N.B.R. (2d) 91 (Q.B.), affd 68 N.B.R. (2d) 370 (C.A.); *Islington Investments Ltd. v. Day, Ault & White* (1978), 7 C.C.L.T. 46 (Ont. H.C.). In *Page v.
Solicitor* (1971), 3 N.B.R. (2d) 773, 20 D.L.R. (3d) 532 (C.A.), affd [1972] S.C.R. vi *sub nom.
Pelletier v. Page,* 29 D.L.R. (3d) 386*n,* the court held that in the absence of any evidence as to
any other funds available to satisfy the hypothetical judgment against the original tortfeasor,
the maximum loss proven was the sum for which the original tortfeasor had been insured.

[92] S.M. Waddams, *The Law of Contracts,* 3rd ed. (Aurora, Ont.: Canada Law Book Inc., 1993), at
pp. 501-503.

Morris v. Edward,[93] in a rather unique fact situation arising out of a motor vehicle accident, the insurers of the defendant paid the plaintiff's solicitors certain money under the Alberta *Insurance Act*.[94] The relevant section of the Act provided that this type of advance could be made without prejudice to the plaintiff's right to try to recover greater damages. The plaintiff's solicitors erroneously interpreted this provision and returned the money whereupon the defendant pleaded that the action had been commenced out of time. This plea succeeded and the plaintiff successfully sued her solicitors for having negligently returned the advance. Thus the plaintiff was found to have been entitled to damages equal to the amount of the advance despite the fact that, at the time of payment of the advance, her claim was statute-barred.

(2) Other Matters

Where a solicitor's negligence results in a loss of opportunity to obtain some benefit or protection or avoid some risk, the value of the loss may be assessed and damages awarded on a proportionate basis. However, there must be "some reasonable probability" or "substantial chance" that the benefit could have been obtained or the loss avoided for damages for the lost chance to be recoverable.

In *Graybriar Industries Ltd. v. Davis & Co.*,[95] the defendant solicitors acted for the plaintiff on the sale of land to a joint venture. The purchase price was funded in part by a second mortgage on the property in favour of the plaintiff. No guarantees were sought from the co-venturers because the plaintiff thought that there was sufficient equity in other lands held by the joint venture to satisfy judgment in the event of a default. In fact, the lands were not available to satisfy judgment when the joint venture ultimately defaulted because the joint venture held them as bare trustee. The plaintiff claimed that the defendants had not explained the risks of the bare trustee ownership and that it would have insisted on more favourable terms or sold the property to someone else had they done so.

---

[93] (1987), 52 Alta L.R. (2d) 105 (Q.B.). The court determined that it was not clear whether or not the insurer would have been entitled to return of the payment as money paid by mistake. If the court had applied the principles enunciated in *Kitchen*, it would have assessed the chances of this claim succeeding and awarded the plaintiff damages that took this chance into account.

[94] R.S.A. 1980, c. I-5, s. 321.

[95] (1990), 46 B.C.L.R. (2d) 164 (S.C.), affd 72 B.C.L.R. (2d) 190 (C.A.). The court reviewed several cases in determining whether the loss of an opportunity can give rise to damages. These cases included: *Chaplin v. Hicks* [1911], 2 K.B. 786 (C.A.) (established the principle that simply because damages cannot be assessed with certainty does not relieve the wrong-doer of liability), endorsed by *Wood v. Grand Valley Railway Co.* (1915), 51 S.C.R. 283; *Schrump v. Koot* (1977), 18 O.R. (2d) 337 (C.A.) (the claim cannot be merely speculative and fanciful); *Ramsay v. Holt*, unreported, October 29, 1987, McEachern C.J.B.C., Doc. B852588 [1987] B.C.J. No. 2043 (S.C.) (there must be a real and significant possibility that the plaintiff may suffer such a loss in the future); *Kovats v. Ogilvie*, [1971] 1 W.W.R. 561 (B.C.C.A.) (the plaintiff may be compensated if he proves, on the balance of probabilities, that there is a possibility of some adverse future development); *Clark v. Kereiff* (1983), 43 B.C.L.R. (2d) 157 (C.A.) (once a reasonable probability has been established, damages flow).

With respect to the proof of damages resulting from the lost opportunity, Mr. Justice Thackray held:

> . . . . the law is clear and that I must make an award if it is established that the claim is not merely "fanciful" but establishes as a possibility that there is a loss of a chance to benefit. [96]

The difficulty in calculating the amount does not justify declining to award substantial damages for the lost opportunity. Thackray J. concluded that there was a good chance that the plaintiff could have negotiated a better deal had it been properly advised, but took into consideration the fact that the joint venture would have had the upper hand in the negotiations.

In *Fasken Campbell Godfrey v. Seven-Up Canada Inc.*,[97] the defendant B was a partner in the plaintiff law firm when he was appointed executor of an estate which owned shares in the defendant corporation. He subsequently left the firm and became president of the corporation. As president, without obtaining the consent of the beneficiaries, B negotiated a transaction which benefited himself and all of the other shareholders except the estate. The law firm closed the deal. A claim brought by the beneficiaries against B for breach of fiduciary duty in respect of the transaction was settled. Shortly thereafter, the law firm brought an action against B and the corporation for unpaid fees. B and the corporation counterclaimed for damages for the cost of settling the beneficiaries' claim, alleging that the firm had an obligation to advise B of the potential liability to the estate. One of the losses alleged in the counterclaim was the opportunity to secure the beneficiaries' consent.

The court reviewed the jurisprudence on assessing damages for "lost chance" and adopted the two part test articulated by the Ontario Court of Appeal in an action involving the breach of an agreement for the purchase and sale of land.[98] First, the plaintiff must establish on the balance of probabilities, that as a reasonable and probable consequence of the breach of contract, the plaintiff suffered the damages claimed. Secondly, where causation is established but the loss is difficult to quantify because it was a loss of chance, the court must estimate the value of the lost chance and award damages on a proportionate basis.[99] Difficulty in assessing damages is no reason for denying recovery. However, it is not sufficient for the plaintiff to show the loss of a mere chance — there must be "some reasonable probability" that a benefit could have been realized or a loss avoided. The court held that, although the plaintiffs by counterclaim satisfied the first part of the test, it was not a reasonable probability that the loss could have been avoided had appropriate advice been given. In fact, the court assessed

---

[96]   *Graybriar Industries Ltd. v. Davis & Co., supra,* note 95, at 193.

[97]   (1997), 142 D.L.R. (4th) 456 (Ont. Gen. Div.).

[98]   *Eastwalsh Homes Ltd. v. Anatal Developments Ltd.* (1993), 12 O.R. (3d) 675 (C.A.).

[99]   *Fasken Campbell Godfrey v. Seven-Up Canada Inc., supra,* note 97 at 482.

the possibility that the beneficiaries would have consented as "close to zero".[100] Nominal damages in the amount of $1,000 were awarded.

The English Court of Appeal recently confirmed in *Allied Maples Group Ltd. v. Simmons & Simmons (a firm)*[101] that the issue of loss of chance to obtain a benefit or avoid a risk is an issue of quantum of damages rather than causation, and that the test to be applied is that of a "substantial chance" of success, not success on the balance of probabilities. The defendant solicitors acted for the plaintiffs in the acquisition of a subsidiary of a company. They did not warn the plaintiffs of the effect of the deletion from the agreement of a warranty by the company that there were no existing or contingent liabilities in respect of any leaseholds held by the subsidiary. The plaintiffs brought an action against the solicitors for the failure to provide this advice when they were saddled with the subsidiary's first tenant liability for the breach of a lease by a sub-lessee. The trial judge found on the balance of probabilities that the plaintiffs would have successfully negotiated some level of protection from this potential liability had they been properly advised. Otherwise, they would not have proceeded with the transaction. On appeal, the solicitors alleged that these causal links between the breach and damage had not been established.

The Court of Appeal characterized the likelihood that the negotiations would have been successful as a damages issue, as opposed to causation. The headnote effectively summarized this approach to causation and the assessment of damages in loss of chance cases in this way:

> Where the plaintiff's loss resulting form the defendant's negligence depended on the hypothetical action of a third party, either in addition to action by the plaintiff or independently of it, the issue fell within the sphere of quantification of damages dependent on the evaluation of the chance that the third party would have taken the action which would have enabled the loss to be avoided, rather than causation, where the plaintiff could only succeed if he showed on the balance of probability that the third party would have taken that action. Accordingly, once it is proved on the balance of probability as a matter of causation that he would have taken action to obtain a benefit or avoid a risk, he did not have to go on to prove on the balance of probability that the third party would have acted so as to confer the benefit or avoid the risk to the plaintiff. Instead, the plaintiff was entitled to succeed provided he showed that there was a substantial, and not merely a speculative, chance that the third party would have taken the action to confer the benefit or avoid the risk to the plaintiff. The evaluation of a substantial chance was a question of quantification of damages, the range lying somewhere between something that just qualified as real or substantial on the one hand and near certainty on the other.[102]

---

[100] *Supra*, note 97 at 487.
[101] [1995] 4 All E.R. 907.
[102] *Ibid.*, at 908.

A majority of the court dismissed the appeal because the plaintiffs had shown that they would have negotiated the issue had they been properly advised and there was a substantial chance that they would have been successful in obtaining partial or total protection.

The court in *835039 Ontario Inc. v. Fram Development Corp.*[103] extensively canvassed the law on damages for loss of opportunity to complete a contract:

> First, the onus lies with the person alleging a breach of contract to prove on a balance of probabilities the breach and not some intervening factor caused the loss. Second, where causation has been established the difficulty in assessing the loss is not an impediment to the recovery of it. Third, the proof of a loss of a chance is not enough — the chance must be a reasonable probability of realizing a significant advantage. Fourth, proof of a "reasonable probability" is not to be equated with proof of a 51% chance — proof of a real possibility is sufficient as a matter of law . . . Fifth, where the Court is satisfied the transaction could not have been completed within the time frame of the contract nothing more than nominal damages should be awarded.[Cases citations omitted.][104]

e. Wasted Expenditure

Claims for wasted expenditure and anticipated gains are regarded as alternative claims, and a client who has suffered losses must elect between the two.[105] Where the claim for loss of profit is not proved, damages may be awarded on the basis of wasted expenditures, whether they were incurred before or after a contract aborted by the solicitor's negligence was formed.[106] The onus is on the defendant to prove the expenditures are not recoverable because the revenues would not have been sufficient to cover them.[107] In addition, expenses that are reasonably incurred in an effort to remedy the problem created by a lawyer's negligence are recoverable.[108]

---

[103] August 9, 1994, Trufford J., Doc. 53207/90, [1994] O.J. No. 1725 (Gen. Div.).

[104] *Ibid.*, at para. 259.

[105] *Anglia Television Ltd. v. Reed*, [1972] 1 Q.B. 60, [1971] 3 All E.R. 690 (C.A.); *Cullinane v. British Rema Mfg. Co. Ltd.*, [1954] 1 Q.B. 292, [1953] 2 All E.R. 1257 (C.A.).

[106] *835039 Ontario Inc. v. Fram Development Corp. supra*, note 103.

[107] *Ibid.*, at para. 263, citing *CCC Films (London) Ltd. v. Impact Quadrant Films Ltd.*, [1984] 3 All E.R. 298 at 312 (Q.B.); *Bowlay Logging Ltd. v. Domtar Ltd.* (1982), 135 D.L.R. (3d) 179 at 180 (B.C.C.A.).

[108] *Boyd v. Ewachniuk*, [1975] 4 W.W.R. 210 (B.C.S.C.). The client commenced an action for wrongful dismissal against his employer. A settlement was negotiated but repudiated by the employer when the client's solicitor attempted to sell documents in the client's possession (without the client's instructions) to the employer. It was held that the client was entitled to recover from his solicitor the costs thrown away in an attempt to recover the amount of the settlement from the employer.

f. Calculation of Interest

There is no hard and fast rule which determines either the rate of interest or the method of calculating interest in a damage claim against a negligent professional.[109] The goal is to remedy the loss caused by the negligent professional, or to deprive him of any benefit derived from the use of the money.[110] When solicitors misappropriated money from their client and used the money as their own, the court held that only by including compound interest as part of the damage award would the plaintiff be returned to the position he would have been in had he not been defrauded.[111] The Ontario Court of Appeal has held in *Confederation Life Insurance Co. v. Shepherd, McKenzie, Plaxton, Little & Jenkins*[112] that compound interest should not be awarded on damages for breach of fiduciary duty.

g. Settlements

To the extent that a client settles an action for an amount less than she would have been entitled to if there had been no negligence by her lawyer, the loss is of her own choosing and cannot be attributed to the defendant solicitors. Damages will then be calculated from the date of default to the date of settlement.[113]

If a solicitor is negligent in failing to obtain the client's consent to settlement or in negligently settling the action, damages should reflect the amount that would have been assessed had there been no negligence.[114] However, courts

---

[109] *McKay v. Cowan* (1989), 39 B.C.L.R. (2d) 192 at 200 (S.C.), citing *Re Taerk* (1959), 15 D.L.R. (2d) 443 (Ont. C.A.) at 447:

> There is no rule of law or rule of practice applicable in every case to ascertain the rate of interest or the method of calculating the amount of interest chargeable against an executor or trustee who has used money or other property belonging to an estate for his own purposes. Each case must be considered and decided in the light of the particular facts and circumstances.

[110] *Ibid.*, at 200, citing *Wightman v. Helliwell* (1867), 13 Gr. 330, at 344:

> The principle and the object in every case is to make good the loss caused [*sic*] the acts of omission or commission of the trustee, or to wrest from him any benefit he had, or is taken to have, derived from the use of the trust moneys . . . Compound interest may in some instance, [*sic*] in such a case as the present, be a convenient mode of making this compensation . . . , but in other cases it may be oppressive, and sound more as punishment than compensation.

[111] *Ibid.*

[112] (1996), 88 O.A.C. 398.

[113] *Elcano Acceptance Ltd. v. Richmond Richmond Stambler & Mills* (1989), 68 O.R. (2d) 165 (H.C.), supp. reasons 68 O.R. (2d) 641, affd (1991), 3 O.R. (3d) 123 (C.A.). The plaintiff settled an action for default of a loan with the borrowers in an amount that was less than the plaintiff would have been entitled to had the plaintiff's solicitor not been negligent.

[114] *Rose v. Mitton* (1994), 128 N.S.R. (2d) 99 (C.A.).

have consistently exhibited reluctance to impose liability for settlement advice except in cases of the most glaring wrongdoing.[115]

2. Non-Pecuniary Losses

a. Mental Distress

For many years, damages could not be awarded for breach of contract causing mental distress, aggravation or disappointment.[116] Until recently, the majority of lawyers' professional liability cases were framed exclusively in contract and compensation for mental suffering was rare.[117] While the adoption of the doctrine of concurrent liability in cases of legal malpractice will largely eliminate this particular problem,[118] the extent to which mental suffering will be adjudged a "foreseeable consequence" of a lawyer's negligence remains unclear. Because it is generally acknowledged that litigation causes anxiety and stress, it is arguable that whenever a lawyer negligently conducts litigation, it is reasonably foreseeable that his client will suffer mental distress; indeed, mental distress is a foreseeable consequence of many negligently performed legal services. However, at least one early decision cast doubt on the foreseeability of this type of damage. In *Kolan v. Solicitor*,[119] although it was accepted that in an action against a solicitor damages were theoretically recoverable for a "physical illness", the court ultimately held that this illness was not a reasonably foreseeable result of the solicitor's failure to ascertain that the plaintiff, an elderly widow, was using her limited cash reserve to purchase a property that was substandard and subject to a demolition order.

The difficulty of predicting the frequency of damages for mental suffering in future cases is compounded by the failure of the courts to provide detailed reasoning when awarding this type of compensation. In *Dorey v. Romney*,[120] a case involving a failure to discover a title defect, the Nova Scotia Supreme Court awarded $1,000 for "emotional suffering due to [the plaintiff's] fear that their title was not good and they would lose their home" without further explanation. In *LeBlanc v. Dewitt*,[121] the plaintiff claimed damages for the rupture of family relationships and depression arising from the defendant's negligent certification of title. After weighing the extent to which the plaintiff's emotional stress could have been prevented or alleviated if the defendant had done the title search

---

[115] See Chapter 6, Section II, "Conduct of a Civil Action", E "Settlement of Actions".

[116] See note 14 and accompanying text, *supra*.

[117] *Heywood v. Wellers*, [1976] Q.B. 446, [1976] 1 All E.R. 300 (C.A.), is the first English case in which damages for mental distress were awarded in a client's breach of contract action against a solicitor. The solicitor had failed to secure protection for a wife against the molestation by a former male friend.

[118] See Chapter 1, Section II, "Definitions", B. "Duties in Tort", 1. "Concurrent Liability".

[119] [1970] 1 O.R. 41, 7 D.L.R. (3d) 481 (H.C.), affd [1970] 2 O.R. 686, 11 D.L.R. (3d) 672 (C.A.).

[120] (1982), 51 N.S.R. (2d) 53 at 61 (S.C.).

[121] (1984), 57 N.B.R. (2d) 141, 34 R.P.R. 196 (Q.B.).

properly and sought to correct the defect immediately rather than insist on his own correctness, and the extent to which the distress was caused by the action against the solicitor itself, the court awarded the plaintiff $5,000.

In *Paton v. Shaw*,[122] a judge of the Prince Edward Island Supreme Court, Trial Division, detailed the factual basis of an award for damages for mental anguish, discomfort and the disruption of the plaintiff's life but did not discuss the appropriate considerations for its assessment of damages. The defendant, who acted for the purchaser of the plaintiff's business, undertook to do all of the corporate work that would ordinarily be done by the vendor's lawyer but negligently failed to remove the plaintiff from the director's register. Two years later, the plaintiff received a notice from Revenue Canada that he personally owed taxes in excess of $6 million as a director of the business. The plaintiff endured the fear that he would no longer be able to support the affluent lifestyle he and his wife had worked for and he devoted much of his time to contesting the assessment until he settled with Revenue Canada, five-and-a-half years later, for $175,000. The only case relied on by the plaintiff in support of his claim for damages for mental distress concerned a civil conspiracy to injure case where the plaintiff lost his marriage, professional reputation, standing in the community and entire family estate valued at $7 million as a result of the defendants' conduct. In that case, damages for mental distress in the amount of $1 million dollars were awarded. The court in *Paton* undertook the "somewhat arbitrary exercise" of assessing damages for mental distress and quantified them at $15,000 a year for five-and-a-half years without any explanation as to how it arrived at that figure.[123]

Similarly, in *Boudreau v. Benaiah*,[124] the defendant criminal defence counsel was found negligent for failing to explore the evidentiary basis for a defence, neglecting to communicate and keep appointments with the plaintiff, pressuring him to plead guilty and failing to document an agreement with the Crown attorney to drop charges against the plaintiff's mother and brother. As a result of defence counsel's conduct, the plaintiff's relationships with his mother and brother were estranged and he suffered serious depression. The court held: "To lose one's familial ties because of the negligence of one's counsel, is a loss of great magnitude, and, in my view, Boudreau must be properly and reasonably compensated for that loss which is tied to his mental distress".[125] Damages for mental distress were assessed at $30,000.

---

[122] (1995), 134 Nfld. & P.E.I.R. 271 (P.E.I.T.D.). For a review of the American case law on this subject, see J.J. Kelleher, "An Attorney's Liability for the Negligent Infliction of Emotional Distress" (1990), Fordham L. Rev. 1309. The author identifies an emerging trend of recovery for emotional distress where the attorney's malpractice injures a personal interest. A personal interest is defined in the article as a non-pecuniary interest.

[123] *Ibid.*, at 307.

[124] (1998), 37 O.R. (3d) 686 (Gen. Div.).

[125] *Ibid.*, at 727.

Damages have been awarded for nervous shock, mental anguish and depression resulting from a lawyer's breach of fiduciary duty in using confidential information to engage in an adulterous affair with the plaintiff's wife.[126] They have also been awarded where a solicitor, in breach of his fiduciary duty, made a secret profit on a real estate transaction with former clients.[127] Two years later, an agreement to sell the property fell through because of a title defect. Damages in the amount of $5,000 were awarded to compensate one of the plaintiffs for the considerable mental distress he suffered as a result of the difficulties they experienced trying to sell the property. The court suggested that damages are more readily available in breach of fiduciary cases: "There is however a basis for an award of damages for mental distress arising out of the breach of fiduciary duty. This is not a case of breach of contract or tort in which only in very rare cases will the court award such damages."[128]

b. Physical Inconvenience and Discomfort

It has long been accepted that a client is entitled to damages as compensation for any physical inconvenience, discomfort or disruption, or indeed for any physical illness or injury, which he suffers as a result of negligently performed legal services.[129] Thus, in *Bailey v. Bullock*,[130] damages were awarded where a delinquent solicitor failed to take steps to obtain possession of premises his client had previously leased knowing that his client and his client's wife and child had to seek temporary accommodation with in-laws in a single room. Similarly, in *Coldwell v. Fitzgerald*, [131] where the defendant solicitors failed to obtain a release of a mortgage to which their clients' newly-purchased property was subject, with the result that they were forced to move off the property temporarily, the clients were awarded general damages for inconvenience and disruption.

c. Loss of Reputation

There are no reported cases in which a client has successfully advanced a claim against her lawyer for damages for loss of reputation. In *Clements v. Wyatt*,[132] the plaintiffs, real estate developers, argued that, because of their solicitors' failure to detect a title defect regarding a property they intended to develop and

---

[126] *Szarfer v. Chodos* (1986), 54 O.R. (2d) 663, 27 D.L.R. (4th) 388 (H.C.), affd (1988), 66 O.R. (2d) 350 (C.A.).

[127] *Kalla v. Wolkowicz*, unreported, February 9, 1994, Haley J., Doc. 30172/91U, [1994] O.J. No. 257 (Gen. Div.).

[128] *Ibid.*, at para. 90.

[129] *Kolan v. Solicitor*, *supra*, note 119. However, as explained in Section II "Damages", A. "Compensatory Damages", 2. "Non-Pecuniary Losses", a. "Mental Distress", the illness must be a reasonably foreseeable consequence of the negligence.

[130] [1950] 2 All E.R. 1167 (K.B.).

[131] (1977), 26 N.S.R. (2d) 140 (S.C.).

[132] (1979), 9 A.P.R. 1 (Ont. H.C.).

market, they and their business suffered a loss of credit rating and reputation. The Ontario High Court rejected this claim on the basis that these problems could not be attributed to any act or default on the part of the defendant law firm and, in any event, were too remote. On a related point, in *Szarfer v. Chodos*,[133] the court was not satisfied on the evidence that the plaintiff's failure to obtain a job promotion was the result of depression caused by his solicitor's breach of fiduciary duty.

B. NON-COMPENSATORY DAMAGES

1. Punitive or Exemplary Damages

There is an ongoing debate as to whether damages awarded in order to punish the defendant for his conduct, referred to variously as punitive or exemplary damages, should be part of a civil liability system.[134] In England, the power to award punitive damages has been restricted by the House of Lords' decision in *Rookes v. Barnard*,[135] and we are not aware of any English legal malpractice case in which punitive damages have been awarded.

In Canada, the weight of authority is against applying the restrictions set out in *Rookes v. Barnard*, although until recently it was generally accepted that punitive damages could not be recovered in a breach of contract action.[136] Yet, it is still a rare case in which they are awarded. The Supreme Court of Canada has mandated that discretion to award exemplary damages should be "most cautiously exercised".[137] The circumstances which would justify the exercise of the discretion were described in general terms by the Supreme Court in a defamation case: "punitive damages may be awarded in situations where the defendant's misconduct is so malicious, oppressive and high-handed that it offends the court's sense of decency".[138]

In the reported cases of legal malpractice in which punitive or exemplary damages have been claimed, we know of only a few that have resulted in an award.[139] Each of them involved a breach of fiduciary duty. In two cases, the defendant owed duties to the plaintiff as his solicitor and in other capacities.

In one case, the defendant solicitor was found in breach of his duty of confidentiality (presumably a breach of fiduciary duty, but the court is not specific on this point) for speaking publicly to the press regarding the confi-

---

[133] *Supra*, note 126.

[134] For a discussion of the arguments both pro and con, see S.M. Waddams, *The Law of Damages* (Aurora, Ont.: Canada Law Book Inc., 1997) at pp. 11.20 - 11.100.

[135] [1964] A.C. 1129, [1964] 1 All E.R. 367 (H.L.).

[136] See note 14 and accompanying text, *supra*.

[137] *Vorvis v. Insurance Corp. of British Columbia*, [1989] 1 S.C.R. 1085 at 1104.

[138] *Hill v. Church of Scientology of Toronto*, [1995] 2 S.C.R. 1130 at 1208.

[139] *Guay v. La Société Franco-Manitobaine* (1985), 37 Man. R. (2d) 16 (Q.B.); *LeBlanc v. Dewitt, supra*, note 121 (failure to conduct a proper title search).

dential affairs of his client and for maliciously issuing a petition for a receiving order against the client for non-payment of fees. Punitive damages of $10,000 appear to have been sanctioned by the court as a deterrent "to bring home to the plaintiff and others in the profession the importance of the duty of confidentiality to a client".[140]

More recently, in *MacDonald Estate v. Martin*,[141] the defendant solicitor Martin incorporated Mac-Mart Holdings Limited with MacDonald, his friend and client, for the purpose of taking advantage of investment opportunities. Martin acted as solicitor for both MacDonald and Mac-Mart and was responsible for managing the company and all of its affairs. MacDonald, on the other hand, was a silent partner. Several years later, following a serious argument, they orally renegotiated their interests in Mac-Mart. MacDonald died shortly thereafter and Martin successfully applied for appointment as one of three executors of his will.

The trial judge found that Martin breached his fiduciary duty to MacDonald and the estate as solicitor, advisor, partner, co-director and co-officer. Throughout their business relationship, he consistently withheld information about, and did not keep proper records of, his dealings on behalf of Mac-Mart, including the transfer of certain interests held by the company to him personally. At no time did he refer MacDonald for independent legal advice in respect of their dealings. While an executor, he made questionable claims against the estate without advising his co-executors to obtain independent legal advice. Further, he devised a complicated asset transfer scheme, which was ultimately rejected by Revenue Canada, whereby the estate's tax liabilities would be substantially reduced and his interests in the remaining assets of Mac-Mart would be preserved. The trial judge held that Martin's conduct offended the court's sense of decency:

> . . . taken cumulatively, Martin's deliberate breaches of his obligations to keep records and to account; his outrageous and disgraceful conduct in acting for and against Mr. MacDonald in the Greensteel transaction; his wilful and wanton presentation of false transactions to the estate tax officials; his false claims against the estate arising from unsupported and oppressive agreements he said he made with MacDonald; and his malicious, and high-handed arbitrary method of dealing with Mac-Mart all convince me his course of conduct was in disregard of every principle that actuates the conduct of a gentleman.[142]

Punitive damages in the amount of $500,000 were awarded by the trial judge against Martin. The Manitoba Court of Appeal found that the award was excessive. It held that punitive damages of $250,000 were sufficient to accomplish

---

[140] *Guay v. La Société Franco-Manitobaine, supra,* note 139, at 27.
[141] (1993), 89 Man. R. (2d) 161, [1993] M.J. No. 396 (Q.B.), supp. reasons 91 Man R.
[142] *Ibid.,* at 212 Man R.

the goals of punishment and deterrence in this case, and, at the same time, conformed with the restraint that Canadian courts have exercised in this developing area of the law.[143] Damages were reduced accordingly. Undoubtedly, the court's contempt for Martin's conduct was compounded by his breaches of his fiduciary duty owed in other capacities. In *Gillis v. Eagleson*, [144] another case in which punitive damages were awarded, the defendant lawyer was the director of the National Hockey League Players' Association ("N.H.L.P.A.") and acted as the plaintiff hockey player's agent and financial advisor. When the plaintiff suffered a career-ending injury, the defendant represented him in a claim against his insurer for disability benefits. There was no arrangement between the parties for the payment of fees and the plaintiff believed that the defendant was representing him in his capacity as director of the N.H.L.P.A., not as separately retained counsel. The defendant worked towards a settlement of the claim but did not provide the plaintiff with the details of his efforts or clarify the capacity in which he was representing him. When the plaintiff's claim was about to be settled, the court found that the defendant "engaged in a devious plan to obtain payment of fees"[145]. In furtherance of this plan, he represented to the plaintiff that the insurer had denied the claim and that he had discussed the matter with outside counsel.

The court found the defendant in breach of the duty of care and fiduciary obligations he owed the plaintiff as his lawyer and professional advisor and awarded the plaintiff the amount of $30,000 in punitive damages. It reasoned that the defendant's conduct in misleading the plaintiff about the settlement negotiations was oppressive and highhanded, though not malicious. The court also referred to the long standing relationship of trust between the parties, the defendant's prominence in the field of professional hockey and the considerable reliance placed on him by the plaintiff in concluding that awarding damages for the purpose of punishment and deterrence was appropriate in the circumstances.

In all other cases, regardless of the severity of the solicitor's negligence, breach of fiduciary duty or breach of contract, courts have declined to award exemplary or punitive damages with very little discussion as to why they were inappropriate on the facts of the case. For example, in *Boudreau v. Benaiah*,[146] although the trial judge found that an award of damages for mental distress was warranted in the circumstances, she held that there was no evidence to support the plaintiff's claim for punitive damages.[147] The solicitor in *MacDonell v. M&M*

---

[143] (1994), 95 Man. R. (2d) 123 (C.A.).

[144] *Gillis v. Eagleson* (1996), 71 C.P.R. (3d) 292 (Ont. Gen. Div.), supp. reasons March 25, 1997 (Ont. Gen. Div.).

[145] *Ibid.,* at 319.

[146] (1998), 37 O.R. (3d) 656 (Gen. Div.). For a review of the facts of this case see Section II, "Damages" A."Compensatory Damages", 2. "Non-Pecuniary Losses", (a) "Mental Distress".

[147] *Ibid.,* at 728. For other solicitors' negligence cases where the court declined to award punitive damages, see *Moorcroft v. Doraty & Kebe* (1990), 71 O.R. (2d) 470 (H.C.), supp. reasons 72

Developments Ltd.[148] breached his fiduciary duty to his client by failing to make full and timely disclosure of a conflict of interest, but the court held that the breach was not so malicious, oppressive or high-handed as to offend its sense of decency and entitle the client to punitive damages.

The defendant solicitor in *Stewart v. Canadian Broadcasting Corp.*[149] committed what the court characterized as a "flagrant" breach of the fiduciary duty of loyalty he owed to a former client when he discussed his case on television over the protestations of the client, causing him serious, reasonably foreseeable emotional harm. Nonetheless, punitive equitable compensation, which was held to be equivalent to punitive damages in the circumstances of the case, was not awarded. In declining to make the award, the court emphasized that the breach arose from the solicitor's honestly held but mistaken belief that the Rules of Professional Conduct exhaustively defined the nature and scope of any fiduciary duty.[150] Punitive damages were also not assessed against a lawyer who breached his contract of retainer by refusing to continue with a trial unless a guardian *ad litem* was appointed for his client against the client's wishes.[151] Courts' reluctance to award damages for the purpose of punishing a lawyer is understandable in light of the fact that the professional discipline process is intended to accomplish this objective.[152]

O.R. (2d) 320; *Okafar v. Bond*, [1995] O.J. No. 3811 (Gen. Div.); *Whitestar Developments v. Chaiton & Chaiton*, unreported, April 7, 1997, Chapnik J., [1997] O.J. No. 1648 (Gen. Div.).

[148] (1997), 164 N.S.R. (2d) 81 (S.C.), supp. reasons *loc. cit.* The Nova Scotia Court of Appeal upheld the conclusion that the solicitor was in breach of fiduciary duty, but remitted other issues back to the trial judge. No appeal was taken from the trial judge's ruling on punitive damages: (1998), 157 D.L.R. (4th) 240 (N.S.C.A.). See also *Szarfer v. Chodos* (1986), 54 O.R. (2d) 663, 27 D.L.R. (4th) 388 (H.C.), affd (1988), 66 O.R. (2d) 350 (C.A.) (breach of fiduciary duty; court concluded that the defendant's conduct was not sufficiently high-handed and arrogant to warrant this type of award); *Ott v. Fleishman* (1985), 46 B.C.L.R. 321, [1983] 5 W.W.R. 721 (S.C.) (breach of the duty of confidentiality; court commented in *obiter* that even if such damages were recoverable in contract, they were only available where the conduct complained of was intentionally directed at the injured person); *McKitterick v. Duco, Geist & Chodos*, unreported, March 22, 1993, Hayes J., Doc. C886158, [1993] O.J. No. 648 (Gen. Div.) (negligence and breach of fiduciary duty of disclosure but facts did not support a claim for punitive damages; no appeal was taken from the trial judge's decision not to award punitive damages for breach of fiduciary duty: (1994), 76 O.A.C. 310).

[149] (1997), 150 D.L.R. (4th) 24 (Ont. Gen. Div.), supp. reasons 152 D.L.R. (4th) 102 (Ont. Gen. Div.). The defendant did not breach the duty of confidentiality because the information he discussed was already in the public domain. This decision is currently under appeal.

[150] *Ibid.*, at 170.

[151] *Kent v. Waldock*, unreported, February 18, 1992, Murphy J., Doc. C886158, [1992] B.C.J. No. 352 (S.C.). Note that this was not an action for damages for breach of contract but for a declaration that the solicitor had no claim for fees or for a solicitor's lien on the proceeds of a settlement. The issue was whether the lawyer had withdrawn or the client had discharged him.

[152] See *Terrace Developments Ltd. v. Terry*, unreported, April 5, 1994, Doc. C12383, [1994] O.J. No. 653 (C.A.), in which the court held that a reprimand by Convocation was serious and sufficient penalty for the conduct complained of. In *Payne v. Carr* (1996), 20 O.T.C. 289 (Gen. Div.), in dismissing a claim for punitive damages, the court noted that the defendant had al-

2. Nominal Damages

Nominal damages are awarded in cases in which the plaintiff has failed to prove any real loss or injury but has established that a legal right has been infringed. Traditionally, they could be awarded in all cases of breach of contract but were not recoverable in a tort action for negligence. In the latter context, if the plaintiff failed to prove a loss, his action was dismissed. Given that in the majority of reported cases against barristers and solicitors the action is framed in contract, there are many examples of nominal damage awards, the client having proved that the lawyer's conduct fell below the standard of care but not that any damages flowed from the breach.[153] Courts began awarding nominal damages for negligence in missed limitation period cases where the plaintiff could not show that her action would have succeeded had it been commenced in time.[154] Somewhat more recently, nominal damages have been assessed against solicitors who negligently represented their clients in the purchase of a business[155] and in the purchase of real property.[156] The award of nominal damages may entitle the plaintiff to costs.[157]

C. LIMITING PRINCIPLES

1. Remoteness

a. Causation

Whether an action against a lawyer is framed in contract or in tort or, indeed, concurrently in contract and in tort, damages will be adjudged too remote if they were not caused by the lawyer's breach of duty. Generally, the plaintiff bears the onus of establishing that her losses were caused by the defendant's negligence[158] although exceptions to this rule are evolving.

---

ready suffered from the adverse publicity surrounding his discipline by the Law Society of Upper Canada in connection with the same conduct.

[153] *Messineo v. Beale* (1978), 20 O.R. (2d) 49, 86 D.L.R. (3d) 713 (C.A.) (nominal damages for failure to discover defect in title in land); *Ott v. Fleishman, supra,* note 148 (nominal damages for solicitor's breach of his contractual obligation to maintain confidentiality); *Marko v. P.,* (1980), 18 B.C.L.R. 263, [1980] 3 W.W.R. 565 *sub nom. Marko v. Perry* (Co. Ct.) (nominal damages for solicitor's failure to register a mortgage); *Scott v. Sills,* unreported, October 11, 1990, Scott J., Doc. 12/89, [1990] O.J. No. 2085 (Gen. Div.) (nominal damages for failure to detect the existence of the easement which caused no loss in value of the land).

[154] *Fisher v. Knibbe* (1992), 3 Alta. L.R. (3d) 97 (C.A.) (amount of nominal damages varied); *Gardi v. MacIsaac, Clark & Co.,* unreported, Cowan J., Doc. Duncan 2033, [1990] B.C.J. No. 1595 (S.C.).

[155] *Kerr & Richard Sports Inc. v. Fulton* (1993), 146 A.R. 59 (Q.B.).

[156] *Spencer v. King* (1992), 131 N.B.R. (2d) 235 (Q.B.), affd (1992), 131 N.B.R. (2d) 243 (C.A.).

[157] S.M. Waddams, *The Law of Damages* (Aurora, Ont.: Canada Law Book Inc., 1997), at p. 10.20.

[158] *Hagg v. Marshall* (1989), 1 C.C.L.T. (2d) 99 (B.C.C.A.) (solicitor breached duty to clients; no damages awarded as no evidence led to show that the breach caused the loss).

(1) The "But For" Test

The "but for" test of causation typically employed by the court is simply stated[159] but difficult to apply and often yields little more than speculation as to what would have happened if the defendant had fulfilled his obligations.[160] The problem is particularly heightened where the court is required to assess hypothetically the plaintiff's motivation in the transaction in question.

At one extreme, a number of cases seem to require persuasive evidence that the plaintiff would have acted differently if the defendant had not been negligent, and the courts regard suspiciously any direct testimony from the plaintiff to that effect.[161] In *Ruxton v. Kelly, Peters & Associates. Ltd.*,[162] the court held that the defendant had negligently failed to advise the plaintiff to seek independent advice respecting a transfer of the plaintiff's interest in her home to her husband, but refused to accept the plaintiff's testimony that she would have refused to sign the transfer if she had received independent advice.

At the other extreme, there are cases in which the court appears to have ignored the plaintiff's causation burden, virtually assuming that the plaintiff would have acted differently in the face of prudent advice. For example, in *Edward Wong Finance Co. Ltd. v. Johnson, Stokes & Master*,[163] the respondent law firm argued that the appellant had not established that it would have declined to close a real estate transaction on the basis of the vendor's solicitor's undertaking to discharge prior encumbrances, a standard practice in the jurisdiction, even if the appellant had been advised of the risk of accepting the undertaking. Interestingly, the Privy Council in allowing the appeal made no mention of the argument and awarded damages.

In *Polischuk v. Hagerty*,[164] which also involved a law firm's acceptance of the vendor's solicitor's undertaking in a real estate transaction, the trial judge's conclusion that the plaintiffs had failed to discharge the onus on them to demonstrate that they would not have authorized the law firm's conduct even if they

---

[159] The plaintiff must establish that his loss would not have occurred "but for" the negligence of the defendant.

[160] Few cases easily resolve this issue; unlike the case of *Mini-Mansion Construction Co. v. Agnew* (1983), 24 Sask. R. 1 (Q.B.), affd 38 Sask. R. 100 (C.A.), in which the evidence clearly established that the plaintiff had knowledge of the building restriction *caveat* prior to agreeing to purchase the property such that the solicitor's failure to advise of this problem did not affect the outcome.

[161] *Sykes v. Midland Bank Executor & Trustee Co. Ltd.*, [1971] 1 Q.B. 113 (C.A.); *Income Trust Co. v. Watson* (1984), 26 B.L.R. 228, 35 R.P.R. 71 (Ont. H.C.), affd unreported, February 14, 1986; *Foster v. Barry* (1983), 46 B.C.L.R. 59, [1983] 5 W.W.R 315 (S.C.); *Markal Investments Ltd. v. Morley Shafron Agencies Ltd.* (1990), 67 D.L.R. (4th) 422 (B.C.C.A.).

[162] (1984), 58 B.C.L.R. 317, [1985] 1 W.W.R. 66 (S.C.).

[163] [1984] A.C. 296, [1984] 2 W.L.R. 1 (P.C.).

[164] (1983), 42 O.R. (2d) 417, 149 D.L.R. (3d) 65 (H.C.), affd 49 O.R. (2d) 71, 14 D.L.R. (4th) 446 (C.A.).

had been informed of the risks was overturned on appeal on the curious footing that this "finding . . . was pure speculation and lack[ed] any evidentiary basis".[165]

A few recent solicitors' malpractice cases have dealt with the difficulties sometimes encountered when applying the "but for" analysis by instead requiring the plaintiff to show that the defendant's conduct materially contributed to the loss. In *835039 Ontario Inc. v. Fram Development Corp.*,[166] the court held that a plaintiff must generally prove, on the balance of probabilities, that the breach by the defendant caused the loss. However, causation is established where the court is satisfied that the defendant materially contributed to the loss.[167] The defendant solicitors in *Midland Mortgage Corp. v. Jawl & Bundon*[168] failed to inform the plaintiff lenders that the security for a loan was deficient or advise them of their alternatives. The court cited a recent Supreme Court of Canada personal injury decision to the effect that, where the "but for" test is unworkable, causation is established if the defendant's negligence materially contributed to the loss.[169] On either analysis, the defendant's conduct had not caused the plaintiff's loss.

A related category of cases which fit under the "but for" rubric are those in which the issue is not whether the plaintiff *would* have proceeded any differently if there had been no breach of duty, but rather whether the she *could* legally have proceeded any differently in the circumstances. In *Cady v. Hanson*[170], the British Columbia Court of Appeal held that the solicitor for the purchasers of a property was careless in not explaining the ramifications of a by-law infringement, the consequences of the failure to obtain a comfort letter from the municipality and their legal alternatives. However, the plaintiffs could not have withdrawn from the transaction without the risk of forfeiting their deposit or being sued for specific performance or damages nor was there any advice the solicitor could have given which would have enabled them to obtain an adjustment of the purchase price. The requisite evidence of causation was absent.

(2) The "Chance" Approach

Another approach to the issue of causation avoids the all-or-nothing results of the "but for" test by treating the issue as a question of quantum of damages

---

[165] *Ibid.*, at 72, 49 O.R. Given the language of the Court of Appeal, the test in *Major v. Buchanan* (1975), 9 O.R. (2d) 491 at 514, 61 D.L.R. (3d) 46 (H.C.), should still be seen as governing this kind of situation: "a solicitor has the duty of warning a client of the risk involved in a course of action. . . . If he fails to warn the client of the risk involved in the course of action *and it appears probable that the client would not have taken the risk if he had been so warned, the solicitor will be liable.*" (Emphasis added.)

[166] Unreported, August 9, 1994, Trafford J., Doc. 53207/90, [1994] O.J. No. 1725 (Gen. Div.).

[167] *Ibid.*, citing *Snell v. Farrell* (1990), 72 D.L.R. (4th) 289 (S.C.C.), and other cases.

[168] (1997), 28 B.C.L.R. (3d) 288 (S.C.).

[169] *Athey v. Leonati*, [1996] 3 S.C.R. 458.

[170] (1988), 26 B.C.L.R. (2d) 169 (C.A.). See also, *Davis v. Fiddes* (1989), 34 B.C.L.R. (2d) 137 (C.A.).

rather than one of liability, and by making allowance for the "chance" that the loss claimed would have occurred in any event. As previously discussed,[171] an award of damages based on an evaluation of the chance that the plaintiff's action would have been successful is the standard method of measuring the plaintiff's loss when a lawyer has failed to conduct litigation properly. While in the majority of these cases it is not the plaintiff's conduct or motivation that is the subject of uncertainty, this approach has also been applied where the question is what the plaintiff would have done with proper advice.[172]

For example, there are a few loss of chance decisions where the loss suffered by the plaintiff as a result of the solicitor's malpractice was the opportunity to obtain a benefit or avoid a risk. In these cases, the court awarded damages because there was some reasonable probability or substantial chance that a benefit could have been realized or a loss avoided if the plaintiff had been properly advised.[173] Professor Waddams suggests that this analysis accords with the approach taken by the Supreme Court of Canada to the assessment of hypothetical events in other types of cases.[174] Past hypothetical events are to be determined in the same manner as future events — not by an all-or-nothing approach but according to the degree of probability that the defendant was responsible for them.

Unfortunately, outside of the cases where the loss alleged is a loss of opportunity, it is difficult to know when the "chance approach" will be adopted and when the plaintiff will be obliged to establish, on the balance of probabilities, that his losses would have occurred "but for" the defendant's negligence. In *Sykes v. Midland Bank Executor & Trustee Co.*,[175] the English Court of Appeal expressly rejected the plaintiffs' argument that they ought to recover damages in proportion to the chance that if properly advised they would have acted differently:

> [Counsel for the plaintiffs] contended that, even if it were probable that the plaintiffs, if properly advised, would have executed the underleases, yet if there were a chance, however slim, that they would not have done so, the plaintiffs were entitled to some damages for the loss of that chance. I cannot accept that proposition, attractively though it was put. It would lead to the strange result that, unless the defendants could prove with certainty that they had not caused damage, they would be liable for the remote chance that they might have done so. This seems to me to turn the onus of proof on its head. In my view, the plaintiffs cannot succeed

---

[171] See Section II, "Damages", A. "Compensatory Damages", 1. "Pecuniary Losses", (d) "Loss of Opportunity".

[172] See *Otter v. Church, Adams, Tatham & Co.*, [1953] Ch. 280, [1953] 1 All E.R. 168.

[173] See Section II "Damages", A. "Compensatory Damages", 1. "Pecuniary Losses", (d) "Loss of Opportunity", (2) "Other Matters".

[174] Waddams, *supra*, note 157 at 13.360 - 13.365.

[175] *Supra*, note 161.

unless they prove that the negligence was probably a cause of their executing the underleases. Since they failed to do so, their claim does not get off the ground.[176]

(3) Reverse Onus of Proof

There are cases on causation in which the onus has been shifted to the defendant lawyer to prove that no loss was sustained by the plaintiff as a result of the defendant's conduct.[177] The defendant solicitors in *Heywood v. Wellers*[178] failed to commence proceedings to protect the plaintiff from molestation. The court rejected the defendants' argument that even had they done so, the protection obtained might not have been effective:

> It was suggested that even if the solicitors had done their duty and taken the man to court he might still have molested her. But I do not think they can excuse themselves on that ground. After all, it was not put to the test: and it was their fault that it was not put to the test. If they had taken him to court as she wished — and as they ought to have done — it might well have been effective to stop him from molesting her anymore. We should assume that it would have been effective to protect her, unless they prove that it would not.[179]

A presumption in favour of the client was also applied in *Wilson v. Rowswell*,[180] in which the defendant solicitor failed to obtain proper security for a client's loan. The loan was secured by an assignment of the borrower's remainder interest in an estate. When the borrower defaulted and failed to satisfy the plaintiff's claim, the defendant argued that future events might establish the adequacy of the security and an award of damages was premature. Although this argument succeeded at trial, the Ontario Court of Appeal and Supreme Court of Canada held that the plaintiff was entitled to recover the full amount of the unpaid debt. McGillivray J.A. stated: "The plaintiff having shown the variation in the securities from those he was entitled to anticipate the onus fell upon the defendant to prove affirmatively that no loss resulted to the plaintiff thereby."[181] Speaking for the Supreme Court of Canada, Spence J. said: "With respect, I . . . view as absurd the proposition that the Respondent Rowswell had in this case to wait until the termination of the life interest before he could prove any damages due to the solicitor's negligence."[182]

---

[176] *Ibid.*, at 129.

[177] See for example, *285614 Alberta Ltd. v. Burnet, Duckworth & Palmer* (1993), 139 A.R. 31 (Q.B.).

[178] [1976] Q.B. 446, [1976] 1 All E.R. 300 (C.A.).

[179] *Ibid.*, at 459 Q.B., *per* Lord Denning M.R.

[180] [1970] S.C.R. 865, 11 D.L.R. (3d) 737.

[181] [1969] 1 O.R. 22 at 23, 1 D.L.R. (3d) 268 at 269 (C.A.), affd [1970] S.C.R. 865, 11 D.L.R. (3d) 737 (*sub nom. Wilson v. Rowswell*).

[182] *Ibid.*, note 181, at 876 S.C.R., at 745 D.L.R.

The reverse onus has been applied most consistently in breach of fiduciary duty cases where there has been a material non-disclosure. In Chapter 3, we reviewed the concept of materiality and the cases in which the onus has been reversed where a breach of fiduciary duty has been established.[183]

Outside of situations involving a breach of fiduciary duty, it is somewhat difficult to predict when the reverse onus will apply in solicitors' malpractice cases. The circumstances appropriate for the reversal of the onus of proof of causation in contract and tort have not been adequately defined in the jurisprudence since *Wilson*. In *Ron Miller Realty v. Honeywell, Wotherspoon*,[184] the court declared that the reverse onus articulated in *Wilson* applied to tort and contract cases without offering any explanation for this approach. Summary judgment was granted against the defendant solicitors for advancing funds which were to be secured by a mortgage in spite of the fact that a title search revealed a registered lien. In *285614 Alberta Ltd. v. Burnet, Duckworth & Palmer*,[185] another case framed in negligence, the court concluded that the onus was on the lawyer to show that the client's loss would have occurred in any event without discussing the rationale for applying the reverse onus in negligence actions on which it ostensibly relied. Because they could not discharge the reverse onus, the defendants were found negligent for failing to advise the plaintiffs of the tax consequences of structuring a shareholders' loan for the purchase of a home by securing it with a promissory note.

On the other hand, the British Columbia Supreme Court held in *Graybriar Industries Ltd. v. Davis & Co.*[186] that, in the absence of an evidentiary gap, the onus remains on the plaintiff. It may be possible to reconcile the *Heywood* and *Wilson* line of cases with the results in *Graybriar* in so far as they can be said to possess an evidentiary gap because the evidence was destroyed, unavailable or hypothetical.

(4) The Chain of Causation

Other difficult questions of causation arise where the issue is whether the so-called chain of causation can be said to have been broken. A reasonable settlement will not break the causation link.[187] A client's knowledge of the negligent

---

[183] See Chapter 3, Section III, "Fiduciary Obligations Defined", B. "Duty of Disclosure", 3. "Materiality, Causation and the Duty of Disclosure".

[184] (1991), 4 O.R. (3d) 492 (Gen. Div.) at 501, revd in part 16 O.R. (3d) 255n (C.A.).

[185] *Supra*, note 177, citing *Ferris v. Rusnak* (1983), 50 A.R. 297 (Q.B.). For another example in which a reverse onus was imposed in respect of a negligence claim see *Hussey v. Parsons* (1997), 152 Nfld. & P.E.I.R. 1 (Nfld. T.D.).

[186] (1990), 46 B.C.L.R. (2d) 164 (S.C.), affd 72 B.C.L.R. (2d) 190.

[187] The sole reason the case arose was because of the solicitor's negligence. Even in a situation where the plaintiff has a very strong case, there is no obligation to see the dispute to a judicial disposition before pursuing the negligent solicitors, as long as the settlement is reasonable. *Confederation Life Insurance Co. v. Shepherd, McKenzie, Plaxton, Little & Jenkins* (1996), 88 O.A.C. 398.

act does not break the causation link.[188] The receipt of a second opinion does not necessarily sever the causal link that exists between the original negligent act and the damage suffered.[189] The dissolution of a partnership (with appropriate notification) will break the causation chain with respect to liability arising from distinct circumstances; however, liability will continue to arise for damages which flow from a breach that occurred during the partnership[190].

The chain of causation may be broken by the intervening negligence of a third party. The case of *Inder Lynch Devoy & Co. v. Subritzky*[191] is illustrative. A vendor of real estate was negligently advised by her solicitors to relinquish possession prior to receiving the sale proceeds. A dispute subsequently arose with the purchasers, and the plaintiff was not paid for nine months, which prevented her from building a new home as planned. The solicitors argued that it was the conduct of the plaintiff's subsequent solicitors and the resulting negotiations with the purchaser that were the immediate and dominant causes of the delay. The court rejected this argument, holding that the plaintiff had acted reasonably in following the advice of her new solicitors, and the intervening events could not be seen as breaking the chain of causation. In *Cook v. Swinfen*,[192] the defendant solicitors negligently failed to defend divorce proceedings commenced by the plaintiff's husband. The defendant firm sought the advice of counsel, who opined that the decree could not be set aside. Despite the court's conclusion that this advice was erroneous, it held that it was not negligent and, therefore, did not break the causation chain.[193]

The defendant solicitor in *Conrad v. Thompson-Shepherd*[194] prepared a conveyance of land from the plaintiffs with a restrictive covenant retaining a right of first refusal for them. The grantees were the son and daughter-in-law of the plaintiffs. When the mortgagee of the property foreclosed, the plaintiffs could not exercise the right of first refusal because it was personal and did not run with the land and, therefore, did not take priority over the mortgage. They were forced to purchase the property at a foreclosure sale. In the meantime, the grantees separated and the daughter-in-law removed fixtures and appliances from the house. The plaintiffs sued the lawyer to recover the depreciated value of the house and the value of a conditional promissory note given by the son and daughter-in-law as consideration for the conveyance. The court held that the

---

[188] *Royal Bank of Canada v. Fogler, Rubinoff* (1991), 5 O.R. (3d) 734 at 746 (C.A.).
[189] In *Roberge v. Bolduc*, [1991] 1 S.C.R. 374, the plaintiffs acted on the first negligent opinion. Subsequently they received a second opinion which confirmed what the first opinion told them. Receiving the second opinion did not affect the causal link between the fault and the damage suffered.
[190] *McKay v. Cowan* (1989), 39 B.C.L.R. (2d) 192 (S.C.).
[191] [1979] 1 N.Z.L.R. 87 (C.A. Wellington).
[192] [1966] 1 All E.R. 248, [1966] 1 W.L.R. 635 (Q.B.), revd on other grounds [1967] 1 All E.R. 299, [1967] 1 W.L.R. 457 *sub nom. Cook v. S.* (C.A.).
[193] This conclusion was not challenged when the case went to the Court of Appeal: *ibid.*
[194] (1998), 167 N.S.R. (2d) 282 (S.C.).

daughter-in-law's conduct was a supervening cause of the diminution in value, and the inability to collect on the promissory note was due to the impecuniosity of the grantees and the fact that they had borrowed in excess of the equity in the property. There was no continuous chain of causation between the lawyer's negligence and the plaintiff's loss. Only special damages for legal fees and expenses directly related to the solicitor's error were awarded.

b. Foreseeability

In order to succeed, the client must prove not only that her losses were caused by her lawyer's negligence but also that they were foreseeable. As explained earlier,[195] while the tests of foreseeability in contract and in tort are differently worded, the prevailing tendency of the courts is to treat these differences as "semantic and not substantial".[196] The Supreme Court of Canada has held: "the test for remoteness may be of no practical difference from the test of reasonable foreseeability applicable in tort".[197]

In *Ferreira v. Amado*,[198] the plaintiffs were unable to build on a newly purchased piece of property because of their solicitor's negligence in failing to discover a title defect. Although the defendant was aware that the plaintiffs intended to finance the purchase on an interim basis, the British Columbia Supreme Court held that the plaintiffs were not entitled to recover the interest they paid on the interim loan during the period they held the property. Since the defendant was entitled to assume the loan would be repaid from the proceeds of the sale of the plaintiffs' original home, it was not within the reasonable contemplation of the parties that long-term financing would be required. No doubt the result would have been the same if the test of foreseeability in tort had been applied.

A similar conclusion was reached in *Pilkington v. Wood*,[199] where a title defect that the defendant failed to disclose delayed the plaintiff's sale of a newly purchased home. The defect only came to light when the plaintiff needed to move because of a new job. The plaintiff obtained temporary accommodation in another county and returned home to be with his wife on weekends. The court held that the plaintiff could not recover the costs of travel between this temporary accommodation and his home nor his interest on a loan necessitated by the delay in selling, because these expenses were not within the reasonable con-

---

[195] See Section I, "General Principles", A. "Contract and Tort".
[196] *H. Parsons (Livestock) Ltd. v. Uttley Inghem & Co. Ltd.*, [1978] Q.B. 791 at 807, [1978] 1 All E.R. 525; *Kienzle v. Stringer* (1981), 35 O.R. (2d) 85 (C.A.), leave to appeal to the Supreme Court of Canada refused, 130 D.L.R. (3d) 272. See also, S.M. Waddams, *The Law of Damages* (Aurora, Ont.: Canada Law Book Inc., 1997) at p. 14.640.
[197] *BG Checo International Ltd. v. British Columbia Hydro & Power Authority*, [1993] 1 S.C.R. 12.
[198] [1985] 1 W.W.R. 78, 33, R.P.R. 213 (B.C.S.C.).
[199] [1953] Ch. 770, [1953] 2 All E.R. 810.

templation of the parties when the solicitor was retained. Conversely, in *Froude v. Nash,*[200] where a solicitor failed to advise the purchasers of a title defect, losses resulting from a subsequent aborted sale of the property were reasonably foreseeable and therefore recoverable.

In *835039 Ontario Inc. v. Fram Development Corp.*[201] a case where a lawyer's negligence and breach of fiduciary duty resulted in the collapse of an agreement for the sale of lots in a residential subdivision, liability was imposed for damages arising from the aborted contract. However, the defendant was not responsible for the loss of the entire subdivision when the real estate market collapsed. The downturn in the market was not reasonably foreseeable.

Likewise, in *Ekkebus v. Lauinger,*[202] a solicitor who acted for the purchasers of a residential property and did ensure that a hot-tub on the property complied with municipal by-laws was not liable to indemnify the purchasers for liability they incurred when a young child fell in the hot-tub and was injured. The injury was not reasonably foreseeable at the time they entered into the contract for legal services respecting the real estate transaction. The plaintiff in *Higgins v. Naugler*[203] retained the defendant lawyer to draft a contract providing that a third person would hold 70 per cent of the stock in a company in trust for the plaintiff and employ him to manage the business. The contract proved unenforceable. An action in negligence and breach of retainer by the plaintiff against the solicitor was allowed but damages relating to a foregone business investment opportunity and the foreclosure of the plaintiff's home were denied as too remote and not reasonably foreseeable.

However, in *Jerol Investments Ltd. v. Burnet, Duckworth & Palmer,*[204] interest on a loan required for bridge financing during a delay in the sale of the plaintiff's land due to the defendant's failure to discharge a caveat was determined to be reasonably foreseeable.

One problem with the contractual test of foreseeability will, it is hoped, be avoided with the advent of concurrent liability in legal malpractice cases. Traditionally, the foreseeability of the plaintiff's loss is assessed at the time the contract is made, that is, when the lawyer is first retained. The artificiality of this rule in cases of lawyers' professional liability, where the period of retainer may extend over a number of years, prompted the court in *Malyon v. Lawrance, Messr. & Co.,*[205] to award damages for neuroses resulting from a solicitor's negligence, even though it may not have been foreseeable at the time the firm was

---

[200] Unreported, May 11, 1994, Crane J., Doc. 1883/94, [1994] O.J. No. 1100 (Gen. Div.).

[201] Unreported, August 9, 1994, Trafford J., Doc. 53207/90, [1994] O.J. No. 1725 (Gen. Div.).

[202] (1990), 73 O.R. (2d) 743 (H.C.).

[203] (1994), 133 N.S.R. (2d) 167 (S.C.), affd (1995), 142 N.S.R. (2d) 104 (C.A.). The Court of Appeal commented that the trial judge's methodology in assessing damages was questionable but not wholly erroneous in light of the difficulty of assessing damages in this case. The comment does not relate to the trial judge's findings with respect to foreseeability.

[204] (1984), 35 Alta. L.R. (2d) 358, 57 A.R. 342 (Q.B.).

[205] [1968] 2 Lloyd's Rep. 539 (Q.B.).

first retained. The court refused to accept that liability should be determined in relation to the situation "which existed at the moment when the plaintiff, as it were, walked into the defendant's office."[206]

In breach of fiduciary duty cases, the plaintiff's recovery will not be limited to losses that were reasonably foreseeable.[207]

2. Mitigation

While the plaintiff has an obligation in law to take all reasonable steps to mitigate his damages, the courts tend to favour the plaintiff on this issue.[208] Specifically, there is no principle that the plaintiff must exhaust all other remedies before suing his solicitor; where alternative remedial action is fraught with difficulty or uncertainty, the plaintiff has no duty to undertake it. In *Pilkington v. Wood*,[209] the court rejected the defendant's argument that the plaintiff purchaser ought to have remedied the title defect, which his solicitors had failed to identify, by instituting litigation against the vendor: "the . . . duty to mitigate does not go so far as to oblige an injured party, even under an indemnity, to embark on a complicated and difficult piece of litigation against a third party."[210] However, the court in *Brownstone Press Ltd. v. Rosenfeld, Malcolmson, Lampkin & Levine*[211] held that one of the two alternative courses of action the plaintiff should have taken to mitigate its damages was to litigate ownership of a trademark. The defendants negligently failed to register the trademark for the plaintiff before a competitor began using the same name. The plaintiff failed to mitigate because it began production and distribution under the name after it had been advised of the error by the defendants, and subsequently settled litigation with the competitor over the trademark. To discharge the obligation to mitigate, the plaintiff should have either chosen a different name as soon as the problem arose, or "if [the plaintiff] had a reasonable chance of success in the litigation it should have attempted to enjoin [the competitor] from interfering with the distribution and sale . . . and also pressed a claim for damages".[212]

---

[206] *Ibid.*, at 550-51.

[207] See Section I "General Principles", B. "Equitable Remedies", for a discussion of this issue.

[208] *Brownstone Press Ltd. v. Rosenfeld, Malcolmson, Lampkin & Levine* (1988), 31 C.P.R. (3d) 142 (Ont. H.C.), affd (1992), 40 C.P.R. (3d) 575n (Ont. C.A.), citing the Supreme Court of Canada decision in a medical malpractice case, *Janiak v. Ippolito*, [1985] 1 S.C.R. 146.

[209] *Supra*, note 200; see also *Ron Miller Realty v. Honeywell Wotherspoon* (1991), 4 O.R. (3d) 492 (Gen. Div.), revd in part 16 O.R. (3d) 255n (C.A.).

[210] *Supra*, note 200, at 777 Ch; *Ron Miller Realty v. Honeywell, Wotherspoon, supra*, note 209 (the plaintiff was not obliged to appeal a ruling that lien claimants took priority over its mortgage before proceeding against the solicitor whose negligence caused the loss of priority). See also *Midland Mortgage Corp. v. Jawl & Bundon*, (1997), 28 B.C.L.R. (3d) 258 (S.C.).

[211] *Supra*, note 208.

[212] *Ibid.*, at 149.

In *Major v. Buchanan*,[213] it was held that the plaintiff need not enforce his vendor's lien before claiming damages from his solicitor because enforcement of the lien might actually aggravate the plaintiff's damages. The solicitor had failed to warn the plaintiff vendor against permitting the purchaser to demolish a house on the property. Other illustrations of the principle can be found in *Ferris v. Rusnak*[214] and *Whiteman v. Hawkins*.[215]

However, in *Bjorninen v. Mercredi*,[216] where the defendant solicitor neglected to obtain adequate security on the plaintiff's sale of her business, the plaintiff was held to have failed to mitigate her loss because she had refused to repossess the business and salvageable assets when it became clear that the purchasers could not fulfil their obligations. Her damages were reduced accordingly. In *Amar Cloth House Ltd. v. La Van & Co.*,[217] a plaintiff's damages for a solicitor's failure to register a subdivision and strata plan were assessed as of the date he should have sold the property in fulfilment of his obligation to mitigate. Similarly, in *Elcano Acceptance Ltd. v. Richmong Richmond Stambler*,[218] when a solicitor's negligence inhibits a lender from collecting the full amount of interest payable on a loan, the lender's obligation to mitigate requires him to recover the money loaned as quickly as reasonably possible, as the damages suffered will continue to arise for as long as the loan is outstanding. Finally, in *Hallmark Financel Insurance Brokers Ltd. v. Fraser & Beatty*,[219] a plaintiff who, because he did not favour its terms, refused an offer by the other party to an agreement of purchase and sale to correct a provision drafted by his solicitor which did not reflect the parties' intent was found to have failed to mitigate his damages.

A plaintiff is obligated to choose between proceeding with a claim for damages and a claim for specific performance. Principles of mitigation prevail unless there is a substantial and legitimate interest in specific performance, as the injured party must act reasonably.[220] The reasonableness of any action will depend to some extent on the surrounding circumstances:

> Clearly, at some point in time, the pursuit of relief by way of specific performance may lose its legitimacy in a complex case even where the breach relates to the purchase of land. However, the complexity of such cases is not an absolute impediment to equitable relief. In any event, an assessment of the reasonableness of the

---

[213] (1975), 9 O.R. (2d) 491, 61 D.L.R. (3d) 46 (H.C.).

[214] (1983), 50 A.R. 297, 9 D.L.R. (4th) 183 (Q.B.).

[215] (1878), 4 C.P.D. 13 (no obligation to enforce securities available rather than sue solicitor).

[216] (1983), 21 Man. R. (2d) 229, [1983] 4 W.W.R. 633 (Q.B.), varied 27 Man. R. (2d) 67, [1984] 2 W.W.R. 646 (C.A.).

[217] (1997), 83 B.C.L.R. (3d) 312.

[218] (1989), 68 O.R. (2d) 165 (H.C.), supp. reasons 68 O.R. (2d) 641 (H.C.), affd (1991), 3 O.R. (3d) 123 (C.A.).

[219] (1990), 1 O.R. (3d) 641 (Gen. Div.).

[220] *Asamera Oil Corp. v. Sea Oil & General Corp.*, [1979] 1 S.C.R. 633 as cited in *835039 Ontario Inc. v. Fram Development Corp.*, unreported, August 9, 1994, Trafford J., Doc. 53207/90, [1994] O.J. No. 1725 (Gen. Div.).

conduct of the plaintiff requires a review of all of the circumstances of the case including the plaintiff's actual knowledge of the facts and his/her legal position.[Cases citations omitted.] [221]

The burden of proof lies with the party who breached his duty of care.[222]

3. Apportionment with a Third Party

Increasingly, defendants in legal malpractice actions are attempting to limit the damages owed to plaintiffs by asserting claims for contribution against third parties, for example, other lawyers or other professionals involved in the provision of forensic services, such as land surveyors or process servers.

Before considering the circumstances in which apportionment with a third party has been determined appropriate, it is necessary to review its availability. At common law, the general rule was that there could be no contribution among tortfeasors.[223] Thus, a defendant's right to claim contribution from a third party largely depends upon the statutory scheme that exists in the applicable jurisdiction.

In England, a statutory right to contribution is provided by the *Law Reform (Married Women and Joint Tortfeasors) Act, 1935*,[224] in respect of damage occurring or obligations undertaken before January 1979, and the *Civil Liability (Contribution) Act, 1978*[225] in respect of obligations undertaken after that. While the 1935 Act precludes claims for contribution in cases where the liability of one of the wrongdoers is contractual and not tortious (a major obstacle when lawyers' liability was characterized as exclusively contractual), the 1978 Act permits a claim for contribution regardless of the basis of liability.

In Canada, each province has its own statute or statutes that permit apportionment with a third party.[226] The jurisprudence in certain provinces has estab-

---

[221] *Supra,* note 220, at para. 261.

[222] *Ibid.*

[223] J.G. Fleming, *The Law of Torts,* 9th ed. (Toronto: Carswell, 1997), at pp. 271 and 302; W.V.H. Rogers, ed., *Winfield & Jolowicz on Tort,* 14th ed. (London: Sweet & Maxwell, 1994).

[224] (U.K.), c. 30.

[225] (U.K.), c. 47.

[226] *Negligence Act,* R.S.O. 1990, c. N.1, s. 2; *Contributory Negligence Act,* R.S.A. 1980, c. C-23, ss. 1, 2; *Negligence Act,* R.S.B.C. 1996, c. 333, ss. 1, 2, 4; *Tortfeasors and Contributory Negligence Act,* R.S.M. 1987, c. T90, ss. 2, 5; *Contributory Negligence Act,* R.S.N.B. 1973, c. C-19, ss. 1, 2; *Tortfeasors Act,* R.S.N.B. 1973, c. T-8, ss. 2, 3; *Contributory Negligence Act,* R.S.N. 1990, c. C-30, ss. 2, 3; *Contributory Negligence Act,* R.S.N.W.T. 1988, c. C-18, ss. 2, 3; *Contributory Negligence Act,* R.S.N.S. 1989, c. 95, ss. 3, 4; *Tortfeasors Act,* R.S.N.S. 1989, c. 471, ss. 3, 4(1); *Contributory Negligence Act,* R.S.P.E.I. 1988, c. C-21, ss. 1, 2; *Contributory Negligence Act,* R.S.S. 1978, c. C-31, s. 2; *Contributory Negligence Amendment Act, 1992,* S.S. 1992, c. C. 24, s. 3; *Contributory Negligence Act,* R.S.Y.T. 1986, c. 32, ss. 1, 2.

lished that the statute applies only to actions in tort;[227] in other provinces, the courts have concluded that the relevant provisions apply to all types of negligent conduct, whether the action is framed in contract or in tort.[228] In any event, it is our view that the legislation should be applicable whenever the wrong can be characterized as both tortious and contractual, that is, in cases of concurrent liability regardless of the way in which the case is actually pleaded.[229] The Supreme Court of Canada has recently held that loss cannot be apportioned according to the degree of causation where it is created by tortious and non-tortious causes.[230]

Claims for contribution from a third party were asserted in *Webb Real Estate Ltd.v. McInnis, Meehan & Tramble*[231] and *Rempel v. Parks,*[232] in both cases unsuccessfully. In *Webb*, the Supreme Court of Canada overturned a New Brunswick Court of Appeal decision which apportioned liability two-thirds to the plaintiff's solicitor and one-third to counsel retained by the solicitor for failure to commence an action within the relevant limitation period. The New Brunswick Court of Appeal had held that the counsel, who was hired expressly because of his knowledge and experience in insurance matters, had an obligation to ensure that the action was commenced in time. The Supreme Court of Canada, Pigeon and Beetz JJ. dissenting, held that the insurance counsel was retained to advise on the proper preparation of proofs of loss and accordingly was not required to give any advice on the appropriate limitation period for actions based on this type of loss. Had the facts been slightly different, for example, had counsel's retainer been less well defined, it is easy to see how the court may have arrived at a different conclusion.

In *Rempel*, the defendant solicitors sought contribution from the sheriff and his deputy, alleging that failure to serve a writ in timely fashion was caused by the failure of the sheriff's office to advise the defendants of its inability to effect service prior to the writ's expiry. The British Columbia Court of Appeal, Lambert J.A. dissenting, overturned the trial court's decision to apportion liability equally between the defendants and the sheriff. The Court of Appeal decision has been justly criticized as premised on an unduly restrictive characterization of the sheriff's obligations.[233]

---

[227] *E.g.,* in Ontario, see D. Cheifetz, *Apportionment of Fault in Tort* (Aurora, Ont.: Canada Law Book Inc., 1981), at pp. 24-25; L.N. Klar, *Tort Law,* 2nd ed. (Toronto: Carswell, 1996), at p. 398.

[228] *E.g.,* in British Columbia, see Cheifetz, *supra,* note 227, at p. 25, and Klar, *supra,* note 227, at p. 398.

[229] Cheifetz, *supra,* note 227, at p. 27.

[230] *Athey v. Leonati,* [1996] 3 S.C.R. 458.

[231] [1978] 2 S.C.R. 1357, 91 D.L.R. (3d) 190 *sub nom. Smith v. McInnis,* revg 20 N.S.R. (2d) 98 (C.A.).

[232] 53 B.C.L.R. 167, [1984] 4 W.W.R. 689 (C.A.), revg in part 34 B.C.L.R. 253, [1982] 3 W.W.R 670 (S.C.).

[233] J. Cassels, "Annotation" (1985), 35 R.P.R. 90.

Liability has been apportioned where the purchaser in a real estate transaction has suffered damages not only as a result of the negligence of her solicitor but also due to the conduct of the vendor or real estate broker. That was the case in *Begusic v. Clark, Wilson & Co.*[234] Neither the plaintiff's real estate broker nor her lawyer informed her of a rent revision provision in the head lease of a co-operative unit she purchased. This failure amounted to a breach of the realtor's contractual duty to ascertain and disclose all pertinent facts concerning the property, and of the solicitor's duty to review the transaction with the plaintiff. Because the realtor acted pre-contractually, the court reasoned that it bore greater responsibility for the plaintiff's loss and apportioned liability 60 per cent to the realtor and 40 per cent to the solicitors. In *669283 Ontario Ltd. v. Reilly*,[235] the plaintiffs purchased an apartment building in reliance on representations by the property management company, which also acted as the real estate broker in the transaction, that the rents were legal. The purchasers subsequently discovered that the rents charged were in excess of the legal maximums and the building was subject to rent review orders. An application for rent increases was brought by the property manager on behalf of the plaintiff but in fact resulted in rent reductions. The court found the purchaser's lawyer 40 per cent liable for the plaintiff's damages for failing to conduct the appropriate searches, and the realtor/property manager 60 per cent liable for negligent and fraudulent misrepresentation. Disproportionate liability was justified by the property manager's involvement with the disastrous rent review application. The vendors were vicariously liable for the conduct of the property manager, but were entitled to indemnification from it.

4. Contributory Negligence

If the client's own negligence contributed to the loss, a lawyer may claim that the damages should be reduced accordingly. In every Canadian jurisdiction there is now legislation that has replaced the common law rule that contributory negligence by the plaintiff constituted a complete bar to an action in tort with a rule that damages should be apportioned between plaintiff and defendant.[236]

---

[234] (1992), 57 B.C.L.R. (2d) 273 (S.C.). See also *Flandro v. Mitha* (1992), 93 D.L.R. (4th) 222 (B.C.S.C.).

[235] Unreported, January 22, 1996, Herold J., Doc. 3670/92, [1996] O.J. No. 273 (Gen. Div.).

[236] *Negligence Act*, R.S.O. 1990, c. N. 1, s. 5; *Contributory Negligence Act*, R.S.A. 1980, c. C-23, ss. 1, 2(1); *Negligence Act*, R.S.B.C. 1979, c. 298, ss. 1, 2; *Tortfeasors and Contributory Negligence Act*, R.S.M. 1987, c. T90, s. 4; *Contributory Negligence Act*, R.S.N.B. 1973, c. C-19, ss. 1, 2(1); *Contributory Negligence Act*, R.S.N. 1990, c. C-30, ss. 2, 3; *Contributory Negligence Act*, R.S.N.W.T. 1988, c. C-18, ss. 2, 3; *Contributory Negligence Act*, R.S.N.S. 1989, c. 95, ss. 3, 4; *Contributory Negligence Act*, R.S.P.E.I. 1988, c. C-21, ss. 1, 2; *Contributory Negligence Act*, R.S.S. 1978, c. C-31, s. 2; *Contributory Negligence Act*, R.S.Y.T. 1986, c. 32, ss. 1, 2.

Analogous legislation has been enacted in England,[237] Australia[238] and New Zealand.[239]

The common law rule for claims in contract is unclear, and there remains some controversy as to whether contributory negligence legislation applies to these claims. The English Court of Appeal has held that contributory negligence can be raised in contract actions "where the defendant's liability in contract is the same as his liability in the tort of negligence independently of the existence of any contract".[240] Australia[241] and New Zealand[242] have taken a similar approach.

In Canada, the legislation is ordinarily interpreted as precluding contribution in cases where the cause of action is exclusively contractual but as permitting a claim of contributory negligence in a case of concurrent liability.[243] In addition, there is support for the proposition that apportionment between a plaintiff and a defendant in a contract action does not depend on apportionment legislation but may be based in common law.[244] On the basis of the decision of the Supreme Court of Canada in *Canson Enterprises Ltd. v. Boughton & Co.*,[245] contributory negligence principles also appear to be applicable in cases of breach of fiduciary duty.

In *Doiron v. La Caisse Populaire D'Inkerman Ltee*,[246] the plaintiff's damages were reduced because of his contributory negligence. The New Brunswick Court of Appeal held that, although the defendant solicitor had been negligent in failing to procure personal guarantees as security for a loan made by the plaintiff, the plaintiff, a financial institution, had also been negligent in giving the defendant misleading instructions and failing to inspect the loan documents which would have disclosed that the guarantees were missing. Liability was,

---

[237] *Law Reform (Contributory Negligence) Act 1945*, (U.K.), c. 28, s. 1(1). See *Winfield & Jolowicz on Tort, supra*, note 223 at p. 176, for a discussion of the English statute.

[238] Victoria: *Wrongs Act, 1958*, No. 6420, s. 26(1); New South Wales: *Law Reform (Misc. Provisions) Act, 1965*, No. 32, s. 10(1).

[239] *Contributory Negligence Act, 1947*, No. 3, s. 3(1).

[240] *Forsikfringsaktieselskapet Vesta v. Butcher*, [1988] 2 All E.R. 43 (C.A.). See, M.P. Furmston, ed., *Cheshire, Fifoot and Furmston's Law of Contract*, 13th ed. (London: Butterworths, 1996) at 633-34 for a review of the English case law on this subject; see also Fleming, *The Law of Torts, supra*, note 223 at pp. 316-18.

[241] *Austrust Pty Ltd. v. Astley and ORS* (1993) 60 S.A.S.R. 354.

[242] *Mouat v. Clark Boyce*, [1992] 2 N.Z.L.R. 559 (C.A., Wellington), revd on other grounds [1993] 4 All E.R. 268 (P.C.).

[243] Cheifetz, *supra*, note 227, at pp. 181-82.

[244] *Doiron v. La Caisse Populaire D'Inkerman Ltee* (1985), 61 N.B.R. (2d) 123, 17 D.L.R. (4th) 660 (C.A.); *Coopers & Lybrand v. H.E. Kane Agencies Ltd.* (1985), 62 N.B.R. (2d) 1, 17 D.L.R. (4th) 695 (C.A.); *Tompkins Hardware Ltd. v. North Western Flying Services* (1982), 139 D.L.R. (3d) 329, 22 C.C.L.T. 1 (Ont. H.C.); *Ribic v. Weinstein* (1982), 140 D.L.R. (3d) 258, 26 R.P.R. 247 (Ont. H.C.); *Cosyns v. Smith* (1983), 146 D.L.R. (3d) 622, 25 C.C.L.T. 54 (Ont. C.A.).

[245] [1991] 3 S.C.R. 534.

[246] *Supra*, note 244, at 673, 676 D.L.R.

accordingly, apportioned on a fifty-fifty basis. In arriving at this conclusion, La Forest J.A. (as he then was) reasoned that a sophisticated financial institution has greater obligations to ensure the accuracy of legal documents than does the "simple person who is looking to a solicitor to ensure that whatever documents are necessary to a transaction are prepared."[247]

This is not to suggest that financial institutions will be denied recovery in full whenever they fail to detect their solicitors' negligence. The defendant solicitor in *Bank of Montreal v. Chedore*[248] argued that the plaintiff bank bore some responsibility for its loss since it had failed to detect that the mortgages he had prepared contained an incorrect legal description of the secured property. Although the New Brunswick Queen's Bench dismissed the argument on the basis that the defendant had failed to prove any negligent omission on the part of the bank, the result is also explicable and justifiable on the basis that the correctness of a legal description of property generally cannot be ascertained by bank personnel, however sophisticated.

Indeed, in *Central Trust Co. v. Rafuse*,[249] the Supreme Court of Canada held the defendant law firm entirely responsible for the plaintiff trust company's losses, despite the fact that certain company administrative officers had legal qualifications:

> The [plaintiff's] executive officers . . . and the members of the Executive Committee . . . did not have a duty of care with respect to the legal aspects of the transaction other than to retain qualified solicitors to perform the necessary services . . . they were administrative officers who, despite their legal qualifications, were not expected to provide the company with legal advice. They and the Executive Committee were concerned with the business or financial aspects of a loan — whether the borrower was a good risk — and quite properly left the legal aspects of a transaction to the retained solicitors. They might well have been negligent had they relied on their own legal judgment in such a case.[250]

A client has an obligation to properly inform and instruct his solicitor and the failure to do so may result in a finding of contributory negligence. The judgment in *Earl v. Wilhelm*[251] illustrates this principle. The defendant solicitors incorporated a client's farm. All of the assets of the farming operation were transferred to the corporation and the client retained bare legal title to the land. The solicitors reviewed the corporation's financial statements and tax returns on an annual basis. Some ten years after the incorporation, at the client's request, the firm

---

[247] *Supra*, note 244, at 668 D.L.R. See *Begusic v. Clark, Wilson & Co., supra,* note 234 for an example of an unsophisticated client who was not contributorily negligent for failing to review the terms of a head lease.

[248] (1985), 63 N.B.R. (2d) 361 (Q.B.), affd 76 N.B.R. (2d) 99, 34 D.L.R. (4th) 177 (C.A.).

[249] [1986] 2 S.C.R. 147, 75 N.S.R. (2d) 109.

[250] *Ibid.*, at 215-16 S.C.R.

[251] (1997), 160 Sask. R. 4 (Q.B.), supp. reasons 164 Sask. R. 4, 166 Sask. R. 148 (Q.B.).

prepared a will bequeathing the land to one of his employees. Of course, the gift failed because the corporation owned the land and the intended beneficiary sued the solicitors in negligence. Apportioning 25 per cent liability to the estate, the court held:

> While a solicitor is not relieved, because of inadequate instructions, from the responsibility to ensure that his instructions are complete and sufficiently accurate in law or otherwise that the work the solicitor undertakes on behalf of a client will be effectual and appropriate in the result, nevertheless, a solicitor is entitled to place an appropriate degree of reliance upon the client and the information he provides having regard to all the circumstances of the engagement.[252]

Once a client discharges this obligation to instruct her solicitor adequately, it will be difficult to establish contributory negligence unless the client is sophisticated or legally trained. In *Fasken Campbell Godfrey v. Seven-Up Canada Inc.*,[253] B, the client, was both the president of a corporation and the executor of an estate which owned shares in the corporation. He was also a solicitor of many years' experience. The solicitors who were retained by the corporation to close a transaction which benefited all of the shareholders, including B, but excluded the estate, were found liable for failing to warn B to obtain the beneficiaries' consent to the transaction. However, 80 per cent contributory liability was apportioned to B because he was sophisticated, negotiated the transaction without consulting the solicitors and had sown the seeds of the problem by agreeing to act in a conflict of interest. Similarly, in *Marbel Developments Ltd. v. Pirani*,[254] the defendant solicitors negligently failed to warn the plaintiff builders of the dangers of allowing a land surveyor's certificate to expire before securing stratification approval, but the plaintiff was 50 per cent contributorily negligent. Its principal had some basic education and experience in real estate law and "alarm bells" should have sounded in his mind when stratification was delayed.[255] A client is entitled to assume that her solicitor will act on her instructions and will not be held contributorily negligent for failing to enquire whether they have been carried out.[256] Clients are also entitled to rely on information and advice they receive from their solicitors. It would be antithetical to the very purpose of the solicitor-client relationship if liability could be apportioned to a client for following her solicitor's advice. This principle was illustrated in the re-

---

[252] *Ibid.*, at 24.
[253] (1997), 142 D.L.R. (4th) 456 (Ont. Gen. Div.).
[254] (1994), 18 C.C.L.T. (2d) 229 (B.C.S.C.).
[255] *Ibid.*, at p. 244.
[256] *120 Adelaide Leaseholds Inc. v. Thomson, Rogers*, (1995), 43 R.P.R. (2d) 79 (Gen. Div.), supp. reasons (1995), 38 C.P.C. (3d) 69 (Gen. Div.); *Paton v. Shaw* (1995), 134 Nfld. & P.E.I.R. 271 (P.E.I.T.D.).

cent case of *Hollander v. Stern*, [257] where a solicitor recommended that a client invest in a second mortgage on a property which he represented to be worth $1.2 million. At the time he made the recommendation, the solicitor was aware that the property had been appraised at $860,000. The court ruled that the client was not contributorily negligent for failing to request an appraisal, inspect the property or investigate the borrower. Instead, he was entitled to rely on his solicitor's representations.

Where a solicitor owes a duty of care to a third party *qua* solicitor, the third party's failure to obtain independent legal advice may not support a finding of contributory negligence. In one case, *Midland Mortgage Corp. v. Jawl & Bundon*, [258] the court declined to apportion liability against a third party, to whom the defendant solicitor owed a duty of care, for failing to seek independent legal advice. The solicitor had undertaken to apply his special skill for the plaintiff's benefit and the plaintiff reasonably relied on the undertaking. In *Hongkong Bank of Canada v. Phillips*[259] the solicitor owed a duty of care to a third party because he held a mortgage in trust for the third party and other investors. One of the solicitor's clients had induced the third party by fraudulent misrepresentations to invest in a project secured by a mortgage against a building. The solicitor breached his duty to the third party by failing to disclose that the security was inadequate and was found liable when the plaintiff lost his investment. Although the third party was negligent in relying on the client's representations without obtaining independent legal advice, liability was not apportioned because it was not a proximate cause of the loss. The court commented that, had the solicitor recommended independent legal advice, the finding with respect to contributory negligence may have been different.

The mere fact that a client was aware of the conduct on the part of the solicitor which is the subject of the malpractice action is not sufficient in itself to establish that she consented to or acquiesced in the conduct and to justify a finding of contributory negligence. As the court in *McKay v. Cowan*[260] held:

> The very underpinning upon which the lawyer-client professional relationship exists is that the client can trust his lawyer to carry out instructions honestly and in a manner above reproach. This is the standard expected of members of the legal profession and, in the absence of clear circumstances where it can be said that a client knew, or ought to have known, that his lawyer was acting dishonestly, there can be no finding of acquiescence by the client in the lawyer's dishonest conduct.[261]

---

[257] Unreported, September 23, 1994, Garton J., Doc. 62430/90Q, [1994] O.J. No. 2137 (Gen. Div.).

[258] *Midland Mortgage Corp. v. Jawl & Bundon* (1997), 28 B.C.L.R. (3d) 288 (S.C.), at 326.

[259] (1997), 119 Man. R. (2d) 243 (Q.B.), supp. reasons 119 Man. R. (2d) 243.

[260] (1989), 39 B.C.L.R. (2d) 192 (S.C.).

[261] *Ibid.*, at 204.

The fact that a client has an in-house legal department will not excuse negligence on the part of an outside solicitor if the client relies on the outside solicitor's expertise and not that of in-house counsel.[262] Where, however, no outside solicitor is retained, a company director who is also a lawyer may be held to have been acting *qua* solicitor and to bear some responsibility for the loss. Thus in *Kendall Wilson Securities Ltd. v. Burrowclough and Anor*,[263] S, a lawyer, acting on behalf of his company, reviewed a real estate appraisal that had been prepared by the defendant appraiser for another firm of solicitors. S, without examining it in any detail, advanced the company's money on the basis of his interpretation of statements contained in the appraisal about proposed industrial zoning. When the zoning did not materialize, the company suffered a loss. The High Court of Auckland found the defendant negligent in the preparation of the appraisal but found that the plaintiff company was also negligent in putting complete reliance upon the conclusion of the report and in failing to investigate the financial viability of the borrower. The court concluded that, in agreeing to the advance, S was, in fact, acting as solicitor on behalf of the company in an advance of trust funds, and that the company was, therefore, contributorily negligent and responsible for 60 per cent of its own losses.

III. DISENTITLEMENT TO FEES

A lawyer may be disentitled to her fees in three situations. First, the lawyer may be deprived of recovery in a suit to enforce payment of her fees; or in a suit by the client to recover fees already paid if the services provided were negligently performed. Secondly, in an assessment or a taxation, a lawyer's fees may be reduced in whole or in part. Finally, in some provinces the court may, in the course of a proceeding conducted by a lawyer, disallow recovery by the lawyer of her fees from the client by reason of the lawyer's delay, neglect or other default.

A. RECOVERY OF FEES

In *Heywood v. Wellers*[264] the plaintiff brought an action against the defendant solicitors for damages for breach of contract in failing to secure an order restraining a man from molesting her. In addition to the claim for damages, the plaintiff claimed return of the fees she had already paid to the solicitors. The English Court of Appeal upheld the claim on the basis that there was a complete

---

[262] *Confederation Life Insurance Co. v. Shepherd, McKenzie, Plaxton, Little & Jenkins* (1996), 88 O.A.C. 389; *Alberta (Workers' Compensation Board) v. Riggins* (1992), 95 D.L.R. (4th) 279 (Alta. C.A.).

[263] [1984] Recent Law (N.S.) 124 (High Ct., Auckland).

[264] [1976] Q.B. 446, [1976] 1 All E.R. 300 (C.A.).

failure of consideration on the part of the solicitors: they had not done what they contracted to do. As well, no useful work had been performed for the client at all, and the solicitors were compelled to return the fees.

There are numerous Canadian examples of clients recovering fees in legal malpractice actions.[265] Where a solicitor acted for a client on a legal aid certificate, the solicitor may be required to reimburse the provincial legal aid plan upon a finding of disentitlement to fees.[266] Although there is not much jurisprudence on the point, where there was some value to the services rendered by the solicitor in spite of the malpractice, fees are only partially recoverable.[267]

B. ASSESSMENT OF FEES

The assessment or taxing officer has the authority to reduce a solicitor's fees or eliminate them entirely. The factors considered in an assessment include the complexity of the matter, the degree of skill and competence demonstrated by the lawyer and the results achieved, as well as the client's expectations of the fee.[268] Thus, if work done or service rendered by the lawyer is completely non-beneficial to the client, although the work may not necessarily have been performed negligently, the lawyer will not be allowed to recover from the client any fees at all. Still, the lawyer is entitled to be paid for that portion of the work performed which was of value to the client,[269] provided there is not an inordinate delay by the lawyer in billing the client.[270]

Simply following the client's instructions may not provide a complete defence. A solicitor has an obligation to inform a client when her ventures are unrealistic by making a written report detailing his findings and detailing prudent advice. Failure to do so may result in disallowance of fees incurred after what is

---

[265] See, for example, *Martin v. Goldfarb* (1997), 31 B.L.R. (2d) 265 (Gen. Div.), revd in part August 26, 1998, Doc. C27477, [1998] O.J. No. 3405 (C.A.). *Grant v. Bains*, unreported, December 9, 1994, Gordon J., Doc. Williams Lake 949004, [1994] B.C.J. No. 3138 (S.C.); *Hickey v. Bowes*, unreported, March 2, 1995, Deschênes J., Doc. N/C/213/93, [1995] N.B.J. No. 105 (Q.B.).

[266] *Boudreau v. Benaiah* (1998), 37 O.R. (3d) 686 (Gen. Div.).

[267] See, for example, *Irwin v. Howard Smith & Co.* (1997), 88 B.C.A.C. 138.

[268] *Re Solicitors*, [1972] 3 O.R. 433 (T.O.), esp. at 436. See now r. 58 of the Ontario *Rules of Civil Procedure*, R.R.O. 1990, Reg. 194; *Cohen v. Kealey & Blaney* (1985), 10 O.A.C. 344; *Wiens (Next Friend of) v. Gallant* (1995), 104 Man. R. (2d) 278 (Q.B.); *Lautrec Acquisition Co. v. Snyder & Co.*, unreported, July 5, 1996, Taxing Officer Christensen, Doc. 9503-20508, [1996] A.J. No. 623 (Q.B.); *Jenkins v. Aitken* (1997), 42 O.T.C. 152 (Gen. Div.).

[269] *Re Solicitor*, [1971] 1 O.R. 138 (T.O.). And see also *Ormindale Holdings Ltd. v. Ray, Wolfe, Connell, Lightbody & Reynolds* (1980), 116 D.L.R. (3d) 346 (B.C.S.C.), affd 36 B.C.L.R. at 390, 135 D.L.R. (3d) 577 (C.A.).

[270] If the delay deprives the client of the opportunity to effectively assess the bill, the bill will be reduced because of the consequences of the delay. *Paletta v. Mackesy, Syme, Turnbull, Grilli & Jones* (1989), 70 O.R. (2d) 404 (H.C.).

deemed to have been a reasonable time in which to dissuade the client from her futile pursuits.[271]

Lack of success will deprive a lawyer of fees only when it is shown she acted improperly in some way.[272] In *Re Solicitor*,[273] the solicitor counselled the client to terminate maintenance payments that he had been making to his wife on a gratuitous basis. The client reluctantly accepted the advice and litigation ensued, with the result that the client was essentially in no better position than he had been before the court proceedings. The taxing officer, in allowing no fees at all, criticized the solicitor for acting against the interests of his client in provoking the unnecessary litigation.

A judge has discretion under the *Solicitors Act*[274] to refer a solicitor's fees for assessment under exceptional circumstances.[275]

C. DISALLOWANCE OF COSTS

In some provinces the court may disallow costs as between a solicitor and his client or direct him to repay to the client money paid on account of costs: that is, the solicitor may be deprived of his fees otherwise chargeable to the client as a sanction against the solicitor's dilatory or neglectful conduct.[276] By way of illustration, r. 63.15(2)(*a*) of the Nova Scotia *Civil Procedure Rules* provides:

> 63.15 (2) Where in a proceeding, costs are incurred improperly, or without reasonable cause, or arise because of undue delay, neglect or other default, the court may, when the solicitor whom it considers to be responsible, whether personally or through a servant or agent, is before the court or has notice, make an order,
>
> (*a*) disallowing the costs as between the solicitor and his client.

---

[271] *Stephenson v. Rollo*, unreported, February 14, 1990, Assessment Officer Eperon, Doc. 1903/89, [1990] O.J. No. 204 (H.C.).

[272] *Morayniss v. McArthur* (1984), 46 C.P.C. 256 (Ont. H.C.); *Re Savignac*, [1993] O.J. No. 543 (Gen. Div.); *Keel Cottrelle v. Stoneburgh* (1997), 46 O.T.C. 298 (Gen. Div.).

[273] *Supra*, note 268.

[274] R.S.O. 1980, c. 478 s. 33, now R.S.O. 1990 c. S.15, s. 31.

[275] *Weir & Foulds (Re)* (1989), 68 O.R. (2d) 342 at 344 (H.C.). The court found that there were exceptional circumstances justifying a referral of the solicitors' account for assessment because the majority of the fees related to special efforts by outgoing management of a company to resist a take-over. The C.E.O. who authorized the bills may not have given them the attention that he should have on behalf of all the shareholders, and not just on behalf of himself as controlling shareholder.

[276] Rule 59.13(1)(a), New Brunswick *Rules of Court*, N.B. Reg. 82-73; r. 57.06(1), Prince Edward Island *Civil Procedure Rules*, OIC EC 492190; r. 348(1)(a), *Federal Court Rules*, C.R.C. 1978, Reg. 663; r. 551, Saskatchewan *Queen's Bench Rules*; r. 57.37, British Columbia *Supreme Court Rules*, B.C. Reg. 221/90.

And in Ontario, r. 57.07(1) of the *Rules of Civil Procedure*[277] similarly provides for a disallowance of costs between a solicitor and client:[278]

IV. LIABILITY TO PAY COSTS

As a corollary to the disallowance of costs as between a lawyer and her client, and as another form of judicial sanction for careless or negligent conduct by the lawyer, the court has discretion to order the lawyer to reimburse the client, or former client,[279] for any costs he has been ordered to pay to the other party or to order the lawyer to pay the costs of the other party personally. The discretion existed at common law as part of courts' jurisdiction to control and discipline its officers[280] and is now contained in the rules of civil procedure in the various provinces.[281] There are two purposes to the rule: (1) to prevent the imposition of a penalty on the client or other party for costs incurred which were not their responsibility and which could have been avoided, and (2) to express disapproval of the handling of the case by the solicitor. The Supreme Court of Canada has held that costs should only be awarded against a solicitor personally on a compensatory, not punitive, basis and that courts must exercise extreme caution in making these awards.[282]

Much of the jurisprudence in this area emanates from Ontario. Two lines of authority have developed in the province with respect to the nature of the conduct that will justify an award of costs against a solicitor personally. The first relies on the decision of Lord Denning M.R. in *R & T Thew Ltd. v. Reeves*.[283] It

---

[277] R.R.O. 1990, Reg. 194.

[278] 57.07 (1) Where a solicitor for a party has caused costs to be incurred without reasonable cause or to be wasted by undue delay, negligence or other default, the court may make an order,

> (*a*) disallowing costs between the solicitor and client or directing the solicitor to repay to the client money paid on account of costs;
>
> (*b*) directing the solicitor to reimburse the client for any costs that the client has been ordered to pay to any other party; and
>
> (*c*) requiring the solicitor personally to pay the costs of any party.

[279] *Fekete v. 415585 Ontario Ltd.* (1988), 64 O.R. (2d) 542 (H.C.).

[280] M.M. Orkin, *The Law of Costs*, 2nd ed. (Aurora, Ont.: Canada Law Book Inc., 1997) at para. 220.2.

[281] Rule 602, Alberta *Rules of Court*, Alta. Reg. 390/68; r. 542, Northwest Territories *Supreme Court Rules*; r. 59(13)(b) and (c), New Brunswick *Rules of Court, supra*, note 276; r. 57.06(1), Prince Edward Island *Civil Procedure Rules, supra*, note 276; r. 57.07(1)(b) and (c), Ontario *Rules of Civil Procedure, supra*, note 277; r. 63.15(2)(b) and (c), Nova Scotia *Civil Procedure Rules*; r. 348(1)(b) and (c), *Federal Court Rules, supra*, note 276; r. 551 Saskatchewan *Queen's Bench Rules, supra*, note 276; r. 57.37, British Columbia *Rules of Court, supra*, note 276. See also Rule 8 of the *Rules of the Supreme Court*, 1965 (U.K.), which codified the jurisdiction available at common law: *Myers v. Elman*, [1940] A.C. 282, [1939] 4 All E.R. 484 (H.L.).

[282] *Young v. Young*, [1993] 4 S.C.R. 3 *per* McLachlin J. at 135-136.

[283] [1982] 3 All E.R. 1086 at p. 1089 (C.A.).

holds that a court should generally limit the exercise of its discretion to those situations where the lawyer's conduct may be viewed as egregious as opposed to merely negligent. The court in *Chrysler Credit Canada Ltd. v. 734925 Ontario Ltd.*[284] agreed with this reasoning and held that an award of costs should only be made against a solicitor personally when she is guilty of outrageous conduct or incompetence amounting to outrageous conduct.[285] Relying on *Thew*, the court in *Cini v. Micallef*[286] held that solicitors who purported to act for a corporation which had been dissolved were not sufficiently negligent to justify an order for costs. Finally, in *931473 Ontario Ltd. v. Coldwell Banker Canada Inc.*,[287] solicitors who did not make full disclosure to a master on an *ex parte* application were found not to have engaged in conduct so inexcusable as to merit having costs awarded against them personally.[288]

Another line of cases holds that based on the wording of r. 57.07 of the Ontario *Rules of Civil Procedure*, "negligence or other default" will cause a professional to be liable to his client for compensatory damages, even though the conduct may not be described as egregious. In *Donmor Industries Ltd. v. Kremlin Canada Ltd.. (No. 2)*,[289] a solicitor prepared a statement of claim which included allegations of behaviour that did not make out a cause of action in Ontario. It was clear the solicitor was attempting to indirectly relitigate the costs of earlier actions. More importantly, the claim contained allegations which could have been raised in the first action. The solicitor admitted to drafting the statement of claim, but said he was in the United Kingdom when it was issued. Thus, he argued that he had no responsibility for the contents of the statement of claim, even though it bore his name and address. When he became aware that the statement was issued, he made no effort to remove himself as solicitor of record. The court held that, as solicitor, he was under a duty to advise his clients concerning the law and the use of the court process. The defendants met the burden of proving, through clear and cogent evidence, that costs were incurred "without reasonable cause" and were entitled to full indemnity. The court held that solicitor-and-client costs incurred by the defendant to strike out the statement of claim were to be paid on a joint and several basis by the plaintiffs and the solicitor in his personal capacity. Costs of the motion regarding costs were to be paid by the solicitor personally on a party-and-party basis.

---

[284] (1991), 5 O.R. (3d) 65 (Gen. Div.).

[285] See also *Hunt v. Brantford City* (1994), 34 C.P.C. (3d) 379 (Gen. Div.), wherein a solicitor who did not file a statement of defence in a reasonable time, despite the fact that the solicitor on the other side repeatedly told him that he would be noted in default, was ordered to pay the costs of the motion.

[286] (1987), 60 O.R. (2d) 584 (H.C.).

[287] (1992), 5 C.P.C. (3d) 271 (Ont. Gen. Div.); see also *San Francisco Pizza v. Granata*, unreported, May 8, 1995, Eberhard J., Doc. 32527/94, [1995] O.J. No. 1408 (Gen. Div.), affd unreported, February 12, 1998, Doc. C21337 (C.A.).

[288] Even though the non-disclosure extended to relevant facts and relevant case law which was contrary to their position.

[289] (1992), 6 O.R. (3d) 506 (Gen. Div.).

In *Worsley v. Lichong*,[290] the court held that "rule 57.07 simply permits the court to make an order for costs against a solicitor where it is fairly determined that the proper responsibility for the payment of such costs rests with the solicitor". Its application should not be limited by the principles enunciated in the line of cases relying on *Thew* because its language clearly provides for costs consequences caused by "undue delay, negligence or other default" and does not require outrageous conduct. These words should be given their ordinary meaning. The defendant solicitors in *Worsley* did virtually nothing to move the actions forward until forced by motion to do so, and when they did act they erred. The court held that it was appropriate that they should personally bear the costs of the proceedings. The solicitor for the plaintiff in *Molevelt v. Sowinski*[291] was required to personally bear the opposing party's costs of a motion to set aside the dismissal of an action even though his negligence in failing to list the matter for trial had not been outrageous. A similar approach was taken in *Faber-Castell Canada Ltd. v. Woods*.[292]

Most recently, the inconsistency in the authorities was resolved in favour of the *Donmor Industries Ltd.* and *Worsley* approach by Mr. Justice Granger of Ontario Court (General Division) in *Marchand (Litigation Guardian of) v. Public General Hospital*.[293] In this case, the defendant sought to have responsibility for some of the costs of a very lengthy trial imposed on counsel for the plaintiff personally. The trial lasted 165 days, almost two times longer than the court felt was reasonable in the circumstances, allegedly as a result of the solicitor's conduct. Granger J. undertook a detailed review of the authorities on the issue and concluded that lawyers may be personally liable for costs in respect of conduct which is merely negligent, and not egregiously so. Further, personal liability may be imposed where there has been no negligence at all:

> As I am satisfied that Rule 57.07 is not a codification of the common law, the ordinary meaning of the words contained therein can be applied to determine if an order for costs should be made against the solicitor personally. Applying the ordinary meaning to the words found in Rule 57.07, costs incurred without reasonable cause, or by reason of undue delay, negligence or other default can be charged back to the solicitor who is responsible for such costs being incurred. Pursuant to Rule 57.07 mere negligence can attract cost consequences. In addition, actions or omissions which fall short of negligence may also attract cost consequences. Causing undue delay in a trial could be the result of bad judgment as opposed to negligence. The reference to "negligence or some other default" indicates that the

---

[290] (1994), 17 O.R. (3d) 615 at 619 (Gen. Div.).
[291] (1991), 6 O.R. (3d) 112 (Gen. Div.).
[292] Unreported, March 9, 1994, Matlow J., Doc. 3681/83, [1994] O.J. No. 475 (Gen. Div.).
[293] (1998), 16 C.P.C. (4th) 201 (Gen. Div.).

categories for making an award under Rule 57.07 against a solicitor are within the discretion of the court.[294]

However, Granger J. also held that these orders should only be made in rare circumstances and should not discourage lawyers from pursuing unpopular or difficult cases. He articulated the test for the assessment of costs against a solicitor personally as follows: "[i]t is only when a lawyer pursues a goal which is clearly unattainable or is clearly derelict in his or her duties as an officer of the court that resort should be had to Rule 57.07."[295] The defendant's conduct contributed significantly to the inordinate length of the trial, and in fact fell within the plain meaning of the wording of r. 57.07. However, a major contributing factor was the hostility between counsel for the plaintiff and counsel for the defendants. Thus, despite the expansive approach preferred by Granger J., he did not award costs against the solicitor personally.

There are many examples of costs awards against solicitors in their personal capacity. Where the solicitor conducts the case lethargically[296] or ineptly,[297] pursues irrelevant questioning of a witness before a jury, which case results in a mistrial,[298] commences or defends a claim without instructions from the client,[299] knowingly advances a claim without foundation,[300] fails to monitor the progress of an action, unreasonably interferes with cross-examinations,[301] fails to recognize a conflict of interest[302] or fails to appear at trial,[303] the court may order costs

---

[294] *Ibid.*, at 270.

[295] *Ibid.*, at 270.

[296] *Aliferis v. Parfeniuk* (1985), 9 O.A.C. 215, 1 C.P.C. (2d) 41. The lawyer failed to serve a writ within time such that the writ expired and had to be renewed. The costs to renew were awarded against the lawyer personally. See also *Worsley v.* Lichong, *supra*, note 290.

[297] *Dobud v. Herbertz* (1985), 50 C.P.C. 283 (Ont. Dist. Ct.), in which the court ordered the solicitor, who had to seek leave to set aside a certificate of readiness and amend the pleadings, to pay personally the costs of the other party for his "inept handling of the case" (at 291). See also *Worsley v. Lichong supra*, note 290. In *Swiderski v. Broy Engineering Ltd.* (1992), 11 O.R. (3d) 594 (Div. Ct.), costs were awarded against the solicitor personally because it was his inadvertence in neglecting to include some parties as defendants which led to the subsequent applications.

[298] *O'Neil v. Pacific Great Eastern Ry.* (1971), 24 D.L.R. (3d) 628 (B.C.C.A.). See also *Sonntag v. Sonntag* (1979), 24 O.R. (2d) 473, 11 C.P.C. 13 (H.C.), in which the solicitor was ordered to pay the costs of an aborted examination for discovery.

[299] *Semenoff v. Pidwerbesky* (1955), 14 W.W.R. (N.S.) 322 (Sask. Q.B.); *Evans v. Savarin Ltd.* (1980), 24 O.R. (2d) 705, 109 D.L.R. (3d) 510 (C.A.), and *Yonge v. Toynbee*, [1910] 1 K.B. 215 (C.A.).

[300] See, *eg.*, *Orleski v. Reid* (1985), 38 Sask. R. 38, 2 C.P.C. (2d) 300 (Q.B.), affd (1989), 31 E.T.R. 249 (Sask. C.A.); *Re Bisyk (No. 2)* (1980), 32 O.R. (2d) 281 (H.C.), affd 32 O.R. (2d) 281n (C.A.); *Donmor Industries Ltd. v. Kremlin Canada Inc. (No. 2)*, *supra*, note 289.

[301] *Kennedy v. Guardian Insurance Co. of Canada* (1991), 1 C.P.C. (3d) 291 (Ont. Gen. Div.), leave to appeal to Ont. C.A. refused (1991), 1 C.P.C. (3d) 291n.

[302] *Chesney v. Hanson*, unreported, November 25, 1994, Thackray J., Doc. Powell River 50186, [1994] B.C.J. No. 2672 (S.C.). But see *McDougall (Township) v. Municipal Contracting Services Ltd.* (1994), 51 A.C.W.S. (3d) 804 (Ont. Gen. Div.).

to be paid by the solicitor personally. And a solicitor may also be liable personally for costs arising out of the negligence of her agent.[304] In *Orleski v. Reid*,[305] the propounding of the will of a testator who lacked mental capacity amounted to a gross dereliction of the solicitor's duty in the circumstances and justified an order of costs against the solicitor personally.

In *Naeyaert v. Elias*,[306] a solicitor who was faced with the prospect of being ordered personally to pay costs filed an affidavit by the client to the effect that the client decided to proceed to trial in the face of the solicitor's advice. Costs were awarded against the client.

Interestingly, an attack on the constitutional validity of the Ontario rule permitting the award of costs against a solicitor personally[307] was launched in *Danson v. Ontario (Attorney General)*,[308] but the application was quashed for having been brought without the requisite factual basis, and the issue remains to be determined.

---

[303] *Faber-Castell Canada Ltd. v. Woods, supra* note 292. Matlow J. held that it was irrelevant that the judgment may have gone against the client if the solicitor had appeared at the trial; the client was entitled to a full defence. See also *Penner v. Palumbi* (1996), 67 A.C.W.S. (3d) 461 (Alta. C.A.).

[304] *Myers v. Elman*, [1940] A.C. 282 at 321 [1939] 4 All E.R. 484 (H.L.), *per* Lord Wright:
  It is no doubt true that a solicitor will not be struck off the Rolls or suspended, unless he is personally implicated, but . . . I can find neither reason nor authority for the view of the Court of Appeal that the discretionary and remedial jurisdiction of the Court to order reimbursement of costs or expenses thrown away owing to his improper conduct in a case cannot be exercised unless the solicitor is personally implicated.

[305] (1989), 74 Sask. R. 79 (C.A.).

[306] (1985), 4 C.P.C. (2d) 298 (Ont. H.C.). *Quaere* whether the solicitor is in a position of conflict of interest with the client in these circumstances.

[307] Known colloquially as the "Torquemada Rule".

[308] [1990] 2 S.C.R. 1086.

Chapter 8

INSURANCE CONSIDERATIONS

I. INTRODUCTION

Lawyer's professional liability insurance policies are governed by provincially-enacted legislation dealing with all types of insurance policies as well as by general insurance law principles. Not only are there variations in the Insurance Acts from one province to the next, but also fine differences in the wording of the policies that result in divergent interpretation of the particular policies. While we consider certain aspects of general insurance law, it is beyond the scope of this chapter to provide an in-depth study of all relevant statutory provisions and insurance law principles. Nevertheless, most of the issues discussed in this chapter are common to the lawyers' insuring agreements in force throughout Canada, except for Quebec.[1]

The legal professions in Ontario, Newfoundland and British Columbia are self-insured. The Law Societies in these provinces provide mandatory coverage for each of their members.

The policies covering lawyers in both Ontario[2] and Newfoundland[3] are issued and administered by the Law Society of Upper Canada's insurance company, the Lawyers' Professional Indemnity Company. The policy period for the Ontario policy is the calendar year. In Newfoundland, the policy period began on January 1, 1995 and will be in effect until it is cancelled. The Law Society of British Columbia administers the policy in that province. It is issued by the LSBC Captive Insurance Company Ltd. for a period covering the calendar year.[4]

Canadian Lawyers Insurance Association ("C.L.I.A.") is a "not-for-profit" insurer designed by lawyers for lawyers. It provides professional liability insurance to the legal profession in Alberta, Saskatchewan, Manitoba, Nova Scotia,

---

[1]   We do not deal at all with the insurance policy provided for Quebec lawyers.
[2]   The policy in effect in Ontario at the time of writing is Policy No. 98-001. All further references to the Ontario policy are to Policy No. 98-001.
[3]   The policy in effect in Newfoundland at the time of writing is Policy No. 95-003. All further references to the Newfoundland policy are to policy No. 95-003
[4]   The policy in effect in British Columbia at the time of writing is Policy No. LPL98-01-01. All further references to the British Columbia policy are to Policy No. LPL98-01-01.

Prince Edward Island, New Brunswick, the Northwest Territories and the Yukon. The C.L.I.A. policies are administered by the relevant provincial or territorial Law Society and are very similar to one another.[5]

In general, the policies cover members, former members for professional services provided while they were members, law partnerships for services provided by partners and employees, law corporations and their shareholders for services provided by shareholders and employees and law societies.

II. THE POLICY

A. SCOPE OF COVERAGE

1. Nature of Services Performed

a. Policies

Coverage depends upon the nature of the services provided. Although the precise wording of the policies differs somewhat, they generally provide coverage for damages arising as a result of an error, omission or negligent act in the performance or the failure to perform "professional services".[6] "Professional services" is defined as the practice of law including services for which the insured is responsible as a lawyer arising out of the insured's activity as a trustee, administrator, executor, guardian, director, custodian receiver or any similar fiduciary capacity. It also includes services performed by the insured in his capacity as an arbitrator, mediator or patent or trademark agent.

Alberta and British Columbia specifically exclude coverage for in-house counsel.[7] The other C.L.I.A. policies do not have this exclusion. Historically, in-house counsel in Ontario and Newfoundland are covered, but not for claims brought by their employers.[8] Coverage was recently expanded in Ontario to include claims by corporate employers for professional services provided by in-house counsel after January 1, 1997.[9]

---

[5]　Given the similarity between the policies, we will refer to them collectively as the "C.L.I.A. policies". When we refer to specific provisions in the C.L.I.A. policies, we cite the provisions of Alberta Policy No. 10005.

[6]　Ontario Policy No. 98-001, Insurance Coverage A; Newfoundland Policy No. 95-003, Insuring Agreement A; British Columbia Policy No. LPL98-01-01, Insuring Agreement 1; Alberta Policy No. 10005, Insuring Agreement I and "Occurrence" definition.

[7]　Alberta Policy No. 10005, Exclusion 3.11; British Columbia Policy No. LPL98-01-01, Exclusion 7.

[8]　Ontario Policy No. 98-001, Exclusion to the Insured's Coverage (c); Newfoundland Policy No. 95-002, Exclusion (c).

[9]　See Ontario Policy No. 98-001, Endorsement No. 8.

b. Judicial Consideration

Difficult questions arise in determining whether the insured acted "as a lawyer" or whether the professional services were rendered in some other capacity, for example, as a mortgage broker or an investment counsellor.

The American case of *H.M. Smith v. Travellers Co.*[10] suggests a rather narrow definition of the practice of law. The insured attorney sought out a client at the client's place of business and suggested that he be allowed to invest the client's money. The client gave the attorney $15,000 and received in return a six-month demand note. In an action by the insured attorney against his liability insurer, the court held that because the investment required no legal skill or training, the attorney was not acting in the capacity of a lawyer.[11]

One of the first Canadian cases to consider this issue was *Hazelwood v. Travellers Indemnity Co. of Canada.*[12] The plaintiff, a lawyer, had received and deposited money on behalf of a syndicate and by way of remuneration received a percentage of the monthly interest payable to his clients, the members of the syndicate. The syndicate was defrauded, the plaintiff made good the loss and then sought indemnification from his insurer. The British Columbia Supreme Court held that the plaintiff was acting as a broker or commission agent and not as a lawyer, and dismissed his action. In arriving at this conclusion, the court reasoned that the fee the plaintiff had received "far exceed[ed] that which he could have taxed for solicitor's services"[13] and that the manner in which the fee was calculated was in sharp contrast with the manner in which legal fees are normally calculated.

The Ontario Court of Appeal has recently applied a less restrictive definition to the term "professional services". In *Pollon v. American Home Assurance Co.,*[14] the solicitor gave a personal undertaking as a solicitor on behalf of her client to the Ministry of Revenue to effect a closing. The tax was to be paid by the client. However, the client was placed into receivership shortly after the closing and prior encumbrances depleted the client's funds before either the lawyer or the Ministry could be paid. The Ontario Court of Appeal distinguished *Hazelwood* on the grounds that, in that case, the lawyer carried on an investment business and the losses flowed from the business, not from the performance of

---

[10]   343 F. Supp. 605 (U.S. Dist. Ct., 1972).

[11]   For further discussion of the American test, see *Ellenstein v. Herman Body Co.*, 23 N.J. 348, 129 A. 2d 268 (1957), in which the New Jersey Supreme Court stated the controlling factor should be whether the attorney was engaged for his legal services or for work which is not inherently the practice of law, and if it is the latter, it is non-legal services even if the attorney's knowledge of the law came into play during the transaction.

[12]   [1978] 1 W.W.R. 93 (B.C.S.C.), affd [1979] 2 W.W.R. 271 (C.A.).

[13]   *Ibid.*, at 96 (S.C.).

[14]   (1991), 3 O.R. (3d) 59 (C.A.), application for leave to appeal to S.C.C. dismissed November 14, 1991.

professional legal services.[15] The court held that, on the facts of *Pollon*, it was clear that the lawyer's losses arose from the performance of professional services in her capacity as a lawyer; thus she was entitled to recover her loss under the insurance policy. The court's decision was supported by a decision of the Manitoba Court of Queen's Bench, *Wolinsky v. General Security Insurance Co.*,[16] which involved similar circumstances and an identically worded clause in the lawyers' professional policy. The Manitoba court held that the solicitor was entitled to recover his loss from an undertaking to pay taxes.

Although the activities that will qualify as "professional services" are sometimes hard to predict, the Manitoba Court of Appeal has determined in *Rice v. Canadian Lawyers Insurance Assn.* [17] that a solicitor who does not deliver any service normally provided by a lawyer within the context of the usual solicitor-client relationship but merely pretends to do so, does not provide professional services within the meaning of the policy. A solicitor persuaded the plaintiffs to invest in a syndicate which he claimed had an interest in a hotel in California. As a result of the plaintiffs' investment, he was able to dispose of units in the syndicate held by a management company he owned. The only "service" provided by the solicitor to the investors was a certificate and cover letter falsely confirming the existence of security for their investments. Ultimately, the investors lost their money. An action brought by the investors against the solicitor in negligence and fraud was resolved by the solicitor consenting to judgment and assigning his right to claim indemnity against his professional liability insurer to the investors.

The investors' action against the insurer was allowed by the trial judge on the basis that there was a solicitor-client relationship between the solicitor and his own management company when he gave the opinion.[18] On appeal, the court noted that the solicitor had not taken any of the steps a lawyer is obliged to take before providing an opinion on the quality of security — he did not open a file, charge a fee, examine any documents or make any investigations or enquiries about the opinion. He had applied "not a scintilla of legal skill or knowledge".[19] The court ruled that an insured is not covered where he merely pretends to provide professional services, even though third parties are fooled by the pretence, and allowed the appeal.

Another interesting aspect of the judgment is the court's comment on the trial judge's ruling that the insurer was not entitled to raise or rely upon an exclusion in the policy about dishonest or fraudulent conduct because it was raised too late in the day. The trial proceeded based on issues outlined in the pleadings which had been agreed upon before trial, namely, whether the lawyer performed

---

[15] See also *Wolinsky v. General Security Insurance Co.* (1983) 21 Man. R. (2d) 138, [1983] 2 W.W.R. 761 (Q.B.), a case giving a similar interpretation to a like-worded policy.

[16] *Ibid.*

[17] (1996), 113 Man. R. (2d) 224 (C.A.).

[18] (1995), 106 Man. R. (2d) 100 (Q.B.).

[19] *Supra*, note 17, at 228.

"professional services". No appeal was taken from this ruling, but the Court of Appeal commented: "[the solicitor's] dishonesty in what he said and in terms of the written material that he provided is relevant evidence in determining whether he was proving "professional services". The issues run together. It is evident that he gave an opinion which had no foundation in fact or in law, which removes it from the ambit of professional services."[20]

In other contexts, the concept of legal services or acting in a legal capacity has been given a considerably broader construction. The issue commonly arises in claims by clients, who have suffered monetary loss by reason of the fraud or defalcation of their solicitors, against provincial compensation plans. For example, in *Patchett v. Law Society of British Columbia*,[21] the British Columbia Supreme Court was called upon to consider whether the Society had properly dismissed a claim against the provincial compensation fund by clients who had been defrauded by a solicitor. The clients had been introduced to the solicitor for the purpose of obtaining assistance in investing in mortgages. An agreement was concluded whereby the clients provided the solicitor with investment funds and the solicitor agreed to find appropriate mortgages and to do all related accounting and legal work. As remuneration, the solicitor was to receive 20 per cent of the profits but would not share any losses. The solicitor absconded with the money and the Law Society refused the clients compensation on the grounds that the solicitor had not received the funds in his capacity as a member of the Law Society.

In upholding the clients' petition for an order quashing this decision, Mr. Justice Anderson set out a series of principles to be considered in determining when a lawyer is engaged in the practice of law.[22] Of particular significance are his conclusions that: (1) it is a "normal and traditional function of the solicitor to place funds left with him in trust to be invested on behalf of his client"[23]; and (2) generally, funds turned over to a lawyer for the purchase of mortgages, particularly, specific mortgages or mortgages to be approved by the client, are funds received by the lawyer in his capacity as a member of the Law Society.[24]

Anderson J. distinguished *Hazelwood v. Travellers Indemnity Co. of Canada*[25] on the basis that the solicitor in that case had acted as an insurer or guarantor of the proposed investments, that he performed no legal services and that he was dealing with loans made for the purpose of purchasing speculative securities and not mortgages. Whatever the factual distinctions between *Hazelwood* and *Patchett*, it is clear that the concept of "lawyering" espoused in the latter includes the provision of certain kinds of brokering or investment services.

---

[20]   *Ibid.,* at 229.
[21]   [1979] 1 W.W.R. 585, 92 D.L.R. (3d) 12 (B.C.S.C.).
[22]   *Ibid.,* at 622 W.W.R.
[23]   *Ibid.*
[24]   This conclusion is of particular importance in interpreting the B.C. policy.
[25]   *Supra,* note 12.

Similarly, in *Riveria Development Corp. v. Law Society of Saskatchewan*,[26] a lawyer joined an investment syndicate involved in the construction of apartment buildings. He was to provide legal services in exchange for title to a building constructed by the syndicate. First mortgage funds from a bank were deposited in the solicitor's mixed trust account. The lawyer misappropriated the money, leaving the other members of the syndicate liable to the bank. The Court of Appeal concluded that, even though the lawyer's involvement in the business agreement could not be characterized as that of a solicitor, the Law Society's Compensation Fund had to compensate the syndicate members because the money was advanced from the bank to the trust account and received by the lawyer in his capacity as a lawyer.

2. Coverage for Liability to Third Parties

Assuming the error or omission arises out of the performance of professional services, does the policy only cover claims made by clients of the insured or does it also respond to claims against the lawyer brought by third parties? None of the policies expressly exclude coverage for claims brought by non-clients. The Ontario, Newfoundland and British Columbia policies provide coverage for damages arising out of the performance or the failure to perform professional services "for others".[27] Similarly, the C.L.I.A. policies cover errors in the rendering of professional services "to others".[28]

In *Wolinsky v. General Security Insurance Co.*,[29] the insurer argued that the phrase "for others" precluded coverage because the injured party was not a client of the insured.[30] Wilson J., of the Manitoba Queen's Bench, held that this phrase was ambiguous and, therefore, was to be interpreted against the insurer. This effectively means that the policy protects a solicitor against a third party claim.[31]

The Ontario Court of Appeal in *Pollon v. American Home Assurance Co.*[32] found no ambiguity in the phrase "for others". In this case, the court held that the breach of a solicitor's personal undertaking to Revenue Canada on behalf of her client in respect of land transfer tax was covered by the policy. It held: "liability under the policy is based on whether the loss arises from the performance of professional services and not on whether it flows from an obligation

---

[26]   [1992] 4 W.W.R. 289 (Sask. C.A.).
[27]   Ontario Policy No. 98-001, Insurance Coverage A; Newfoundland Policy No. 95-003, Insuring Agreement A; British Columbia Policy No. LPL98-01-01, Insuring Agreement 1.
[28]   Alberta Policy No. 10005, Definition of "occurrence".
[29]   *Supra*, note 15.
[30]   In this case, the insured firm of solicitors, acting for a mortgagor, incurred liability to the mortgagee by virtue of an undertaking to pay tax arrears.
[31]   See Chapter 4.
[32]   *Supra*, note 14.

owed to clients or other parties".[33] At least one commentator agrees with this interpretation of "for others":

> "Others" simply limits the coverage for services performed for persons other than the lawyer. The policy does not apply when the lawyer represents himself in a transaction or proceeding. Even if a lawyer ends up obligated to a third party because of such self-representation, the policy provides no coverage. "Others", therefore, has no reference to whom a duty may be owed.[34]

Nevertheless, the same commentator observed that while the policy clearly covers damages owed to a third party for whose benefit services were rendered (that is, where a duty of care arises), it may not cover tort liability to a third party as a consequence of representing the client.[35] The Ministry of Revenue was neither a client nor someone to whom the lawyer assumed a duty of care. In any event, he maintained that coverage should not be extended to obligations voluntarily assumed. Alternatively, he suggested:

Another way of approaching the problem is to break down in categories the various types of claims which might be made against a lawyer while providing professional services. They are claims by:

(a) clients or persons benefiting from legal services;

(b) parties opposite to the lawyer's client in a proceeding or transaction, *e.g.*, vendor and purchaser;

(c) persons providing goods or services for the benefit of either the client or the lawyer.

In the instance of the first category, the policy must cover the loss. While the issue is not so clear for (b), claims in the last category ought to be excluded.[36]

In our view, even where an assumption of responsibility is voluntary, a solicitor should be covered if it is made in her capacity as a lawyer. This is especially true in situations such as *Pollon v. American Home Assurance Co.*[37] where the Ministry of Revenue would only accept the undertaking of a solicitor licensed to practise in the province. The fact that there were other courses of action the lawyer could have pursued to fulfil her professional obligation to

---

[33] *Ibid.*, at 64.

[34] K.W. Golish, "Case Comments: Lawyers' Errors and Omissions Insurance: *Pollon v. American Home Assurance*" (1992), 13 *Advocates' Q.* 507 at p. 509.

[35] *Ibid.*, at p. 510.

[36] *Ibid.*, at p. 509.

[37] (1991), 3 O.R. (3d) 59 (C.A.), application for leave to appeal to S.C.C. dismissed November 14, 1991.

"extricate her client from such a predicament" is not sufficient reason to deny coverage.

3. Coverage Period

Unlike fire and accident policies, which provide coverage for liability arising from an act or event occurring only during the term of the policy, lawyers' liability policies, like other professional liability policies, operate on a "claims made" basis. That is, the policy responds to claims made, not errors or omissions committed, during the policy period. In *St. Paul Fire & Marine Insurance Co. and Guardian Insurance Co. of Canada*,[38] the majority of the Ontario Court of Appeal rejected the insurer's argument that a claim was "made" upon issuance of a writ of summons because the writ had not been served or otherwise brought to the attention of the insured.

Generally, lawyers who cease practising, retire or are appointed to the bench continue to be covered under the policy in effect in their jurisdiction, or any preceding policy, for professional services provided while they were practising members of the relevant Law Society if the services would have been covered under the policy.[39]

4. Coverage for Partners, Shareholders, Employees and Agents

Coverage is available for the errors or omissions of any person for whose acts the insured is legally responsible, namely, partners, shareholders, employees and agents, even if the partner, shareholder, employee or agent is guilty of a dishonest, fraudulent, criminal or malicious act, so long as the insured did not participate or acquiesce in or conceal the conduct.[40] The acts and omissions of both real and ostensible partners are covered in all jurisdictions.[41] However, the Lawyers' Professional Indemnity Co.'s recent decision to reduce the per claim limit of liability to $250,000 and the aggregate limit per policy period to $250,000 for judges, retired members and former members, has been the subject of some controversy.[42]

---

[38] (1983), 43 O.R. (2d) 326, 1 D.L.R. (4th) 342 (C.A.).

[39] Ontario Policy No. 98-001, Definition (h); Newfoundland Policy No. 95-003, Definition d(i); Alberta Policy No. 10005, Definition of "Individual Insured".

[40] Newfoundland Policy No. 95-003, Exclusion (a); British Columbia Policy No. LPL98-01-01, Condition 6.1; Alberta Policy No. 10005, Exclusion 4.5(a).

[41] Ontario Policy 98-001, Definition h(iii); Newfoundland Policy No. 95-003, Definition d(iii); Alberta Policy No. 10005, Definitions of "Law Firm" and "Additional Insured"; British Columbia Policy No. LPL98-01-01, Definitions of "Law Firm" and "Additional Insured".

[42] Ontario Policy No. 98-001, Endorsement 7; R. Westhead, "Retired Lawyer Fights LPIC's "Breach of Contract" *Law Times* (12-18 February 1996) 1.

5. Geographical Limitations

Most lawyers' professional liability policies have geographical limitations. The Ontario and Newfoundland policies cover members practising anywhere in Canada, as well as members who perform professional services outside of Canada respecting the laws of Canada, provided that those services do not constitute more than 10 per cent of the members' docketed time (or, in Ontario, gross billings) in a calendar year.[43]

The policy in British Columbia applies to errors occurring anywhere in the world.[44] The insurer has the duty to defend claims first made or suits first brought within Canada and the United States of America and the right, but not the duty, to investigate, settle and defend any claim made or suit brought elsewhere than within Canada or the United States.[45]

The C.L.I.A. policies do not cover professional services provided from an office located within Canada, but outside the province in which the insured is licensed to practise, unless those services are provided on an occasional basis only.[46] Professional services provided from an office located outside Canada are excluded altogether.[47] Most C.L.I.A. policies do not apply to any claims instituted outside Canada or the United States of America.[48]

6. Limit of Liability

The Ontario and Newfoundland policy limits liability to $1 million (including the deductible), per claim or occurrence.[49] This limit applies to a claim or suit which names more than one insured for an occurrence arising out of the same (or, in Ontario, related) professional service, unless the claim or suit is brought jointly or severally against two or more partnerships, law corporations or sole practitioners, in which case the $1 million limit applies separately to each.[50] Additionally, the annual aggregate for which the insurer is liable is limited to $2 million for each insured, including any vicarious liability arising from profes-

---

[43] Ontario Policy No. 98-001, Special Provision A; Newfoundland Policy No. 95-003, Special Provision (a).

[44] British Columbia Policy LPL 98-01-01, Insuring Agreement 3.1.

[45] *Ibid.*, Insuring Agreement 2.1 and 2.2.

[46] Alberta Policy No. 10005, Exclusion 3.1. Note the provision for Interjurisdictional Coverage in Condition 4.7.

[47] *Ibid.*, Exclusion 3.2.

[48] See, for example, Saskatchewan Policy No. 10004, Exclusion 3.11 and Nova Scotia Policy No. 10000, Exclusion 3.11.

[49] Note that the limit in Ontario is subject to any sublimit for innocent party coverage, restricted area of practice or part-time practice coverage or for claims brought by corporate employers against in-house counsel. There is also a real estate transaction levy surcharge, civil litigation transaction levy surcharge, volume levy surcharge and claims history levy surcharge set out in Endorsements 2, 3, 4 and 5 respectively of Ontario Policy No. 98-001.

[50] Ontario Policy No. 98-001, General Condition A; Newfoundland Policy No. 95-003, Condition (a)(i).

sional services performed by any other insured. The insurer's obligation to pay on behalf of an insured generally applies only to amounts in excess of the insured's deductible.[51]

British Columbia's policy also limits liability to $1 million per error, including damages, expenses and the deductible.[52] The limit of liability will not be increased even in the event that the error gives rise to more than one claim or a claim is brought against more than one insured.[53] The annual aggregate is limited to $2 million for each insured, including any vicarious liability imposed upon the insured.[54] The B.C. policy specifically states that the insurer will not be responsible for any damages or claims expenses or for continuing to defend any proceeding once the limit of liability has been exhausted.[55]

Finally, the C.L.I.A. policies limit liability to $1 million per occurrence, less the deductible.[56] When a claim is brought jointly or severally against two or more law firms, the $1 million limit applies separately to each.[57] The aggregate limit is $2 million. The C.L.I.A. policies specify that the limit is inclusive of defence costs.[58]

Each of the policies limits liability for more than one act, error or omission arising from the same professional services to $1 million by deeming them to be a single claim, occurrence or error.[59] This sort of provision was interpreted by the Alberta Court of Appeal in *Yang v. Canadian Lawyers' Insurance Assn.*[60] The court considered whether there was one or several occurrences involved in a lawyer's representation of seven investors in a syndicate developed by the lawyer for the construction of shopping malls. The policy in effect provided that a single liability limit applied where the act, error or omission occurs in relation to "the same professional services". After a review of the American jurisprudence, the court held that these issues should be considered in determining whether the claims involve the "same professional services": (1) the nature of the professional services involved; (2) whether there was a commonality of interest between the clients for whom the services were performed; (3) the acts, errors or omissions that gave rise to a finding of negligence; and (4) whether the

---

[51] Ontario Policy No. 98-001, General Condition C; Newfoundland Policy No. 95-003, Condition (b).

[52] British Columbia Policy No. LPL98-01-01, Condition 1.1.1.

[53] *Ibid.*, Condition 1.1.2.

[54] *Ibid.*, Condition 1.2.

[55] *Ibid.*, Condition 1.5.

[56] *Ibid.*, Insuring Agreement 2.4(c).

[57] *Ibid.*, Condition 4.1.

[58] *Ibid.*, Insuring Agreement 2.4(c).

[59] Ontario Policy No. 98-001 covers "claims" (see Insurance Coverage A), British Columbia Policy No. LPL98-01-01 covers "errors" (see Insuring Agreement 1), Newfoundland Policy No. 95-001 and Alberta Policy No. 10005 cover "occurrences" (see, respectively, Condition (a)(i) and Insuring Agreement 2.4(c)).

[60] (1996), 50 Alta. L.R. (3d) 179 (C.A.), application for leave to appeal to the Supreme Court of Canada dismissed (1997), 226 N.R. 394n, [1997] S.C.C.A. 318.

negligence caused the damage which was the subject of the claim. In this case, to assess whether there was a commonality of interest between the investors, the court compared the type and timing of their investments, and whether their interests were substantially the same or came into conflict at any time throughout the provision of the services. It also considered when and how the clients became involved with one another. The court concluded that there was insufficient commonality of interest among the clients to justify a finding that there had only been one occurrence under the policy.

All provinces except Newfoundland now provide that a single limit of liability applies in respect of claims that arise out of the same *or related* act, error or omission. Thus, courts may now be more willing impose a single limit of liability in cases involving multiple claims.

7. Exclusions

Each Canadian policy expressly excludes coverage for claims against an insured resulting from any dishonest, fraudulent, criminal or malicious act, unless the insured did not participate or acquiesce in or conceal the conduct.[61] For the exclusion to operate, the excluded conduct must be the proximate cause of the client's loss.[62] The onus is on the insurer to establish the applicability of the exclusionary clause, with any doubt to be resolved in favour of the insured.[63] The Saskatchewan Court of Queen's Bench interpreted this type of exclusion in *Kallos v. Saskatchewan Government Insurance*,[64] and held that it requires a wilful and deliberate act:[65]

> The [insurer] submits that the conduct of the solicitor towards the plaintiffs went beyond negligence and amounted to conduct of the type excluded by the policy. It is important to bear in mind that the act or omission we are talking about here was

---

[61] The coverage for lawyers under professional liability policies has been considerably expanded since the time of *Davies v. Hosken*, [1937] 3 All E.R. 92 (K.B.), in which a lawyer failed to obtain indemnification for his clerk's misappropriation of a client's funds since the policy only covered acts arising from "neglect, omission or error".

[62] See, for example, *Clark, Drummie & Co. v. Law Society of New Brunswick* (1993), 138 N.B.R. (2d) 332 (T.D.); *New Brunswick Power Corp. v. Canadian Lawyers Insurance Assn.* (1996), 184 N.B.R. (2d) 329 (T.D.).

[63] *Litton Systems Canada v. Olympia Engineering Ltd.* (1990), 1 O.R. (3d) 780 (Gen. Div.).

[64] [1984] 2 W.W.R. 183 (Sask. Q.B.).

[65] The word "dishonest" has also been construed in contexts other than but related to lawyers' professional liability. *e.g.*, in cases dealing with the availability of coverage under a fidelity bond such as *Lynch & Co. v. U.S. Fidelity & Guarantee Co.*, [1971] 1 O.R. 28, 14 D.L.R. (3d) 294 (H.C.) and *Jarvis v. Van-Martin Realty Ltd.* (1987), 25 C.C.L.I. 13 (B.C.S.C.). See also *Leo Goodman Investments Ltd. v. Pidlubny* (1980), 15 R.P.R. 87 (Ont. S.C.). In the annotation accompanying the report of this case, Professor Swan suggests that the solicitor's conduct characterized by the judge as "serious and willful misconduct" and as "unconscionable [and] manifesting deliberate and complete disregard for the interests of his client" raises a coverage problem.

the failure of the solicitor to commence legal action within the prescribed limitation period. Can it be said this occurred in a manner specified in the exclusion, as
opposed to negligently? *The words used in the exclusion denote an act or omission that is willful and deliberate.* There is nothing in the evidence which would
lead to the conclusion the solicitor's failure to commence action within the prescribed limitation period was wilful and deliberate as opposed to negligent. The
onus of establishing the applicability of this exclusion is on the [insurer]; it has not
met this onus . . . [66] [Case citations omitted, emphasis added.]

A recent Ontario Court (General Division) decision reveals that the exclusion
will apply not only in the case of acquiescence in the dishonest, fraudulent, criminal or malicious acts of another insured but also of one's clients. In *Wisebrod v.
American Home Assurance Co.,*[67] the plaintiff solicitors sought reimbursement
from their insurers for the expenses they incurred in defending an action brought
against them, their partners and law firms. The claim alleged wrongful interference with contractual relations, conspiracy to injure and fraud with respect to
events surrounding an aborted real estate transaction involving the plaintiffs'
clients. The insurer undertook to defend the plaintiffs' partners and law firms
but would only agree to defend the plaintiffs under a non-waiver agreement
which they refused to provide. They obtained leave to defend themselves. In
dismissing the plaintiffs' motion for a declaration that the insurers were obliged
to defend them, the court held:

> Having concluded that [the plaintiffs] were the individual members of the firms
> that represented the companies involved in this so-called scheme the defendant in-
> surers correctly applied the exclusion clause and concluded that it was required to
> apply the policy only to those members of the two law firms who were neither the
> authors (*i.e.*, [the plaintiffs]) nor their accomplices. This applied to the remaining
> lawyers in the action.[68]

No details of the transaction or allegations were provided, but the court was
clearly of the view that the plaintiffs had been the authors or accomplices of the
clients' dishonest acts and sanctioned the exclusion of coverage on this basis. At
trial, coverage under an excess professional liability insurance policy was also
denied even though it only excluded "actual and deliberate fraud and dishonesty" committed by the insured with "actual fraudulent or dishonest purpose and
intent". The court reasoned that, by definition, excess coverage presumes that
there is primary coverage; since primary coverage was excluded, there could be
no excess coverage.[69] On appeal, the denial of coverage under the primary pol-

---

[66]   *Supra,* note 64, at 188.
[67]   (1996), 29 O.R. (3d) 243 (Gen. Div.).
[68]   *Ibid.,* at 249.
[69]   *Ibid.,* at 250.

icy was upheld but the court ruled that the excess insurer had an obligation to defend the insured.[70] There was no exclusion for fraud in the excess policy unless a judgment or other final adjudication established fraud by the insured.

a. Dishonest Acts

The court found in *Fisher v. Guardian Insurance Co. of Canada*[71] that the word "dishonest" in a lawyers' professional liability insurance policy should be given its ordinary meaning:

> The word "dishonest" is a word of common usage and, in the context of this policy, no special meaning is to be attributed to it. Both criminal conduct and conduct which falls short of criminal conduct can be characterized as "dishonest". Whether the conduct in a particular case should be so characterized will depend upon the factual circumstances of that case considered in light of the coverage involved.[72]

In this case, the court considered an excess insurance policy which excluded coverage where "actual dishonest purpose or intent" was proven. A client of the insured made a mortgage loan to a company in which the insured had a substantial interest. The insured failed to disclose his interest or refer the client for independent legal advice. The court held that these breaches of fiduciary duty may have been motivated by dishonesty or negligence. Thus, coverage was not excluded as no actual dishonest purpose had been proven. "Dishonest activity" cannot be equated with actual dishonest purpose or intent.

Conversely, the Saskatchewan Court of Appeal held that an insured who failed to prepare security documentation and disbursed mortgage money contrary to the lender's instructions, in a transaction in which he was personally interested, was guilty of dishonest conduct within the meaning of the errors and omissions policy in that province.[73] The court denied coverage.

b. Fraudulent Acts

When dealing with an allegation of fraudulent conduct, the lawyer's state of mind is relevant.[74] A lawyer who conceals material facts from her client, either by failure to report or actual concealment, and prefers her own interests to those

---

[70] (1997), 35 O.R. (3d) 733 (C.A.).

[71] (1993), 87 B.C.L.R (2d) 34 (S.C.), varied (1995), 3 B.C.L.R. (3d) 161 (C.A.).

[72] *Ibid.*, at 45 82 B.C.L.R., citing a passage from Robins J.A. in *Higgins v. Orion* (1985), 50 O.R. (2d) 352 at 356 (C.A.). Note that the primary insurance policy in British Columbia currently excludes coverage for "actual or *alleged* dishonest or fraudulent conduct" (Exclusion 2). The insured would not likely have been covered under this policy. The Ontario, Newfoundland and C.L.I.A. policies appear to exclude only actual dishonest conduct.

[73] *63398 Alberta Ltd. v. Saskatchewan Government Insurance* (1995), 137 Sask. R. 246 (C.A.).

[74] *Agip (Africa) Ltd. v. Jackson*, [1989] 3 W.L.R. 1367 (Ch.).

of her client is guilty of fraudulent conduct.[75] Similarly, using a client's funds without full disclosure of material facts may be a fraudulent misrepresentation.[76] A representation which is literally true but is, in substance, a misrepresentation may amount to a fraudulent misrepresentation.[77]

The scope of the concept of "fraud" in professional liability insurance for lawyers was recently discussed in *Schwartz v. Longview Motel & Saloon Corp.*[78] The plaintiff clients loaned money to a hotel company which was owned in part by their solicitor. He represented the clients in the negotiation of the loan and in the preparation of the loan documents. The court found that the solicitor made several misrepresentations to the clients in the course of their dealings, including misrepresentations as to the ownership of shares pledged as security, the ownership of the hotel, whose money was at risk when he sought the loan from the clients, the sale of the shares pledged as security, the use of the share sale proceeds for his personal purposes, his ability to repay the loan over the short term and the availability of replacement security after the sale of the shares.

An action for damages for fraud was tried in Schwartz[79] by the clients against the solicitor, together with an application by the solicitor's insurer for declaration that it had no obligation to indemnify him for any judgment against him in the clients' action. In deciding whether the solicitor's conduct amounted to fraud, the court considered the legal definition, namely, "an intentional perversion of truth for the purpose of inducing another in reliance upon it to part with some valuable thing belonging to him or to surrender a legal right".[80] The court also referred to the definition in *Derry v. Peek*[81] to the effect that fraud is established where a false representation is made knowingly, or without belief in its truth, or with reckless carelessness as to its truth. The motive of the person committing the fraud is immaterial; it does not matter that there was no intention to cheat or injure the person to whom the statement was made. The solicitor's conduct amounted to a fraudulent breach of fiduciary duty. The policy's coverage of acts and omissions in a fiduciary capacity was subject to all of the exclusions in the policy. A declaration was made in favour of the insurer that the acts were excluded from coverage as fraudulent or dishonest.

---

[75] *Terry v. Law Society of Upper Canada,* unreported, August 12, 1992, Mandel J., Doc. C7284/91, [1992] O.J. No. 1678 (Gen. Div.). See also *Jakovljevic v. Law Society of Upper Canada* (1995), 129 D.L.R. (4th) 761 (Ont. Gen. Div.), affd (1996), 139 D.L.R. (4th) 574 (C.A.), leave to appeal to S.C.C. refused (1997), 215 N.R. 400n, [1997] S.C.C.A. No. 23.

[76] *Garofoli v. Kohm,* (1989), 77 C.B.R. (N.S.) 84 (Q.B.). The lawyer was found guilty of misappropriation and fraudulent misrepresentation within the meaning of the *Bankruptcy Act,* R.S.C. 1985, c. B-3.

[77] *Kerr on the Law of Fraud and Mistake,* 7th ed. (1952) at p. 43, as cited by Blair J.A. in *Greenglass v. Rusonik,* unreported, March 18, 1983, [1983] O.J. No. 40 (C.A.).

[78] (1994), 136 A.R. 290 (Q.B.).

[79] *Ibid.*

[80] *Black's Law Dictionary,* 5th ed. (St. Paul, Minn.: West Publishing Co., 1990).

[81] (1889), 14 App. Cas. 337 (H.L.).

The term "fraud" has also been interpreted in other contexts.[82] In *Greenglass v. Rusonik*,[83] the court held:

A representation in order to be fraudulent must be one (1) which is untrue in fact; (2) which defendant knows to be untrue or is indifferent as to its truth; (3) which was intended or calculated to induce the plaintiff to act upon it; and (4) which the plaintiff acts upon and suffers damages.[84]

If an insured obtains insurance by fraudulent misrepresentation, the policy is void from inception. The insurer has a right to rely on the applicant lawyer to provide complete disclosure on the basis of the highest good faith. However, the British Columbia Court of Appeal has held that, where one of multiple insureds made false representations in applying for insurance, his dishonesty will not be imputed to the other insured so as to render the policy void as against them if this result conflicts with the policy language.[85]

c. Theft or Misappropriation of Trust Funds

The "innocent insured" provisions in the C.L.I.A. policies cover insureds for "dishonest, fraudulent, criminal or malicious act or omissions by [another insured] other than one relating in any way to theft or misappropriation of trust funds or property" provided that the insured did not conceal, acquiesce or participate in the conduct or fail to notify the insurer when he became aware of it.[86] In Ontario, British Columbia and Newfoundland, theft or misappropriation of trust funds is not expressly excluded from innocent insured coverage.

The C.L.I.A. exclusion was interpreted in *Clark, Drummie & Co. v. Law Society of New Brunswick*,[87] a case involving more than one proximate cause of the client's loss. All the members of a law firm applied for judicial review of an arbitrator's decision that they were not covered for conversion of funds by an associate. The associate represented to a lawyer at another firm that he was the administrator of a client's estate. The other solicitor sent a cheque to the associate for a large sum of money payable to the client, whom he knew to be deceased, without confirming that the associate was in fact the administrator of the client's estate or making any other enquiries. The New Brunswick Court of Queen's Bench agreed with the arbitrator's decision that the conversion of the funds by the associate was the proximate cause of the loss to the client's estate and the members of the associate's firm were therefore not covered.

---

[82] See, for example, *Harland v. Fancsali* (1993), 13 O.R. (3d) 103 (Gen. Div), revd (1994), 21 O.R. (3d) 798 (Div. Ct.); *R. v. Silver*, unreported, May 17, 1993, Salhany J. (Ont. Gen. Div.); *R. v. Sahaidak*, unreported, January 10, 1990, Doherty J. (Ont. H.C.).

[83] *Supra*, note 77.

[84] *Ibid.*, at para. 50, citing *Kerr on the Law of Fraud and Mistake, supra*, note 77, at p. 25.

[85] *Fisher v. Guardian Insurance Co. of Canada*, *supra*, note 71.

[86] Alberta Policy No. 10005, Condition 4.5.

[87] (1993), 138 N.B.R. (2d) 332 (T.D.).

Further, in situations where there is more than one cause of a loss, one of which falls within a policy exclusion, the exception prevails and precludes recovery.

d. Criminal Acts

Outside of the lawyers' professional liability insurance context, there is authority for the proposition that a criminal conviction is *prima facie* proof that the act complained of is not one for which indemnity is provided. In one case, *Heck v. Prudential Assurance Co.*,[88] an insured shot a third party and was convicted of assault under the *Criminal Code*.[89] The third party sued for negligence and the insured attempted to compel his insurer to defend the suit. The court held that, as no material was filed to repudiate the *prima facie* inference that arose from the criminal conviction, the policy's exclusion ought to apply.

A recent case, *New Burnswick Power Corp. v. Canadian Lawyers Insurance Assn.*,[90] suggests that courts will be reluctant to provide coverage for negligent acts that occur in the course of a criminal scheme where the proximate cause of the client's loss is a criminal conduct. A solicitor acting for the purchasers in a real estate transaction raised a title concern with the vendors and, without his client's knowledge or consent, negotiated a postponement of closing and a second agreement of purchase and sale. He was subsequently convicted of various counts of theft and sentenced to a term of imprisonment for misappropriating trust funds, including most of the money the client had provided to close the transaction. In an action against the solicitor's insurer, the clients alleged that the extra expenses they incurred to close the transaction were caused by the solicitor's negligence in failing to obtain their consent to the subsequent agreement of purchase and sale and were therefore covered by the policy. The court held that the test in these circumstances is whether the criminal conduct was the proximate cause of the loss. In this case, the second agreement was negotiated because of the depressed state of the solicitor's trust account resulting from his misappropriations. The conduct "cannot be viewed in isolation but were all part of a continuing criminal scheme" and the expenses were therefore not covered by the policy.

e. Business Exclusion

Ontario, Newfoundland and British Columbia all exclude coverage for claims by organizations which are beneficially owned or controlled, directly or indi-

---

[88] *Heck v. Prudential Assurance Co.* (1991), 77 Man. R. (2d) 200 (Q.B.), relying on *West Wake Price & Co. v. Ching*, [1956] 3 All E.R. 821 (Q.B.), and *Cansulex Ltd. v. Reed Stenhouse Ltd.* (1986), 70 B.C.L.R. 273 (S.C.).

[89] R.S.C. 1985, c. C-46.

[90] (1996), 184 N.B.R. (2d) 329 (T.D.).

rectly, in excess of 10 per cent, by the insured, the insured's spouse or partners.[91] Coverage under the C.L.I.A. policies is excluded for the portion of a payment resulting from a claim by an enterprise equal to the proportionate direct or indirect beneficial interest held by an insured in an enterprise in excess of 5 per cent. An insured is considered to have an indirect interest in an enterprise if the interest is held by a relative of the insured, or a corporate entity that is controlled by the insured, a relative of the insured, the insured's law firm or any combination of them.[92]

B. RIGHTS AND OBLIGATIONS OF THE INSURER

1. Obligation to Defend

a. Policies

The insurer is obliged to defend any civil suit against the insured that is covered by the policy.[93] The British Columbia policy states the insurer is obliged to defend even where the allegations are "groundless, false or fraudulent".[94] The insurer in British Columbia has the right, but not the obligation, to defend, investigate or pay on any claim that is brought elsewhere than within Canada or the United States of America,[95] but all of the policies provide that "no action" shall lie against the insurer unless, as a condition precedent to, the insured has fully complied with all terms of the policy.[96] Additionally, in British Columbia and the jurisdictions covered by the C.L.I.A., an action will not lie against the insurer until the amount of the insured's obligation to pay has been finally determined by judgment, binding arbitration or by written agreement.[97] This requirement does not preclude the insured from obtaining a declaration, prior to judgment, arbitration or agreement.[98] The obligation to defend is independent of the insurer's obligation to indemnify the insured for damages assessed against him.

---

[91] Ontario Policy No. 98-001, Exclusion (d); Newfoundland Policy No. 95-003, Exclusion (d); British Columbia Policy No. LPL98-01-01, Exclusion 6.2.

[92] Alberta Policy No. 10005, Exclusion 3.16.

[93] Ontario Policy No. 98-001, Part I.B; Newfoundland Policy No. 95-003, Insuring Agreement, Coverage C; British Columbia Policy No. LPL98-01-01, Insuring Agreement 2.1.1; Alberta Policy No. 10005, Insuring Agreement 2.2.

[94] British Columbia Policy No. LPL98-01-01, Insuring Agreement 2.2.1.

[95] *Ibid.*, Insuring Agreements 2.2.

[96] Ontario Policy No. 98-001, General Condition I; Newfoundland Policy No. 95-003, Condition V(h); British Columbia Policy No. LPL98-01-01, Condition 9; Alberta Policy No. 10005, Condition 4.10(d)(i).

[97] British Columbia Policy No. LPL 98-01-01, Condition 9; Alberta Policy No. 10005, Condition 4.10(d)(ii).

[98] *Great West Steel Industries v. Simcoe & Erie General Insurance Co.* (1979), 27 O.R. (2d) 379, 106 D.L.R. (3d) 347 (C.A.). See also, *e.g., Schwartz v. Longview Motel & Saloon Corp.* (1994), 136 A.R. 290 (Q.B.).

The indemnity obligation is triggered by a settlement or trial judgment[99]. In all cases, the right to be defended depends on the right to coverage. Thus, if the insured has breached a policy condition and thus relinquished his right to be covered, the insurer has no obligation to defend him in an action.

When an insured's right to coverage is in issue, there must be a separate action between the insurer and the insured to determine whether the insured has forfeited her right to coverage.[100] Only then can the tort action proceed, the insurer defending or not, depending on the outcome of the first action.[101] Generally, the insurer will not be allowed to have coverage issues determined in the tort action. However, an insured may bring third party proceedings claiming coverage from the insurer; it is not necessary for the insured to commence a separate action.[102]

b. Pleadings

As a general rule, the obligation to defend applies exclusively to of damages claims that potentially fall within the policy.[103] However, the insurer's obligation to defend an action is decided only by reference to the allegations in the pleadings. As the Supreme Court of Canada held in *Nichols v. American Home Assurance Co.*:

> I conclude that considerations related to insurance law and practice, as well as the authorities, overwhelmingly support the view that the duty to defend should, unless the contract of insurance indicates otherwise, be confined to the defence of

---

[99] This is implicit in the definition of "damages" contained in the Ontario and Newfoundland policies as amounts the insured is "legally obliged to pay" arising out of a claim, and explicit in the definition in the British Columbia policy. It is also implicit in Insuring Agreement 2.1 in Alberta Policy No. 10005.

[100] It would be prudent for an insurer to obtain a non-waiver agreement or a letter of reservation of rights at this stage. This will help the insurer to maintain its contention that the claim is off coverage. For further discussion, see Section II.B.4., "Duty of Good Faith and Equal Consideration".

[101] In *Carter v. Kerr* (1990), 45 B.C.L.R. (2d) 160 (C.A.), the court held that *Boxeur v. Smith*, [1989] I.L.R. 1-2530 (B.C.S.C.), revd (1992), 66 B.C.L.R. (2d) 356 (C.A.), was incorrectly decided because the Supreme Court judge opined that the reasoning in *Bacon v. McBride* (1984), 51 B.C.L.R. 228 (S.C.) was applicable to a case involving a breach of condition. In fact, when the court in *Bacon* held that the pleadings govern the duty to defend, the court was determining whether the alleged facts, if proven, fell within the policy's coverage. The *Bacon* case did not deal with the issue of a breach of condition. See also *SCS Western Corp. v. Dominion of Canada v. General Insurance Co.*, (1998), 59 Alta. L.R. (3d) 73 (Q.B.); *Colletti v. Popp*, unreported, May 6, 1998, Forestell J., Doc. 9103/97, [1998] O.J. No. 1898 (Gen. Div.).

[102] *Bliefernich v. Freeman* (1989), 38 B.C.L.R. (2d) 128, 60 D.L.R. (4th) 385 (C.A.), as cited in *Carter v. Kerr, supra*, note 101.

[103] *American Home Assurance Co. v. Stinchcombe* (1992), 136 A.R. 290 (Q.B.); *Jon Picken Ltd. v. Guardian Insurance Co. of Canada* (1993), 66 O.A.C. 39 (C.A.), supp. reasons September 12, 1993 (Ont. C.A.); *Nichols v. American Home Assurance Co.*, [1990] 1 S.C.R. 801; *Slough Estates Canada Ltd. v. Federal Pioneer Ltd.* (1994), 20 O.R. (3d) 429 (Gen. Div.).

claims which may be argued to fall under the policy. That said, the widest latitude should be given to the allegations in the pleadings in determining whether they raise a claim within the policy.[104]

This is known as the "pleadings rule".[105] As already noted,[106] difficult questions arise when determining whether the insured acted "as a lawyer" or whether the services were rendered in some other capacity. Before the insurer will be relieved of its obligation to defend, it must be clearly established, within the meaning of *Nichols*,[107] that the activities complained of are not part of the business of a solicitor, and, therefore, are outside of the definition of "professional services" in the policy.[108]

It is unclear whether an insurer must defend a claim which, although pleaded within the terms of the policy, is not one for which the policy provides indemnity. Some authorities hold that it is open to an insurer to show that a claim, however pleaded, is not one for which indemnity is provided.[109] This requires an investigation and assessment of the facts underlying the claim and is therefore known as the "underlying facts exception" to the pleadings rule.[110] Under the exception, the insurer is relieved of its obligation to defend when the underlying facts indicate that the policy does not cover a particular situation. However, the weight of authority appears to favour the proposition that the insurer cannot refuse to defend a claim which is pleaded within the terms of the policy, even if the underlying facts suggest that the incident is not one for which coverage is provided.[111] In *Karpel v. Rumack*,[112] the court found that as the underlying facts exemption does not appear to be recognized in Ontario, the Lawyers' Profes-

---

[104] *Supra*, note 103, at 329. See also *Dyne Holdings Ltd. v. Royal Insurance Co. of Canada* (1996), 138 Nfld. & P.E.I.R. 318 (P.E.I.C.A.), supp. reasons (1997), 155 Nfld. & P.E.I.R. 181 (P.E.I.C.A.).

[105] For a detailed discussion of the rule, see G. Hilliker, *Liability Insurance Law in Canada*, 2nd ed. (Toronto: Butterworths, 1996) at p. 65.

[106] See Section II, "The Policy", A "Scope of Coverage", 1. "Nature of Services Performed", for an in-depth discussion of when an insured acts "as a lawyer" and when an insured acts in another capacity.

[107] Than is, the widest latitude should be given to the allegations in the pleadings in determining whether, they give rise to a claim within the policy.

[108] *Karpel v. Rumack* (1994), 19 O.R. (3d) 555 (Gen. Div.).

[109] *West Wake Price & Co. v. Ching*, [1956] 3 All E.R. 821 (Q.B.); *Cansulex Ltd. v. Reed Stenhouse Ltd.* (1986), 70 B.C.L.R. 273 (S.C.); *Heck v. Prudential Assurance Co.* (1991), 77 Man. R. (2d) 200 (Q.B.); *Bathurst (City) v. Royal Insurance Co. of Canada* (1994), 154 N.B.R. (2d) 86 (C.A.); *Privest Properties Ltd. v. Foundation Co. of Canada* (1992), 6 C.C.L.I. (2d) 15 (B.C.S.C.).

[110] See Hilliker, *supra*, note 105 at 65.

[111] See *Nichols v. American Home Assurance Co.*, *supra*, note 103; *Bacon v. McBride*, *supra*, note 101; *Jon Picken Ltd. v. Guardian Insurance Co. of Canada*, *supra*, note 103; *Leger v. Canadian Lawyers Insurance Assn.*, [1993] I.L.R. 1-2954 (N.B.T.D.); *Longarini v. Zuliani* (1994), 17 O.R. (3d) 527 (C.A.); *Karpel v. Rumack*, *supra*, note 108.

[112] *Supra*, note 108. See also *Leger v. Canadian Lawyers Insurance Assn.* (1993), 132 N.B.R. (2d) 79 (Q.B.), affd (1993), 140 N.B.R. (2d) 395 (C.A.).

sional Indemnity Co. ("L.P.I.C.") was obligated to defend an action in which the pleadings were framed in negligence, breach of contract and fiduciary duty. Evidence of underlying facts was not admitted to establish fraudulent, criminal, malicious or dishonest behaviour.[113]

Further difficulties arise if the allegations in the claim are ambiguous or framed in the alternative alleging both negligence and fraud. The insurer can refuse to defend the excluded claims but not those which are covered by the policy.[114] If the insurer chooses to defend the entire action, it will often do so under a non-waiver agreement or letter of reservation of rights.[115] The insured should obtain independent legal advice about claims which clearly fall outside the terms of the policy.[116] This practice alleviates the concern of a conflict of interest. If an insurer defends both those allegations which fall within the policy and those which clearly fall outside the scope of the policy, a conflict may arise between the insurer and the insured as it is in the insurer's interests to have the claim succeed on allegations that are not covered by the policy and fail on allegations properly covered by the policy.

c. Scope of Duty

There is little judicial consideration of the scope of the insurer's duty to defend, but, at a minimum, an insurer is obligated to exercise reasonable care in investigating and defending a claim.[117] In *Fredrikson v. Insurance Corp. of British Columbia*,[118] the British Columbia Supreme Court adopted this excerpt from *Appleman's Insurance Law and Practice*,[119] an American publication:

---

[113] *Karpel v. Rumack, supra,* note 108; *Jon Picken Ltd. v. Guardian Insurance Co. of Canada, supra,* note 103; *Longarini v. Zuliani, supra,* note 111.

[114] *Bacon v. McBride, supra,* note 101; *American Home Assurance Co. v. Stinchcombe, supra,* note 103; *Waterloo (Regional Municipality) v. Guarantee Co. of North America* (1990), 1 C.C.L.I. (2d) 290 (Ont. H.C.).

[115] If the insured refuses to sign the non-waiver, the insurer has a difficult decision to make. If it is subsequently determined that the denial of coverage was improper, the insurer will have lost control of the suit and will be liable to fully reimburse the insured. Conversely, if the insurer chooses to defend a claim that is "off coverage" by reason of the obligation to defend any suit however groundless, it may be estopped from later refusing to indemnify the insured: Smith, "Legal Professional Malpractice" (1986), 4 Can. J. Insurance L. 7.

[116] *American Home Assurance Co. v. Stinchcombe, supra,* note 103; *Jon Picken Ltd. v. Guardian Insurance Co. of Canada, supra,* note 103. See also *Nichols v. American Home Assurance Co., supra,* note 103. McLachlin J., writing for a unanimous court, approved such a practice. Hilliker, *supra,* note 105 at 78, refers to the practical difficulties of having two counsel defend the claim on behalf of the insured. Further, a conflict would still arise with respect to the presentation of evidence and cross-examination of witnesses. Thus, he suggests that it is preferable to appoint one counsel to defend the entire proceeding.

[117] Hilliker, *supra,* note 105 at 83. *Joe v. Insurance Corp. of British Columbia* (1984), 55 B.C.L.R. 118 (C.A.).

[118] (1990), 44 B.C.L.R. (2d) 303 (S.C.).

[119] Appleman, *Insurance Law and Practice* (revised ed.) (St. Paul: West Publishing Co., 1981) para. 4687, at pp. 181-83.

It is not an extraordinary degree of care but the care that is required under these particular circumstances. It must use skill diligently and adequately to investigate a case, it must use skill in negotiation, it must select skilled trial counsel — not the lowest priced member of the bar — and that individual, so selected by it, may bind the insurer by his derelictions. It is not a comfortable spot for a liability insurer to occupy, but it seeks the business upon the basis of its skill.[120]

In *Shea v. Manitoba Public Insurance Corp.*[121], a decision of the British Columbia Court of Appeal, the court found that the duty to defend entails a duty to disclose in a timely manner all information relating to the litigation and the settlement process, advise the insured of the nature and extent of any conflicting interests, instruct counsel to give equal consideration to the interests of the insured, and seek to minimize the damages awarded against the insured. The insured sued the insurers for bad faith in failing to settle the claim within policy limits. Settlement was not reached because the two insurers could not agree on a mechanism for resolving the issue of who had responsibility for amounts owing in excess of the policy limits. The insurers were liable for failing to act in good faith and for failing to consider the insured's interests equally with their own during settlement and defence.

The Ontario Court of Appeal emphasized in *Kerr v. Lawyers' Professional Indemnity Co.*[122] that the solicitor's obligation to defend is broader than the obligation to indemnify, and arises if the coverage provisions might become engaged. In this case, a solicitor was sued by his employer in his capacity as corporate secretary. The Ontario Court (General Division) dismissed an application by the solicitor for a declaration that the insurer had an obligation to pay his defence costs because the acts complained of were those of a corporate secretary and not a solicitor.[123] The duty to defend only arises from the performance of professional services as a solicitor. The solicitor appealed and, in the meantime, the plaintiff amended its pleadings to include claims against the solicitor in his capacity as the corporation's solicitor as well as its secretary. LPIC acknowledged its duty to defend in light of the amended pleadings but argued that defence costs should be split so that the solicitor would pay for the defence of the allegations against him as corporate secretary.

Following the Supreme Court of Canada decision in *Nichols v. American Home Assurance Co.*,[124] the court found that all the allegations contained in the pleadings came within the ambit of the policy coverage. Thus, it was "possible" that the coverage provisions of the policy would be engaged because it could be

---

[120] *Supra,* note 118 at 330.
[121] (1990), 1 C.C.L.I. (2d) 61 (B.C.S.C.).
[122] (1995), 25 O.R. (3d) 804 (C.A.).
[123] (1994), 22 C.C.L.I. (2d) 28 (Gen. Div.).
[124] (1990), 1 S.C.R. 801. See, *supra,* Section II, B: "Rights and Obligations of the Insurer", 1. "Obligation to Defend", (b) "Pleadings", for a discussion of this case and the other jurisprudence on the "pleadings rule" in determining whether a duty to defend is owed.

found that the solicitor was liable as a consequence of his performance of or failure to perform professional services for the corporation. The court concluded:

> The fact that the various allegations of breaches of duty are also related by the pleadings to the appellant's duties as [the corporation's] corporate secretary does not alter the fact that the amended pleadings leave it open to the court to connect all alleged breaches of duty to the appellant's retainer as [the corporation's] solicitor providing professional services.[125]

An insurer under an obligation to defend cannot deliver a defence that conflicts with the insured's interests. In *Gatt v. Rumack*, [126] the Ontario Court (General Division) held that to do so is both a breach of the duty to defend and an abuse of process. In this case, the defendant, a solicitor and mortgage broker, was sued for negligence and breach of fiduciary duty. LPIC denied coverage, alleging that the claim fell within the exclusion for dishonest, malicious and fraudulent acts, but was ordered to defend. The defendant solicitor brought third party proceedings against LPIC seeking a defence and indemnity respecting the plaintiff's claims. In response, LPIC delivered a defence to the main action denying negligence but alleging dishonesty, fraud and malice on the solicitor's part.

Madam Justice MacDonald struck the third party pleadings on the basis that it intermingled the duty to defend with the right to raise defences to any claim for indemnification which may be advanced by the insurer after the trial of the main actions. The determination of coverage issues was premature, and, moreover, "create[d] a scandalous result for the defendant in that the persons who were obligated to provide a defence, in accordance with the insurance contract are, at the same time, embarrassing the insured in the defence of the action . . ."[127] The rule of civil procedure permitting a third party to deliver a defence to the main action cannot be interpreted as enabling the insurer to breach its duty to defend. Further, to allow the liability and indemnity issues to be adjudicated together would be highly prejudicial to the solicitor.

d. Failure to Defend

The obligation to defend is an important part of the insurance agreement, and courts will be loathe to allow a primary insurer to contract out of, or even limit, the obligation if it would unfairly prejudice the insured. In *Pacific Employers*

---

[125] *Supra,* note 122, at 812.

[126] (1994), 21 O.R. (3d) 655 (Gen. Div.).

[127] *Ibid.,* at 660. MacDonald J. also reasoned on procedural grounds that the third party pleadings should be struck because it is a fundamental rule of pleading that a defendant may not plead to causes of action which do not appear in the statement of claim. *Ibid.,* at 662.

Insurance Co. v. Non Marine Underwriters[128], the primary insurer provided coverage for lawyers up to a limit of $100,000. The defendant law firm obtained excess insurance of $900,000. The primary insurer added a proviso that if "any other insurance policy" applied to a claim, the primary insurer's obligation to defend would cease once a proceeding had exhausted the $100,000 limit. The defendant law firm was sued for tens of millions of dollars in damages. It was anticipated that the action could cost over $1 million to defend. The primary insurer claimed that, under the proviso, its obligation to defend was discharged once the defence costs reached $100,000. The court determined that the reasonable expectation of the insured law firm was that they would be indemnified on any claim up to $100,000, in addition to being defended against the claim. The law firm expected to increase its coverage to $900,000, not to be put in a worse position respecting its defence costs.[129] Thus, the Court held that the excess insurance policy was not an "other insurance policy" within the meaning of the primary policy and the primary insurer's obligation to defend continued.

The consequences of failing to defend in a proper case are amply illustrated by *Murphy Oil Co. Ltd. v. Continental Ins. Co.*[130] The defendant insurer refused to defend a claim on the grounds that the policy excluded coverage. The court determined that the insurer had wrongfully denied coverage, the denial of coverage constituted a fundamental breach of the policy and, accordingly, the insurer had lost its right to contest the appropriateness of a settlement entered into between the insured and the client. The insurer was obligated to fully reimburse the insured.

The Ontario Court of Appeal subsequently considered this situation in *Jon Picken Ltd. v. Guardian Insurance Co. of Canada*[131]. The insured negotiated a reasonable settlement after the insurer refused to defend the claim on the grounds that coverage was excluded. Coverage was wrongfully denied and the insurer was obligated to indemnify the insured for the amount the insured paid on settlement. The court held that a reasonable settlement can be viewed as a foreseeable consequence of the insurer's breach of contract in refusing to defend the action against the insured.[132] However, the court did not expressly hold that *any* settlement is reasonably foreseeable.

---

[128] (1990), 47 B.C.L.R. (2d) 254, 45 C.C.L.I. 42; 71 D.L.R. (4th) 726 (C.A.). For recent applications of this case not involving solicitors' professional liability insurance, see *Lurette v. Wellington Insurance* (1996), 181 N.B.R. (2d) 304 (C.A.), and *University of Saskatchewan v. Fireman's Fund Insurance Co. of Canada* (1997), 158 Sask. R. 223 (C.A.).

[129] The excess insurance policy did not contain an obligation to defend an action, although the excess insurers were required to share the costs of the defence with the primary insurer in certain circumstances.

[130] (1981), 33 O.R. (2d) 853 (Co. Ct.).

[131] (1993), 66 O.A.C. 39 (C.A.), supp. reasons September 17, 1993 (Ont. C.A.).

[132] The court relied on *Cansulex Ltd. v. Reed Stenhouse Ltd.* (1986), 70 B.C.L.R. 273 (S.C.), for the proposition that a reasonable settlement is a foreseeable consequence of breach of contract.

When an insurer improperly denies coverage, it loses control of the suit and its exclusive right to settle and will be liable to fully reimburse the insured's costs if coverage was improperly refused. For example, in *St. Andrew's Service Co. v. McCubbin*[133], an insurer who refused to defend an action was required to pay the costs of defending the allegations covered by the policy. In this case, it was agreed that 10 per cent of the costs related to insured claims, 10 per cent to uninsured claims and 80 per cent to the defence of issues common to both. The court relieved the insurer of its obligation to defend only with respect to claims clearly not covered by the policy. Thus, the insurer was obliged to pay 90 per cent of the costs.

e. Estoppel

The insurer must ascertain without delay whether it is appropriate to deny coverage in a particular situation. This determination is crucial, because although the consequences of improperly denying coverage may be significant, an insurer who unduly delays in appropriately denying coverage may be estopped from denying coverage in future.

Before this estoppel applies to the insurer, it must know of facts which indicate that the claim is "off coverage". The insurer must also have engaged in a course of conduct upon which the insured has relied to its detriment.[134]

In *Rosenblood Estate v. Law Society of Upper Canada*,[135] the insurer was estopped from denying coverage because it knew of facts indicating that certain conditions of the policy had been breached, yet the insured's estate received no notice of the potential coverage problem until after settlement negotiations had commenced. Further, the insured's estate was clearly relying on the insurer to act in its best interests of estate. Had the estate been notified of the coverage issue earlier, settlement discussions would have been commenced sooner and examinations for discovery would have been conducted with a different emphasis. The court held that these facts created a presumption that the estate was prejudiced by the delay:

> It is not possible to point to actual prejudice but in the circumstances of this case where the insurer persisted in the defence through production and discovery into settlement negotiations prejudice must be presumed.

> When a claim is presented to an insurer the facts giving rise to the claim should be investigated. If there is no coverage then the insured should be told at once and the insurer should have nothing further to do with the claim if it wishes to main-

---

[133] (1987), 22 B.C.L.R. (2d) 38 (B.C.S.C.), supp. reasons (1988), 29 B.C.L.R. (2d) 305 (B.C.S.C.).

[134] *Western Canada Accident & Guarantee Insurance Co. v. Parrott* (1921), 59 D.L.R. 307 (S.C.C.), as cited in *Rosenblood Estate v. Law Society of Upper Canada*, [1989] I.L.R. 1-2416 (H.C.), affd (1992), 16 C.C.L.I. (2d) 226 (Ont. C.A.).

[135] *Supra*, note 134, at 9340 [1989] I.L.R.

tain its off coverage position. If coverage is questionable the insurer should advise the insured at once and in the absence of a non-waiver agreement or of an adequate reservation of rights letter defends the claim at its risk. In the present case the insurer finally took an off coverage position but against Mr. Atlin's advice and much too late.[136]

2. Obligation to Pay

In addition to the insurer's obligation to pay damages,[137] including pre- and post-judgment interest,[138] the policies require the insurer to pay all reasonable expenses incurred to defend the claim and any costs assessed against the insured to the extent that they do not exceed the policy limits.[139] The policies generally exclude liability for legal fees, personal fines and penalties, and exemplary and aggravated damages.[140] Disputes between insureds or between the insured and the insurer as to the apportionment of liability are required to be arbitrated in all of the jurisdictions except British Columbia.[141] There appears to be no obligation on the insurer to pay damages and expenses, or to continue the defence after the liability limit has been reached.[142]

The British Columbia insurer is also required to reimburse the insured for reasonable costs of investigation, settlement and defence of any suit brought elsewhere than within Canada or the United States of America which the insurer has elected not to investigate, settle or defend.[143]

3. Non-Waiver Agreements / Letter of Reservation of Rights

In situations where it is not clear that the professional has coverage available to her under the policy, the insurer may enter into a non-waiver agreement with the

---

[136] *Supra*, note 134, at 9340 [1989] I.L.R.
[137] Ontario Policy No. 98-001, Insurance Coverage A; Newfoundland Policy No. 95-003, Insuring Agreement A; British Columbia Policy No. LPL98-01-01, Insuring Agreement 1; Alberta Policy No. 10005, Insuring Agreement 2.1.
[138] Ontario Policy No. 98-001, Definition (d); Newfoundland Policy No. 95-003, Definition (b); British Columbia Policy No. LPL98-01-01, Definition of "damages"; Alberta Policy No. 10005, Definition of "Damages". Note that the Alberta policy appears to only cover pre-judgment interest.
[139] Ontario Policy No. 98-001, Insurance Coverage B; Newfoundland Policy No. 95-003, Insuring Agreement C; British Columbia Policy No. LPL98-01-01, Definition of "Claims expenses"; Alberta Policy No. 10005, Definition of "Defence Costs".
[140] Ontario Policy No. 98-001, Definition (d); Newfoundland Policy No. 95-003, Definition (b); British Columbia Policy No. LPL98-01-01, Definition of "Damages"; Alberta Policy No. 10005, Definition of "Damages".
[141] Ontario Policy No. 98-001, Condition P; Newfoundland Policy No. 95-003, Condition (o); Alberta Policy No. 10005, Condition 4.10(e).
[142] Ontario Policy No. 98-001, Insurance Coverage A & B; British Columbia Policy No. LPL98-01-01, Condition 1.5; Alberta Policy No. 10005, Insuring Agreement 2.4(f).
[143] British Columbia Policy No. LPL98-01-01, Insuring Agreement 2.2.2.

insured. This agreement permits the insurer to investigate and defend or settle a claim, without waiving its rights under the policy, in particular, its right to deny coverage.[144]

There are at least three kinds of agreements currently in use in Ontario: the "preferred", the "accepted", and a non-waiver agreement which is individually negotiated by the insurer and insured to cover unusual situations. Under a preferred non-waiver, once the insurer denies coverage, the insured is obliged to reimburse the insurer for defence costs incurred to the date of the denial; no similar obligation is contained in the accepted non-waiver. Although not expressly stated, all of the agreements contemplate that if judgment is granted against the insured, the insured is liable to pay the judgment subject only to a successful action against the insurer for indemnification.

If the insured solicitor refuses to negotiate or sign a non-waiver agreement in the belief that coverage is available to him, the insurer may attempt, albeit unilaterally, to protect its interests and begin its investigation under a letter of reservation of rights. This is simply a letter from the insurer to the insured advising him that the insurer is commencing its investigation of the claim without prejudice to its rights to later deny coverage. A key difference between a non-waiver agreement and a letter of reservation of rights is that, in the former, the insurer can negotiate rights not contained in the policy, such as a right to claim and seek reimbursement from the insured.[145]

The British Columbia policy specifically provides for the defence of an action under a reservation of rights. In this case, each party has the right to obtain independent legal advice at its own expense.[146]

An insurer is not entitled to investigate the facts surrounding a claim and at the same time conduct an investigation as to whether there exist sufficient grounds to deny coverage.[147] However, an insurer may obtain a non-waiver agreement in order to investigate the factual underpinnings of a claim so as to demonstrate that coverage is not available. This is also true of a letter of reservation of rights. At least one case has held that an insurer cannot defend an action under a non-waiver agreement and seek a declaration in separate proceedings that it is not liable under the policy. The application for a declaration is a repudiation of the non-waiver agreement and the continued defence of the insured is tantamount to an election to provide coverage.[148]

The importance of a non-waiver agreement or an adequate reservation of rights letter cannot be over-emphasized from the insurer's point of view. When an insurer investigates and defends a claim for which coverage is questionable without the protection of a non-waiver agreement or a reservation of rights let-

---

[144] Hilliker, *Liability Insurance Law in Canada,* 2nd ed. (Toronto: Butterworths, 1996), at 95.
[145] *Ibid.*
[146] British Columbia Policy No. LPL98-01-01, Insuring Agreement 2.3.
[147] *Rowe v. Mills* (1986), 72 N.B.R. (2d) 344, [1986] I.L.R. 1-2116 (Q.B.).
[148] *Federal Insurance Co. v. Matthews* (1956), 18 W.W.R. 193 (B.C.S.C.).

ter, it does so at its own risk. It may be estopped from taking an off coverage position in future.[149]

4. Duty of Good Faith and Equal Consideration

An insurance contract is distinct from other contracts in that the utmost of good faith is required of the parties because of each party's vulnerability at different stages of the relationship. The insured is in sole possession of material facts that must be communicated to the insurer when the initial contract is entered into, and as circumstances change. The insured must be certain that all these facts are fully disclosed. On the other hand, the insurer usually has exclusive control over the defence and settlement of any claim against the insured. The insured must be able to rely on the insurer to fulfil this duty without compromising the insured's best interests.[150] Thus, although the relationship between an insurer and an insured is a commercial one, the duty of honesty which is required in a typical commercial relationship is insufficient in the context of an insurance relationship.

The few authorities that have considered the nature and scope of the special duties owed under insurance contracts have determined that an insurer owes its insured a duty of good faith, fair dealing and equal consideration. Generally, fiduciary obligations are not owed, although in some circumstances, a higher duty may be owed than would ordinarily apply in business relationships. One of the first Canadian decisions to consider this issue extensively is *Shea v. Manitoba Public Insurance Corp.*[151] At issue was the duty owed by an insurer to an insured with respect to settlement within the policy limits. After a comprehensive analysis of the authorities, the court found that the duty is greater than that which is typically owed in a commercial relationship but less than that required of a fiduciary.

Thus, in a typical insurance relationship, an intermediate level of duty is required to provide appropriate protection for the insured while leaving the insurer free to look after its own interests. In *Shea*, Finch, J. determined that the intermediate level is one at which the insurer has an obligation to act in good faith and to give equal consideration to the interests of the insured:

> [There is clearly a commercial relationship between the parties.] It can, however, reasonably be inferred that the insurer knew it had a "fiduciary like" obligation to its insureds. It held by statute and regulation exclusive control over settlement negotiations. It knew that the insured was within its power so far as settlement was

---

[149] See Section II, B. "Rights and Obligations of the Insurer", 1. "Obligation to Defend", (d) "Failure to Defend".

[150] *Fredrikson v. Insurance Corp. of British Columbia* (1990), 44 B.C.L.R. (2d) 303 (S.C.); *Plaza Fiberglass Manufacturing Ltd. v. Cardinal Insurance Co.* (1994), 18 O.R. (3d) 663 at 669 (C.A.).

[151] (1990), 1 C.C.L.I. (2d) 61 at 124 (B.C.S.C.).

concerned, and was therefore "at its mercy." The insurer must in such circumstances be taken to know that the law would view it as something akin to a trustee in the exercise of those powers on the insured's behalf, and that while it could legitimately assert and protect its own interests, even where they were in conflict with those of its insureds, it would not do so at the expense or prejudice of the insureds, at least without advising them of the conflict and the position it proposed to take.[152]

Finch J. summarized his view of the law respecting the insurer's duty to its insured as follows:

1. The relationship between the insurer and insured is a commercial one, in which the parties have their own rights and obligations;
2. Within the commercial relationship, special duties may arise over and above the universal duty of honesty, which do not reach the fiduciary standard of selflessness and loyalty;
3. The exclusive discretionary power to settle liability claims given by statute to the insurer in this case, places the insured at the mercy of the insurer;
4. The insured's position of vulnerability imposes on the insurer the duties:
   a) of good faith and fair dealing;
   b) to give at least as much consideration to the insured's interests as it does to its own interests; and
   c) to disclose with reasonable promptitude to the insured all material information touching upon the insured's position in the litigation, and in the settlement negotiations.
5. The fact that the insured is at the mercy of the insurer for the purposes of settlement negotiations gives rise to a justified expectation in the insured that the insurer will not act contrary to the interests of the insured, or will, at least, fully advise the insured of its intention to do so;
6. While the commercial nature of the relationship permits an insurer to assert or defend interests which are opposed to, or are inconsistent with, the interests of its insured, the duty to deal fairly and in good faith requires the insurer to advise the insured that conflicting interests exist, and of the nature and extent of the conflict;
7. The insurer's statutory obligation to defend its insured imposes on the insurer, where conflicting interests arise, a duty to instruct counsel to treat the interests of the insured equally with its own; and where one counsel cannot adequately represent both conflicting interests, an obligation to instruct separate counsel to act solely for the insureds, at the insurer's own cost;
8. The insurer's duty to defend includes the obligation to defend on the issue of damages, and to attempt to minimize by all lawful means the amount of any judgment awarded against the insured. In this case that would include arguing

---

[152] *Ibid.*, at 114.

that court order interest and no fault benefits are payable in addition to the policy limits, where such an argument is available in law; and

9. Defence preparations and settlement negotiations must take place in a timely way, and, where last minute negotiations are required, advance planning must be made to ensure that the insured's interests are given equal protection with those of the insurer.[153]

These principles have been broadly accepted. *In Adams v. Confederation Life Insurance*[154] a case involving the wrongful termination of long term disability benefits, the Alberta Court of Queen's Bench held: "However defined at this time, it is clear from these authorities that an insurer owes a yet undefined duty of good faith to its insured. It is a duty which in certain circumstances, resembles a fiduciary duty but is always governed by fair play in every dealing". More recently, in *Bullock v. Trafalgar Insurance Co. of Canada*,[155] a case involving the wrongful denial of autombile insurance benefits, the Ontario Court (General Division) reviewed the jurisprudence and concluded:

The duty is not a fiduciary duty but includes certain elements akin thereto. A fiduciary who owes a duty of individual loyalty to his/her principal and in exercising powers of discretion arising from the fiduciary relationship must treat the principal's interest as paramount. In contrast, an insurer in fulfilling its contractual obligations may give consideration to its own interests. However, the insurer must give as much consideration to the welfare of the insured as it gives to its own interests. The insurer cannot do anything to injure the rights of the insured to receive the benefits under the policy.[156]

The duties will be akin to those owed by a fiduciary when the insurer has the power to exercise discretion which affects the interests of the insured, such as in the context of settlement. On the other hand, when the insured is merely discharging obligations under the insurance contract in a manner which does not involve an exercise of discretion, it will only be bound by the duties of good faith, fair dealing and equal consideration, something less than a true fiduciary obligation. This rule was recently confirmed by the British Columbia Court of Appeal in *Warrington v. Great-West Life Assurance Co.*[157] The insurer wrongfully terminated the insured's long term disability benefits after two weeks when it ought to have been aware that his entitlement continued. Because the extension of benefits involves the fulfilment of contractual obligations and not the

---

[153] *Ibid.*, at 124.
[154] [1994] 6 W.W.R. 662 at 685 (Alta. Q.B.).
[155] Unreported, July 12, 1996, Cumming J., Doc. 22938/87Q, [1996] O.J. No. 2566 (Gen. Div.).
[156] *Ibid.*, at para. 100.
[157] (1996), 24 B.C.L.R. (3d) 1 (C.A.).

exercise of discretion, the Court of Appeal concluded that fiduciary obligations were not owed in the circumstances:

> To my mind, the insurer's obligation to pay benefits under the policy upon receiving such proof is virtually indistinguishable from any other contractual duty undertaken by a contracting party and it is a long stretch indeed to characterize its role in this regard as a fiduciary one, even where the insured is "vulnerable" in the sense that he is in dire need of benefits. . . .
>
> . . . . .
>
> [The insurer] was bound by the policy to pay the benefits upon the requisite proof, i.e., proof satisfactory to a reasonable person, being presented to it. The insurer was not required, or authorized, to exercise any other judgment of the kind that would necessitate the operation of Equity on its conscience.[158]

While the relationship between insurer and insured is not one of the categories of relationships which are *prima facie* fiduciary in nature, a fiduciary relationship may arise between them on the facts.[159] If the *indicia* outlined by the Supreme Court of Canada for the identification of fiduciary relationships are present in the circumstances, the insurer may owe fiduciary obligations to its insured.

The content of the duty of good faith and equal consideration has not been extensively explored in the jurisprudence but *Shea v. Manitoba Public Insurance Corp.*[160] provides some guidance on this issue. Some authorities conflate these duties; for example, Barker, Glad and Levy canvassed the law on insurer's duties in California and came to the conclusion that "it is the duty of good faith which applies, and that duty merely requires equal consideration of the insureds' interests".[161] *Couch on Insurance* suggests that *indicia* of bad faith include the failure to: (1) adequately investigate the grounds for the claim against its insured; (2) advise the insured of settlement decisions that could adversely affect his interests; (3) regard the advice of counsel or other agents; (4) settle when the probability of success at trial is low and the risk of personal liability to the insured is high; and (5) institute or participate in settlement negotiations.[162]

---

[158] *Ibid.*, at 10-11. See also *Shewchuk v. London Life Insurance Co.*, [1996] B.C.J. No. 1886 (S.C.).

[159] See, for example, *Plaza Fiberglass Manufacturing Ltd. v. Cardinal Insurance Co.*, *supra*, note 150.; *Warrington v. Great-West Life Assurance Co.*, *supra*, note 157. We discuss the jurisprudence respecting the identification of fiduciary relationships outside of the traditional categories in Chapter 3, Section I, "Fiduciary Relationship Defined", A. "Fiduciary Relationships Generally".

[160] *Supra*, note 151.

[161] William T. Barker, Paul E.B. Glad and Steven M. Levy, "Is an Insurer a Fiduciary to its Insureds?" (1989), 25 *Tort & Ins. L.J.* 1 at p. 8.

[162] *Couch on Insurance*, 2nd rev. ed. (1982), paras. 51:15, as cited in *Fredrikson v. Insurance Corp. of British Columbia*, *supra*, note 150, at p. 284.

5. Settlement of Claims

In each province, the insurer has the right to settle a claim or suit without the consent of the insured.[163] In cases where a claim is settled without the insured's consent, the insured still remains liable to contribute the deductible. An insured who objects to the recommended settlement may be permitted to contest or continue legal proceedings in connection with the claim. However, any damages and expenses in excess of the amount for which the claim could have been settled are not recoverable under the policy.

One of the leading American cases respecting an insured's duty to settle, *Crisci v. Security Insurance Co. of New Haven, Connecticut*, [164] set out three standards which may be used to assess the conduct of the insurer: absolute liability, liability for failing to act reasonably, and liability for bad faith.[165]

Canadian cases dealing with lawyers' professional liability often consider American jurisprudence. In *Pelky v. Hudson Bay Insurance Co.*,[166] Mr. Justice Catzman, then of the Ontario High Court, reviewed the three standards set out in *Crisci* but found it unnecessary in the case before him to determine whether the insurer owed an absolute duty to the insured to settle within the policy limits. Mr. Justice Catzman found the insurer's solicitors (the third parties) liable for the damages sustained by the insured for failing to submit the settlement offer to the insurer for consideration. In another decision of the Ontario High Court, *Dillon v. Guardian Insurance Co. Ltd.*,[167] Mr. Justice Fitzpatrick expressed a preference for the standard of absolute liability set out in *Crisci* but concluded on the facts before him that the insurer was liable by any standard.[168]

More recently, the British Columbia Supreme Court held in *Fredrikson v. Insurance Corp. of British Columbia*:[169]

> Although the California Court [in *Crisci*] expressed itself as sympathetic to the proposed rule [of absolute liability], it did not apply it. I am told by counsel, who have researched this area of the law in great depth, that no court has ever applied

---

[163] Ontario Policy No. 98-001, Condition O; Newfoundland Policy No. 95-003, Condition O; British Columbia Policy LPL98-01-01, Insuring Agreement 2.1.2(a); Alberta Policy 10005, Condition 11(f). In Ontario, the insurer must give the insured notice of its intention to settle.

[164] 426 P. 2d 179 (1967).

[165] Under the standard of absolute liability, whenever an insurer receives an offer to settle within the policy limits and rejects it, the insurer is liable for the amount of any final judgment whether or not within the policy limits. Under the second standard, the insurer is liable whenever it unwarrantedly refuses an offer of settlement if the most reasonable manner of disposing of the claim is by accepting the settlement. In the American cases, bad faith is usually equated with fraud, dishonesty or concealment: see *Crisci v. Security Insurance Co. of New Haven, Connecticut, supra*, note 164.

[166] (1981), 35 O.R. (2d) 97 (H.C.).

[167] [1983] I.L.R. 1-1706 (H.C.).

[168] *Ibid.*, at 6587.

[169] *Supra*, note 150 at 333-34.

such a rule. To do so would, of course, be a striking example of judicial legislation.

> [I]n my view, [the rule of absolute liability as stated in *Crisci*] is not the law and need not be further considered.

There is no single rule in the United States necessary to establish liability for judgments in excess of insurance policy limits, although many jurisdictions hold that the insurer and insured's interests should be weighed fairly and equally.[170] The *Crisci* decision with respect to the absolute liability rule has not been judicially considered in Canada since Fitzpatrick J.'s decision in *Dillon*.

Instead, Canadian courts are developing a doctrine of good faith and equal consideration in insurance relationships.[171] Further, when the conduct of the insurer involves the exercise of discretion as opposed to the mere fulfilment of contractual obligations, such as in the exercise of a right to settle, obligations akin to fiduciary duties will be owed. The court in *Shea v. Manitoba Public Insurance Corp.*[172] found an affirmative duty on the insurer to explore settlement possibilities. It is no defence that the insurer was waiting for the opposing party to make a settlement offer. If it is very likely that liability will be imposed and the judgment will exceed policy limits, the insurer has a duty to offer to pay the third party the amount of the policy limit in exchange for a release of the insured:

> In my view, the exclusive power to settle conferred on MPIC by the regulations requires it to use reasonable efforts on the insureds' behalf to settle within policy limits. Those reasonable efforts include affirmative attempts to settle, and, where a finding of liability is highly probable, and where the judgment to be awarded will probably exceed the policy limits include the affirmative duty to offer to pay the third party liability policy limits in exchange for a release of its own insureds.[173]

In light of this trend, and the minimal judicial attention paid to the decision in *Crisci*, it is probably fair to conclude that the absolute liability doctrine cannot be sustained in Canada.

One commentator extensively reviewed the Canadian jurisprudence and suggested the following guideline for the discharge of the insurer's duty on the settlement of claims:

> Where the risk of liability is remote, as was reasonably perceived to be the case in *Fredrikson*, then the matter may be fairly contested. Where there is "an over-

---

[170] *Ibid.*

[171] See Section II, "The Policy", B. "Rights and Obligations of the Insurer", 4. "Duty of Good Faith and Equal Consideration".

[172] (1990), 1 C.C.L.I. (2d) 61 (B.C.S.C.).

[173] *Ibid.*, at 141; *Warrington v. Great-West Life Assurance*, *supra*, note 157; *Shewchuk v. London Life Insurance Co.*, *supra*, note 158.

whelming probability" of liability as in *Dillon*, settlement for a reasonable sum should be accepted. Where the case is more like 50/50 and difficult to predict as to liability, a typical damage discount exercise should be undertaken. For example, in a 50/50 case where damages are reasonably expected to be about $1.5 Million, the insurer would not be unreasonable in holding to a settlement position of $750,000 in respect of a Million Dollar policy. On the other hand, if there were a realistic topside exposure that might take damages well beyond $1.5 Million in the last example, it might be viewed as unreasonable to reject a $1 Million policy limit offer. With respect, the burden of proof of bad faith viewed essentially as unreasonableness should rest on the insured.[174]

6. Obligations of the Insurer's Solicitor

a. Settlement and Defence of a Claim

Liability for negligence in the defence of an action usually falls on the insurer's solicitor,[175] whereas liability for lack of diligence with respect to settlement rests with the insurer. This allocation is appropriate because a lawyer draws on professional skills in defending an action, and will usually control the process of the trial. On the other hand, settlement negotiations do not require a lawyer's professional services, and a lawyer often does not have ultimate control over the settlement negotiations. The Court in *Shea* observed:

> It is, I think, probably correct to say that with respect to its obligation "to defend" an action, an insurer can in general discharge the obligation by employing competent counsel with a level of experience appropriate to the case. If counsel is in breach of some duty owed in the exercise of his professional skills when defending a case, any liability is his and not that of the insurer . . .
>
> The position of defence counsel with respect to settlement of liability claims is quite different. To begin with, settlement negotiations need not be conducted by lawyers. The insurer may discharge its statutory responsibility to assist the insured by negotiating settlement of claims equally well by its own employees, or by independent adjusters . . . No matter who conducts the settlement negotiations on an insurer's behalf,...all authority to settle up to the limits of the liability coverage must come from the insurer.[176]

---

[174] Warren H.O. Mueller, Q.C., "Defending Lawyers Against Professional Negligence Claims"; The Canadian Institute (20 November, 1992) at p. 106.

[175] *Fredrikson v. Insurance Corp. of British Columbia* (1990), 44 B.C.L.R. (2d) 303 at 330 (S.C.).

[176] *Shea v. Manitoba Public Insurance Corp.* (1990), 1 C.C.L.I. (2d) 6 at 97 (B.C.S.C.).

b. Dual Obligations

A lawyer acting for an insurer has a dual role: she owes a duty not only to the insurer but also to the insured solicitor.[177] Thus, a lawyer representing the insurer, even while acting under a non-waiver agreement, must alert the insured that if a conflict arises, she will continue to act as counsel for the insurer.[178] In a situation where a possible conflict of interest is established, the insured may be entitled to separate representation at the insurer's expense.[179] Further, the insurer's lawyer will be liable to the insured if she fails to submit to the insurer a settlement offer within the policy limits and judgment is granted in excess of those limits.[180]

Hilliker has offered insurers' counsel the following useful guidelines for the avoidance of conflicts:

> Counsel appointed by an insurer to defend the claim on behalf of the insured must be careful to avoid representing the insurer in those areas where its interests are at odds with those of the insured. As a practical matter, this is accomplished at the outset by a clear delineation of the scope of the retainer. Counsel appointed to defend the claim against the insured should restrict the retainer to the defence of issues of liability and damages in the underlying action. Issues as to coverage or as to the obligations of one party to the other under the insurance contract must be considered to be outside the scope of counsel's retainer.[181]

The extent of the obligations of the insurer's lawyer to the insured is best illustrated by the decision of *Paupst v. Henry*.[182] In an action for damages arising out of a fire, the insurer's lawyers appeared on behalf of two insured defendants, one of whom had disappeared and, hence, had never been served with the statement of claim. Realizing that certain admissions made by the defendant who had not been served would be used by the plaintiffs in their case, the lawyers for the insurer sought to be removed as counsel for that defendant. The judge of first instance refused the application on the basis that the insurer was the real defendant and the defendant who had vanished was irrelevant to the proceedings. In allowing the appeal, Mr. Justice Henry concluded:

---

[177] *Groom v. Crocker*, [1939] 1 K.B. 194, [1938] 2 All E.R. 394 (C.A.). This parallels the duty of an insured lawyer not only to her client but also to the insurer. See Commentary 15 of Rule 5 of the *Rules of Professional Conduct* of the Law Society of Upper Canada.

[178] *Citadel General Assurance Co. v. Wolofsky*, unreported, September 4, 1984 (Que. C.A.), leave to appeal to S.C.C. refused February 1, 1985.

[179] *Laurencine v. Jardine* (1988), 64 O.R (2d) 336, [1988] I.L.R. 1-2292 (S.C.); *Shea v. Manitoba Public Insurance Corp.*, *supra*, note 176.

[180] *Pelky v. Hudson Bay Insurance Co.* (1981), 35 O.R. (2d) 97 (H.C.).

[181] G. Hilliker, *Liability Insurance Law in Canada*, 2nd ed. (Toronto: Butterworths, 1996), at p. 108.

[182] (1983), 43 O.R. (2d) 748, 2 D.L.R. (4th) 682 (H.C.).

... assuming that [the solicitors for the insurer] embarked upon the defence of the actions on instructions of [the insurer], that did not extinguish [the disappeared defendant's] right not to be subjected to the proceedings and possibly to judgment without having been properly served with the writ. The solicitors had a duty independent of their duty to the insurer to protect that right in the absence of contrary instructions from her. Even at this late date they are...quite properly seeking to carry out that duty.[183]

In light of this decision, and decisions respecting the insurer's duty of good faith,[184] one commentator has summarized the obligations of counsel for the insurer as follows:[185]

(1) An insured must be advised of his right to separate counsel on any excess claim over the policy limits.

(2) Counsel must communicate all offers of settlement to the insurer.[186]

(3) Copies of significant documents must be forwarded to the insurer.[187]

(4) To avoid a claim of bad faith, a second opinion ought to be obtained in cases where there is a possibility of judgment in excess of the policy.

(5) Counsel must act reasonably and responsibly, ensuring that she bears in mind the dual obligation to both insurer and insured.

C. Obligations of the Insured

1. Notice and Reporting Requirements

Although there are some minor differences in the wording of the provisions, all of the policies require the insured to notify the insurer when it first becomes aware that it is reasonably foreseeable that a claim might be made.[188] The British Columbia and C.L.I.A. policies include the caveat that notice is required however unmeritorious the claim may be.[189] Of course, when a claim is actually received by an insured, it must be immediately forwarded to the insurer, as must

---

[183] *Ibid.*, at 753 O.R.

[184] See Section II "The Policy", B. "Rights and Obligations of the Insurer", 4. "Duty of Good Faith and Equal Consideration".

[185] M. Lerner, "Bad Faith — The Insurer's and the Lawyer's Obligations" in *Law Society of Upper Canada Special Lectures* (Richard De Boo: Toronto, 1987), at pp. 172-73.

[186] Offers of settlement should also be communicated to the insured.

[187] Of course, these should also be reviewed with the insured.

[188] Ontario Policy No. 98-001, General Condition F; Newfoundland Policy No. 95-003, Condition (f); British Columbia Policy No. LPL98-01-01, Condition 4.1; Alberta Policy No. 10005, Condition 4.3(a).

[189] British Columbia Policy No. LPL98-01-01, Condition 4.1; Alberta Policy No. 10005, Condition 4.3.

any demand, notice, summons or other process the insured receives.[190] Under each policy, the insured is additionally obliged to furnish the insurer with all information on the subject which is in the insured's possession or knowledge.[191]

Under the Newfoundland and C.L.I.A. policies, the Law Society may also give notice to the insurer.[192] Coverage of a claim reported by the Law Society rather than the insured directly will protect the insured only to the extent that the insurer is not prejudiced by lack of notice. Accordingly, if the Law Society gives notice of a claim or potential claim, the delinquent solicitor will be protected except for those losses that could have been rectified by timely notice or that would not have been sustained if prompt notice had been given. In British Columbia, notice given by a third party may be deemed to be notice given by the insured.[193]

If the insured fails to report, the insurer may be able to deny coverage.[194] However, in the absence of bad faith or a deliberate misrepresentation, a court may grant equitable relief from forfeiture for imperfect compliance with a term of the policy (such as a delay in reporting or failure to give notice) if it does not result in prejudice to the insurer.[195] The onus is on the insurer to prove breach of a condition, while the onus of establishing the grounds for relief from forfeiture is on the insured. It may be discharged if the insured can show that she did not act in bad faith and there is no prejudice to the insurer.

In *Moore v. Canadian Lawyers Insurance Assn.*,[196] the Nova Scotia Court of Appeal considered the notice provisions in the lawyers' liability insurance policy in effect at the time, which provided that an insured must notify the insurer

---

[190] Ontario Policy No. 98-001, General Condition F; Newfoundland Policy No. 95-003, Condition (f); British Columbia Policy No. LPL98-01-01, Condition 4.2; Alberta Policy No. 10005, Condition 4.3(b).

[191] Ontario Policy No. 98-001, General Condition F; Newfoundland Policy No. 95-003, Condition (f); British Columbia Policy No. LPL98-01-01, Condition 4.1; Alberta Policy No. 10005, Condition 4.3(b).

[192] Newfoundland Policy No. 95-003, Condition (f); Alberta Policy No. 10005, Condition 4.3(c).

[193] British Columbia Policy No. LPL98-01-01, Condition 4.3. In Ontario, this is implicit in the Law Society's right to take the place of the insured where the insured refuses to comply with the policy: Ontario Policy No. 98-001, General Condition G.

[194] See *Perry v. General Security Insurance Co. of Canada* (1984), 47 O.R. (2d) 472, 11 D.L.R. (4th) 516 (C.A.); *McNish & McNish v. American Home Assurance Co.* (1989), 68 O.R. (2d) 365 (H.C.), affd (1991), 5 C.C.L.I. (2d) 222 (Ont. C.A.); *Richards v. Continental Casualty Co.* [1993] I.L.R. 1-2947 (Alta. Q.B.); and *El-Amad v. Goldberg* (1997), 24 O.T.C. 325 (Gen. Div.).

[195] See *Royal Trust Corp. of Canada v. American Home Assurance Co.* (1992), 90 D.L.R. (4th) 582 (N.S.T.D.), affd (1993), 100 D.L.R. (4th) 447 (N.S.C.A.); *McNish & McNish v. American Home Assurance Co.*, *supra*, note 194; *Moore v. Canadian Lawyers' Insurance Assn.* (1993), 105 D.L.R. (4th) 258 (N.S.C.A.). See also *Fisher v. Guardian Insurance Co. of Canada* (1993), 87 B.C.L.R. (2d) 34 (S.C.), varied (1995), 3 B.C.L.R. (3d) 161 (C.A.), wherein the insurance company received notice from a "custodian" who had taken over the practice of a dishonest solicitor. One of the "innocent partners" was not identified in the notice until after the policy had expired. This notice was sufficient as the insurer was not prejudiced nor were its potential losses increased by the subsequent addition of the "innocent partner".

[196] *Supra*, note 195.

"as soon as practicable after learning of a claim or of a circumstance which would likely give rise to a claim". In February 1988, the plaintiff solicitor drew up an invalid mortgage. In December of that year, the mortgage company questioned the validity of the mortgage and proceedings were commenced to have it validated. By late summer 1990, it became apparent that the mortgagor would not execute an affidavit necessary for the validation and shortly thereafter the plaintiff learned that there had been a default. He finally notified his insurer of the situation in October 1990. When the mortgagor became bankrupt in January 1991, the trust company brought an action in negligence against the plaintiff.

The trial judge granted a declaration that the plaintiff was entitled to coverage for the claim. On appeal, Hallett J.A. held that where an obvious error that would likely lead to a claim has been brought to a solicitor's attention, he ought to meet the standard of a reasonably prudent solicitor in reporting. The insurer must prove the following to establish a breach of the reporting requirement at issue:

> To prove a breach of the reporting requirement of this policy, where a claim has not been made, the insurer must prove three things, first that the insured lawyer had actually become aware that he had likely breached a duty to his client in the performance of legal services. Otherwise, it could not be said that he had "learned" of such a circumstance. A court could infer such knowledge from the evidence. Secondly, after learning of his probable breach of duty, a lawyer must measure up to the standard of a reasonably prudent lawyer in assessing whether his deficient conduct will likely give rise to a claim; at this stage an objective test applies. The insurer must adduce evidence from which a court could conclude that the lawyer did not meet this test. The lawyer cannot be absolved from the contractual responsibility of reporting as soon as practicable simply because, although he had learned of his probable breach of duty to his client, he did not believe a claim was likely; such a belief must be a belief that would be reasonably held by a prudent solicitor under the circumstances. Thirdly, the insurer must prove the insured failed to report as soon as practicable. If the delay in reporting, after leaning of an apparent breach of duty is lengthy, as in this case, the lawyer, as a rule, must adduce some evidence that would support a finding that he acted as a reasonably prudent solicitor would have under the circumstances.[197]

In this case, a reasonably prudent solicitor would have concluded from the outset that a claim was probable because the mortgage was invalid and the likelihood of obtaining retroactive approval was not great. The solicitor had a duty to determine from his own research or by consulting a solicitor experienced in the area whether there was a likelihood that the mortgage would be validated by the court. With respect to the timeliness of the notice, the court held: "While an insured can be given some leeway in reporting so as to allow him to take action

---

[197] *Ibid.,* at 261-62.

to correct a problem he has created through his breach of duty to his client so as to avoid a claim, he must act immediately and decisively."[198] Hallett J.A. concluded that the lengthy delay in this case was not justified and coverage was denied.

The *Moore* decision will likely govern the interpretation of the notice requirement in the C.L.I.A. policies as it is substantially the same as the provision before the court in that case. Hallett J.A.'s objective test for assessing whether a breach of duty will likely give rise to a claim is reflected in the wording of the Ontario, Newfoundland and British Columbia policies. They generally impose an obligation to report where it is reasonably foreseeable that the circumstances might give rise to a claim.[199] Furthermore, unlike the provision discussed in *Moore* and those now in the C.L.I.A. and British Columbia policies which require notice "as soon as practicable", the Ontario and Newfoundland cases require the insured to give notice "immediately". It may be that courts in Ontario and Newfoundland will not allow insureds the opportunity to attempt to correct an error before reporting it to the insurer. In a case decided under a predecessor to the Ontario policy, coverage was denied to a solicitor who did not notify the insurer until she was actually served with a statement of claim because a solicitor of ordinary prudence would have foreseen nine months to a year earlier that a claim might arise.[200]

Each of the policies generally provides coverage only in respect of claims made against the insured during the policy period, regardless of when the actual or alleged error, omission or negligent act or acts took place. Again, the wording of the provisions varies to some degree, but their general effect is that coverage will not be provided if prior to the policy period, the insured knew or could have reasonably foreseen that the circumstances might give rise to a claim.[201] The court in *Kallos v. Saskatchewan Government Insurance*[202] interpreted this exclusion to mean what a solicitor could reasonably have known having regard to all the circumstances. It reasoned that it would be unreasonable to interpret the clause to refer to what an ordinarily competent solicitor would have known, as this would result in coverage being denied for errors to which the policy was intended to apply.[203] Further, even if the solicitor could reasonably have known that the negligent act had occurred, it must be shown that the solicitor knew or

---

[198] *Ibid.*, at 265.

[199] Ontario Policy No. 98-001, Condition F obligates an insured to report "any circumstance which any reasonable person or firm would expect to subsequently give rise to a claim".

[200] *Terry v. Law Society of Upper Canada*, unreported, August 12, 1992, Mandel J., Doc. C7284/91, [1992] O.J. No. 1678 (Gen. Div.).

[201] Ontario Policy No. 98-001, Special Provision B; Newfoundland Policy No. 95-003, Condition (d); British Columbia Policy No. LPL98-01-01, Insuring Agreement 3.2; Alberta Policy No. 10005, Condition 4.2.

[202] *Kallos v. Saskatchewan Government Insurance*, [1984] 2 W.W.R. 183 (Sask. Q.B.).

[203] Errors such as missing a limitation period.

could reasonably have known that the plaintiff might institute a claim based on the negligent act.

2. Assistance, Cooperation and Subrogation

The insured is obliged to cooperate with the insurer in making settlements, conducting the defence[204] and enforcing any right of contribution or indemnity[205] against any person.[206] Substantial breaches of the duty to cooperate will disentitle the insured to relief from forfeiture.[207] Where the breaches are deliberate, the insured may not be entitled to relief from forfeiture even if there is no prejudice to the insurer.[208]

Understandably, the insured's obligation to cooperate with the insurer is subject to all other obligations under which a solicitor acts. In *Swiderski v. Broy Engineering Ltd.*,[209] a solicitor inadvertently failed to include some defendants in a claim. When the omission was discovered, the solicitor notified the Law Society and the insurers. The insurers instructed the lawyer to attempt to rectify the error and to report back to them with the results. The court found that there were significant risks to a solicitor remedying his own errors, not the least of which is the potential for a conflict of interest. It was improper for the insurer to make this request, and equally improper for the solicitor to comply with it.

The insured must not voluntarily assume or admit liability, settle any claim, make any payment, assume any obligation or incur any expense, except at her own expense.[210] In instances where the insurer makes payment under the policy on behalf of the insured, the insurer becomes subrogated to the insured's right of recovery against any other person.[211] Under the Ontario, Newfoundland and C.L.I.A. policies, the insurer cannot attempt by way of subrogation to recover against another insured except to the extent that the insurer has been prejudiced

---

[204] Ontario Policy No. 98-001, General Condition G; Newfoundland Policy No. 95-003, Condition (g); British Columbia Policy No. LPL98-01-01, 5.1; Alberta Policy No. 10005, Condition 4.4(b).

[205] Ontario Policy No. 98-001, General Condition G; Newfoundland Policy No. 95-003, Condition (g); British Columbia Policy No. LPL98-01-01, Condition 5.1.6; Alberta Policy No. 10005, Condition 4.4(b).

[206] The Ontario and Newfoundland policies specifically exclude an obligation to co-operate in enforcing subrogation against an employee of the insured who may be liable to the insured.

[207] *Canadian Newspapers Co. v. Kansa General Insurance Co.* (1996), 30 O.R. (3d) 257 (C.A.), application for leave to appeal to the Supreme Court of Canada dismissed (1997), 220 N.R. 80*n*, [1996] S.C.C.A. No. 553.

[208] *Terry v. Law Society of Upper Canada, supra*, note 200.

[209] (1992), 11 O.R. (3d) 594 (Div. Ct.).

[210] Ontario Policy No. 98-001, General Condition G; Newfoundland Policy No. 95-003, Condition (g); British Columbia Policy No. LPL98-01-01, Condition 5.3; Alberta Policy No. 10005, Condition 4.4(d) and (e).

[211] Ontario Policy No. 98-001, General Condition K; Newfoundland Policy No. 95-003, Condition (j); British Columbia Policy No. LPL98-01-01, Condition 11; Alberta Policy No. 10005, Condition 4.9 (a).

by the failure of the other insured to comply with the policy or by reason of any dishonest, fraudulent, criminal or malicious act on the part of the other insured, the Law Society or employees of either.[212] There is no similar specific prohibition under the policy in British Columbia.

3. Duty of Good Faith

An insurance contract is a contract *uberrima fides*, that is, of the utmost good faith.[213] Although breaches of the duty of good faith are most commonly alleged by an insured respecting its insurer's handling of a claim, the principle of *uberrima fides* applies to both parties at the time they enter into the contract. The insured's good faith is most likely to be questioned in connection with the manner in which she secured and retained insurance. When an insured obtains insurance by means of a fraudulent misrepresentation, the policy is voided upon inception; the insurer has a right to rely on the applicant lawyer to provide complete disclosure on the basis of the highest good faith.[214]

4. Conflict of Interest

Insurance relationships may raise unique conflict of interest issues. One example of a situation in which a conflict may arise is when the insured tries to rectify an error which may give rise to a claim. It may seem reasonable to allow an insured to take action to correct his error or omission in order to avoid a claim.[215] On the other hand, there is a risk that a conflict may arise as a result. In some circumstances, a significant risk of a conflict will make it improper for the insured to remedy his own error.[216]

Conflicts may also arise when the insurer has relinquished management of the defence to the insured. In this case, there is obviously potential for conflict between the interests of the insured and the insurer, particularly in situations in which the insurer remains responsible for a portion of the costs and damages awarded.

5. Obligations of the Insured's Solicitor

Occasionally, the insurer will relinquish management of the defence to the insured. In this situation the insured's solicitor owes a duty not only to the insured solicitor but also to the insurer. There is potential for conflict between the interests of the insured and the insurer, and the insured's solicitor must not be seen as

---

[212] Ontario Policy No. 98-001, General Condition K; Newfoundland Policy No. 95-003, Condition (j); Alberta Policy No. 10005, Condition 4.9 (b).

[213] G. Hilliker, *Liability Insurance Law in Canada*, 2nd ed. (Toronto: Butterworths, 1996), at 19.

[214] See, Section II, "The Policy", A. "Scope of Coverage", 7. "Exclusions", (b) "Fraudulent Acts".

[215] See, for example, *Moore v. Canadian Lawyers' Insurance Assn* (1993), 105 D.L.R. (4th) 258 (N.S.C.A.).

[216] *Swiderski v. Broy Engineering Ltd., supra*, note 209.

preferring the interests of the insured. One case, *Canadian Newspapers Co. v. Kansa General Insurance Co.*[217] has concluded that the fact that the insured and its solicitors had a long-standing relationship does not in itself support an inference that counsel preferred the insured's interests. The insurer complained that the solicitors failed to report to and consult with it about the conduct of the defence. As a result, the insurer was liable for costs and damages far in excess of those warranted by its economic interests. The court held that the insurer was a sophisticated litigant with knowledge of difficulties inherent in predicting the course and outcome of a litigation. It must be taken to have known the potential conflict between its interest in the economic aspects of the litigation and the insured's interests in defence as a matter of principle. In the circumstances, the solicitors' performance was satisfactory.

III. OTHER CONSIDERATIONS

A. THIRD-PARTY CLAIMS AGAINST THE INSURER

Whether a person who sustains pecuniary loss arising from a solicitor's negligence has recourse against the insurer has been an issue of some debate. Although the wording of the provisions varies somewhat, all of the provincial Insurance Acts permit recovery against an insurer where a person obtains a judgment against an insured in respect of injury or damage to person or property, execution on the judgment is returned unsatisfied and the insured's liability falls within the coverage afforded by policy.[218] The debate entails whether purely economic loss suffered as a result of a solicitor's malpractice constitutes loss or damage to person or property. The provisions have been interpreted differently in different provinces.

The Ontario Court of Appeal in *Perry v. General Security Insurance Co. of Canada*[219] held that a person who sustains pecuniary loss arising from the negligence of a solicitor has no direct recourse against the insurer. In this case, the plaintiff had retained a solicitor to place a second mortgage on a property; the solicitor failed to register the plaintiff's charge. When power of sale proceedings were taken by the first mortgagee, the plaintiff lost his investment. The solicitor's insurer denied coverage because of the solicitor's failure to give notice of claim and his refusal to cooperate with the insurer. When the plaintiff's judgment against the solicitor went unsatisfied, the plaintiff sued the insurer directly

---

[217] (1991), 5 C.C.L.I. (2d) 66 (Gen. Div.), supp. reasons (1991), 1 C.P.C. (3d) 16 (Ont. Gen. Div.). The proceedings against the insured's solicitor were third party proceedings. The appeal from the third party claim was dismissed and leave to appeal to the Supreme Court of Canada was denied (*supra,* note 207).

[218] See, for example, R.S.B.C. 1996, c. 226, s. 24; R.S.A. 1980, c. I-5, s. 219, am. 1994, c. C-10.5, s. 129; R.S.O. 1990, c. I.8, s. 109.

[219] (1984), 47 O.R. (2d) 472, 11 D.L.R. (4th) 516 (C.A.).

under the mandatory recovery section of the Ontario *Insurance Act.*[220] Unhappily
for the plaintiff, the majority of the Court of Appeal, endorsing the reasoning of
Mr. Justice R.E. Holland at trial, held that the plaintiff's loss, being purely economic, did not constitute "injury or damage to property" within the statutory
definition.[221] The court rejected the reasoning of *Kallos v. Saskatchewan Government Insurance,*[222] which reached the opposite conclusion in construing a virtually
identical provision in the Saskatchewan *Insurance Act.*[223] Instead, the court called
for legislative intervention which has not occurred to date.

Perry was followed in the British Columbia Supreme Court case of *Starr
Schein Enterprises Inc. v. Gestas Corp.,*[224] a decision dealing with the equivalent
section of the British Columbia *Insurance Act.*[225] The British Columbia Supreme
Court affirmed in *Freemont Development Co. Ltd. v. Travellers Indemnity
Co.,*[226] that no direct cause of action exists between the insurers and the lawyer's
client. The *Insurance Act* permits a direct right of action for damage suffered to
person or property but not for mere pecuniary loss.

Conversely, courts in Saskatchewan, Alberta and New Brunswick have followed the *Kallos* decision and permitted recovery directly from the insurer for
economic loss. Most recently, in *63398 Alberta Ltd. v. Saskatchewan Government Insurance,*[227] the Saskatchewan Court of Queen's Bench permitted a client
who obtained judgment against a solicitor which could not be enforced, to recover against the solicitor's insurer. In *Richards v. Continental Casualty Co.,*[228]
the Alberta Court of Queen's Bench attributed the different results to minor differences in wording between the Ontario and British Columbia statutes on the
one hand and the Alberta and Saskatchewan statutes on the other. Further, in
Resznick v. Ziterman,[229] the Manitoba Court of Appeal commented in *obiter* that
there were well-reasoned dissents in both *Perry* and *Starr Shein.*

Academic opinion also favours the *Kallos* line of cases and other provinces
may eventually adopt a more expansive reading of the legislation. The problem

---

[220] R.S.O. 1980, c. 218.
[221] The court also considered whether the plaintiff had a claim for relief from forfeiture against the
insurer under s. 106 of the Act. It was unanimously agreed that this claim must fail since the
plaintiff could stand in no better position than the insured solicitor whose conduct was determined to be unworthy of relief.
[222] [1984] 2 W.W.R. 183, 14 D.L.R. (4th) 34 (Q.B.).
[223] R.S.S. 1978, c. S-26, s. 122.
[224] (1986), 70 B.C.L.R. 362, [1986] 3 W.W.R. 366 (S.C.), affd 13 B.C.L.R. (2d) 85, [1987] 4
W.W.R. 664 (C.A.).
[225] R.S.B.C. 1979, c. 200, s. 26.
[226] (1993), 82 B.C.L.R. (2d) 256 (S.C.).
[227] (1995), 127 Sask R. 261 (Q.B.), supp. reasons *loc. cit.* (Q.B.), revd (1995), 137 Sask. R. 246
(C.A.). See also *Caisse Populaire de St.-Isodore Ltée v. Assoc. d'Assurance des Juristes cana-
diens,* (1992), 129 N.B.R. (2d), 227 (Q.B).
[228] (1986), 22 C.C.L.I. 91 (Alta. Q.B.), affd 25 C.C.L.I. 237 (Alta. C.A.), leave to appeal to the
Supreme Court of Canada refused (1987), 55 Alta. L.R. (2d) 1*n*.
[229] (1994), 27 C.C.L.I. (2d) 294 (Man. C.A.).

posed by the *Perry* decision led to an amendment to the Ontario Policy in July, 1982 that permitted the Law Society to give notice to the insurer when the insured fails to do so. For an injured client, the message is clear: if there is reason to believe the solicitor is ignoring a potential problem, it is prudent to notify the Law Society or its Department of Insurance of a claim or potential claim against the inattentive solicitor.

Third parties have also attempted to claim against the insurer as beneficiaries of the insurance policy. In *Bode (Administrator appointed by Law Society of Upper Canada) v. Chubb Insurance Co. of Canada*,[230] the court held that although the clients were the ultimate beneficiaries of the policy, they could not be construed to be "insured" under the policy as this characterization would distort the actual intent of the contract. On the other hand, in *QuickRun Courier Ltd. v. Abbe Insurance Brokers Ltd.*,[231] Feldman J. held on a motion to strike a statement of claim that it can be argued that members of the public are beneficiaries of certain statutorily mandated insurance plans, and thus have a direct right of action against the insurer as no other remedy is provided. However, the court in *Lee v. Law Society of Upper Canada*[232] expressly disagreed with Feldman J.'s conclusions and preferred the reasoning found in *Perry*.

B. OTHER INSURANCE

The Ontario and Newfoundland policies provide that, if an insured has other insurance against a loss covered by the policy, other than insurance specifically arranged to apply as excess insurance, the insurance provided by the policy applies only as excess insurance, and cannot be called upon in contribution.[233] Conversely, in the same circumstances, the British Columbia insurer is responsible for the proportion of loss and claims expenses that the applicable limit of liability bears to the total applicable limits of all collectible insurance against the loss.[234] If an insured is required to purchase lawyer's professional liability insurance in another Canadian jurisdiction, the two policies apply as agreed by the Law Societies. However, the maximum insurance available under the British Columbia policy and all other Canadian lawyers' compulsory professional liability insurance together cannot exceed $1 million for all claims arising out of an error.[235]

The C.L.I.A. policies provide that if an insured has other lawyers' professional insurance, other than excess insurance, through one or more Law Socie-

---

[230] (1991), 3 O.R. (3d) 752 (Gen. Div.). See also *Freemont Development Co. v. Travellers Indemnity Co.*, *supra*, note 226.

[231] (1993), 14 O.R. (3d) 150 (Gen. Div.).

[232] [1994] O.J. No. 1468 (Gen. Div.).

[233] Ontario Policy No. 98-005, General Condition J; Newfoundland Policy No. 95-003, Condition (i).

[234] British Columbia Policy No. LPL98-01-01, Condition 8.1 and 8.2.

[235] Condition 8.3, *supra*, note 234.

ties, all insurance shall apply in a manner agreed between the Law Societies.[236] Further, the aggregate coverage provided under all policies cannot exceed the occurrence limit of $1 million. If insurance against a loss covered by the C.L.I.A. policy, other than excess insurance, is not arranged through a Law Society, the C.L.I.A. policy applies only as excess insurance, and cannot be called upon in contribution.[237]

C. EXCESS INSURANCE

A cautious solicitor will obtain excess insurance, which is available privately,[238] for coverage over the effective policy limits of the group plan. As between the primary and the excess insurer, however, the former is obliged to conduct the claims investigation.

In some cases, where liability is not in issue and the claim will clearly fall outside of the compulsory policy limits, the primary insurer may simply turn over the defence to the excess insurer.

Although the excess insurer is generally not under a duty to participate in the insured's defence until the primary insurance is exhausted, it may be important to involve the excess insurer in the early stages of the defence process. If not, problems may arise:

> . . . without the active involvement of [the excess insurer], it is impractical to discuss with the other defendants the formulation of a common defence strategy or a possible joint settlement package.[239]

Thus, where the primary and excess insurer are under a concurrent obligation to defend, and where the true value of the claim clearly puts both insurers at risk, they are often held to share responsibility for the costs of the defence.[240] When the result is not certain and the litigation is likely to be protracted, there is authority for the proposition that the costs ought to be divided equally between the insurers.[241] However, if the final outcome has been determined, it may be

---

[236] Alberta Policy No. 10005, Condition 4.6(a).

[237] Condition 4.6(b), *supra*, note 236.

[238] The C.L.I.A. policies provide optional excess coverage.

[239] *Broadhurst & Ball v. American Home Assurance Co.* (1990), 1 O.R. (3d) 225 at 241 (C.A.), motion for leave to appeal to the Supreme Court of Canada dismissed (1991), 3 O.R. (3d) xii.

[240] In cases where there is no contractual agreement between the insurers with respect to the allocation of costs, the court can use the remedy of equitable subrogation to achieve a fair result.

[241] See *Continental Casualty Co. v. Zurich Insurance Co.*, 17 Cal. Rptr. 12 (1961) (Cal. S.C.); *Canadian Indemnity Co. v. Simcoe & Erie General Insurance Co.* (1979), 103 D.L.R. (3d) 485, [1979] I.L.R. 1-1147, 33 N.S.R. (2d) 310, 57 A.P.R. 310; *Broadhurst & Ball v. American Home Assurance Co.*, *supra*, note 239.

more appropriate to allocate the costs with reference to the respective policy limits.[242]

The Canadian Bar Excess Liability Association ("C.B.E.L.A.") is an organization which provides excess liability insurance to practitioners in Ontario, British Columbia and Quebec. The C.B.E.L.A. organization is a subscriber to the umbrella C.L.I.A. organization, which provides primary and excess insurance in all Canadian jurisdictions except British Columbia, Ontario, Quebec and Newfoundland. The C.L.I.A. excess insurance offers coverage on a "follow form" basis, so that the excess insurance follows the form of the underlying coverage provided by the Law Society. The C.B.E.L.A. excess insurance policy is distinct from the primary insurance provided by the Law Societies of British Columbia and Ontario.

D. RE-INSURANCE

The primary insurer may broker part of the risk to another insurance company. That, however, will not relieve the primary insurer of any obligation it may have to the insured under the policy.

E. INEVITABILITY OF LOSS

The inevitability of loss is yet another contentious area of insurance law. It arises when the plaintiff in a tort claim is awarded a judgment to be paid by a number of parties. These parties usually include some combination of the primary insurer, the excess insurer and the tortfeasor. In the ordinary course, each party pays only the portion of the judgment for which it is responsible. Complications arise when one of the defendants has breached a duty owed to another. This will typically occur when the insurer breaches its duties with respect to the defence and settlement of the tort claim against the insured. If the insurer's breach of duty results in the insured's liability for a portion of the judgment, or results in the insured being liable for a greater portion of the judgment than would have been the case had the duty not been breached, the insurer must indemnify the insured for the insured's damages. The issue which arises is how to quantify the insured's damages. Do the damages equal the amount by which the insured's liability increased because of the breach of duty, or are they equal to the amount which the third party claimant could have realized from the insured had there been no action for indemnity? This is, of course, only an issue when the insured does not have sufficient assets to satisfy the judgment. The court in *Shea* extensively canvassed this issue, and came to the conclusion that inevita-

---

[242] *American Fidelity Insurance Co. v. Employees Mutual Casualty Co.*, 593 P. 2d 14 (Kansas C.A., 1979).

bility of loss is irrelevant with respect to the amount recoverable from the insurer:

> Whether the insured estate is insufficient to pay the entire judgment or whether the insured is hopelessly insolvent and the judgment is uncollectible is immaterial; the fact that there is such a judgment outstanding against the insured is considered to be sufficient harm to justify recovery from the insurer.[243]

The rationale is that the insured's legal rights and the scope of the insurers' obligations arising under a policy of insurance ought not to depend upon the financial means of the particular insured. To measure the loss that way is to create an obvious double standard, is uncertain and inconvenient.[244]

On the other hand, there is a line of reasoning that challenges the full indemnity principle. For example, Keeton states:

> The appropriate measure of damages when an insured is entitled to a recovery that is in excess of the applicable liability insurance policy limits, should be the amount needed to make the insured whole by placing the insured in the same position that would have existed had there been no breach of the duty to settle. Furthermore, this sum should be established after taking into account the amount, if any, that the third party claimant could have realized upon rights against the insured if there had been no cause of action for liability in excess of policy limits — that is, after taking into account how much could have been recovered above the insurance policy limits against an insured who had some assets, but not enough that the third party could recover more than could have been recovered against the insured. This might be done by permitting a single recovery against the insurer on the excess liability claim, at the instance of either the insured or the third party claimant, in an amount equal to the insured's net assets which are not exempt from legal process, and holding that the claimant's tort judgment against the insured is fully discharged by payment of this sum to the claimant either by the insured or by the insurer on the insured's behalf.[245]

The concern appears to be that the insured or the third party claimant will be in a "windfall" position if full recovery is the rule.

---

[243] Appleman, *Insurance Law and Practice*, vol. 7C, at pp. 490-92, cited in *Shea v. Manitoba Public Insurance Corp.* (1990), 1 C.C.L.I. (2d) 61 at 149 (B.C.S.C.).

[244] *Shea v. Manitoba Public Insurance* Corp., *supra*, note 243, at 119.

[245] Robert E. Keeton, *Insurance Law: A Guide to Fundamental Principles, Legal Doctrines and Commercial Practices* (1988) at p. 903, as cited in *Shea v. Manitoba Public Insurance Corp.*, *supra*, note 243, at 151.

Index